Schizotypy

For several decades there has been an increasing move towards viewing the psychotic illnesses from a dimensional perspective, seeing them as continuous with healthy functioning. The idea, concentrating mostly on schizophrenia, has generated considerable theoretical debate as well as empirical research, conducted under the rubric of 'schizotypy'. This book offers a timely discussion of the most significant themes and developments in this research area.

Divided into four parts that represent current concerns in schizotypy research – Measurement, brain and biology; Development and environment; Consequences and outcomes; and Future directions – chapters reflect a broad range of approaches and discuss varied theoretical perspectives on schizotypy. Topics include:

- cognitive and perceptual biases
- psychometric assessments
- creativity and schizotypy
- genetic associations
- developmental perspectives.

Schizotypy: New dimensions will appeal to academics, researchers and postgraduate students in the area of psychotic illnesses, as well as professionals such as psychiatrists and clinical psychologists who are concerned with the basis of serious mental disorder. The book will inform readers who are new to the topic, and update and expand the knowledge base of those more experienced in the field.

Oliver J. Mason is Senior Lecturer at University College London, UK. He also works at the North East London Foundation NHS Trust as a clinical researcher and clinical psychologist.

Gordon Claridge is Emeritus Professor of Abnormal Psychology in the Department of Experimental Psychology, University of Oxford, UK and Emeritus Fellow, Magdalen College. He is Fellow of the British Psychological Society, Associate of the Royal College of Psychiatrists, UK.

Advances in Mental Health Research series

Books in this series:

The Clinical Effectiveness of Neurolinguistic Programming
A critical appraisal
Edited by Lisa Wake, Richard M. Gray and Frank S. Bourke

Group Therapy for Adults with Severe Mental Illness
Adapting the Tavistock method
Diana Semmelhack, Larry Ende and Clive Hazell

Narratives of Art Practice and Mental Wellbeing
Reparation and connection
Olivia Sagan

Video and Filmmaking as Psychotherapy
Research and practice
Edited by Joshua L. Cohen and J. Lauren Johnson with Penelope P. Orr

Schizotypy
New dimensions
Edited by Oliver J. Mason and Gordon Claridge

Schizotypy
New dimensions

Edited by Oliver J. Mason and
Gordon Claridge

LONDON AND NEW YORK

First published 2015
by Routledge
27 Church Road, Hove, East Sussex, BN3 2FA

and by Routledge
711 Third Avenue, New York, NY 10017

Routledge is an imprint of the Taylor & Francis Group, an informa business

© 2015 O. Mason and G. Claridge

The right of the editors to be identified as the authors of the editorial material, and of the authors for their individual chapters, has been asserted in accordance with sections 77 and 78 of the Copyright, Designs and Patents Act 1988.

All rights reserved. No part of this book may be reprinted or reproduced or utilised in any form or by any electronic, mechanical, or other means, now known or hereafter invented, including photocopying and recording, or in any information storage or retrieval system, without permission in writing from the publishers.

Trademark notice: Product or corporate names may be trademarks or registered trademarks, and are used only for identification and explanation without intent to infringe.

British Library Cataloguing in Publication Data
A catalogue record for this book is available from the British Library

Library of Congress Cataloging in Publication Data
Schizotypy (Mason)
Schizotypy : new dimensions / edited by Oliver Mason and Gordon Claridge.
  p. ; cm.
Includes bibliographical references and index.
I. Mason, Oliver, 1967- , editor. II. Claridge, Gordon, 1932- , editor. III. Title.
[DNLM: 1. Schizotypal Personality Disorder. 2. Schizophrenic Psychology. WM 203]
RC569.5.S36
616.85′81—dc23
2014046166

ISBN: 978-0-415-72203-2 (hbk)
ISBN: 978-1-315-85856-2 (ebk)

Typeset in ITC New Baskerville Std
by Swales & Willis Ltd, Exeter, Devon, UK

Contents

List of illustrations   vii
List of contributors   viii

Introduction   1
OLIVER J. MASON AND GORDON CLARIDGE

PART I
Measurement, brain and biology   5

1 The psychometric assessment of schizotypy   7
THOMAS R. KWAPIL AND CHARLOTTE A. CHUN

2 The role of dopamine in schizotypy   33
CHRISTINE MOHR AND ULRICH ETTINGER

3 Genetic associations: the basis of schizotypy   48
PHILIP GRANT

4 Hemispheric asymmetries in schizotypy   62
GINA M. GRIMSHAW AND LAURA KRANZ

PART II
Development and environment   81

5 Schizotypy: a developmental perspective   83
MARTIN DEBBANÉ

6 Childhood trauma and schizotypy: a systematic review   99
TJASA VELIKONJA, OLIVER J. MASON AND HELEN L. FISHER

7 Mechanisms mediating the pathway from environmental adversity to psychosis proneness 116
TAMARA SHEINBAUM AND NEUS BARRANTES-VIDAL

8 Schizotypy and substance use 132
EMMA BARKUS

9 Inducing psychotic-like experiences: the role of schizotypy 147
CHRISTINA DANIEL AND OLIVER J. MASON

PART III
Consequences and outcomes 163

10 Dimensional approaches to delusional beliefs 165
CHARLIE HERIOT-MAITLAND AND EMMANUELLE PETERS

11 Schizotypy and psychopathology 180
JO HODGEKINS

12 Schizotypy: a creative advantage? 197
NICOLA J. HOLT

PART IV
Future directions 215

13 Old thoughts: new ideas: future directions 217
GORDON CLARIDGE

Index 228

Illustrations

Figures

5.1	Diagram illustrating the developmental core of models accounting for the emergence of psychotic disorders	85
13.1	Two historical traditions in proposals to dimensionalise psychosis	218

Tables

1.1	Summary of psychometric measures of schizotypy – wide spectrum	11
1.2	Summary of psychometric measures of schizotypy – single trait excluding delusions and paranoia	16
1.3	Summary of psychometric measures of schizotypy – paranoia and delusions	22
4.1	Visual half-field studies of hemispheric asymmetries in language	71
4.2	Dichotic listening studies of hemispheric asymmetries in language	72
4.3	Studies of hemispheric asymmetry in attention	74
6.1	Summary of studies on childhood trauma and schizotypal traits (ordered by weight [W])	101
9.1	Auditory paradigms	149
9.2	Sensory deprivation and other paradigms	150

Contributors

Neus Barrantes-Vidal is an associate professor in the Department of Clinical Psychology at the Universitat Autònoma de Barcelona (Spain), Adjunct Associate Professor at the University of North Carolina at Greensboro, a researcher of the Spanish Ministry of Health Network on Mental Health Research (CIBERSAM) and a research consultant of the Sant Pere Claver Health Foundation. She is currently a member of the advisory board of the Spanish Agency for the Assessment of Scientific Research (ANEP) and holds a research distinction awarded by the Catalan Institution for Research and Advanced Studies (ICREA Acadèmia).

Emma Barkus is a senior lecturer in psychology at the University of Wollongong, Australia, where she has been a faculty member since 2010. Emma completed her PhD at Manchester Metropolitan University investigating schizotypy, auditory hallucinations and other risk factors for psychosis. Her research interests include factors that exacerbate and ameliorate risk for psychosis – for example, biological factors such as cannabis and environmental factors such as stress. Her papers cover topics that include hallucinations, experiences after cannabis and personality psychology.

Charlotte A. Chun is a graduate student in clinical psychology at the University of North Carolina at Greensboro (UNCG). She received a Fulbright Fellowship to complete a research project examining creativity, personality and cognition in synesthesia at the Centre de Recherche Cerveau et Cognition while completing a Master's in neuroscience, cognition and behaviour at the Université de Toulouse III-Paul Sabatier. Her current research at UNCG examines the role of neurocognition in the development of schizophrenia-spectrum psychosis.

Gordon Claridge is Emeritus Professor of Abnormal Psychology in the Department of Experimental Psychology, University of Oxford, and Emeritus Fellow, Magdalen College, Oxford. He is a Fellow of the British Psychological Society and an Associate of the Royal College of Psychiatrists, UK. Despite being long retired, he continues to brood and sometimes write about schizotypy. His current interest is in its relationship to creativity, especially humour.

Christina Daniel is a graduate student in psychology at University College London. Her current research involves inducing psychotic-like experiences using sensory deprivation, including the use of electroencephalographic recording.

Martin Debbané is Associate Professor at the Faculty of Psychology and Educational Sciences and Director of the Developmental Clinical Psychology Research Unit at the University of Geneva in Switzerland. His research activities focus on developmental psychopathology through the integrative lens of clinical psychology and cognitive neuroscience. Dr Debbané is also Honorary Reader at University College London. He is an associate and trainer in mentalisation-based therapies at the Anna Freud Centre in London. He teaches and practises psychotherapy from a contemporary psychodynamic perspective.

Ulrich Ettinger is Professor of Psychology at the University of Bonn. He holds degrees in psychology and neuroscience. He completed his PhD on endophenotypes of schizophrenia. His primary research interest include (a) cognition, brain structure and brain function in schizophrenia and schizotypy, (b) the cognitive and neural control of eye movements, and (c) the pharmacological modulation of cognition and brain function.

Helen L. Fisher has been a lecturer at King's College London since 2011. She is also a chartered research psychologist and consultant with the children's charity, NSPCC. She has received interdisciplinary research training in psychology, social psychiatry, genetics and epidemiology, funded through pre- and post-doctoral fellowships from the Medical Research Council (MRC) and the Economic and Social Research Council (ESRC). Helen's initial research involved evaluating early intervention services for young people with psychosis, and then focused on the interplay between childhood maltreatment and genetic factors in the development and course of psychosis. She has recently been awarded an MQ Fellowship to extend this work by exploring the social, psychological and epigenetic factors that increase and decrease the risk of psychotic experiences persisting during adolescence among victimised children.

Phillip Grant is currently working as Associate Professor in the Department of Personality and Biological Psychology at the Justus-Liebig University in Giessen (JLU) and as Honorary Professor for Functional Anatomy at the University of Applied Sciences in Giessen, Germany. He is supervisor of the Department of Personality and Biological Psychology's molecular genetics and biochemical lab, and coordinator of the psychological faculty's neuroanatomical education for students at JLU.

x   List of contributors

Gina M. Grimshaw is Director of the Cognitive and Affective Neuroscience lab at Victoria University of Wellington, New Zealand. Her research is focused on hemispheric differences in cognitive and emotional processing, and she has a particular interest in the assessment of handedness. She completed her PhD at the University of Waterloo in 1996. Her research has been funded by the National Institute of Mental Health, the Marsden Fund, and the Neurological Foundation of New Zealand.

Charlie Heriot-Maitland is an MRC Clinical Research Training Fellow at King's College London and an Honorary Clinical Psychologist at the South London and Maudsley NHS Foundation Trust. He is currently researching the role of social-rank threats and compassion-focused therapy in psychosis for a Fellowship project, while also providing interventions for people with psychosis in NHS services and running workshops for various staff groups. His academic interests include the occurrence and function of anomalous experiences, and the role of social processes in determining their helpful or unhelpful consequences.

Jo Hodgekins is a clinical lecturer in clinical psychology at Norwich Medical School at the University of East Anglia. She completed a PhD in 2009 examining factors associated with social recovery following early psychosis, including the role of schizotypal symptoms and the development of a measure to assess these phenomena. This remains her specialist area of interest both within research and clinical practice. She is also a qualified clinical psychologist with an interest in developing and evaluating psychological interventions for individuals at risk of long-term social disability both before and after the onset of psychosis.

Nicola J. Holt is a senior lecturer in psychology at the University of the West of England, Bristol, where she has been a faculty member since 2008. She completed her PhD on creativity and unusual experiences at the University of Northampton in 2007, and subsequently worked as a research fellow at the Anomalous Experiences Research Unit at the University of York. Nicola has published over forty books, chapters and articles on the topics of creativity, consciousness, anomalistic psychology and anomalous experiences.

Laura Kranz has been a member of the Cognitive and Affective Neuroscience lab at Victoria University of Wellington, New Zealand since 2012. She is currently completing her Master's of Science specialising in cognitive and behavioural neuroscience: she is using both behavioural and event-related potential (ERP) measures to explore the neural mechanisms involved in inhibiting emotional information when it is irrelevant to the current goal.

Thomas R. Kwapil is the Associate Dean for Research in the College of Arts and Sciences and Professor in the Department of Psychology at the University of North Carolina at Greensboro. His programme of research investigates risk for schizophrenia and bipolar-spectrum psychopathology from both experimental and developmental psychopathology perspectives. He coordinated the Chapmans' landmark 10-year longitudinal study of psychosis proneness and his current research focuses on developing and testing symptom, personality, daily life, neurocognitive and genetic indicators of schizotypy and bipolar-spectrum psychopathology. He has published over a hundred peer-reviewed articles and invited chapters, and maintained a long-standing record of external funding for his research.

Oliver J. Mason is a senior lecturer in clinical psychology at University College London where he has been a faculty member since 2003. He is also Deputy Director of Research and Development for the North East London NHS Foundation Trust where he works as a consultant clinical psychologist. He completed his D.Phil. at the University of Oxford investigating schizophrenia and schizotypy, and subsequently trained clinically at the University of Wales. His research interests include vulnerability factors for psychosis, as well as its treatment and recovery. He is author of over seventy articles and chapters across several areas of clinical and personality psychology.

Christine Mohr was made a full Professor for Cognitive Psychology at the University of Lausanne, Switzerland, in 2010. Subsequent to the completion of her doctoral thesis at the University of Zürich in 2001, she worked as a postdoctoral student at the University Hospital of Geneva and the University of Alberta (Canada). In 2004, she took up a position as lecturer and subsequently as senior lecturer at the University of Bristol (UK). Her major interest is in the cognitive, neuropsychological and psychopharmacological correlates of high-risk conditions in the general population, with a particular focus on schizotypy and the schizophrenia spectrum. Currently, she has contributed to over seventy scientific articles and book chapters.

Emmanuelle Peters is Reader in Clinical Psychology at the Institute of Psychiatry, Psychology and Neuroscience (IoPPN), King's College London, and an Honorary Consultant Clinical Psychologist for the South London and Maudsley NHS Foundation Trust (SLaM), where she is the director of a specialist outpatients psychological therapies service for psychosis (PICuP). She has specialised in psychosis for the past 25 years as a clinician, researcher and trainer. Her research interests include the continuum view of psychosis, cognitive models of psychotic symptoms, and cognitive behaviour therapy for psychosis.

Tamara Sheinbaum is from Mexico and is currently a postdoctoral researcher at the Universitat Autònoma de Barcelona in Spain. She received an MSc in Research Methods in Psychology from University College London in 2010, and a PhD in Clinical and Health Psychology from the Universitat

Autònoma de Barcelona in 2014. Her research interests include the role of adverse developmental environments and psychological factors in relation to the risk and expression of schizophrenia-spectrum phenotypes.

Tjasa Velikonja is an early career researcher having recently completed her PhD at University College London (UCL). Her interests include childhood trauma, schizotypy and psychosis, and especially the psychological underpinnings of the trauma–psychosis association. She has previously been working on psychosis studies for the NHS, UCL and Institute of Psychiatry (King's College London).

Introduction

Oliver J. Mason and Gordon Claridge

Apart from presumably guessing that it has something to do with schizophrenia, most people – even in psychopathology – know relatively little about schizotypy. This is reflected in its lack of public exposure to and among professionals. In the 60 years since the term was coined (Rado, 1953), there have only been two major conferences to discuss the topic: in 1994 and as recently as 2013 in Geneva. The proceedings of these conferences constitute the bulk of the published collections of writings on schizotypy (Raine, Lencz, & Mednick, 1995), and, in the case of the Geneva conference, as a special issue of *Schizophrenia Bulletin* (http://schizophreniabulletin.oxfordjournals.org/content/41/suppl_2.toc). The only other collated source is the edited volume (Claridge, 1997), of which the present book is a kind of sequel. Only a sequel, however, in the sense that one of the current editors was also responsible for the earlier volume. In other respects its provenance was very different from that of the present book. The 1997 book was very much an 'in-house' production, designed to foster a particular view of schizotypy, by contributors who were either ex-students or close collaborators of the editor.

We will not dwell in detail here on what the perspective of the 1997 book was. Suffice it to say that it offered a challenge to the then prevailing view about the nature of the dimensionality of schizotypy, the latter's status as part of the spectrum of schizophrenic disease, and the wider issue about how best to view psychotic personality traits generally in relation to clinical psychosis. These questions are still a matter for lively debate; indeed they have become even more so in the 30 years since they were first posed, and they lie in the background whenever the nature of 'schizotypy' is discussed. It is important, therefore, that they are aired here. However, we decided that, unlike the 1997 collection, these questions should come at the end of the book, as a final theoretically focused chapter. Placing the chapter there makes two points. First, it absolves us, as editors, from appearing to pre-empt, or influence in other ways, the contents of the earlier chapters and the views of their writers, some of whom may have a different theoretical stance on schizotypy from our own. Second, it underlines how, even in the absence of agreeing on some fundamental issues about the dimensionality of clinical psychosis, research on the topic over the past few decades has greatly expanded, taking in most areas of psychological, social and biological science – and making a book such as this timely.

The chapters are arranged around several themes that represent current concerns in schizotypy research, and there is a refreshing diversity of views contained therein. They are not intended to cohere to a single perspective, but to reflect a broad range of approaches. In particular, we were concerned not to advance a narrow view of schizotypy – either as a biogenic personality trait or as a quasi-clinical construct of sole relevance to schizophrenia. Rather, we take the view that the term subsumes a range of approaches to studying psychotic-like phenomena largely outside the clinic, but which have genuine relevance both inside and outside the clinical domain. To give some idea of this, we will briefly summarise the chapter contributions.

Any construct wanting to survive among the plethora of psychiatric and psychological concepts in mental health needs reliable and valid measurement as the bedrock to its existence. The first chapter by Thomas Kwapil and Charlotte Chun sets out the now very broad landscape with regards to psychometric assessment. The genetic, neurobiological and neurocognitive foundations of the construct are outlined by Christine Mohr and Ulrich Ettinger, Philip Grant, and Gina Grimshaw and Laura Kranz. These now 'traditional areas' of schizophrenia/schizotypy research nevertheless lead to some surprising illuminations, as Grimshaw and Kranz's deconstruction of the commonly advanced hemisphere asymmetry accounts goes to show.

The subsequent part of the book turns from exclusively biogenically focused accounts to include the roles of development and the environment. Moving beyond experimental psychopathology, Martin Debbané describes how a uniquely developmental psychopathology perspective is able to link schizotypy to other, more explicitly psychiatric, accounts of risk. Until relatively recently, childhood adversity and abuse in particular were overlooked in relation to psychotic disorders (in contrast to other psychopathology). This view is rapidly changing, and Tjasa Velikonja, Oliver Mason and Helen Fisher's systematic review clearly evidences that this also pertains very substantially to schizotypy. Extending this argument, Tamara Sheinbaum and Neus Barrantes-Vidal describe the evidence for a wide range of psychosocial adversities, and the psychological mechanisms by which they may come to have their impact on proneness to psychoses. It should be firmly asserted that is not an 'either biology or environment' debate – we suspect that all the authors here would espouse a highly 'interactionalist' position – and this is explicitly argued for by Sheinbaum and Barrantes-Vidal, who in some ways 'join up' the preceding contributions.

At the interstices of biology and environment, and of much current scientific and political debate, the role of recreational drug use in psychosis exemplifies the complexities in this arena. Drawing on a wide range of evidence, Emma Barkus provides a comprehensive and balanced overview, concentrating on agents plausibly able to trigger psychosis, and the role of schizotypy here. Although pharmacological agents are of great value to research, they are not the exclusive means to bring psychotic-like phenomena into the laboratory. Christina Daniel and Oliver Mason review the evidence for other methods, and their relevance to schizotypy research. The idea that not all within the psychosis continuum is 'pathological' is perhaps made explicit here for the first time.

The third part of the book turns to a range of consequences or outcomes from individual differences in schizotypy. Charlie Heriot-Maitland and Emmanuelle Peters describe how the seemingly categorical and irreducible symptoms of delusions actually lend themselves well to a dimensional and clinical psychological view that has promising leads for developments in treatment. It is critical to the view taken in this volume that schizotypy can lead to both pathological and benign outcomes as exemplified by the final two chapters in this part of the book. Jo Hodgekins describes the wide range of psychopathological outcomes for which schizotypy may be pertinent: that these can span such a wide range of psychiatric disorders, both psychotic and non-psychotic, and neurodevelopmental disorders such as the autistic spectrum and epilepsy, is evidence of the perhaps surprising relevance of schizotypy today. The 'positive' outcomes for schizotypy are most substantially covered in Nicola Holt's account of a plausible creative advantage. Although the book's chapters probably represent something of the balance of research in the field, it is nevertheless a regret that so-called 'benign' or 'healthy' schizotypy is not more substantially represented – just as it must be in the general population.

References

Claridge, G. E. (Ed.). (1997). *Schizotypy: Implications for illness and health*. Oxford University Press.

Rado, S. (1953). Dynamics and classification of disordered behavior. *American Journal of Psychiatry, 110*, 406–426.

Raine, A., Lencz, T., & Mednick, S. A. (Eds.). (1995). *Schizotypal personality*. Cambridge University Press.

Part I
Measurement, brain and biology

1 The psychometric assessment of schizotypy

Thomas R. Kwapil and Charlotte A. Chun

History of schizotypy

The term 'schizotypy' was introduced more than 60 years ago to describe a broad phenotype of schizophrenic-like psychopathology and impairment. However, the concept extends back to the late nineteenth and early twentieth centuries. Kraepelin (1913/1919) and Bleuler (1911/1950) both described schizophrenic-like traits in patients prior to their illness, and in the relatives of patients. Kraepelin suggested these psychotic-like experiences were precursors to *dementia praecox*, but added that in some cases they represented an arrested form of the illness. Bleuler described that 'entirely crazy acts in the midst of normal behaviour' can presage the development of schizophrenia (p. 252). Other scholars have noted that mild forms of schizophrenia frequently appear in the non-psychotic relatives of patients (e.g. Kallman, 1938) and precede the onset of the disorder (e.g. Chapman, 1966), but that they often represent stable forms of pathology that do not advance into psychosis. The twentieth-century descriptive psychopathology tradition described numerous schizophrenic-like conditions such as borderline, ambulatory and pseudoneurotic schizophrenia that captured characteristics of the schizotypy continuum (Kwapil & Barrantes-Vidal, 2012).

Rado (1953) introduced the term 'schizotype' to represent the schizophrenic phenotype, indicating a continuum of schizophrenic-like or schizotypic behavioural impairment. Meehl (e.g. 1962) conjectured that a single dominant 'schizogene' gave rise to a neurointegrative defect, referred to as 'schizotaxia' that was necessary, although not fully sufficient, for the development of schizotypy (and, by extension, schizophrenia). He described schizotypy as the personality organisation that culminated from schizotaxia and left the individual vulnerable to the development of schizophrenia. Meehl (1990) substantially updated his original model by diminishing the role of anhedonia and expanding the contribution of polygenetic potentiators. He suggested that schizotypy was taxonic in nature, adding that approximately 10 per cent of the population was schizotypic and that about 10 per cent of schizotypes decompensated into schizophrenia (corresponding with the 1 per cent lifetime prevalence rate of schizophrenia).

Claridge and colleagues (e.g. Claridge, 1997; Claridge & Beech, 1995) offered an alternative model of schizotypy that built upon dimensional models of personality and psychopathology, and conjectured that schizotypy was fully dimensional in nature and included adaptive manifestations. Claridge's model indicated that schizotypy resulted from a combination of genetic, environmental and personality variations that were normally distributed in the general population. Thus, Claridge argued that it included the pathological, quasi-dimensional components, but also encompassed healthy manifestations (e.g. creativity).

Meehl and Claridge's models differed on whether schizotypy was taxonic or fully dimensional in the population. The basis of Meehl's taxonic model was that a single dominant gene was necessary, albeit not sufficient, for schizotypy and schizophrenia. However, this etiological model has not received support in the literature (e.g. McGue & Gottesman, 1989; Schizophrenia Working Group of the Psychiatric Genomics Consortium, 2014). More than a dozen studies have employed taxometric analyses to study the structure of schizotypy, primarily using psychometric questionnaires. Many of these studies (e.g. Korfine & Lenzenweger, 1995; Linscott, 2013) have provided at least partial support for a schizotypy taxon (or taxa) with base rates in non-clinical samples generally approximating Meehl's 10 per cent estimate, although there have been exceptions (Meyer & Keller, 2001; Rawlings, Williams, Haslam, & Claridge, 2008). Widiger (2001) raised concerns that taxonic models were inconsistent with views that psychopathology arose from multifactorial genetic and non-genetic origins. Ultimately, support for any taxonic model requires a compelling etiological basis for discontinuity, not simply results of taxometric analyses (a basis that appears lacking at this point for schizotypy). Additionally, Edmundson and Kwapil (2013) suggested that schizotypy and schizophrenia were markedly heterogeneous in symptom presentation, etiology and treatment response. This heterogeneity raises questions about the extent to which separate etiological processes are occurring, and how many taxa would be represented in our current conceptualisation of schizotypy.

Current conceptualisation of schizotypy

Current conceptualisations indicate that schizotypy is a multidimensional construct that represents the underlying vulnerability to schizophrenia-spectrum psychopathology that is expressed across a broad range of personality, subclinical, and clinical phenomenology (Kwapil & Barrantes-Vidal, 2014). Schizotypy offers a useful and unifying construct – useful in that it has explanatory power for understanding the development, expression, trajectory, risk and resilience, and treatment of schizophrenia-spectrum conditions, as well as for understanding variation in normal behaviour, and unifying because it encompasses a broad spectrum of conditions – schizophrenia, related psychotic disorders, spectrum personality disorders, the prodrome, and subclinical expressions – under a single conceptual framework. Schizotypy allows us to examine the etiological and developmental factors underlying schizophrenia-spectrum psychopathology, while minimizing many of the confounding effects (e.g. hospitalisation, medications, marginalised social status) that complicate the study of patients. There are a number of related terms that are frequently used interchangeably with schizotypy. We suggest that many of these represent specific manifestations along the schizotypy continuum (e.g. schizotypal, prodrome, at-risk mental states) and that care should be used to distinguish such constructs.

Schizotypy and, by extension, schizophrenia are heterogeneous. This heterogeneity occurs at the phenotypic level, as well as at the etiological, developmental and treatment-response levels (Kwapil & Barrantes-Vidal, 2012, 2014). Therefore, treating schizotypy and schizophrenia as homogeneous constructs runs the risk of diminishing our ability to understand the origins, development and expression of these complex conditions. Schizotypy and schizophrenia appear to share a common multidimensional structure. Numerous studies support the view that positive, negative and disorganised dimensions underlie schizophrenia (e.g. Lenzenweger & Dworkin, 1996), and these dimensions have been replicated in non-clinically ascertained schizotypy (e.g. Bentall, Claridge, & Slade, 1989; Kwapil, Barrantes-Vidal, & Silvia, 2008; Raine et al., 1994; Vollema & van den Bosch, 1995).

Measurement of schizotypy

Lenzenweger (1998) discussed the relative strengths and weaknesses of three broad (and by no means mutually exclusive) methods for identifying schizotypy: (a) familial, (b) clinical, and (c) psychometric laboratory index approaches. Of the three methods, the familial is the best known, due in large part to landmark studies of the offspring of schizophrenic patients (e.g. Cannon & Mednick, 1993). The clinical method identifies high-risk individuals based upon schizophrenia-spectrum or prodromal diagnoses, as has been conducted by the North American Prodrome Longitudinal Study (NAPLS) consortium (e.g. Cannon et al., 2008). The final method involves the use of psychometrically sound research instruments designed to identify symptom, trait, neurocognitive and biobehavioural markers of vulnerability. While all three methods have their strengths and limitations, the psychometric questionnaire or screening method provides several notable advantages. First, these measures can be used to screen large numbers of individuals from the general population, rather than selecting participants based upon clinical status or consanguinity. In contrast, family studies provide a somewhat stratified group of at-risk participants, because only a fraction of patients with schizophrenia have a known first-degree relative with the disorder – thus providing a sample that is not wholly representative of future sufferers. Psychometric screening inventories also tend to be relatively non-invasive and inexpensive to administer and score, and thus can be used to screen large numbers of participants at one time. Finally, they can be used in conjunction with other measures of risk, including family studies.

As discussed by Kwapil and Barrantes-Vidal (2014), psychometric assessment of schizotypy has provided a powerful tool for assessing schizophrenic-like symptoms and impairment. Numerous studies have reported that psychometric schizotypy in non-disordered individuals is associated with psychotic-like (Gooding, Tallent, & Matts, 2005), prodromal (e.g. Barrantes-Vidal, Chun, Myin-Germeys, & Kwapil, 2013), and schizophrenia-spectrum (e.g. Blanchard, Collins, Aghevli, Leung, & Cohen, 2011) symptoms. Furthermore, longitudinal studies (e.g. Chapman, Chapman, Kwapil, Eckblad, & Zinser, 1994; Kwapil, 1998) have demonstrated that positive schizotypy predicts the development of psychotic disorders, whereas negative schizotypy predicts the development of schizophrenia-spectrum disorders. Schizotypy is associated with schizophrenic-like patterns of cognitive impairment (e.g. Tallent & Gooding, 1999), neurological soft signs (e.g. Kaczorowski, Barrantes-Vidal, & Kwapil, 2009) and social cognition (e.g. Morrison, Brown, & Cohen, 2013). Schizotypy is also associated with schizophrenic-like impairment assessed with neuroimaging (e.g. Modinos et al., 2010) and eye tracking (e.g. Lenzenweger & O'Driscoll, 2006). In addition, schizotypy is associated with normal personality traits (e.g. Kwapil, Barrantes-Vidal, & Silvia, 2008), impaired attachment (e.g. Sheinbaum, Bedoya, Ros-Morente, Kwapil, & Barrantes-Vidal, 2013), creativity (see Holt, Chapter 12 in this volume), and schizophrenic-like symptoms and impairment in daily life (e.g. Barrantes-Vidal et al., 2013).

Psychometric measures of schizotypy

Although measures of schizophrenic-like characteristics date back at least as far as the Minnesota Multiphasic Personality Inventory (MMPI; University of Minnesota, 1943), the psychometric assessment of schizotypy began in earnest in the 1970s and 1980s with the development of the Schizotypal Traits Questionnaire (Claridge & Broks, 1984) and the Wisconsin Schizotypy Scales, including the Perceptual Aberration (Chapman, Chapman, & Raulin, 1978), Magical Ideation (Eckblad & Chapman, 1983), Physical Anhedonia (Chapman, Chapman, & Raulin, 1976) and Revised Social Anhedonia (Eckblad, Chapman, Chapman, & Mishlove, 1982) Scales. The remainder of this chapter provides a review of psychometric assessments of schizotypy, although readers are also directed to previous reviews by Chapman, Chapman, & Kwapil (1995), Fonseca-Pedrero et al. (2008) and Mason, Claridge, & Williams (1997). Tables 1.1 and 1.2 provide a summary of more than two dozen psychometric measures of schizotypy and related constructs, with measures of paranoia shown later in Table 1.3. Note that we have not included measures specifically designed to assess schizotypic and prodromal features in children and adolescents, or interview-based measures.

Table 1.1 Summary of psychometric measures of schizotypy – wide spectrum

Test	Authors and Year	Authors' Stated Purpose	Content	Subscales	Items	Test-Retest Reliability	Cronbach's Alpha	Validity Studies
Schizotypal Traits Scale (STA)	Claridge & Broks, 1984	Identify individuals with schizotypal personality traits	DSM-III SPD traits	None	37, Yes/No			STA correlates: hemispheric, PEN Psychoticism, PEN Neuroticism.
Oxford-Liverpool Inventory of Feelings and Experiences (O-LIFE)	Mason, Claridge, & Jackson, 1995	Create new scales for the factors based on factor analysis of several scales, with 20-30 items per factor	*UnEx*: Perceptual aberrations, magical thinking, hallucinations. *CogDis*: Purposelessness, moodiness, social anxiety, poor attention and decision-making. *IntAn*: Independence, solitude, social and physical anhedonia, avoidance of intimacy. *ImpNom*: Violent, impulsive, anti-social, eccentric behaviour, lack of self-control	Unusual Experiences, Cognitive Disorganisation, Introvertive Anhedonia, Impulsive Non-conformity	104, True/False: 30 UnEx, 24 CogDis, 27 IntAnh, 23 ImpNon	3-6 months later. 0.86 UnEx, 0.93 CogDis, 0.84 IntAn, 0.77 ImpNon	0.89 UnEx, 0.87 CogDis, 0.82 IntAnh, 0.77 ImpNon	UnEx, CogDis, ImpNon correlated with STA. IntAnh weakly correlated with STA. O-LIFE subscales all linked with genetic heritability.

(continued)

Table 1.1 (continued)

Test	Authors and Year	Authors' Stated Purpose	Content	Subscales	Items	Test-Retest Reliability	Cronbach's Alpha	Validity Studies
O-LIFE Short Forms	Mason, Linney, & Claridge, 2005	To make a shortened form of the O-LIFE maximising genotypic variance	Same as O-LIFE	As above	43, True/False: 12 UnEx, 11 CogDis, 10 IntAnh, 10 ImpNon		0.90 to 0.94	
Wisconsin Schizotypy Scales (WSS) Short Forms	Winterstein, Silvia, Kwapil, Kaufman, Reiter-Palmon, & Wigert, 2011	To develop abbreviated versions of the WSS that are more time efficient and include stronger items		Magical Thinking, Perceptual Aberration, Social Anhedonia, Physical Anhedonia	60 True/False (15 items/scale)		Subscale alphas: 0.74 MagId, 0.83 PerAb, 0.75 SocAnh, 0.62 PhysAnh	Positive symptom schizotypy strongly correlated with affective dysregulation, and approach-oriented traits. Negative symptom schizotypy correlated negatively with curiosity, sensation seeking and hypomania, and strongly negatively correlated with emotionality and extraversion.

Schizotypal Personality Questionnaire (SPQ)	Raine, 1991	To develop short subscales to assess each of the nine features of schizotypal personality from *DSM-III-R* features	Modeled on *DSM-III-R* criteria for schizotypal personality disorder and containing subscales for all nine schizotypal traits.	Ideas of reference; Excessive social anxiety; Odd beliefs or magical thinking; Unusual perceptual experiences; Odd or eccentric behavior; No close friends; Odd speech; Constricted Affect; Suspiciousness	74, Yes/No	0.82	0.91	Correlated with Schizophrenism, STA, *DSM-III-R* SPD diagnosis, and continuous SPD interview scores; weakly with Psychoticism and Anhedonia scales. 55% of subjects scoring in top 10% of SPQ scores had clinical diagnosis of SPD.
Schizotypal Personality Questionnaire-Brief (SPQ-B)	Raine, & Benishay, 1995	To develop a briefer self-report scale that assesses the three main factors of schizotypal personality and may be used as an initial screening for *DSM-IV* SPD	Items tapping SPD traits; does not tap all 9 SPQ subscales but only 3 domains (see subscales)	Cognitive-Perceptual, Disorganised, and Interpersonal	22, True/False		0.83 Total scale. *Subscale alphas:* 0.72 & 0.72 Cognitive-Perceptual, 0.78 & 0.76 Interpersonal, 0.75 and 0.73 Disorganisation.	SPQ-B correlated with *DSM-III-R* SPD SCID dimensional scores. *Factor Analysis:* 3-factor structure not supported, found 4 factors. Constraining to 3 factors led to high cross-loadings

(*continued*)

Table 1.1 (continued)

Test	Authors and Year	Authors' Stated Purpose	Content	Subscales	Items	Test-Retest Reliability	Cronbach's Alpha	Validity Studies
Schizotypal Personality Questionnaire-Brief Revised (SPQ-BR)	Cohen, Matthews, Najolia, & Brown, 2010	To develop a revised SPQ-Brief with more sensitive response format, expanded trait coverage, a higher order 4-factor structure of Social Anxiety, Social Anhedonia, Disorganization, and Cognitive-Perceptual dimensions.	Items tapping SPD traits from all 9 SPQ subscales	Ideas of Reference/Suspiciousness, No Close Friends/Constricted Affect, Eccentric Behaviour, Social Anxiety, Magical Thinking, Odd Speech, Unusual Perceptions	32, 5-point Likert scale (ranging from Strongly Disagree to Neutral to Strongly Agree)		*Subscale alphas:* 0.84 Ref/Susp, 0.81 Friends/Affect, 0.86 EccBx, 0.84 SocAnx, 0.82 MagThink, 0.82 OddSpeech, 0.70 UnPercep	All SPQ factors significantly associated with poor QOL. *Factor Analysis:* subordinate 7-factor structure, both 3-factor superordinate (Cognitive-Perceptual, Interpersonal, and Disorganised factors) and 4-factor superordinate (Cognitive-Perceptual, Disorganised, No Close Friends/Constricted Affect, Social Anxiety).
Aberrant Salience Inventory (ASI)	Cicero, Kerns, & McCarthy, 2010	To create a measure of lifetime occurrence or trait aberrant salience that can be used in non-clinical samples	Items measuring the assignment of salience, significance or importance to otherwise innocuous stimuli, i.e. report of enhanced sensory, cognitive or emotional perception of the world.	Feelings of increased significance, Senses sharpening, Impending understanding, Heightened emotionality, Heightened cognition	29, Yes/No		0.89	ASI correlated with positive schizotypy and measures associated with dopamine level. Correlated weakly with social anhedonia. High psychosis-proneness group had elevated ASI scores compared with controls. Group with history of psychosis had elevated ASI scores compared with psychiatric comparison group.

Community Assessment of Psychic Experiences (CAPE)	Stefanis, Hanssen, Smirnis, Avramopoulos, Evdokimidis, Stefanis, ... Van Os, 2002	To examine how positive and negative psychosis are independent of depression and whether they have a normal distribution in the general population	Hallucinations and delusions; lack of emotions, motivation, and social interest; cognitive symptoms of depression	Positive, Negative, Depression	40, 4-point scale for frequency and distress 18 Positive, 14 Negative, 8 Depression	1 to 26 months, CAPE Pos: 0.71, CAPE Neg: 0.78, CAPE Depression: 0.76.	CAPE Pos: 0.63, CAPE Neg: 0.64, CAPE Depression: 0.62.	CAPE positive with perceptual aberration. CAPE negative with SPQ negative symptom scales. CAPE depression with SCL-90 Depression scale. However, scales correlate highly with one another, and CAPE negative correlates highly with depression.
Psychoticism Scale	Eysenck & Eysenck (1975) revised: Eysenck et al. (1985)	To measure traits believed to be linked to increased vulnerability to psychosis	Aggressive, cold, egocentric, impulsive, antisocial, creative, unempathic, tough-minded, impulsive.		Original: 25 Revised: 32	Original Male: 0.83 Female: 0.71	Original: Male: 0.74 Female: 0.68 Revised: Male 0.78 Female 0.76	Correlations with range of schizotypy scales. Higher scores of 153 psychotic patients on original scale.

Table 1.2 Summary of psychometric measures of schizotypy – single trait excluding delusions and paranoia

Test	Authors and Year	Authors' Stated Purpose	Content	Subscales	Items	Test-Retest Reliability	Cronbach's Alpha	Validity Studies
Magical Ideation Scale (MIS)	Eckblad & Chapman, 1983	To measure magical ideation, the belief in invalid or unconventional causation	Thought transmission, psychokinesis, precognition, astrology, spirit influences, reincarnation, good luck charms, psychical energies transfer, secret messages	None	30, True/False		0.83 – 0.85	Magical ideation group exceeded controls on range of schizotypal experiences. Predicts psychotic disorders.
Perceptual Aberration Scale (PAS)	Chapman, Chapman & Raulin, 1978	A self-report scale of experience of body-image aberration, independent from hypochondriasis and feelings of inadequacy	Unclear body boundaries; unreality, estrangement, deterioration of body parts; change in the size, proportions, or space of body parts; hanges in body appearance	None	23, True/False		0.88 – 0.94	Discriminated schizophrenia patients and controls, and between poor premorbid schizophrenia from good premorbid schizophrenia. Predicts psychotic disorders.
Physical Anhedonia Scale (Pha)	Chapman, Chapman, & Raulin, 1976	A self-report scale of experience of physical pleasures	Long-term ability to experience physical pleasures of eating, touching, feeling, sex, temperature, movement, smell, sound	None	40, True/False		0.78 – 0.84	Discriminated schizophrenia patients and controls, and premorbid state. Not correlated with depression, delusions, or hallucinations

Revised Social Anhedonia Scale (R-SAS)	Eckblad, Chapman, Chapman, & Mishlove, 1982	To revise the SAS by eliminating social anxiety items and adding new schizoid asociality items	Schizoid indifference to other people	None	40, True/False	0.84–0.88	Associated with psychotic-like experiences and schizotypal and schizoid symptoms, predicts schizophrenia-spectrum disorders
Cognitive Slippage Scale (CSS)	Miers & Raulin, 1987	To measure cognitive impairment	Cognitive slippage: speech deficits and confused thinking	None	35, True/False	1 month later, 0.75 in schizophrenic patients, 0.80 in college students	0.88–0.90	Correlated with executive functioning, perceptual aberration, intense ambivalence, social fear, magical ideation, somatic symptoms and distrust. Identifies people with increased communication impairments and poor executive control.
Poor Cognitive Control Scale (PCCS)	Cicero & Kerns, 2010	To create a measure of disorganised schizotypy to assess the kinds of executive functioning deficits observed after frontal lobe damage	Attentional difficulties, confusion, language impairments, difficulty with beginning and finishing complex tasks, with following directions, with impulse control, and with memory	None	30, 5-point scale	0.89	Correlated strongly with other measures of disorganised schizotypy; moderately with measures of positive schizotypy, dissociation, neuroticism, inattentiveness, difficulty with emotional processing; weakly with measures of negative schizotypy and childhood maltreatment.

(continued)

Table 1.2 (continued)

Test	Authors and Year	Authors' Stated Purpose	Content	Subscales	Items	Test-Retest Reliability	Cronbach's Alpha	Validity Studies
Referential Thinking Scale (REF)	Lenzenweger, Bennett, & Lilenfeld, 1997	To create a self-report schizotypy measure covering a broader range of simple and guilty ideas of reference that are relatively severe, uncommon, and distinct from self-consciousness and self-monitoring	Referential experiences interacting with people or animals, referential reflections on common or causal experiences, and guilty referential interpretation of interpersonal or intrapersonal nature	Laughing/Commenting, Attention/Appearance, Guilt/Shame, Songs/Newspapers/Books, Reactions	34, True/False	0.86 (1+ month)	0.83 to 0.85. 0.80	REF correlated strongly with perceptual aberration, magical ideation and paranoia; moderately with trait anxiety and depression; weakly with self-monitoring, self-consciousness, state anxiety, and negative social desirability. *Factor analysis*: REF loaded on schizotypy factor but not on affect or normal self-awareness.
Schizotypal Ambivalence Scale (SAS)	Raulin, 1986	To develop a scale to measure the ambivalence that Meehl (1964) described as a sign of schizotypy	Strong simultaneous/rapidly interchangeable positive and negative feelings toward the same object, activity, or person	None	45, True/False	0.81 (10 to 12 weeks, n = 76)	0.87 (n = 394), 0.86 (n = 1177), 0.87 (n = 1349)	SAS scores: Depressed inpatients > Schizophrenic inpatients = Psychology clinic outpatients > Controls. 70% of acute patients were ≥2 SD above control group on SAS. SAS correlated with PerAb in all four groups.

Measures based on Claridge's fully dimensional model

The fully dimensional approach to characterising psychopathology holds that psychotic traits are normally distributed in the general population and, while still representative of psychosis proneness, are an aspect of normal variation in healthy personality. Measurement in this area initially grew out of the differentiation of schizotypal and borderline personality traits. Specifically, Claridge and Broks (1984) created the Schizotypal Traits Questionnaire (STQ) that included the Schizotypal Personality Scale (STA) and the Borderline Personality Scale (STB). Unlike the current definition of schizotypal personality, the STA did not include descriptions of negative symptoms.

In order to create a broader assessment tool, the Combined Schizotypal Traits Questionnaire (CSTQ; Bentall, Claridge, & Slade, 1989) was created by combining items from more than a dozen measures of schizotypy and personality. The CSTQ provided a more comprehensive measurement of schizotypal traits, but with 420 items it was relatively impractical. In order to create a more manageable measure, Mason, Claridge, and Jackson (1995) created the Oxford-Liverpool Inventory of Feelings and Experiences (O-LIFE) from a factor analysis of the CSTQ. The resulting scale had four factors, Unusual Experiences, Cognitive Disorganisation, Introvertive Anhedonia and Impulsive Non-conformity. Note that a short form version was subsequently developed (Mason, Linney, & Claridge, 2005).

The O-LIFE and related fully dimensional scales are advantageous in that they measure schizotypy multidimensionally and allow for broad screening of traits in the general population. The O-LIFE has solid psychometric properties and its validity is supported by numerous cross-sectional questionnaire (e.g. Goulding, 2004), psychophysiological (Mason, Claridge, & Clark, 1997) and neurocognitive (e.g. Burch, Hemsley, Corr, & Gwyer, 2006) studies. The O-LIFE Unusual Experiences and Impulsive Non-conformity scales have also been associated with measures of creativity (e.g. Batey & Furnham, 2008), which some have hypothesised to be an adaptive feature of schizotypy (e.g. Claridge, 1997).

Limitations of using these scales include mixed evidence for the proposed factor structure and for associations with related interview measures (Cochrane, Petch, & Pickering, 2010). Furthermore, there is question of whether Impulsive Non-conformity is a meaningful dimension of schizotypy (Cochrane et al., 2010; see also Chapman, Chapman, & Kwapil, 1994). (For further discussion of this issue, see Chapter 13 in this volume). Finally, like many of the psychometric assessment measures, the O-LIFE scales lack longitudinal data demonstrating their relation to long-term outcomes such as the development of schizophrenia-spectrum disorders.

Measures based upon Meehl's model of schizotypy

A number of measures have come directly from Meehl's (1962) formulation of schizotypy and his (1964) Checklist of Schizotypic Signs. Primary among these has been the family of Wisconsin Schizotypy Scales developed by the Chapmans and their colleagues. They employed Jackson's (1970) model of rational scale development to create measures assessing different characteristics described in Meehl's checklist and Hoch and Cattell's (1959) description of pseudoneurotic schizophrenia. The four most widely used scales, the Perceptual Aberration, Magical Ideation, Physical Anhedonia, and Revised Social Anhedonia scales, can be used to compute positive and negative schizotypy dimensional scores (Kwapil et al., 2008) and are also available in shortened versions (Winterstein et al., 2011).

The Wisconsin Schizotypy Scales have good psychometric properties and extensive support of the validity of both the individual scales and their underlying dimensions. The strongest evidence comes from the Chapmans' 10-year longitudinal study, which indicated that the Perceptual Aberration and Magical Ideation scales predict the development of psychotic disorders (Chapman et al., 1994) and the Revised Social Anhedonia scale predicts the development of schizophrenia-spectrum disorders (Kwapil, 1998). Note that Kwapil, Gross, Silvia, and Barrantes-Vidal (2013) demonstrated that the positive and negative dimensional scores provided improved longitudinal prediction over the individual scales. Numerous other studies have shown that positive and negative schizotypy, as assessed by the Chapman scales, are associated with schizophrenia-like outcomes and impairment, as demonstrated by interview (e.g. Kwapil et al., 2008), daily life (e.g. Barrantes-Vidal et al., 2013; Kwapil, Brown, Silvia, Myin-Germeys, & Barrantes-Vidal, 2012) and laboratory studies (e.g. Tallent & Gooding, 1999).

Despite strong empirical validity, the Wisconsin Schizotypy Scales have several limitations –namely, they provide inadequate trait coverage: the scales do not assess disorganised schizotypy or paranoia, and their assessment of negative schizotypy is largely limited to anhedonia. The Physical Anhedonia scale has not demonstrated good predictive validity for the development of psychotic disorders and the Revised Social Anhedonia scale loads on positive as well as negative schizotypy, suggesting that the scale may tap characteristics such as social anxiety and affective dysregulation, in addition to negative symptoms.

Schizotypal Personality Questionnaire

The Schizotypal Personality Questionnaire (SPQ; Raine, 1991) was designed to assess schizotypal personality in the general population and includes nine subscales derived from *DSM-III-R* (American Psychiatric Association, 1987) criteria for schizotypal personality disorder (SPD). However, it has been widely used as a more general measure of schizotypy. Raine et al. (1994) indicate that three factors underlie the scales (cognitive–perceptual, interpersonal and disorganised); however, the factor structure has been inconsistently replicated (see Gross, Mellin, Silvia, Barrantes-Vidal, & Kwapil, 2014). Raine and Benishay (1995) subsequently created a short form of the SPQ (SPQ-B) that produces three factor scores and a total score. The SPQ-B has benefited from improved psychometric properties in a recent Likert-scale version (Wuthrich & Bates, 2005) and modified Likert-scale revision (SPQ-BR; Cohen et al., 2010).

Convergent validity of the SPQ has been demonstrated through its correlations with other schizotypy measures, and its relation to interview-based SPD diagnoses and trait ratings (Raine, 1991). Raine (1991) indicated that 55 per cent of subjects scoring in the top tenth percentile on the scale met criteria for SPD diagnoses. The SPQ, SPQ-B and SPQ-BR have demonstrated validity in cross-sectional interview (e.g. Raine, 1991; Raine & Benishay, 1995) questionnaire (e.g. Chun, Minor, & Cohen, 2013; Minor & Cohen, 2010; Morrison, Brown, & Cohen, 2013), and psychophysiological (e.g. Prévost et al., 2010) and neurocognitive (e.g. Chun, Minor, & Cohen, 2013) studies.

The SPQ and its brief scale are advantageous in that they provide a continuous, multidimensional measure of schizotypal symptoms in subclinical individuals. However, limitations of these scales include lack of longitudinal data, high inter-correlations among factors (e.g. Cohen et al., 2010), poor replicability of the proposed factor structure (e.g. Chmielewski & Watson, 2008; Stefanis et al., 2004; Wuthrich & Bates, 2006) and high correlations of all the factors with neuroticism (Gross et al., 2014).

Measures of paranoia

Dating back to Kraepelin, paranoia has been considered a feature of schizophrenia-spectrum pathology. However, it also appears along a continuum of expression in the general population (e.g. Freeman et al., 2005; Horton, Barrantes-Vidal, Silvia, & Kwapil, 2014). Suspiciousness or paranoid ideation is one of the nine features of schizotypal personality disorder and a common characteristic of persecutory delusions in positive symptom schizophrenia according to *DSM-5* (American Psychiatric Association, 2013). Paranoia has alternatively been conceptualised as part of positive schizotypy or as a separate dimension of schizotypy (that is strongly associated with the positive dimension) (Horton et al., 2014). Historically, there were a variety of clinical measures designed to assess pathological paranoia, primarily derived from the MMPI. However, several scales (see Table 1.3) have been developed in the past two decades to assess attenuated paranoia and suspiciousness, including the Paranoia Scale (Fenigstein & Vanable, 1992), the Paranoia/Suspiciousness Questionnaire (PSQ; Rawlings & Freeman, 1996) and the Paranoia Checklist (Freeman et al., 2005). The paranoia measures have demonstrated good convergent validity with cross-sectional questionnaire measures; however, they have no known longitudinal data and little converging evidence with psychophysiological, neurocognitive and genetic assessment.

Table 1.3 Summary of psychometric measures of schizotypy – paranoia and delusions

Test	Authors and Year	Authors' Stated Purpose	Content	Subscales	Items	Test-Retest Reliability	Cronbach's Alpha	Validity Studies
Paranoia Checklist	Freeman, et al., 2005	To assess a range of paranoid thoughts, more clinical than those assessed on the Paranoia Scale, and to examine their distribution	Frequency, conviction and distress of paranoid thoughts, including persecutory thoughts.		18, 5-point scale for frequency, degree of conviction, distress		≥ 0.90. Rarer items associated with higher total score than the common items.	PS correlated with Paranoia Checklist frequency, conviction and distress. Frequency correlated with conviction and distress; conviction correlated with distress.
Paranoia Scale	Fenigstein & Vanable, 1992	To assess paranoid thought in non-clinical college students	Belief that people or external forces are trying to influence one's behaviour/control one's thinking, that people are against one, belief that people talk about, refer to, or watch one, suspicion or mistrust of others' motives, feelings of resentment or bitterness.		20, 5-point scale	0.7 (6 months, n=107/180)	0.84 overall (0.81 to 0.87 in 4 independent samples). r=0.42 mean corrected item-total correlation (r=0.27 to 0.51)	Paranoia negatively correlated with interpersonal trust, trust in close relationships, social desirability; positively with experience and expression of anger, belief in the control of powerful others, need for personal control and self-consciousness. Paranoid individuals more likely to report feeling watched in a behavioural study.

Paranoia/ Suspiciousness Questionnaire (PSQ)	Rawlings & Freeman, 1996	To produce a substantial measure of paranoia/suspiciousness representative of schizotypy, suitable for a non-psychiatric sample	Suspiciousness and hostility in daily interpersonal interactions, tendency to be mistrustful and wary, perception that life is harsh and unfair, feelings of general unhappiness, loneliness, anger and lack of control.	Interpersonal Suspiciousness/Hostility, Negative Mood/Withdrawal, Anger/Impulsiveness, Mistrust/Wariness, Perceived Hardship/Resentment	47, Yes/No	0.82 (3 months, n=74/264). *Subscale reliability*: 0.82 IS, 0.68 NM, 0.59 AI, 0.64 MW, 0.79 PH	0.87 to 0.9. *Subscale alphas*: 0.77 IS, 0.66 NM, 0.71 AI, 0.65 MW, 0.74 PH. *Subscales correlations*: r=0.33 (MW with AI) and 0.50 (IS with AI; IS with PH)	Created 5 subscales based on the factor structure, using low factor loading criterion "in an attempt to include as many items as possible in these subscales."
Peters et al. Delusional Inventory (PDI)	Peters, Joseph, & Garety, 1999	To create a quasi-dimensional measure assessing a wide range of attenuated delusions, filling the gap between common superstition and clinical delusions	Distress, preoccupation and conviction of a variety of delusions.	Delusions of control; misinterpretations, misidentification and delusions of reference; delusions of persecution; expansive delusions; delusions of influence and primary delusions; other delusions; simple delusions of guilt, de-personalisation, hypochondriasis; disturbed thinking	40, Yes/No. If Yes: 5-point scale for distress, preoccupation, conviction.	0.82 PDI yes/no (6 months to 1 year, n=83)	0.88	PDI correlated with positive schizotypy. Psychotic inpatients had higher scores than controls PDI total and dimensions.

(continued)

Table 1.3 (continued)

Test	Authors and Year	Authors' Stated Purpose	Content	Subscales	Items	Test-Retest Reliability	Cronbach's Alpha	Validity Studies
Peters Delusional Inventory (PDI-21)	Peters, Joseph, Day, & Garety, 2004; Peters et al., 1999	To develop a shorter version of the PDI with the same psychometric properties	Distress, preoccupation and conviction of a variety of delusions (see subscales).	Persecution, Suspiciousness, Paranoid ideation, Religiosity, Grandiosity, Paranormal beliefs, Thought disturbances, Negative self, Depersonalisation, Catastrophic ideation and thought broadcast, and Ideation of reference and influence.	21, Yes/No. If Yes: 5-point scale for distress, preoccupation, conviction.	0.78 PDI yes/no (6 months to 1 year. *Subscale reliability*: 0.81 Distress, 0.81 Preoccupation 0.78 Conviction	0.82 (n=444 mixed sample + 33 deluded patients). 0.90 (33 deluded patients only). *Item-scale correlations*: 0.35 to 0.60.	PDI-21 correlated positive schizotypy. Uncorrelated with Eysenck's Extroversion, IntAn, or CogDis. Deluded patients higher than mixed student/community sample on PDI total and dimensions. Correlated with state and trait anxiety and negative affect. *Factor analysis*: 3-factor structure

Disorganisation measures

Despite the strong empirical validity for a three-factor model of schizotypy (e.g. Raine et al., 1994; Vollema & van den Bosch, 1995), there are relatively few measures designed to assess cognitive and behavioural disorganisation. To date, the primary measures are the SPQ-Disorganisation, O-LIFE Cognitive Disorganisation and the Cognitive Slippage Scale (CSS; Miers & Raulin, 1987). This dimension has proven difficult to assess because such scales often tap volitional oddness associated with positive schizotypy, rather than a breakdown in the ability to control thought, speech and behaviour. Furthermore, disorganisation may not be as easily assessed by self-report questionnaires, because disorganised individuals may be impaired in their ability to report disruptions in thought and behaviour. Such scales can easily be confounded with other factors that disrupt cognition such as attention deficit hyperactivity disorder (ADHD), anxiety and substance use.

A newer measure, the Poor Cognitive Control Scale (PCCS; Cicero & Kerns, 2010), was developed to provide further coverage of the conceptualisation of disorganised schizotypy by assessing day-to-day manifestations of executive functioning deficits. Although the PCCS demonstrated good convergent validity in its development study, it remains to be incorporated in other empirical work.

Questionnaire and laboratory studies using SPQ-Disorganisation, O-LIFE Cognitive Disorganisation, and the CSS have found disorganised traits to be associated with factors such as executive functioning deficits (e.g. Cappe, Herzog, Herzig, Brand, & Mohr, 2012), communication disturbances in stressful or negative conditions (Kerns & Becker, 2008; Minor & Cohen, 2010), atypical semantic activation (Minor, Cohen, Weber, & Brown, 2011), low working memory (Kerns & Becker, 2008) and poor cognitive control (e.g. Kerns, 2006). As with the paranoia scales, the current measures of schizotypic disorganisation have no known longitudinal data and have far fewer empirical validation studies than positive and negative trait measures.

Additional measures of schizotypy and related constructs

As our understanding of the schizophrenia spectrum expands, new aspects of schizotypy and related constructs continue to be included in its nomological network. Recent psychometric tools that have been designed to measure these constructs include the Community Assessment of Psychic Experiences (CAPE; Stefanis et al., 2002) to assess positive, negative and depressive symptoms of psychosis; the Peters et al. Delusional Inventory (PDI; Peters, Joseph, & Garety, 1999) and its short form, the Peters Delusional Inventory (PDI-21; Peters, Joseph, Day, & Garety, 2004) to assess distress, preoccupation and conviction of eight different delusion categories; the Referential

Thinking Scale (REF; Lenzenweger, Bennett, & Lilenfeld, 1997) to assess simple and guilty ideas of reference; the Aberrant Salience Inventory (ASI; Cicero, Kerns, & McCarthy, 2010) to assess the assignment of salience, significance or importance to innocuous stimuli; the Schizotypal Ambivalence Scale (SAS; Raulin, 1986) to assess strong simultaneous or rapidly interchangeable positive and negative feelings toward one person or activity; and the Personality Inventory for *DSM-5* (PID-5; American Psychiatric Association, 2013; Krueger, Derringer, Markon, Watson, & Skodol, 2012) psychoticism domain to assess unusual beliefs and experiences, eccentricity and perceptual dysregulation.

In summary, these new measures are advantageous in that they allow for a broader coverage of schizotypic traits; however, they lack longitudinal data. Several of the measures have relatively limited support to date and would benefit from further empirical validation.

Summary

Schizotypy is a promising construct for understanding both normal variation and the development of schizophrenia-spectrum psychopathology. It successfully integrates a variety of subclinical and clinical conditions and offers a useful (and essential) multidimensional framework. Psychometric assessment has been a centerpiece of the empirical study of schizotypy and numerous cross-sectional and longitudinal findings attest to the importance of this method. However, there are several limitations that must be addressed for schizotypy to remain an important construct and the psychometric method to remain a useful tool for its study. First of all, a comprehensive, multidimensional model of schizotypy is needed – this model should be integrated with developmental psychopathology models of schizophrenia. Researchers increasingly treat schizotypy as a multidimensional construct; however, at times it appears that their conceptualisation of this structure is driven by the measure they choose, rather than the measure being driven by an a priori model. Thus, the development of a comprehensive and multidimensional model of schizotypy should drive the development of a new generation of psychometric measures. Many of our current measures are showing their age and limitations. Specifically, the language in some has grown outdated, they do not fully cover the domains of schizotypy and they have differential item functioning, especially in terms of sex and ethnicity. Furthermore, very few of these measures were developed using modern measurement models such as item response theory. Finally, the process of construct validation should include greater longitudinal assessment, consider the identification of endophenotypes, and integrate psychometric approaches with interview, laboratory, biogenetic and daily life assessments. We fully expect that schizotypy will continue to be a useful construct and that psychometric assessment will provide a valuable tool for tapping this complex phenotype.

References

American Psychiatric Association. (1987). *Diagnostic and statistical manual of mental disorders (DSM-IIIR)* (3rd ed., rev.). Washington, DC: Author.

American Psychiatric Association. (2013). *Diagnostic and statistical manual of mental disorders (DSM-V)* (5th ed.). Arlington, VA: Author.

Barrantes-Vidal, N., Chun, C., Myin-Germeys, I., & Kwapil, T. R. (2013). Psychometric schizotypy predicts the experience of psychotic-like, paranoid, and negative symptom experiences in daily life. *Journal of Abnormal Psychology, 122*, 1077–1087.

Batey, M., & Furnham, A. (2008). The relationship between measures of creativity and schizotypy. *Personality and Individual Differences, 45*, 816–821.

Bentall, R. P., Claridge, G. S., & Slade, P. D. (1989). The multidimensional nature of schizotypal traits: a factor analytic study with normal subjects. *British Journal of Clinical Psychology, 28*, 363–375.

Blanchard, J. J., Collins, L. M., Aghevli, M., Leung, W. W., & Cohen, A. S. (2011). Social anhedonia and schizotypy in a community sample: The Maryland Longitudinal Study of Schizotypy. *Schizophrenia Bulletin, 37*, 587–602.

Bleuler, E. P. (1950). *Dementia praecox or the group of schizophrenias* (J. Zinkin, Trans.). New York: International Universities Press. (Original work published in 1911.)

Burch, G., Hemsley, D., Corr, P., & Gwyer, P. (2006). The relationship between incidental learning and multi-dimensional schizotypy as measured by the Oxford-Liverpool Inventory of Feelings and Experiences (O-LIFE). *Personality and Individual Differences, 40*, 385–394.

Cannon, T. D., Cadenhead, K., Cornblatt, B., Woods, S. W., Addington, J., Walker, E., . . . Heinssen, R. (2008). Prediction of psychosis in youth at high clinical risk: a multisite longitudinal study in North America. *Archives of General Psychiatry, 65*, 28–37.

Cannon, T. D., & Mednick, S. A. (1993). The schizophrenia high-risk project in Copenhagen: three decades of progress. *Acta Psychiatrica Scandinavica, 87*, 33–47.

Cappe, C., Herzog, M. H., Herzig, D. A., Brand, A., & Mohr, C. (2012). Cognitive disorganisation in schizotypy is associated with deterioration in visual backward masking. *Psychiatry Research, 200*, 652–659.

Chapman, J. (1966). The early symptoms of schizophrenia. *British Journal of Psychiatry, 112*, 225–251.

Chapman, J. P., Chapman, L. J., & Kwapil, T. R. (1994). Does the Eysenck Psychoticism Scale predict psychosis: a ten-year longitudinal study. *Personality and Individual Differences, 17*, 369–375.

Chapman, J. P., Chapman, L. J., & Kwapil, T. R. (1995). Scales for the measurement of schizotypy. In A. Raine, T. Lencz, & S. Mednick (Eds.), *Schizotypal personality disorder*, Cambridge University Press.

Chapman, L. J., Chapman, J. P., & Raulin, M. L. (1976). Scales for physical and social anhedonia. *Journal of Abnormal Psychology, 85*, 374–382.

Chapman, L. J., Chapman J. P., & Raulin M. L. (1978). Body image aberration in schizophrenia. *Journal of Abnormal Psychology, 87*, 399–407.

Chapman, L. J., Chapman, J. P., Kwapil, T. R., Eckblad, M., & Zinser, M. C. (1994). Putatively psychosis-prone subjects ten years later. *Journal of Abnormal Psychology, 103*, 171–183.

Chmielewski, M., & Watson, D. (2008). The heterogeneous structure of schizotypal personality disorder: item-level factors of the schizotypal personality questionnaire and their associations with obsessive-compulsive disorder symptoms, dissociative tendencies, and normal personality. *Journal of Abnormal Psychology, 117*, 364–376.

Chun, C., Minor, K., Cohen, A. (2013). Neurocognition in psychometrically-defined college schizotypy samples: we are NOT measuring the 'right stuff'. *Journal of the International Neuropsychological Society, 19*, 1–14.

Cicero, D. C., & Kerns, J. G. (2010). Can disorganized and positive schizotypy be discriminated from dissociation? *Journal of Personality, 78*, 1239–1270.

Cicero, D. C., Kerns, J. G., & McCarthy, D. M. (2010). The Aberrant Salience Inventory: a new measure of psychosis proneness. *Psychological Assessment, 22*, 688–701.

Claridge, G. (1997). Theoretical background issues. In G. Claridge (Ed.), *Schizotypy: Implications for illness and health* (pp. 3–18). Oxford University Press.

Claridge, G., & Beech, T. (1995). Fully and quasi-dimensional constructions of schizotypy. In A. Raine, T. Lencz, & S. A. Mednick (Eds.), *Schizotypal personality* (pp. 192–216). Cambridge University Press.

Claridge, G., & Broks, P. (1984). Schizotypy and hemisphere function – I: Theoretical considerations and the measurement of schizotypy. *Personality and Individual Differences, 5*,(6), 633–648.

Cochrane, M., Petch, I., & Pickering, A. D. (2010). Do measures of schizotypal personality provide non-clinical analogues of schizophrenic symptomatology? *Psychiatry Research, 176*, 150–154.

Cohen, A. S., Matthews, R. A., Najolia, G. M., & Brown, L. A. (2010). Toward a more psychometrically sound brief measure of schizotypal traits: introducing the SPQ-Brief Revised. *Journal of Personality Disorders, 24*, 516–537.

Eckblad, M., & Chapman, L. J. (1983). Magical ideation as an indicator of schizotypy. *Journal of Consulting and Clinical Psychology, 51*, 215–225.

Eckblad, M. L., Chapman, L. J., Chapman, J. P., & Mishlove, M. (1982). The Revised Social Anhedonia Scale. Unpublished test.Edmundson, M., & Kwapil, T. R. (2013). A five-factor model perspective of schizotypal personality disorder. In P. T. Costa, & T. A. Widiger (Eds.), *Personality disorders and the five factor model of personality* (3rd ed.) (pp. 147–162). Washington, DC: American Psychological Association.

Eysenck, H. J., & Eysenck, S. B. G. (1975). *Manual of the Eysenck Personality Questionnaire.* Sevenoaks: Hodder and Stoughton.

Eysenck, S. B., Eysenck, H. J., & Barrett, P. (1985). A revised version of the psychoticism scale. *Personality and Individual Differences, 6*(1), 21–29.

Fenigstein, A., & Vanable, P. A. (1992). Paranoia and self-consciousness. *Journal of Personality and Social Psychology, 62*, 129–138.

Fonseca-Pedrero, E., Paíno, M., Lemos-Giráldez, S., García-Cueto, E., Campillo-Álvarez, Á., Villazón-García, Ú., & Muñiz, J. (2008). Schizotypy assessment: state of the art and future prospects. *International Journal of Clinical And Health Psychology, 8*, 577–593.

Freeman, D., Garety, P. A., Bebbington, P. E., Smith, B., Rollinson, R., Fowler, D., . . . Dunn, G. (2005). Psychological investigation of the structure of paranoia in a non-clinical population. *British Journal of Psychiatry, 186*, 427–435.

Gooding, D. C., Tallent, K. A., & Matts, C. W. (2005). Clinical status of at-risk individuals 5 years later: further validation of the psychometric high-risk strategy. *Journal of Abnormal Psychology, 114*, 170–175.

Goulding, A. (2004). Schizotypy models in relation to subjective health and paranormal beliefs and experiences. *Personality and Individual Differences, 37*, 157–167.

Gross, G. M., Mellin, J., Silvia, P. J., Barrantes-Vidal, N., & Kwapil, T. R. (2014). Comparing the factor structure of the Wisconsin Schizotypy Scales and the Schizotypal Personality Questionnaire. *Personality Disorders: Theory, Research, and Treatment, 5*, 397–405.

Hoch, P. H., & Cattell, J. P. (1959). The diagnosis of pseudoneurotic schizophrenia. *Psychiatric Quarterly, 33*, 17–43.

Horton, L. E., Barrantes-Vidal, N., Silvia, P. J., & Kwapil, T. R. (2014). Worries about being judged versus being harmed: disentangling the association of social anxiety and paranoia with schizotypy. *PLoS ONE, 9*(6).

Jackson, D. N. (1970). A sequential system for personality scale development. In C. N. Spielberger (Ed.), *Current topics in clinical and community psychology* (Vol. 2, pp. 61–96). New York: Academic Press.

Kaczorowski, J. A., Barrantes-Vidal, N., & Kwapil, T. R. (2009). Neurological soft signs in psychometrically identified schizotypy. *Schizophrenia Research, 115*, 293–302.

Kallman, F. (1938). *The genetics of schizophrenia*. New York: J. J. Augustin.

Kerns, J. G. (2006). Schizotypy facets, cognitive control, and emotion. *Journal of Abnormal Psychology, 115*(3), 418–427.

Kerns, J. G., & Becker, T. M. (2008). Communication disturbances, working memory, and emotion in people with elevated disorganized schizotypy. *Schizophrenia Research, 100*(1–3), 172–180.

Korfine, L., & Lenzenweger, M. F. (1995). The taxonicity of schizotypy: a replication. *Journal of Abnormal Psychology, 104*, 26–31.

Kraepelin, E. (1919). *Dementia praecox and paraphrenia*. Edinburgh, Scotland: Livingstone. (Original work published in 1913.)

Krueger, R. F., Derringer, J., Markon, K. E., Watson, D., & Skodol, A. E. (2012). Initial construction of a maladaptive personality trait model and inventory for DSM-5. *Psychological Medicine, 42*, 1879–1890.

Kwapil, T. R. (1998). Social anhedonia as a predictor of the development of schizophrenia-spectrum disorders. *Journal of Abnormal Psychology, 107*, 558–565.

Kwapil, T. R., & Barrantes-Vidal, N. (2012). Schizotypal personality disorder: an integrative review. In T. A. Widiger (Ed.), *The Oxford handbook of personality disorders* (pp. 437–477). Oxford: Oxford University Press.

Kwapil, T. R., & Barrantes-Vidal, N. (2014). Schizotypy: looking back and moving forward. *Schizophrenia Bulletin*. doi: 10.1093/schbul/sbu186

Kwapil, T.R., Barrantes-Vidal, N., & Silvia, P.J. (2008). The dimensional structure of the Wisconsin Schizotypy Scales: factor identification and construct validity. *Schizophrenia Bulletin, 34*, 444–457.

Kwapil, T. R., Brown, L. H., Silvia, P. J., Myin-Germeys, I., & Barrantes-Vidal, N. (2012). The expression of positive and negative schizotypy in daily life: an experience sampling study. *Psychological Medicine, 42*, 2555–2566.

Kwapil, T. R., Gross, G. M., Silvia, P. J., & Barrantes-Vidal, N. (2013). Prediction of psychopathology and functional impairment by positive and negative schizotypy in the Chapmans' ten-year longitudinal study. *Journal of Abnormal Psychology, 122*, 807–815.

Lenzenweger, M. F. (1998). Schizotypy and schizotypic psychopathology: mapping an alternative expression of schizophrenia liability. In M. F. Lenzenweger, & R. H. Dworkin (Eds.), *Origins and development of schizophrenia*. Washington, DC: APA Press.

Lenzenweger, M.F., & Dworkin, R. H. (1996). The dimensions of schizophrenia phenomenology: not one or two, at least three, perhaps four. *British Journal of Psychiatry, 168*, 432–440.

Lenzenweger, M. F., & O'Driscoll, G. (2006). Smooth pursuit eye movement and schizotypy in the community. *Journal of Abnormal Psychology, 115*, 779–786.

Lenzenweger, M. F., Bennett, M. E., & Lilenfeld, L. R. (1997). The Referential Thinking Scale as a measure of schizotypy: scale development and initial construct validation. *Psychological Assessment, 9*, 452–463.

Linscott, R. (2013). The taxonicity of schizotypy: does the same taxonic class structure emerge from analyses of different attributes of schizotypy and from fundamentally different statistical methods? *Psychiatry Research, 210*, 414–421.

Mason, O., Claridge, G., & Clark, K. (1997). Electrodermal relationships with personality measures of psychosis-proneness in psychotic and normal subjects. *International Journal of Psychophysiology, 27*, 137–146.

Mason, O., Claridge, G., & Jackson, M. (1995). New scales for the assessment of schizotypy. *Personality and Individual Differences, 18*(1), 7–13.

Mason, O., Claridge, G., & Williams, L. (1997). Questionnaire measurement. In G. Claridge (Ed.), *Schizotypy: implications for illness and health*. Oxford: Oxford University Press.

Mason, O., Linney, Y., & Claridge, G. (2005). Short scales for measuring schizotypy. *Schizophrenia Research, 78*, 2–3.

McGue, M., & Gottesman, I. I. (1989). A single dominant gene still cannot account for the transmission of schizophrenia. *Archives of General Psychiatry, 46*, 478–479.

Meehl, P. E. (1962). Schizotaxia, schizotypy, schizophrenia. *American Psychologist, 17*, 827–838.

Meehl, P. E. (1964) *Manual for use with checklist of schizotypic signs* (no. PR-73-5). Minneapolis: University of Minnesota Research Laboratories of the Department of Psychiatry.

Meehl, P. E. (1990). Toward an integrated theory of schizotaxia, schizotypy, and schizophrenia. *Journal of Personality Disorders, 4*, 1–99.

Meyer, T., & Keller, F. (2001). Exploring the latent structure of the perceptual aberration, magical ideation, and physical anhedonia scales in a German sample – a partial replication. *Journal of Personality Disorders, 15*, 521–535.

Miers, T. C., & Raulin, M. L. (1987). Cognitive Slippage Scale. In K. Corcoran, & J. Fischer (Eds.), *Measures for clinical practice: A sourcebook* (pp. 125–127). New York: Free Press.

Minor, K. S., & Cohen, A. S. (2010). Affective reactivity of speech disturbances in schizotypy. *Journal of Psychiatric Research, 44*, 99–105.

Minor, K. S., Cohen, A. S., Weber, C. R., & Brown, L. A. (2011). The relationship between atypical semantic activation and odd speech in schizotypy across emotionally evocative conditions. *Schizophrenia Research, 126*, 144–149.

Modinos, G., Mechelli, A., Ormel, J., Groenewold, N., Aleman, A., & McGuire, P. (2010). Schizotypy and brain structure: a voxel-based morphometry study. *Psychological Medicine, 4*, 1423–1431.

Morrison, S. C., Brown, L. A., & Cohen, A. S. (2013). A multidimensional assessment of social cognition in psychometrically defined schizotypy. *Psychiatry Research, 210*, 1014–1019.

Peters, E., Joseph, S., Day, S., & Garety, P. (2004). Measuring delusional ideation: the 21-item Peters et al. Delusions Inventory (PDI). *Schizophrenia Bulletin, 30*, 1005–1022.

Peters, E. R., Joseph, S. A., & Garety, P. A. (1999). Measurement of delusional ideation in the normal population: introducing the PDI (Peters et al. Delusions Inventory). *Schizophrenia Bulletin, 25*, 553–576.

Prévost, M., Rodier, M., Renoult, L., Kwann, Y., Dionne-Dostie, E., Chapleau, I., & Debruille, J. (2010). Schizotypal traits and N400 in healthy subjects. *Psychophysiology, 47*, 1047–1056.

Rado, S. (1953). Dynamics and classification of disordered behaviour. *American Journal of Psychiatry, 110*, 406–416.

Raine, A. (1991). The SPQ: a scale for the assessment of schizotypal personality based on DSM-III-R criteria. *Schizophrenia Bulletin, 17*, 555–64.

Raine, A., & Benishay, D. (1995). The SPQ-B: a brief screening instrument for schizotypal personality disorder. *Journal of Personality Disorders, 9*, 346–355.

Raine, A., Reynolds, C., Lencz, T., Scerbo, A., Triphon, N., & Kim, D. (1994). Cognitive-perceptual, interpersonal and disorganized features of schizotypal personality. *Schizophrenia Bulletin, 20*, 191–201.

Raulin, M. L. (1986). Schizotypal Ambivalence Scale. Unpublished test copies available from M.L. Raulin, Psychology Department, SUNY at Buffalo, Buffalo, NY 14260.

Rawlings, D., & Freeman, J. L. (1996). A questionnaire for the measurement of paranoia/suspiciousness. *British Journal of Clinical Psychology, 35*, 451–461.

Rawlings, D., Williams, B., Haslam, N., & Claridge, G. (2008). Taxometric analysis supports a dimensional latent structure for schizotypy. *Personality and Individual Differences, 44*, 1640–1651.

Schizophrenia Working Group of the Psychiatric Genomics Consortium (2014). Biological insights from 108 schizophrenia-associated genetic loci. *Nature, 511*, 421–427.

Sheinbaum, T., Bedoya, E., Ros-Morente, A., Kwapil, T. R., & Barrantes-Vidal, N. (2013). Association between attachment prototypes and schizotypy dimensions in two independent non-clinical samples of Spanish and American young adults. *Psychiatry Research, 210*, 408–413.

Stefanis, N. C., Hanssen, M., Smirnis, N. K., Avramopoulos, D. A., Evdokimidis, I. K., Stefanis, C. N., . . . van Os, J., 2002. Evidence that three dimensions of psychosis have a distribution in the general population. *Psychological Medicine, 32*, 347–358.

Stefanis, N. C., Smyrnis, N., Avramopoulos, D., Evdokimidis, I., Ntzoufras, I., & Stefanis, C. N. (2004). Factorial composition of self-rated schizotypal traits among young males undergoing military training. *Schizophrenia Bulletin, 30*, 335–350.

Tallent, K. A., & Gooding, D. C. (1999). Working memory and Wisconsin Card Sorting Test performance in schizotypic individuals: a replication and extension. *Psychiatry Research, 89*, 161–170.

University of Minnesota (1943). *Minnesota Multiphasic Personality Inventory.* Minneapolis, MN: Author.

Vollema, M. G., & van den Bosch, R. J. (1995). The multidimensionality of schizotypy. *Schizophrenia Bulletin, 21*, 19–31.

Widiger, T. A. (2001). What can be learned from taxometric analyses? *Clinical Psychology: Science and Practice, 8*, 528–533.

Winterstein, B. P., Silvia, P. J., Kwapil, T. R., Kaufman, J. C., Reiter-Palmon, R., & Wigert, B. (2011). Brief assessment of schizotypy: developing short forms of the Wisconsin Schizotypy Scales. *Personality and Individual Differences, 51*, 920–924.

Wuthrich, V., & Bates, T. C. (2005). Reliability and validity of two Likert versions of the Schizotypal Personality Questionnaire (SPQ). *Personality and Individual Differences, 38*(7), 1543–1548.

Wuthrich, V. M., & Bates, T. C. (2006). Confirmatory factor analysis of the three-factor structure of the Schizotypal Personality Questionnaire and Chapman schizotypy scales. *Journal of Personality Assessment, 87,* 292–304.

2 The role of dopamine in schizotypy

Christine Mohr and Ulrich Ettinger

Introduction

To facilitate research on how personality traits pertain to risk for psychopathology, and schizophrenia in particular, it is important that they be associated with well-established brain correlates of relevant disorders. In schizotypy, for example, researchers often assume that brain correlates involved in schizophrenia or psychosis more widely are also contributing to schizotypal personality traits. The focus of the majority of brain-related studies on personality stresses structural or functional differences, and the same is true of schizotypy. Yet, neuronal information transfer is only possible with functional neurochemical transmission at synapses. Therefore, neurochemical studies involving pharmacological challenges or molecular imaging methods are also of importance for our understanding of personality.

The brain possesses several neurochemicals exerting different actions that depend on the receptor types distributed in different brain areas. The focus of this chapter is on dopamine (DA), which has been linked to schizotypy (e.g. Kopp, Wolff, Hruska, & Reischies, 2002; Mohr, Landis, Bracha, Fathi, & Brugger, 2005; Schmechtig et al., 2013), primarily because (1) classical antipsychotic agents (ameliorating positive psychotic symptoms in patients) are known to block or to stabilise DA activity at moderate levels (Davis, Kahn, Ko, & Davidson, 1991), and (2) DA-promoting substances such as amphetamine induce or exacerbate psychotic symptoms (Laruelle & Abi-Dargham, 1999). This chapter explores this putative link by describing relevant psychopharmacological studies in both patients and healthy individuals where schizotypy is measured. It should be noted that cannabis is also relevant to the DA system and is covered elsewhere (Chapter 9). First, however, we introduce the structure and function of the DA system.

Dopamine – a major cerebral neurotransmitter

While widely distributed, many neurotransmitters exert their particular actions at specific sites and within given systems. With regard to the DA system, we distinguish between the nigrostriatal (important to motor control), mesolimbic (important to reward and motivation), and mesocortical (important to prefrontal functions) pathways, based on where the cell bodies of these systems are located and where their axons project. Two major DA receptor families have been described: the D1-like receptors (D1 and D5 receptors) and the D2-like receptors (D2, D3 and D4 receptors). D1-like receptors are located post-synaptically and D2-like receptors are located both pre- and post-synaptically (Banich, 2004). Post-synaptically, the action potentials can be both excitatory and inhibitory. Pre-synaptically, the actions are exerted via autoreceptors on the dendrites and cell bodies (decreasing neural firing) or in the terminal boutons (decreasing DA production and, by inference, release) (Banich, 2004).

Any alteration in such a complex neurotransmitter system cannot of course be equated with a particular form of psychopathology in a simple way. Instead, the kind of psychopathology observed is likely to depend on the subsystem involved. For instance, DA has been linked to various – and quite diverse – neurological and psychiatric conditions such as Parkinson's disease, schizophrenia, addiction and attention deficit hyperactive disorder (ADHD) (e.g. Mehler-Wex, Riederer, & Gerlach, 2006). Moreover, the different neurotransmitter systems are not modular (i.e. they do not exert their actions in isolation, but are in constant interaction with other systems). The interaction between DA and glutamate, for instance, is a topic of intense debate (Javitt, 2007). Accordingly, if some psychopharmacological substances facilitate the release of DA (e.g. amphetamines), these may equally facilitate the release of the other two monoamines (norepinephrine, serotonin), either directly or indirectly through further metabolism of DA into norepinephrine and the latter into serotonin (Rothman, Baumann, & Dersch, 2001). Keeping this complexity in mind, it should also become obvious that single psychopharmacological studies cannot provide definite answers to the role of DA in schizotypy. Instead, we need to consider series of studies using different but complementary approaches to best indicate whether DA should be treated as an important neurotransmitter in schizotypy.

Dopamine – treatment effects in patients with schizophrenia and its continuum

Subsequent to the discovery of neuroleptics in the early 1950s, it has been shown that DA antagonists ameliorate acute psychotic symptoms (e.g. Klein & Davis, 1969). Currently DA plays a major role in the treatment and, by inference, the pathophysiology of schizophrenia. Clinically successful anti-psychotic medication, including contemporary 'second-generation' neuroleptics, all act on the DA system (Laruelle & Abi-Dargham, 1999; Seeman, 2013). For instance, patients with schizophrenia profit from DA antagonistic treatment and show an exacerbation of psychotic symptoms after DA agonistic treatment (Davidson et al., 1987; Laruelle & Abi-Dargham, 1999). Complementary DA agonists trigger psychotic or psychosis-like symptoms in healthy populations (Sekine et al., 2001). Consequently, acute psychotic symptoms have been assumed to emerge from a hyperactive DA system (Davis et al., 1991; Laruelle & Abi-Dargham, 1999). These studies, in particular those following the seminal paper by Davis et al. (1991), have further contributed to the development of the original DA hypothesis of a hyperactive DA system in schizophrenia. Implementing contradictory findings around the idea that D2 receptors are significantly involved, Davis et al. suggested that abnormalities depend on the brain region, with D1 receptors being mainly distributed cortically and D2 receptors subcortically. In particular, frontal hypodopaminergia would result in a striatal hyperdopaminergia. With regard to symptoms, negative symptoms would result from a frontal hypodopaminergia and positive symptoms from a striatal hyperdopaminergia.

Howes and Kapur (2009) proposed a refined version of the DA theory, which 'rather than being a hypothesis of schizophrenia – version III is more accurately a "dopamine hypothesis of psychosis-in-schizophrenia"' (p. 556). The authors propose that multiple 'hits' (e.g. social, environmental and cultural stressors) lead to DA dysregulation at the presynaptic dopaminergic control level. Thus, the DA system is the final common pathway to psychosis, and potentially even underlies psychosis proneness. The authors argued that such DA dysregulation could lead to a change in the appraisal of events, presumably because of aberrant salience (i.e. the increased attachment of meaning to actually irrelevant stimuli). While these authors review evidence for a predominantly presynaptic DA release in psychosis, other authors debate post-synaptic processes such as hypersensitive post-synaptic receptors (Seeman, 2013). This author outlined how dynamic changes in post-synaptic D2 receptors might importantly contribute to symptoms experienced in schizophrenia. Mainly based on animal studies, the author reports on D2 receptors that can either take a high affinity state for DA (D2High) or a low affinity state for DA (D2Low). Reviewing the literature, he suggests that psychosis is associated with the more active and normally less common D2High state.

In sum, despite various suggestions concerning the involvement of alternative neurotransmitter systems in psychosis and, by inference, schizophrenia (Javitt, 2007), recent evidence still suggests DA to be the final common pathway to psychosis. The site of action remains debated, and continued research reveals ever more complex synaptic dynamics such as the recent ones described for the D2High and D2Low affinity states. It remains to be clarified whether any such alterations of the DA system are specific to the acute and severe psychotic state. Importantly, such alterations are also evident, although less pronounced, along the schizophrenia spectrum including healthy schizotypy. Howes and Kapur (2009) previously reviewed a number of studies showing an involvement of DA in the prodromal state, in ultra-high risk populations, relatives and schizotypy and argued for its role in risk and transition. Such studies show that DA abnormalities are not specific to schizophrenia proper but are equally evident in the extended phenotype, and should thus also include schizotypy.

Methods to assess the role of dopamine in schizotypy in healthy participants

The most promising DA-relevant methodologies in the context of schizotypy research involve (1) pharmacological challenges, (2) neurobiologically informed cognitive measures, (3) molecular neuroimaging, and (4) genetics (see Chapter 3). Here, we will briefly outline these methods and discuss their uses in relation to schizotypy research.

Psychotic patient populations are commonly treated with antipsychotic medication over many weeks, because treatment effects take several weeks to emerge (e.g. Nordström, Farde, & Halldin, 1992). When testing healthy populations, such a long-term drug regime, would be unethical. Hence long-term treatment effects are typically reported only in clinical populations while single-dose studies or a limited number of drug applications are common when testing healthy populations. In principle, one-off pharmacological challenge studies in healthy volunteers allow direct modulation of the DA system. These studies involve the administration of DA antagonists or agonists to healthy individuals in order to assess psychoactive, cognitive and neural effects in well-controlled laboratory settings (e.g. using double-blind procedures, placebo controlled). One advantage of this approach over patient studies is that risks (psychotic relapse, worsening of psychotic symptoms) are lower when providing DA agonists to healthy populations. Conversely, therefore, these designs allow addressing questions that are hard to justify in patients (Davidson et al., 1987; Sekine et al., 2001). Results of these single-dose or short-term administration studies can then be compared with those obtained from longer-term treatments in clinical populations with the aim of providing some insight into general drug actions versus those more specific to the clinical population.

Another common, indirect approach in healthy populations is the assessment of DA-mediated cognitive and behavioural performance and their covariance with personality traits. Various approaches can be drawn upon to inform the implication of DA in a given cognitive or behavioural measure. We present various such measures that have been used to infer on the functioning of the DA system. An important issue for these indirect indices of DA concerns the distinction between basic behavioural and higher cognitive functions, so these are discussed separately. The molecular imaging approach (PET and single photon emission computed tomography [SPECT]) can provide *in vivo* data on markers of the DA system (such as DA synthesis or receptor and transporter availability) in the brain (e.g. Laruelle & Abi-Dargham, 1999; Woodward et al., 2011). As will be detailed below, PET and SPECT methods are starting to be used to study alterations in the DA system in schizotypy.

Dopamine and schizotypy: the evidence

Despite the long-lasting debate on the role of DA in psychosis and schizophrenia in particular, information on the precise role of DA in schizotypy has been scarce. While the involvement of DA in even modest elevations of schizotypal traits has been emphasised (Kopp et al., 2002; Mohr, Bracha, & Brugger, 2003), the relationship between schizotypy and the DA system has rarely been investigated directly (e.g. Williams et al., 1997).

Basic behavioural functions

An established behavioural marker of a hyperactive DA system is **turning behaviour**, which stems from a relatively hyperactive DA system in one hemisphere over the other. Well known from the animal literature and from one study with patients with asymmetrical Parkinson's disease, the preferred side of whole-body turning occurs away from the hemisphere with the more active DA system (see Mohr et al., 2003. Supporting the notion of a relative hyperactive right-hemispheric DA system, acutely psychotic patients and healthy individuals relatively high in positive schizotypal features displayed a significant preference for left- over right-sided turns.

In a pharmacological challenge study, half the participants received a placebo and the other half a non-specific DA agonist (levodopa) (Mohr, Landis, et al., 2005). Turning preferences were analysed as a function of positive and negative schizotypy. In the placebo group, elevated positive schizotypy associated with a left- over right-sided turning preference, while negative schizotypy associated with a right- over left-sided turning preference. Of interest, these relationships were not strengthened in the levodopa group. On the contrary, the side preferences were reversed, as if a higher than normal DA availability balanced out pre-existing DA asymmetries. In an independent study, lateral turning biases were found to be unrelated to schizotypy and levodopa when performing a computer-based object-rotation task (Mohr, Landis, Sandor, Fathi, & Brugger, 2004).

Another basic behaviour indicative of DA activity is the *spontaneous eye blink rate* (SBR). Eye blinks primarily serve the health of the surface of the eye and the clarity of vision. They occur spontaneously, frequently and mostly without awareness during any human behaviour. SBR rate has long been considered a sensitive marker of striatal DA levels and been associated with changes in concurrent cognitive processes, perceptual load and level of arousal (Chermahini & Hommel, 2010; Ettinger & Klein, in press). SBR is enhanced in schizophrenia, in particular in the unmedicated or drug-naïve state, but decreases with antipsychotic treatment (E. Chen, Lam, Chen, & Nguyen, 1996; Mackert, Woyth, Flechtner, & Volz, 1990). In line with Davis et al.'s (1991) notion of a link between negative symptoms and a hypodopaminergia on the one hand and positive symptoms and a hyperdopaminergia on the other, the former symptoms were associated with a decreased SBR and the latter with an increased SBR (E. Chen et al., 1996; Mackert et al., 1990).

In one schizotypy study on SBR, half the participants received a placebo and the others an unspecific DA agonist (levodopa) (Mohr, Sandor, Landis, Fathi, & Brugger, 2005). The SBR was comparable between substance groups. The only significant finding on schizotypy was that SBR correlated positively with negative (but not positive) schizotypy after levodopa intake, presumably because negative schizotypy is a priori related to a hypodopaminergia. This might explain why an experimental elevation of DA became relevant to SBR only as a function of negative schizotypy. However, in another study, SBR was positively related to psychoticism scores, (Colzato, Slagter, van den Wildenberg, & Hommel, 2009). While it has been argued that this Eysenckian dimension is associated with schizotypy (Ettinger, Corr, Mofidi, Williams, & Kumari, 2013), other notions link it to impulsiveness, lack of cooperation, rigidity, low superego control, low social sensitivity, low persistence, lack of anxiety and lack of feelings of inferiority, features associated with borderline and antisocial personality disorder rather than univocally with the schizophrenia spectrum (Pickering et al., 2003). Whatever the psychoticism dimension is measuring, the latter SBR finding would suggest that psychoticism is probably more sensitive to the DA system subserving SBR than is schizotypy (or negative schizotypy) as such.

Stereotyped behaviour can be observed both in schizophrenia (Peralta & Cuesta, 2001) and after amphetamine consumption in healthy individuals (Ridley, Baker, Frith, Dowdy, & Crow, 1988). In schizophrenia, stereotyped behaviour can occur on the motor level (e.g. rocking, walking backwards and forwards, repetitive jaw movements) but also on a higher cognitive level (e.g. perseverative errors in the Wisconsin Card Sorting Test). Such perseverative errors in the Wisconsin Card Sorting Test are also elevated in schizotypal personality disorder (SPD) and healthy schizotypal individuals (see Mohr et al., 2004). When producing random sequences, patients with schizophrenia, healthy participants after amphetamine administration, and healthy participants with elevated schizotypal features show more pronounced stereotypical response biases compared with controls (see in Mohr et al., 2004). When participants had to rotate a figure into a target position on the screen, left or right turns would have to be applied dynamically to obtain a maximal score (Mohr et al., 2004). Thus, sticking stereotypically with one or the other direction would be disadvantageous. In this latter study, Mohr et al. (2004) reported on two experiments with one being between-subject levodopa placebo controlled. The authors observed that individuals with relatively high, compared with low positive, schizotypy were behaving more stereotypically. Yet, in the levodopa group, high positive schizotypy individuals performed less stereotypically than the low positive schizotypy individuals. Comparable to the findings on turning behaviour, the results seem to suggest that a higher than normal DA availability in positive schizotypes balances out pre-existing DA-mediated behavioural abnormalities.

Psychometric measures of schizotypy or psychosis proneness have also been found to be associated with *prepulse inhibition* (PPI). In humans PPI is typically assessed through the startle response to acoustic stimuli. The PPI phenomenon refers to attenuation in the startle response to a strong stimulus (the pulse) if this is preceded shortly (30–500ms) by a weak stimulus (the prepulse). PPI is thought to prevent the interruption of ongoing perceptual and early sensory analysis, and is thus considered a measure of early sensorimotor gating processes both in animals and in humans (Braff, Geyer, & Swerdlow, 2001). PPI is reduced in patients with schizophrenia (Swerdlow et al., 2014), patients with SPD (Cadenhead, Swerdlow, Shafer, Diaz, & Braff, 2000) and individuals with high schizotypy or psychoticism scores (Kumari, Cotter, Checkley, & Gray, 1997; Swerdlow, Filion, Geyer, & Braff, 1995). Attempts to substantiate the neural mechanisms underlying this relationship have employed functional magnetic resonance imaging (fMRI) during PPI and observed reduced activation in the insula, putamen, thalamus, inferior parietal cortex, hippocampal gyrus and fusiform gyrus in people with high levels of psychoticism (Kumari, Antonova, & Geyer, 2008). These activation reductions resemble the data obtained from samples of patients with schizophrenia (Kumari & Ettinger, 2005). Importantly, areas such as the putamen are rich in DA receptors. Accordingly, and in agreement with numerous animal and human studies, PPI has been argued to be at least partially dopaminergically mediated (Braff et al., 2001; Kumari & Ettinger, 2005; Völter et al., 2012).

Finally, *latent inhibition* (LI) represents another cross-species paradigm known to be sensitive to DA challenges (Weiner & Arad, 2009). The LI phenomenon involves mechanisms of selective attention. It refers to the observation that non-reinforced pre-exposure to a stimulus, that is later to be conditioned, causes less efficient conditioning when the same stimulus is subsequently reinforced. This phenomenon has been widely studied in experimental animals and in humans, including patients with schizophrenia as well as controls of varying levels of schizotypy (Kumari & Ettinger, 2010). The latter comprehensive review concluded that patients with schizophrenia show reduced LI in the acute phase, while there is evidence of preserved LI in chronic schizophrenia. It was also concluded that there is a relatively consistent relationship (of small-to-moderate effect) between higher schizotypy and reduced LI in samples of non-clinical volunteers. A study using the O-LIFE questionnaire suggested that the positive dimension of schizotypy may be more strongly related to LI disruption than the negative dimension, and that this effect may be dopaminergically mediated (Evans, Gray, & Snowden, 2007). In agreement with this hypothesis, enhancement or normalisation of human LI via DA antagonism depends on the schizotypy level of the sample (Williams et al., 1997).

Higher cognitive functions

DA has been described as a potent modulator of the signal-to-noise ratio in semantic networks. Specifically, it has been argued that the lack of tonic dopaminergic modulation in the prefrontal cortex (hypofrontality) of patients with schizophrenia would decrease the contrast between a signal and noise leading to a disinhibition of the spreading activation within semantic networks (see Spitzer, 1997, for an overview). The increased spreading activation would manifest itself, on the behavioural level, as remote associations and, in experimental situations, as enhanced semantic priming effects in patients with schizophrenia (Spitzer, 1997) and as more focused priming effects in healthy individuals after levodopa consumption (Kischka et al., 1996). Moreover, given that a hyperdopaminergia might be more prominent in the right than left hemisphere (as mentioned earlier), this enhanced spreading activation would be more relevant for the right than left hemisphere in patients with schizophrenia (Weisbrod, Maier, Harig, Himmelsbach, & Spitzer, 1998) but also in healthy individuals high in positive schizotypy (Mohr, Landis, & Brugger, 2006). Obviously, these DA-mediated functions could manifest themselves as such priming effects, but also more generally as enhanced associative processing and a shift towards the right hemisphere for lateralised hemispheric functions (see Mohr, Krummenacher, et al., 2005, for an overview). Indeed, for a variety of functions, the left hemisphere seems compromised in patients with schizophrenia, but DA antagonists would restore or even reverse these altered hemispheric asymmetries (e.g. Purdon, Woodward, & Flor-Henry, 2001).

Schizotypy studies targeting the DA system more directly showed that, without additional DA challenge, lateralised lexical decision performance is relatively biased towards the right hemisphere in high as compared with low scorers on a positive but not negative schizotypy questionnaire (Brugger, Gamma, Muri, Schafer, & Taylor, 1993; Mohr, Krummenacher et al., 2005). In a levodopa group, however, superior left hemisphere language dominance was associated with elevated negative schizotypy scores (Mohr, Krummenacher et al., 2005). Thus, in the healthy brain, levodopa seemed to have restored the left hemisphere dominance for language through the attenuation of the contribution of the right hemisphere to language with regard to positive schizotypy, and also by increasing the left hemisphere contribution as a function of individuals' negative schizotypy. In another population, using the same lateralised task, signal detection theory measures of sensitivity (d-prime) and response tendency (criterion) were calculated (Krummenacher, Mohr, Haker, & Brugger, 2010). For individuals low in positive schizotypy, d-prime was lower in the levodopa than in the placebo group. Moreover, in the placebo group, those high in positive schizotypy yielded a looser response criterion, while those low in positive schizotypy showed the opposite tendency. In the levodopa group, though, these response tendencies were reduced in both schizotypy groups. Results from this study indicated that levodopa might reduce sensitivity in individuals low in positive schizotypy but make low scorers less conservative and high scorers more conservative in their response tendencies.

Other research has investigated the effects of antipsychotic compounds on 'higher' cognitive functions such as *working memory, verbal fluency* (a measure of executive function) or *response inhibition* (a domain of cognitive control) as a function of the participants' schizotypy levels. For example, in a large, multicentre pharmacological study, it was observed that the clinically effective antipsychotic amisulpride, a D2/D3 receptor antagonist, improved working memory and verbal fluency performance in participants with high levels of schizotypy but worsened them in medium schizotypal controls (Koychev et al., 2012). The same study also examined the effects of 7mg risperidone, a clinically effective atypical antipsychotic with D2 antagonist but also prominent action on 5-HT receptors, on the antisaccade task, a widely studied measure of inhibitory function (Hutton & Ettinger, 2006). Antisaccade performance deteriorated in medium schizotypy controls following risperidone administration, whereas in high schizotypy a non-significant tendency towards improvement was observed (Schmechtig et al., 2013). These data are compatible with the improvements in antisaccade performance seen in schizophrenia with risperidone treatment (Harris, Reilly, Keshavan, & Sweeney, 2006).

Together, these data suggest that people with high schizotypy seem to benefit in cognitive functions from DA agonistic treatment (i.e. they performed like people with low schizotypy). On the other hand, people low in schizotypy seem to experience negative consequences from DA agonistic treatment (i.e. they performed like people with high schizotypy in the psychopharmacological untreated state). With regard to antipsychotic treatments, the current data suggest that people with high schizotypy benefit in cognitive function from antipsychotic compounds similar to patients with schizophrenia, or at least tolerate them, whereas people low and medium in schizotypy do not. Moreover, given the prominence of DA action in the effects of clinically effective antipsychotics, the current data shed light on the likely role of DA in mediating some of the cognitive deficits observed in schizotypy (Ettinger, Meyhöfer, Steffens, Wagner, & Koutsouleris, 2014; Mohr, Landis, et al., 2005).

Molecular imaging of the dopamine system in schizotypy

Both PET and SPECT have frequently been applied to study the dopaminergic basis of schizophrenia. Few molecular imaging studies have investigated relationships in schizotypy. An early study by Gray, Pickering, and Gray (1994) reported a significant *negative* relationship between psychoticism and D2 receptor binding in the basal ganglia (relative to frontal cortex) in nine healthy individuals. On the other hand, a more recent SPECT study testing fifty-five healthy volunteers found a significant *positive* correlation between the Schizotypal Personality Questionnaire (SPQ)-Disorganisation score and D2/3 receptor binding in the right striatum (relative to occipital cortex), a finding that can be reconciled with a small increase in D2/D3 receptors seen in schizophrenia (K. Chen et al., 2012).

In addition to the differences in presynaptic DA function in patients with schizophrenia mentioned earlier (Howes, Kambeitz, & Kim, 2012), a fundamental observation in schizophrenia research is the finding of increased striatal DA release in patients following the acute administration of amphetamine. Imaging studies have shown that patients with schizophrenia, both in the acute phase and in remission, display amphetamine-induced reductions in D2 and D3 DA receptor binding potential in the striatum (Breier et al., 1997). A similar pattern was observed in patients with SPD (Abi-Dargham et al., 2004). Additionally, a significant correlation between striatal DA release after amphetamine administration and overall schizotypy was observed in a sample of healthy volunteers (Woodward et al., 2011), providing support for a shared dopaminergic dysfunction in schizotypy and schizophrenia when assayed with this paradigm.

Finally, dopaminergic molecular imaging methods have been combined with stress induction paradigms, because stress is a possible risk factor for schizophrenia. A study using [11C]raclopride PET showed that participants with negative schizotypy – but not controls or those with positive schizotypy – possessed a significant stress-induced striatal reduction in binding potential (Soliman et al., 2008). This finding is compatible with results from an fMRI study of the neuronal response to stress in participants with high schizotypy (Soliman et al., 2011). In this latter study, differences in striatal and limbic activation patterns were observed in participants with negative schizotypy in comparison to controls.

To conclude, molecular imaging studies have the advantage of providing relatively direct markers of DA system integrity and its relationship to schizophrenia and schizotypy. In schizophrenia, presynaptic DA abnormalities are at least consistent upon meta-analysis. Evidence of associations with schizotypy in healthy individuals is less consistent but points to (1) increased striatal DA release following amphetamine administration or stress induction, and (2) increased striatal D2/3 receptor binding in higher schizotypy.

Conclusion and outlook

DA is the main potential neurotransmitter relevant to schizotypy and its associated cognitive functions, already indisputably linked to schizophrenia. DA-relevant findings have been seen predominantly with regard to behavioural and cognitive functions, and also using brain imaging. However, both behavioural paradigms and results are highly variable. The variety of studies precludes clear-cut conclusions about the role of DA in schizotypy and more studies are needed. These would be most advantageous when using paradigms and measures already well established in clinical and healthy populations allowing direct comparison of study results.

More encouragingly, many studies reported that deficits already observed in schizophrenia are also evident in schizotypy. Moreover, these are consistent with neuronal changes observed in schizophrenia patients. As in patients with schizophrenia, DA antagonists may ameliorate deficits in schizotypy. On the other hand, the consequences of DA agonists seem to depend on individuals' trait proneness. Comparable to DA antagonistic actions, deficits after a DA agonist are absent for moderate-to-high schizotypes, while they are observable in low schizotypes. This latter observation might point to compensatory mechanisms in healthy individuals with elevated positive schizotypy. To what extent healthy schizotypes may be able to compensate for a higher than normal DA availability needs further testing, in particular because DA antagonists also seem to lead to deficit reductions. May it be the case that a simple alteration to the 'status quo' in the DA system leads to an improvement of cognitive and behavioural deficits in individuals with elevated schizotypy? This possibility can only be addressed in future studies. Another conclusion is that we need further studies of larger sample sizes (such as the newly instantiated Schizotypy Consortium) in neuroimaging but also in genetics (see Chapter 3) as well as studies that tease apart the role of different DA systems and how these relate to different cognitive and behavioural deficits in schizotypy. For instance, one can ask whether the above observed amelioration in cognitive functioning in high schizotypy, after either DA antagonists or DA agonists, relate to brain changes in similar areas and with regard to the same DA system.

References

Abi-Dargham, A., Kegeles, L. S., Zea-Ponce, Y., Mawlawi, O., Martinez, D., Mitropoulou, V., & Siever, L. J. (2004). Striatal amphetamine-induced dopamine release in patients with schizotypal personality disorder studied with single photon emission computed tomography and [123I]iodobenzamide. *Biological Psychiatry*, 55(10), 1001–1006.

Banich, M. T. (2004). *Cognitive neuroscience and neuropsychology*. Boston: Houghton Mifflin.

Braff, D., Geyer, M., & Swerdlow, N. (2001). Human studies of prepulse inhibition of startle: normal subjects, patient groups, and pharmacological studies. *Psychopharmacology*, 156(2—3), 234–258.

Breier, A., Su, T.-P., Saunders, R., Carson, R. E., Kolachana, B. S., de Bartolomeis, A., . . . Pickar, D. (1997). Schizophrenia is associated with elevated amphetamine-induced synaptic dopamine concentrations: evidence from a novel positron emission tomography method. *Proceedings of the National Academy of Sciences*, 94(6), 2569–2574.

Brugger, P., Gamma, A., Muri, R., Schafer, M., & Taylor, K. I. (1993). Functional hemispheric-asymmetry and belief in esp – towards a neuropsychology of belief. *Perceptual and Motor Skills*, 77(3), 1299–1308.

Cadenhead, K. S., Swerdlow, N. R., Shafer, K. M., Diaz, M., & Braff, D. L. (2000). Modulation of the startle response and startle laterality in relatives of schizophrenic patients and in subjects with schizotypal personality disorder: evidence of inhibitory deficits. *American Journal of Psychiatry, 157*(10), 1660–1668.

Chen, E. Y. H., Lam, L. C. W., Chen, R. Y. L., & Nguyen, D. G. H. (1996). Blink rate, neurocognitive impairments, and symptoms in schizophrenia. *Biological Psychiatry, 40*(7), 597–603.

Chen, K. C., Lee, I. H., Yeh, T. L., Chiu, N. T., Chen, P. S., Yang, Y. K., . . . Chen, C. C. (2012). Schizotypy trait and striatal dopamine receptors in healthy volunteers. *Psychiatry Research, 201*(3), 218–221.

Chermahini, S. A., & Hommel, B. (2010). The (b)link between creativity and dopamine: spontaneous eye blink rates predict and dissociate divergent and convergent thinking. *Cognition, 115*(3), 458–465.

Colzato, L. S., Slagter, H. A., van den Wildenberg, W. P. M., & Hommel, B. (2009). Closing one's eyes to reality: evidence for a dopaminergic basis of psychoticism from spontaneous eye blink rates. *Personality and Individual Differences, 46*, 377–380).

Davidson, M., Keefe, R. S., Mohs, R. C., Siever, L. J., Losonczy, M. F., Horvath, T. B., & Davis, K. L. (1987). L-dopa challenge and relapse in schizophrenia. *American Journal of Psychiatry, 144*(7), 934–938.

Davis, K. L., Kahn, R. S., Ko, G., & Davidson, M. (1991). Dopamine in schizophrenia: a review and reconceptualization. *American Journal of Psychiatry, 148*(11), 1474–1486.

Ettinger, U., & Klein, C. (in press). Eye movements. In M. Reuter, & C. Montag (Eds.), *Neuroeconomics*. Springer Verlag.

Ettinger, U., Corr, P. J., Mofidi, A., Williams, S. C. R., & Kumari, V. (2013). Dopaminergic basis of the psychosis-prone personality investigated with functional magnetic resonance imaging of procedural learning. *Frontiers in Human Neuroscience, 7*, 130.

Ettinger, U., Meyhöfer, I., Steffens, M., Wagner, M., & Koutsouleris, N. (2014). Genetics, cognition, and neurobiology of schizotypal personality: a review of the overlap with schizophrenia. *Frontiers in Psychiatry, 5*.

Evans, L. H., Gray, N. S., & Snowden, R. J. (2007). A new continuous within-participants latent inhibition task: examining associations with schizotypy dimensions, smoking status and gender. *Biological Psychology, 74*(3), 365–373.

Gray, N. S., Pickering, A. D., & Gray, J. A. (1994). Psychoticism and dopamine D2 binding in the basal ganglia using single photon emission tomography. *Personality and Individual Differences, 17*(3), 431–434.

Harris, M. S. H., Reilly, J. L., Keshavan, M., & Sweeney, J. A. (2006). Longitudinal studies of antisaccades in antipsychotic-naive first-episode schizophrenia. *Psychological Medicine, 36*(4), 485–94.

Howes, O. D., & Kapur, S. (2009). The dopamine hypothesis of schizophrenia: version III – the final common pathway. *Schizophrenia Bulletin, 35*(3), 549–562.

Howes, O. D., Kambeitz, J., & Kim, E. (2012). The nature of dopamine dysfunction in schizophrenia and what this means for treatment: meta-analysis of imaging studies. *Archives of General Psychiatry, 69*, 776–786.

Hutton, S. B., & Ettinger, U. (2006). The antisaccade task as a research tool in psychopathology: a critical review. *Psychophysiology, 43*(3), 302–313.

Javitt, D. C. (2007). Glutamate and schizophrenia: phencyclidine, N-methyl-d-aspartate receptors, and dopamine–glutamate interactions. *International Review of Neurobiology, 78*, 69–108.

Kischka, U., Kammer, T., Maier, S., Weisbrod, M., Thimm, M., & Spitzer, M. (1996). Dopaminergic modulation of semantic network activation. *Neuropsychologia*, *34*(11), 1107–1113.

Klein, D., & Davis, J. (1969). *Diagnosis and drug treatment of psychiatric disorders* (pp. 52–138). Baltimore: Williams & Wilkins.

Kopp, B., Wolff, M., Hruska, C., & Reischies, F. M. (2002). Brain mechanisms of visual encoding and working memory in psychometrically identified schizotypal individuals and after acute administration of haloperidol. *Psychophysiology*, *39*(4), 459–472.

Koychev, I., McMullen, K., Lees, J., Dadhiwala, R., Grayson, L., Perry, C., . . . Barkus, E. (2012). A validation of cognitive biomarkers for the early identification of cognitive enhancing agents in schizotypy: a three-center double-blind placebo-controlled study. *European Neuropsychopharmacology*, *22*(7), 469–481.

Krummenacher, P., Mohr, C., Haker, H., & Brugger, P. (2010). Dopamine, paranormal belief, and the detection of meaningful stimuli. *Journal of Cognitive Neuroscience*, *22*(8), 1670–1681.

Kumari, V., & Ettinger, U. (2005). Prepulse inhibition deficits in schizophrenia: static or amenable to treatment? In M. V Lang (Ed.), *Trends in schizophrenia research* (pp. 95–117). New York: Nova Science Publishers.

Kumari, V., & Ettinger, U. (2010). Latent inhibition in schizophrenia and schizotypy: a review of the empirical literature. In R. Lubow, & I. Weiner (Eds.), *Latent Inhibition: Cognition, Neuroscience, and Applications to Schizophrenia* (pp. 419–447). Cambridge University Press.

Kumari, V., Antonova, E., & Geyer, M. A. (2008). Prepulse inhibition and "psychosis-proneness" in healthy individuals: an fMRI study. *European Psychiatry*, *23*(4), 274–280.

Kumari, V., Cotter, P. A., Checkley, S. A., & Gray, J. A. (1997). Effect of acute subcutaneous nicotine on prepulse inhibition of the acoustic startle reflex in healthy male non-smokers. *Psychopharmacology*, *132*(4), 389–395. Laruelle, M., & Abi-Dargham, A. (1999). Dopamine as the wind of the psychotic fire: new evidence from brain imaging studies. *Journal of Psychopharmacology*, *13*, 358–371.

Mackert, A., Woyth, C., Flechtner, K.-M., & Volz, H.-P. (1990). Increased blink rate in drug-naive acute schizophrenic patients. *Biological Psychiatry*, *27*(11), 1197–1202.

Mehler-Wex, C., Riederer, P., & Gerlach, M. (2006). Dopaminergic dysbalance in distinct basal ganglia neurocircuits: implications for the pathophysiology of Parkinson's disease, schizophrenia and attention deficit hyperactivity disorder. *Neurotoxicity Research*, *10*(3–4), 167–179.

Mohr, C., Bracha, H. S., & Brugger, P. (2003). Magical ideation modulates spatial behavior. *Journal of Neuropsychiatry and Clinical Neurosciences*, *15*(2), 168–174.

Mohr, C., Landis, T., & Brugger, P. (2006). Lateralized semantic priming: modulation by levodopa, semantic distance, and participants' magical beliefs. *Neuropsychiatric Disease and Treatment*, *2*(2), 71–84.

Mohr, C., Landis, T., Bracha, H. S., Fathi, M., & Brugger, P. (2005). Levodopa reverses gait asymmetries related to anhedonia and magical ideation. *European Archives of Psychiatry and Clinical Neuroscience*, *255*(1), 33–39.

Mohr, C., Landis, T., Sandor, P. S., Fathi, M., & Brugger, P. (2004). Nonstereotyped responding in positive schizotypy after a single dose of levodopa. *Neuropsychopharmacology*, *29*(9), 1741–1751.

Mohr, C., Sandor, P. S., Landis, T., Fathi, M., & Brugger, P. (2005). Blinking and schizotypal thinking. *Journal of Psychopharmacology, 19*(5), 513–520.

Mohr, C., Krummenacher, P., Landis, T., Sandor, P. S., Fathi, M., & Brugger, P. (2005). Psychometric schizotypy modulates levodopa effects on lateralized lexical decision performance. *Journal of Psychiatric Research, 39*(3), 241–250. Nordström, A. L., Farde, L., & Halldin, C. (1992). Time course of D2-dopamine receptor occupancy examined by PET after single oral doses of haloperidol. *Psychopharmacology, 106*(4), 433–438.

Peralta, V., & Cuesta, M. J. (2001). Motor features in psychotic disorders. I. *Schizophrenia Research, 47*(2), 107–116.

Pickering, A., Farmer, A., Harris, T., Redman, K., Mahmood, A., Sadler, S., & McGuffin, P. (2003). A sib-pair study of psychoticism, life events and depression. *Personality and Individual Differences, 34*(4), 613–623.

Purdon, S. E., Woodward, N. D., & Flor-Henry, P. (2001). Asymmetrical hand force persistence and neuroleptic treatment in schizophrenia. *Journal of the International Neuropsychological Society, 7*(5), 606–614.

Ridley, R., Baker, H., Frith, C., Dowdy, J., & Crow, T. (1988). Stereotyped responding on a two-choice guessing task by marmosets and humans treated with amphetamine. *Psychopharmacology, 95*(4).

Rothman, R., Baumann, M., & Dersch, C. (2001). Amphetamine-type central nervous system stimulants release norepinephrine more potently than they release dopamine and serotonin. *Synapse, 39*, 32–41.

Schmechtig, A., Lees, J., Grayson, L., Craig, K. J., Dadhiwala, R., Dawson, G. R., . . . Ettinger, U. (2013). Effects of risperidone, amisulpride and nicotine on eye movement control and their modulation by schizotypy. *Psychopharmacology, 227*(2), 331–345.

Seeman, P. (2013). Are dopamine D2 receptors out of control in psychosis? *Progress in Neuro-Psychopharmacology and Biological Psychiatry, 46*, 146–152.

Sekine, Y., Iyo, M., Ouchi, Y., Matsunaga, T., Tsukada, H., Okada, H., . . . Mori, N. (2001). Methamphetamine-related psychiatric symptoms and reduced brain dopamine transporters studied with PET. *American Journal of Psychiatry, 158*(8), 1206–1214.

Soliman, A., O'Driscoll, G. A., Pruessner, J., Holahan, A.-L. V, Boileau, I., Gagnon, D., & Dagher, A. (2008). Stress-induced dopamine release in humans at risk of psychosis: a [11C]raclopride PET study. *Neuropsychopharmacology: Official Publication of the American College of Neuropsychopharmacology, 33*(8), 2033–2041.

Soliman, A., O'Driscoll, G. A., Pruessner, J., Joober, R., Ditto, B., Streicker, E., . . . Dagher, A. (2011). Limbic response to psychosocial stress in schizotypy: a functional magnetic resonance imaging study. *Schizophrenia Research, 131*(1–3), 184–191.

Spitzer, M. (1997). A cognitive neuroscience view of schizophrenic thought disorder. *Schizophrenia Bulletin, 23*(1), 29–5.

Swerdlow, N. R., Filion, D., Geyer, M. A., & Braff, D. L. (1995). "Normal" personality correlates of sensorimotor, cognitive, and visuospatial gating. *Biological Psychiatry, 37*(5), 286–299.

Swerdlow, N. R., Light, G. A., Sprock, J., Calkins, M. E., Green, M. F., Greenwood, T. A., . . . Braff, D. L. (2014). Prestimulus effects on human startle reflex in normals and schizophrenics. *Schizophrenia Research, 152*(2–3), 503–512.

Völter, C., Riedel, M., Wöstmann, N., Aichert, D. S., Lobo, S., Costa, A., . . . Ettinger, U. (2012). Sensorimotor gating and D2 receptor signalling: evidence from a molecular genetic approach. *International Journal of Neuropsychopharmacology/ Official Scientific Journal of the Collegium Internationale Neuropsychopharmacologicum (CINP), 15*(10), 1427–1440.

Weiner, I., & Arad, M. (2009). Using the pharmacology of latent inhibition to model domains of pathology in schizophrenia and their treatment. *Behavioural Brain Research, 204*(2), 369–386.

Weisbrod, M., Maier, S., Harig, S., Himmelsbach, U., & Spitzer, M. (1998). Lateralised semantic and indirect semantic priming effects in people with schizophrenia. *British Journal of Psychiatry, 172*, 142–146.

Williams, J. H., Wellman, N. A., Geaney, D. P., Feldon, J., Cowen, P. J., & Rawlins, J. N. P. (1997). Haloperidol enhances latent inhibition in visual tasks in healthy people. *Psychopharmacology, 133*(3), 262–268.

Woodward, N. D., Cowan, R. L., Park, S., Ansari, M. S., Baldwin, R. M., Li, R., . . . Zald, D. H. (2011). Correlation of individual differences in schizotypal personality traits with amphetamine-induced dopamine release in striatal and extrastriatal brain regions. *American Journal of Psychiatry, 168*(4), 418–426.

3 Genetic associations
The basis of schizotypy

Philip Grant

The question of a genetic basis for schizotypy is at the heart of the original concept as proposed by Rado (1953) and propagated by Meehl (1962). Rado therefore described schizotypy as in essence being the expression of the schizophrenic genotype in interaction with the environment. Meehl suggested revisiting 'the old European notion' (1962, p. 829) of viewing schizophrenia as based on an integrative neural defect, which he christened 'schizotaxia' and assumed to be the only aspect of the schizophrenia spectrum that could be spoken of as inherited. In interaction with the environment and social learning history, schizotaxia could then result in schizotypy, whereby a favourable environment and a preponderance of positive life events would lead to 'a well-compensated "normal" schizotype, never manifesting symptoms of mental illness' (1962, p. 830). In any case, however, the inheritance of what Meehl considered a dominant schizophrenia gene was the *condicio sine qua non* for the development of schizotaxia and, by extension, schizotypy: 'I postulate that a non-schizotaxic individual . . . would not become a schizotype' (1962, p. 831). The Meehlian model is, by definition, taxonic and expectant of shared genetics between schizophrenia and schizotypy. However, it allows for continuity only within the group of schizotypes, and clearly disallows complete continuity across the entire population. Claridge (1997) also notes that considering the proposition of a causal single dominant gene 'probably rules out the *fully* dimensional interpretation' (p. 13).

It has become abundantly clear, though, that the search for a single schizophrenia gene has comprehensively failed; the inheritance of the schizophrenia spectrum is no longer considered to be monogenic but rather polygenic. Therefore, additive and interactive effects of many genes, each with only small respective effect sizes, led behavioural geneticists to the conclusion that 'qualitative disorders can be interpreted simply as being the extremes of quantitative dimensions' (Plomin, Haworth, & Davis, 2009; p. 872). In the case of schizotypy, this is simply to posit that a greater number of genetic risk factors increases the quantitative trait underlying risk. Although the risk for the development of schizophrenia increases with ever higher schizotypy values, the fully dimensional model suggests that there is no clear cut-off or distribution break, but a functional transition between high schizotypy and schizophrenia. In terms of genetics, this could be based on an assumption of two different and major groups of risk factors – namely, those highly specific to the schizophrenia spectrum and those shared between different neuropsychiatric conditions. The advent of DNA microarray technology and, subsequently, genome-wide association studies (GWAS) has led to a vast number of genetic variations being found more commonly in schizophrenic patients compared with healthy controls, but has unfortunately also led to the question of the functional aspects of these respective genetic variants being ignored. Thus, no theoretical explanations exist for many of the genes in question as to how, in detail, they convey their individual risk for the development of schizophrenia. Many genes are involved in pathways that are not considered unique features of psychosis, but are known to regulate various ubiquitous cell functions. It is therefore a plausible 'working hypothesis' that a number of genetic variants convey an overall neural and neuronal resilience. Thus, personality correlates associated with high schizotypy and based on gene × environment interactions may increase the risk of developing clinical psychosis, but do so in interaction with a second set of genes that – in a non-specific fashion – convey the risk of developing any neuropsychiatric condition.

To sum up the major arguments regarding the genetic basis of schizotypy so far: (1) Schizotypy is based partially on genetic risk factors that are common for the whole schizophrenia spectrum. (2) There is a vast number of genes involved, suggestive of a fully dimensional approach to schizotypy. (3) The qualitative disorder of clinical schizophrenia may well result from an interaction between the environment and (at least) two groups of genetic variants – namely, those involved in schizotypy as a quantitative dimension and those involved in general neuronal resilience as a second quantitative dimension.

Terminology

For the uninformed reader, genetics has numerous terms that require at least a brief outline. Our starting point is the definition of the basic unit of genetics – namely, the *gene*. A brief overview of the rapid evolution of the definition of a gene is given in Pearson (2006). Officially, it is defined as a 'locatable region of genomic sequence, corresponding to a unit of inheritance, which is associated with regulatory regions, transcribed regions and/or other functional sequence regions' (p. 398). Within the scope of this chapter, it is sufficient to view genes as specific sequences of deoxyribonucleic acid (DNA) that are transcribed into respective strands of ribonucleic acid (RNA).

Within most genes (and, generally, for those encoding proteins), different sequences exist. The most important ones are the *exons*, *introns* and *promoters*. Promoter regions are sequences of usually 100–1,000 base pairs in length and function as initiators of gene expression. They contain binding sites for the enzyme RNA polymerase, which transcribes the genomic DNA sequence into a precursor version of the messenger RNA (pre-mRNA), as well as binding sites for transcription factors (so-called 'response elements'). Transcription factors are signalling molecules that convey 'information' from other metabolic pathways by influencing the transcription of the respective gene. Activated genes are, during the first step, transcribed fully into the pre-mRNA. In a second step, however, major sequences of the pre-mRNA are excised and the remaining regions are spliced together. Those regions of the genome coding for sequences that are excised from the pre-mRNA are the introns, and those coding for sequences still found in mature mRNAs are the exons.

It is important to realise that genes are generally shared by all members of a species and to a certain degree even between members of different species. One does not have 'good genes' or a 'risk gene', because all healthy members of *Homo sapiens* have the same genes. These genes, however, are not identical within all members of the species, whereby any given possible variant of *the same* gene is referred to as an 'allele'. Thus, while all humans share the gene for catechol-*O*-methyltransferase (the gene COMT), for example, not all humans have identical alleles. Therefore, to amend Meehl's original assumption of a dominant schizophrenia *gene* [sic], we should more accurately be talking about a dominant schizophrenia risk-*allele* of a given gene.

Genetic or allelic variations can occur through various mechanisms and, in some cases, be very rare (and even non-viable) mutations. In many cases, however, mutations in genes are not pathological or life threatening, have only very small (if any) effect sizes and are thus passed on to the next generation. If they become more common throughout evolution and can be detected in at least 1 per cent of the general population, the specific genetic location that has this common amount of variation is referred to as a 'polymorphism'. A polymorphism most commonly exists in one of two forms: either through the exchange of only one base pair of the genome (i.e. a 'single nucleotide polymorphism' [SNP]), or through the variation of the number of repeats of a short genomic sequence (i.e. a 'repeat polymorphism'). Although a great number of polymorphisms have been identified, the true number of possible variable regions within the human genome remains speculative. Thus, the probability of two individuals having exactly identical genetic make-up is almost zero (with the exceptions of monozygotic twins). Furthermore, considering the great genetic variability and the fact that each mammal has two copies of each autosome (i.e. the chromosomes 1 through 22), the likelihood of a single gene being identical in the same human within both autosomes is also highly improbable. In any given case, an individual may be *homozygous* for an allele (i.e. both chromosomes have the identical variant for a specific polymorphism) or *heterozygous* (i.e. both chromosomes have different variants for a specific polymorphism).

Because of the distinct functional consequences associated with a specific allele, it is possible for either the effect to be noticeable on the phenotypical level only – in that case a person is homozygous for the specific allele – or for only one allele to be present (i.e. the person has a heterozygous genotype). In those cases where both chromosomes have to carry a specific allele in order for it to become noticeable on the phenotypical level, the allele is called 'recessive'. Should the effects of a single allele (i.e. in heterozygous persons) be noticeable on the phenotypical level, the allele is either *dominant* or *co-dominant*. In the first case, there is no phenotypical difference between carriers of one or two of the dominant alleles, whereas, in the second case, the heterozygous persons show phenotypical traits of both alleles. Thus, it was Meehl's original belief that all individuals carrying at least one allele of the proposed schizophrenia gene would develop schizotaxia. In the case of co-dominant alleles, an important concept is that of *molecular heterosis* or *hybrid vigour*. This refers to the situation in which the heterozygote genotype is fitter than both homozygotes. Should the heterozygotes have higher values in a trait considered to be adaptive or beneficial, this is referred to as 'positive heterosis'. In those cases were the heterozygotes show lower levels of a trait considered to be maladaptive, one speaks of 'negative heterosis'.

Heritability of schizophrenia and schizotypy

Taking into account that relatives of schizophrenics exhibit higher values in schizotypy, and that schizotypy – at least partially – harbours the liability for schizophrenia (Lenzenweger, 2006), it would appear that the genetics of schizotypy and schizophrenia are highly similar. Thus schizotypy represents an *endophenotype* of schizophrenia, a measurable phenomenon 'along the pathway between disease and distal genotype' (Gottesman & Gould, 2003; p. 636). On reviewing the heritability of clinical schizophrenia (e.g. Sullivan, Kendler, & Neale, 2003), it becomes readily apparent that the risk of developing a spectrum disorder increases with the amount of genetic variance shared with the reference patient: (i.e. highest concordance in monozygotic twins and lowest in non-related individuals). However, there are two problems associated with the observed concordance for schizophrenia observed in monozygotic twins. First, the rates of common occurrence vary strongly between studies, with the highest being just below 70 per cent (Kallmann, 1946), clearly suggesting that environmental factors play a decisive role in aetiology. Second, in twins the role of shared environment, at the very least *in utero*, cannot be disregarded, thereby also supporting the notion that the schizophrenia spectrum is based on gene × environment interactions. A number of adoption studies have, however, managed to disentangle the *postpartum* effects of shared environments somewhat, thus strongly supporting the partial contribution of genetic factors. Finally, as mentioned earlier, the risk not only for schizophrenia but also for schizotypy correlates positively with shared genetic variance (see Tarbox & Pogue-Geile, 2011).

Regarding the heritability of various psychometric measures of schizotypy, to date fewer than ten studies exist; these include a single study by

Battaglia et al. (1999) using a semi-structured interview based on the *DSM III-R* (American Psychiatric Association, 1987) diagnosis of schizotypal personality disorder (SPD). In addition to their scarcity, studies frequently suffer from small sample sizes and, therefore, weak statistical power. One of the largest studies, with over 700 female twin pairs, was performed by Linney et al. (2003) who concluded that 'most schizotypal traits, as measured by self-report questionnaire, have a substantial heritable component in the general population' (p. 812), and that schizotypy is influenced solely by additive genetic and non-shared (i.e. unique to one twin) environmental factors. These findings were mostly concurrent with previous heritability studies, the largest of which – performed by Hay et al. (2001) on over 1,400 twin pairs using a 12-item short form of the Chapman scales – found that *social anhedonia* was explained by dominant genetic effects alone. Heritability estimates for individual schizotypy scales range from 27 per cent (MacDonald, Pogue-Geile, Debski, & Manuck, 2001) to 67 per cent (Kendler & Hewitt, 1992), for social anhedonia leading to an average heritability of approximately 50 per cent. More recent studies by Lin et al. (2007) and Ericson, Tuvblad, Raine, Young-Wolff, and Baker (2011), using the Perceptual Aberration Scale (Chapman, Chapman, & Raulin, 1978) and/or the Schizotypal Personality Questionnaire (SPQ) (Raine, 1991) report average contributions by additive genetic factors to schizotypy facets of 50 per cent. The latter study additionally examined the genetic contribution to the stability of schizotypal traits during adolescence in a longitudinal study (3-year re-test interval) and estimated that genetic influences through a latent factor explained 81 per cent of stability.

While those studies examining latent genetic factors influencing schizotypy in adults often find that positive and negative facets are explained by different genetic and environmental influences (e.g. Linney et al., 2003; MacDonald et al., 2001), the findings of Ericson et al. (2011) suggest that gene-based variance in schizotypal traits in adolescents is rather explained through a single latent factor. The authors therefore estimate that 'perhaps there is something quantitatively different about schizotypal traits during adolescence as compared to during adulthood' (p. 508). Interestingly in this context, only the disorganisation facet loaded on both latent genetic factors in Linney et al. (2003) and it was also the only facet to show differences between age groups in Ericson et al. (2011): that is, increasing with age. Within the final common pathway model of psychosis, Howes and Kapur (2009) note that 'cognitive changes need not necessarily be primary but instead may arise as a consequence of striatal dysfunction' (p. 556) and that 'multiple environmental and genetic risk factors influence diagnosis by affecting other aspects of brain function that underlie negative and cognitive symptoms' (p. 557). The Howes and Kapur (2009) model explains positive psychotic symptoms as a primary consequence of aberrant salience due to a dysregulation of dopaminergic neurotransmission (in part at least attributable to decreased glutamatergic inhibition of the ventral tegmental area [VTA] neurons), and negative symptoms as a subsequent reduction in the signal-to-noise ratio. There are also numerous findings that increased dopaminergic activity leads to atypical neurodegeneration in the frontal lobe. The inconsistent results regarding higher-order latent genetic factors determining schizotypal traits could be explained as follows. Genetic variance in positive schizotypy – as explained through a commonly found latent factor – may be the primary biological core of proneness to psychosis. In interaction with other genetic risk factors (suggested earlier as a 'neur[on]al resilience' factor), negative and disorganised/cognitive traits may emerge in consequence of this biological core.

Identifying genetic loci of the schizotypy continuum

Apart from heritability studies, three major methods exist in humans to examine distinct genetic loci relevant to a given disorder: linkage studies, GWAS and candidate gene or gene of interest (GOI) studies. Linkage studies are based on the fact that the closer genetic loci lie to each other within the genome, the more likely they are to be inherited together. A number of linkage studies published in 2002 by Straub et al., Stefansson et al. and Chumakov et al. led to the identification of the first set of schizophrenia risk loci within the genes DTNBP1 (dysbindin), NRG1 (neuregulin1) and DAAO (D-amino acid oxidase activator), respectively. The lack of specificity of linkage studies (i.e. regions of the genome, but not individual genes or polymorphisms, were identified) proved advantageous for schizophrenia research, because genomic loci found to be significantly more commonly inherited in schizophrenic patients (probably) encompassed a number of polymorphisms with individually small effect sizes. Thus, while linkage studies should not have worked for a complex polygenetic disorder like schizophrenia, regions of the genome were identified that were likely to have conveyed their effects together, even though they may have varied between individual patients. Findings from linkage cites did, however, lead to the proposition of candidate genes or GOI within these regions that were chosen because of theoretical assumptions related to the hypotheses of schizotypal aetiology.

While linkage studies and GWAS are basically blind approaches comparing data from clinical cases with controls, candidate gene or GOI approaches propose specific functional consequences of a given genetic variant and are therefore influenced by theoretical background and choice of a respective GOI. Thus, while GWAS may be suitable for the exploratory identification of genetic variations between cases and controls, only GOI studies can evaluate the complex interactions between distinct polymorphisms. Of course, finding significant effects of a small number of GOIs on schizotypal traits cannot give any information regarding the effects of the enormous number of other relevant risk variants. On the other hand, findings of certain alleles of genes identified by GWAS cannot account for the mechanisms through which these alleles convey their effects in interaction with other polymorphisms. Nor can they ultimately exclude the effects of polymorphisms not identified by GWAS. The most recent GWAS, conducted by Ripke et al. (2013) in a total sample of 21,246 cases and 38,072 controls, identified twenty-two loci of genome-wide significance: each had small individual effect sizes. Through indices of genetic linkage, they 'estimate that 8,300 independent, mostly common SNPs (95 per cent credible interval of 6,300–10,200 SNPs) contribute to risk for schizophrenia and that these collectively account for at least 32 per cent of the variance in liability' (p. 1150). Of these loci, at least ten were also causally associated with other disorders, commonly mental retardation but also a number of somatic disorders. Furthermore, the study did not replicate findings from another large GWAS by O'Donovan et al. (2008) regarding the SNP rs1344706 within the gene ZNF804A, a polymorphism whose effect was replicated by Williams et al. (2011) and Li & Su (2013). The same goes for a number of other proposed candidate genes.

Interestingly, genes identified by GWAS are often not believed to be transcribed, or are non-specifically involved in basal cellular metabolism or anti-oxidant defense mechanisms. Examples here would be the genes involved in calcium-channel formation (e.g. CACNA1C-SNP rs4765905; Ripke et al., 2013), the risk variant of which leads to delayed channel closing and thus to proneness for Ca^{2+}-excitotoxicity. The GWAS by O'Donovan et al. (2008) also identified a SNP within the gene NOS1 as conveying risk for schizophrenia. The encoded protein neuronal nitric oxide synthase 1 (nNOS) is relevant for pro-oxidative and, thus, neurotoxic effects commonly found in a variety of conditions (see Grant, 2011). It could therefore be argued that GWAS-based results 'are decidedly disappointing to those expecting this strategy to yield conclusive evidence of common variants predicting risk for schizophrenia' (Weinberger, 2009). My own explanation would be that those loci may mainly constitute a measure of overall cellular or neur(on)al resilience and therefore be relevant to a number of quantitative traits – schizotypy being one of them; and that they may predict a risk for developing (psycho)pathologies *in general*, but that they do not represent the risk for developing a schizophrenia spectrum disorder. This is supported by first results from healthy adults examining the effects of a polygenic-risk score based on the GWAS-SNPs. This risk score could *not* differentiate between healthy controls and individuals at ultra-high risk for psychosis (Pettersson-Yeo et al., 2013) and was inversely related to psychosis-like experiences (comparing individuals with at least one to those who had never had such an experience; Zammit et al., 2014) as well as SPQ scores (N. Smyrnis [personal communication, 2014]). Arguing that healthy individuals with high schizotypy *could* not have many of these alleles proposed by myself and others to convey lack of neur(on)al resilience (or else they would be schizophrenic), these results fit well into the proposed model of the genetic discontinuity between high schizotypy and spectrum disorders.

Another issue regarding the genome-wide association (GWA) approach is that more often than not it ignores any variability within the schizotypy continuum. This becomes especially striking when keeping in mind the unitary psychosis concept: GWAS often find significant allelic associations shared with bipolar disorder or, alternatively, only if bipolar patients are included – a fact that appears to underscore the great amount of shared quantitative variance between qualitatively *separated* (and I specifically use this participle rather than the adjective *separate*) clinical diagnoses. Also, within the group of schizophrenia cases, schizotypal variance is not regarded. To again quote Weinberger (2009):

> The GWA approach also assumes that diagnosis represents a unitary biological entity, but most clinical diagnoses are syndromal and biologically heterogeneous, and this is especially true in psychiatric disorders .... how could the effect of any common genetic variant acting on only one of the diverse pathophysiological mechanisms implicated in these disorders be anything other than small when measured in large patho-physiologically heterogeneous populations?

I would like to add to this that the GWA approach also assumes that the control sample represents a homogenous population, an assumption that cannot hold true for complex quantitative traits like schizotypy. In other words, persons are grouped according to clinical criteria into cases or controls, but the tremendous amount of variation within both groups is completely ignored.

Regarding self-reported schizotypy, a number of candidate gene studies exist. As mentioned earlier, candidate gene or GOI approaches are highly biased by the a priori selection of a specific polymorphism. This might lead one to believe that any polymorphism, even if chosen poorly, could be falsely positively considered relevant for schizotypy; this is, however and thankfully, not the case. As stated by Richard Straub (cited in McCaffrey, 2010; p. 3) 'It is so much harder for competent investigators to generate a false positive than a false negative in the detection of genes in complex disorders.' I support Straub's statement (from experience) and conclude that the belief often expressed by opponents of the GOI approach – namely, that this approach often leads to false-positive results, is erroneous. Furthermore, since GOI studies usually have considerably less statistical power than GWAS, their positive results are even more compelling. An added advantage of the GOI approach, as also mentioned earlier, is that it has the ability of examining gene × gene-interactions. Furthermore, this approach has the added advantage of using polymorphisms that have been shown to be functional. While GWAS results show that a given allele is more or less common within cases compared with controls, they often render no information regarding the functional significance of this allele. Although the number of candidate gene studies published for self-reported schizotypy is relatively small, the results appear to be consistent. Commonly examined polymorphisms are involved in dopaminergic regulation; for example, polymorphisms in the genes COMT (Avramopoulos et al., 2002; Ettinger, Joober, De Guzman, & O'Driscoll, 2006; Grant et al., 2013; Ma et al., 2007; Schurhoff et al., 2007; Sheldrick et al., 2008; Smyrnis et al., 2007), DRD1 and DRD2 (Gurvich, Louise, Van Rheenen, Neill, & Rossell, 2013), SLC6A3 (Ettinger et al., 2006; Grant et al., 2013) or MAOA (Grant et al., 2013). Most of the aforementioned studies, especially regarding the SNP rs4680 within the COMT-gene, find effects for self-reported schizotypy, not all of which, though, reach statistical significance. The latter is, however, unsurprising. Again to cite Straub (in McCaffrey, 2010, p. 3): 'negative studies should never be weighted as strongly as positive [ones].... I've maintained for many years that a negative really means nothing.' To this McCaffrey adds 'Instead, researchers need to look at the cumulative evidence for a gene's involvement, be it genetic or biological.' The cumulative evidence would therefore suggest that, indeed, dopaminergic polymorphisms – especially the rs4680 of the COMT-gene – truly explain a portion of schizotypal variance.

Apart from polymorphisms directly involved in dopaminergic regulation, other studies have found significant effects of genes identified by early GWAS. In 2011, Yasuda et al. reported significant associations of the ZNF804A-SNP rs1344706 on the total score and the disorganisation factor but not the cognitive/perceptual or interpersonal factors of the SPQ in a relatively small mixed-sex sample (n=176). These analyses were replicated and extended by Stefanis et al. (2013) in a large sample of 1,507 men, although the results of this study support the notion that SNPs in the ZNF804A-gene (rs1344706 and rs7597593) are associated with various indicators of positive but not negative schizotypy. Among the self-report measures used was the SPQ (as in Yasuda et al. 2011), whereby the differences between allelic groups of the rs1344706 in the sample from Stefanis et al. (2013) were also significant for the disorganisation factor before (p=.009), and borderline significant after, correction for multiple testing (p=.081). Keeping in mind that Linney et al. (2003) found strong loading of Cognitive Disorganisation on the positive latent genetic schizoytypy factor and support the aforementioned argument by Straub and McCaffrey, it can therefore be concluded that the gene ZNF804A, and especially the SNP rs1344706, may be a candidate for the modulation of predominantly positive schizotypal traits. Stefanis et al. (2013, p. 1258) also concluded that the 'refined phenotype most sensitive to ZNF804A variability is characterised by ideas of reference and suggestively of distortion of perceptual experiences, which bears a striking resemblance to "aberrant salience"'.

In this context, we have found significant associations of two other polymorphisms repeatedly shown to be involved in attribution of incentive salience (i.e. the serotonin transporter-linked polymorphic region

[5-HTTLPR] and the val[66]met-polymorphism [rs6265] of the gene BDNF) with the Unusual Experiences scale but neither of the other scales of the Oxford-Liverpool Inventory of Feelings and Experiences (O-LIFE). Associations between the BDNF rs6265 and schizotypy were also reported by Ma et al. (2007). Building on these findings, we were also able to demonstrate a significant additive effect of all examined genes shown to be associated directly or indirectly with dopaminergic activity and attribution of incentive salience (Grant, Munk, Kuepper, Wielpuetz, & Hennig et al., in press). Additionally, we were able to find that only positive schizotypy was significantly negatively correlated with levels of mRNA-expression of the genes COMT, MAOA, DRD4, DRD5 and FOS (Grant, Gabriel, Kuepper, Wielpuetz, & Hennig, 2014).

A final method to assess the impact of specific genes on a phenotype uses animals (commonly mice) with genetic knockout (KO). Before going into detail, however, I think it necessary to address the issue of animal models of schizophrenia/schizotypy in general. Animal models find little agreement with a number of researchers, because the human definition of schizotypal traits hinges on faculties that are uniquely measurable only in humans. It has to be noted, however, that a number of animal models exist in research on schizotypy. Animals (including non-human primates) have both the capacity for showing schizotypal manifestations like hallucinations, cognitive impairments, repetitive behaviour, social inadequacy and decreased affective responses (Bauman et al., 2013; Castner & Goldman-Rakic, 2003; Friedman & Selemon, 2010) as well as suffering from the biological dysregulations considered to be both directly and indirectly causal along the schizophrenia spectrum. Thus, the notion of schizotypy in the sense of an underlying biological trait being unique to humans is unlikely, even though this biological trait leads to signs that are different between species. This may give a certain amount of validation to the genetic KO method, which functions through the introduction of the enzyme Cre recombinase into the animal's genome as well as the flanking of a desired sequence of the genome with so-called loxP sites that are recognised by Cre recombinase. Cre can be promoted by specific DNA sequences so that it is only expressed in specific tissues and/or expressed only by activation through specific pharmacological agents. When Cre is expressed, it interacts with the loxP sites and thereby renders the flanked gene dysfunctional (e.g. through excision or inversion of parts of the genome). The KO model nevertheless has its drawbacks, so inferences should be drawn with caution (Grant, 2011). Genetic KOs usually target either genes identified through GWAS or GOIs chosen specifically, mainly because of the dopamine and glutamate hypotheses of schizophrenia. In most KOs, animals show a variety of schizotypal features or animal correlates of clinical manifestations (see Grant, 2011). For a review of a large number of genetic KOs that are considered mouse models of schizophrenia, see Taylor, Taylor, Markham, & Koenig (2009).

Summary and conclusions

It can be ascertained that genetic factors account for a substantial part of variance within the schizotypy continuum. Heritability studies suggest that the amount of variance explained through genetic effects is approximately 50 per cent, although measures and their subscales do differ in this respect. The remainder is explained through (unique) environmental factors, whereby the individual expression of schizotypal traits of a given person is determined through gene × environment interactions. Studies trying to ascertain specific loci involved in the expression of schizotypal traits as well as their extreme manifestation – the qualitative entity of psychosis – suggest a number of roughly 10,000 relevant loci. Therefore, from a genetic point of view, schizotypy can clearly be viewed as an underlying quantitative trait, normally distributed throughout the population and not reserved for individuals who are offspring of schizophrenic parents. Heritability studies as well as genetic association studies suggest that individual facets of schizotypy are moderated through different latent genetic factors that are likely to interact with one other. The genetic/biological core of schizotypy is likely to be the positive facet, which is biologically represented through the mechanism of aberrant salience. Thus, a number of genetic association studies find an involvement of genetic polymorphisms within genes that directly or indirectly influence dopaminergic neurotransmission and the process of attribution of incentive salience. A further genetic factor could be called a 'neur(on)al or cellular resilience' factor and may thus be involved in those schizotypal facets that are not specifically linked to positive expressions of psychosis proneness (e.g. cognitive slippage or the transition from healthy to clinical). It is therefore not surprising that genes possibly relevant to this factor also play major roles in, for example, mental retardation.

In closing, I would like to address what is my personal view of the current situation regarding schizotypal genetic research, and to suggest possible directions for the future. My own experience suggests a large 'division of faiths', especially between advocates of GWAS and those of the candidate gene/GOI approach, whereby the advocates of the one usually tend to be avid opponents of the other. As both methods have their flaws, one can observe voices from both 'faiths' claiming that the respective other method has proven disappointing and lost its value. However, I personally believe that – in this case, at least – overly criticising the individual shortcomings of a given method may lead to inadequate appreciation of its merits.

References

American Psychiatric Association (1987). *Diagnostic and statistical manual of mental disorders* (3rd ed. revised). Washington, DC: Author.

Avramopoulos, D., Stefanis, N. C., Hantoumi, I., Smyrnis, N., Evdokimidis, I., & Stefanis, C. N. (2002). Higher scores of self reported schizotypy in healthy young males carrying the COMT high activity allele. *Molecular Psychiatry, 7*(7), 706–711.

Battaglia, M., Fossati, A., Torgersen, S., Bertella, S., Bajo, & S., Maffei, C. (1999). A psychometric-genetic study of schizotypal disorder. *Schizophrenia Research, 37*(1), 53–64.

Bauman, M. D., Iosif, A. M., Smith, S. E., Bregere, C., Amaral, D. G., & Patterson, P. H. (2013). Activation of the maternal immune system during pregnancy alters behavioral development of rhesus monkey offspring. *Biological Psychiatry, 75*(4), 332–341.

Castner, S. A., & Goldman-Rakic, P. S. (2003). Amphetamine sensitization of hallucinatory-like behaviors is dependent on prefrontal cortex in nonhuman primates. *Biological Psychiatry, 54*(2), 105–110.

Chapman, L. J., Chapman, J. P., & Raulin, M. L. (1978). Body-image aberration in schizophrenia. *Journal of Abnormal Psychology, 87*(4), 399–407.

Chumakov, I., Blumenfeld, M., Guerassimenko, O., Cavarec, L., Palicio, M., & Abderrahim, H. (2002). Genetic and physiological data implicating the new human gene G72 and the gene for D-amino acid oxidase in schizophrenia. *Proceedings of the National Academy of Sciences of the United States of America, 99*(21), 13675–13680.

Claridge, G. (1997). Theoretical background and issues. In G. Claridge (Ed.), *Schizotypy: Implications for illness and health* (pp. 3–18). Oxford University Press.

Ericson, M., Tuvblad, C., Raine, A., Young-Wolff, K., & Baker, L. A. (2011). Heritability and longitudinal stability of schizotypal traits during adolescence. *Behavior Genetics, 41*(4), 499–511.

Ettinger, U., Joober, R., De Guzman, R., & O'Driscoll, G.A. (2006). Schizotypy, attention deficit hyperactivity disorder, and dopamine genes. *Psychiatry and Clinical Neurosciences, 60*(6), 764–767.

Friedman, H. R., & Selemon, L. D. (2010). Fetal irradiation interferes with adult cognition in the nonhuman primate. *Biological Psychiatry, 68*(1), 108–111.

Gottesman, I. I., & Gould, T. D. (2003). The endophenotype concept in psychiatry: etymology and strategic intentions. *American Journal of Psychiatry, 160*(4), 636–645.

Grant, P. (2011). Dopamine neurotoxicity, oxidative stress and schizophrenia – in vitro and in vivo studies of peroxisomal reactions to increased dopamine (doctoral thesis), Justus-Liebig-University, Giessen. Available online at geb.uni-giessen.de/geb/volltexte/2011/8495/index.html (accessed 1 March 2015).

Grant, P., Gabriel, F., Kuepper, Y., Wielpuetz, C., & Hennig, J. (2014). Psychosis-proneness correlates with expression levels of dopaminergic genes. *European Psychiatry, 29*(5), 304–306.

Grant, P., Munk, A. J. L., Kuepper, Y., Wielpuetz, C., & Hennig, J. (in press). Additive genetic effects for schizotypy support a fully-dimensional model of psychosis-proneness. *Journal of Individual Differences.* doi: 10.1027/1614-0001/a000155

Grant, P., Kuepper, Y., Mueller, E., Wielpuetz, C., Mason, O., & Hennig, J. (2013). Dopaminergic foundations of schizotypy as measured by the German version of the Oxford-Liverpool Inventory of Feelings and Experiences (O-LIFE) – a suitable endophenotype of schizophrenia. *Frontiers in Human Neuroscience, 7*(1).

Gurvich, C., Louise, S., Van Rheenen, T., Neill, E., & Rossell., S. (2013). The influence of prefrontal and striatal dopaminergic genes on cognitive control in high and low schizotypy. *Biological Psychiatry, 73*(9), 270.

Hay, D. A., Martin, N. G., Foley, D., Treloar, S. A., Kirk, K. M., & Heath, A. C. (2001). Phenotypic and genetic analyses of a short measure of psychosis-proneness in a large-scale Australian twin study. *Twin Research, 4*(1), 30–40.

Howes, O. D., & Kapur, S. (2009). The dopamine hypothesis of schizophrenia: version III – the final common pathway. *Schizophrenia Bulletin, 35*(3), 549–562.

Kallmann, F. J. (1946). The genetic theory of schizophrenia – an analysis of 691 schizophrenic twin index families. *American Journal of Psychiatry, 103*(3), 309–322.

Kendler, K. S., & Hewitt, J. (1992). The structure of self-report schizotypy in twins. *Journal of Personality Disorders, 6*(1), 1–17.

Lenzenweger, M. F. (2006). Schizotypy – an organizing framework for schizophrenia research. *Current Directions in Psychological Science, 15*(4), 162–166.

Li, M., & Su, B. (2013). Meta-analysis supports association of a non-synonymous SNP in ZNF804A with schizophrenia. *Schizophrenic Research, 149*(1–3), 188–189.

Lin, C. C. H., Su, C. H., Kuo, P. H., Hsiao, C. K., Soong, W. T., & Chen, W. J. (2007). Genetic and environmental influences on schizotypy among adolescents in Taiwan: a multivariate twin/sibling analysis. *Behavior Genetics, 37*(2), 334–344.

Linney, Y. M., Murray, R. M., Peters, E. R., MacDonald, A. M., Rijsdijk, F., & Sham, P. C. (2003). A quantitative genetic analysis of schizotypal personality traits. *Psychological Medicine, 33*(5), 803–816.

Ma, X., Sun, J., Yao, J., Wang, Q., Hu, X., & Deng, W. (2007). A quantitative association study between schizotypal traits and COMT, PRODH and BDNF genes in a healthy Chinese population. *Psychiatry Research, 153*(1), 7–15.

MacDonald, A. W., 3rd, Pogue-Geile, M. F., Debski, T. T., & Manuck, S. (2001). Genetic and environmental influences on schizotypy: a community-based twin study. *Schizophrenia Bulletin, 27*(1), 47–58.

McCaffrey, P. (2010). Schizophrenia genetics: best of times . . . worst of times? Available online at http://www.schizophreniaforum.org/images/SRFSchizophrenia GeneticsSeries.pdf (accessed 1 March 2015).

Meehl, P. E. (1962). Schizotaxia, schizotypy, schizophrenia. *American Psychologist, 17*(12), 827–838.

O'Donovan, M. C., Craddock, N., Norton, N., Williams, H., Peirce, T., & Moskvina, V. (2008). Identification of loci associated with schizophrenia by genome-wide association and follow-up. *Nature Genetics, 40*(9), 1053–1055.

Pearson, H. (2006). What is a gene? *Nature, 441*(7092), 398–401.

Pettersson-Yeo, W., Benetti, S., Marquand, A. F., Dell'acqua, F., Williams, S. C., & Allen, P. (2013). Using genetic, cognitive and multi-modal neuroimaging data to identify ultra-high-risk and first-episode psychosis at the individual level. *Psychological Medicine, 43*(12), 2547–2562.

Plomin, R., Haworth, C. M., & Davis, O. S. (2009). Common disorders are quantitative traits. *Nature Review of Genetics, 10*(12), 872–878.

Rado, S. (1953). Dynamics and classification of disordered behavior. *American Journal of Psychiatry, 110*(6), 406–416.

Raine, A. (1991). The SPQ – a scale for the assessment of schizotypal personality based on DSM-III-R criteria. *Schizophrenia Bulletin, 17*(4), 555–564.

Ripke, S., O'Dushlaine, C., Chambert, K., Moran, J. L., Kahler, A. K., & Akterin, S. (2013). Genome-wide association analysis identifies 13 new risk loci for schizophrenia. *Nature Genetics, 45*(10), 1150–1159.

Schurhoff, F., Szoke, A., Chevalier, F., Roy, I., Meary, A., & Bellivier, F. (2007). Schizotypal dimensions: an intermediate phenotype associated with the COMT high activity allele. *American Journal of Medical Genetics Part B-Neuropsychiatric Genetics, 144B*(1), 64–68.

Sheldrick, A. J., Krug, A., Markov, V., Leube, D., Michel, T. M., & Zerres, K. (2008). Effect of COMT val(158)met genotype on cognition and personality. *European Psychiatry*, *23*(6), 385–389.

Smyrnis, N., Avramopoulos, D., Evdokimidis, I., Stefanis, C. N., Tsekou, H., & Stefanis, N. C. (2007). Effect of schizotypy on cognitive performance and its tuning by COMT val(158) met genotype variations in a large population of young men. *Biological Psychiatry*, *61*(7), 845–853.

Stefanis, N. C., Hatzimanolis, A., Avramopoulos, D., Smyrnis, N., Evdokimidis, I., & Stefanis, C. N. (2013). Variation in psychosis gene ZNF804A is associated with a refined schizotypy phenotype but not neurocognitive performance in a large young male population. *Schizophrenia Bulletin*, *39*(6), 1252–1260.

Stefansson, H., Sigurdsson, E., Steinthorsdottir, V., Bjornsdottir, S., Sigmundsson, T., & Ghosh, S. (2002). Neuregulin 1 and susceptibility to schizophrenia. *American Journal of Human Genetics*, *71*(4), 877–892.

Straub, R. E. (2002). Genetic variation in the 6p22.3 gene DTNBP1, the human ortholog of the mouse dysbindin gene, is associated with schizophrenia. *American Journal of Human Genetics*, *71*(2), 337–348.

Sullivan, P. F., Kendler, K. S., & Neale, M. C. (2003). Schizophrenia as a complex trait – evidence from a meta-analysis of twin studies. *Archives of General Psychiatry*, *60*(12), 1187–1192.

Tarbox, S. I., & Pogue-Geile, M. F. (2011). A multivariate perspective on schizotypy and familial association with schizophrenia: a review. *Clinical Psychology Review*, *31*(7), 1169–1182.

Taylor, A., Taylor, S., Markham, J., & Koenig, J. (2009). Animal models of schizophrenia. Available online at http://www.schizophreniaforum.org/res/models/Animal_Models_04_09.pdf (accessed 1 March 2015).

Weinberger, D. R. (2009). Comment. Available online at http://www.schizophreniaforum.org/pap/readmore.asp?commentID={01F38259-FD4B-460D-9968-488367BC0C6B} (accessed 1 March 2015).

Williams, H. J., Norton, N., Dwyer, S., Moskvina, V., Nikolov, I., & Carroll, L. (2011). Fine mapping of ZNF804A and genome-wide significant evidence for its involvement in schizophrenia and bipolar disorder. *Molecular Psychiatry*, *16*(4), 429–441.

Yasuda, Y., Hashimoto, R., Ohi, K., Fukumoto, M., Umeda-Yano, S., & Yamamori, H. (2011). Impact on schizotypal personality trait of a genome-wide supported psychosis variant of the ZNF804A gene. *Neuroscience Letters*, *495*(3), 216–220.

Zammit, S., Hamshere, M., Dwyer, S., Georgiva, L., Timpson, N., & Moskvina, V. (2014). A population-based study of genetic variation and psychotic experiences in adolescents. *Schizophrenia Bulletin*, *40*, 1254–1262.

4 Hemispheric asymmetries in schizotypy

Gina M. Grimshaw and Laura Kranz

There are two reasons why hemispheric asymmetries are important in the study of schizotypy. First, several theories of schizophrenia include a causal or associated role for atypical lateralisation of anatomy and function (Oertel-Knöchel & Linden, 2011). To the extent that schizotypy and schizophrenia have a shared neurodevelopmental history, one might also expect atypical asymmetry to be present in schizotypy. If so, it may provide a model in which to test hypotheses without confounds produced by the schizophrenic disorder itself (Chun, Minor, & Cohen, 2013; Ettinger, Meyhöfer, Steffens, Wagner, & Koutsouleris, 2014). This rationale is based on the pathology-oriented premise that schizotypy reflects psychosis proneness, or is at least a diathesis for the development of disorder.

A second rationale for exploring hemispheric correlates of schizotypy is premised on the dimensional view of schizotypy as an individual difference that varies continuously in the healthy population (Claridge, 1997). Schizotypy is associated with a number of cognitive and personality traits, both advantageous and disadvantageous. Hemispheric asymmetry may have some explanatory value as the neural correlate of functional organisation that gives rise to schizotypal thought. This rationale does not depend on any direct parallel between hemispheric asymmetries in schizotypy and schizophrenia. A corollary of this is also true: if schizotypy is associated with predictable variability in lateralisation, then we may learn something about the consequences of individual differences in lateralisation by studying people who vary in schizotypal traits.

In the Claridge (1997) book on schizotypy, Richardson, Mason, and Claridge (1997) reviewed the (then) current status of literature. They cautiously concluded that schizotypy (and particularly positive schizotypy) was associated with a reduced degree of lateralisation (or an increase in hemispheric equivalence) as reflected in hand preference and perceptual asymmetries. Our goal in this chapter is to update their analysis by highlighting developments in our understanding of hemispheric asymmetry, and in theoretical models that link it to schizophrenia and schizotypy. We review the current empirical evidence regarding lateralisation in schizotypy as reflected in studies of handedness and perceptual asymmetries.

We conclude with a discussion of imaging methods that have been used primarily to study asymmetries in schizophrenia, but promise to further our understanding of hemispheric processing in schizotypy as well. Throughout, we highlight methodological concerns that complicate any straightforward interpretation of the findings.

Hemispheric asymmetry

The two hemispheres of the brain differ in anatomy and function. Early models assumed asymmetry was essentially a human trait – manifesting most obviously in the uniquely human characteristics of handedness and language (Corballis, 2014). However, comparative studies show asymmetries to be pervasive in the animal kingdom (Rogers, Vallortigara, & Andrews, 2013). Asymmetries are observed in many domains including language and handedness, but also in perception, attention, memory, emotion and motivation. For the most part, these asymmetries are independent of one another (Nielsen, Zielinski, Ferguson, Lainhart, & Anderson, 2013), suggesting that individuals do not possess hemisphericity – a characteristic dominance of one hemisphere over the other. The two most closely related asymmetries are those of language lateralisation and handedness, although even here the relationship is not particularly strong, suggesting that these asymmetries only partially overlap in development (Ocklenburg, Beste, Arning, Petersburs, & Güntürkün, 2014).

Hemispheric specialisation is relative and not absolute, and it is an oversimplification to refer to broad classes of cognition as lateralised (e.g. *language* is lateralised to the left hemisphere; *attention* is lateralised to the right). Rather, any function arises through the coordination of component processes, some of which function most effectively in one hemisphere or the other. For example, in the speech processing domain, both hemispheres are capable of processing the speech signal to the extent required for lexical access (reviewed in Hickok & Poeppel, 2007). But they do so in computationally different ways: auditory processing in the left hemisphere is optimised for the extraction of phonological information that exists in rapid auditory transitions, while auditory processing in the right hemisphere is optimised for detection of slow changes in acoustic properties that signal emotional tone of voice, or prosody. Effective speech processing requires the integration of both components. Similarly, semantic processing involves both left- and right-hemisphere components that differ qualitatively (for a review, see Lindell, 2006). Left-hemisphere semantic processes give rise to rapid activation of meaning, followed by inhibition of inappropriate meanings as guided by context. In contrast, right-hemisphere semantic activation arises more slowly, but sustains diffuse associations allowing for the simultaneous activation of figurative or other non-literal meanings. Semantic processing is typically driven by the fast Left-hemisphere system, but slower right-hemisphere effects can emerge when more distant (or loose) associations are necessary to create meaning.

Individual differences are observed in both the direction and degree of asymmetry. Although much research has focused on individuals with atypical direction (e.g. left-handers, or those with right-hemisphere language lateralisation), it now seems likely that degree of asymmetry may be more psychologically relevant (Corballis, 2014; Prichard, Propper, & Christman, 2013). Reduced asymmetry is associated with a number of developmental disorders (Bishop, 2013; Brandler & Paracchini, 2014). Although it is tempting to consider lateralisation to be a cause of atypical development, it may be a consequence instead (Bishop, 2013). For example, if a disorder causes atypical development in inhibitory language networks that are normally supported by the left frontal cortex, then affected individuals will exhibit reduced asymmetry for language processing as an epiphenomenon of the underlying developmental problem. It is therefore important to try to determine whether reduced asymmetry reflects hemispheric equivalence, or deficit in the normally specialised hemisphere.

Individual differences in lateralisation can also be observed in healthy individuals. Again, it seems that degree of asymmetry is more relevant than direction (Corballis, 2014). However, the relationship between asymmetry and performance is not clear-cut. Greater lateralisation has been associated with both better (Hirnstein, Hugdahl, & Hausmann, 2014) and worse performance (Boles, Barth, & Merrill, 2008) on language and spatial tasks. Individual differences may also be related to sex. Women are less lateralised than men for some aspects of language function, and more likely to be right-handed, although both effects are much smaller than once thought (Hirnstein, Westerhausen, Korsnes, & Hugdahl, 2013; Sommer, Aleman, Somers, Boks, & Kahn, 2008; Voyer, 2011).

A further consideration is the role of interhemispheric interaction. The coordination of left- and right-hemisphere computations clearly involves interhemispheric processing via the corpus callosum; however, our current understanding of the relationship between asymmetry and interhemispheric processing is poor (van der Knaap & van der Ham, 2011). Some callosal connections are excitatory and important for the transmission of information. In this context, better interhemispheric communication would result in less lateralisation of function. However, interhemispheric effects can also be inhibitory, allowing one hemisphere to regulate or dominate the functions of the other. In this context, better hemispheric communication would result in greater lateralisation of function. It is likely that both excitatory and inhibitory callosal functions exist, and that the form of interaction depends on modality, task demands and developmental considerations (Homae, 2014).

Theoretical models linking schizophrenia and schizotypy to hemispheric asymmetry

A full review of the literature on hemispheric asymmetries in schizophrenia is beyond the scope of this chapter (for the review, see Oertel-Knöchel &

Linden, 2011). Empirically, schizophrenia is associated with reduced asymmetry in anatomy and function, across a number of brain areas, functions and behaviours (Sommer, Ramsey, Kahn, Aleman, & Bouma, 2001). Some early models posited that schizophrenia is specifically related to left- or right-hemisphere deficits. An example of both perspectives is seen in Gruzelier (1999) who suggested that positive symptoms derived from overactivity of the left hemisphere and negative symptoms from overactivity of the right. However, given the heterogeneity in hemispheric functions and their relative independence, it is unlikely that schizophrenia is caused by wholesale effects on one hemisphere or the other.

The most comprehensive of contemporary models is Crow's (2013) XY Gene Hypothesis, a variant on an earlier hypothesis (e.g. Crow, 1990) that draws a causal connection between hemispheric asymmetry and schizophrenia. According to the model, important genes for asymmetries in language and handedness (being recent evolutionary developments) are located in autosomal regions of the X and Y chromosomes. Psychosis-proneness arises when epigenetic markers prevent the normal expression of those genes; thus schizophrenia results from a failure of normal lateralisation of anatomy and function. In fact, Crow has claimed that psychosis is the 'price that *Homo sapiens* pays for language (Crow, 2013, p. 816). The model generates specific predictions about asymmetry in schizophrenia, the most obvious being that schizophrenia should be associated with an absence (or reduced degree) of asymmetry, as seems to be the case. However, the model further specifies that those asymmetries should be specific to regions involved in language processing and manual control, and that additionally there may be sex differences in the relationship. Although some aspects of the XY Hypothesis have been challenged (particularly the idea that language and handedness suddenly emerged in a rapid process of speciation [Corballis, 2014]), it does account for a number of findings regarding hemispheric asymmetry and sex differences in schizophrenia.

The XY Gene Hypothesis links hemispheric asymmetry and schizophrenia through genetics; a more proximal theory suggests that schizophrenia is essentially a disorder of connectivity (Friston, 1998; Ribolsi et al., 2009). For example, in a recent functional imaging study, Guo and colleagues (2013) found that schizophrenia was associated with reduced interhemispheric connectivity, and further that the degree of disruption predicted symptom severity. They suggest that the reduced asymmetry in schizophrenia reflects a failure of inhibitory interhemispheric connectivity, allowing activity to arise in both hemispheres when one would normally dominate. These two hypotheses are compatible – in fact, Crow (2013) suggests that one mechanism by which epigenetic markers might achieve their effects is through altering the genes that control callosal development.

These models of hemispheric asymmetry in schizophrenia predict that similar associations should be observed in schizotypy, because they are proposed to share a developmental history. However, an alternative hypothesis links schizotypy to increased activity in the right hemisphere generally (e.g. Richardson et al., 1997). This 'right-hemisphere hypothesis' of schizotypy is premised mostly on findings that cognitive processing in schizotypy (particularly positive schizotypy) has traits that are thought to be typical of the right hemisphere – including creativity, diffuse semantic processing and reduced inhibition (Lindell, 2006, 2011). We reiterate here the caveats about linking an entire hemisphere with broad domains of cognition, and note specifically that contemporary models of creativity emphasise the importance of interhemispheric interactions in creative thought. That is, while the right hemisphere may play an important role in generating some core components of creative thinking, it is the ability to integrate these with Left-hemisphere processes that allows creative behaviour to emerge (Aziz-Zadeh, Liew, & Dandekar, 2013; Lindell, 2011). We turn now to an evaluation of the empirical evidence for altered hemispheric asymmetry in schizotypy, drawn from studies of handedness and perceptual asymmetries.

Evidence for a relationship between schizotypy and hemispheric asymmetry

Handedness

Given the ease of assessment, it is not surprising that the preponderance of data relevant to the relationship between schizotypy and hemispheric asymmetry comes from studies of hand preference. If handedness is defined as writing hand, rates of left-handedness range from about 9–12 per cent (see Corballis, 2014, for a review). However, dichotomous classification of left- and right-handers fails to capture much variability in human hand preference. Inventories that assess a range of activities reveal a sizeable subgroup of mixed-handers who do some activities consistently with the left hand and some with the right. Early studies of handedness in schizotypy frequently used either a dichotomous (left/right) classification, or more commonly combined left- and mixed-handers into a single 'non-right-handed' group. In their 1997 chapter, Richardson and colleagues indicated that there are several 'small indicators' of unusual handedness in schizotypy and schizophrenia. Since then, a number of large studies have confirmed a small but robust relationship between schizotypy and mixed-hand preference. In their 2009 meta-analysis of fourteen effect sizes and more than 10,000 participants, Somers and colleagues (Somers, Sommer, Boks, & Kahn, 2009) concluded that mixed-handers have higher levels of positive schizotypy, and that scores in consistent left- and right-handers do not differ. Since that meta-analysis was published, a number of large-scale studies have similarly reported that associations between schizotypy and mixed-handedness are observed across ages (e.g. Chapman, Grimshaw, & Nicholls, 2011) and cultures (e.g. Asai & Tanno, 2009). The effect furthermore appears to be robust across different handedness questionnaires and measures of schizotypy.

Many studies of handedness have focused exclusively on its relationship with positive schizotypy. Fewer studies have examined relations with other dimensions of schizotypy, but those that have suggest the relationship is specific to positive, and possibly disorganised, factors. In their meta-analysis, Somers and colleagues did not consider other dimensions specifically because too few studies assessed them, but they showed that the effect size for the comparisons of right-handers to mixed-handers was larger in studies that measured only positive schizotypy than in studies that measured total schizotypy. The relationship between mixed-handedness and schizotypy is also maintained across the psychosis-prone spectrum. Rates of mixed-handedness are elevated in non-clinical samples that are high in delusional or psychotic-like experiences, in family members of those with schizophrenia and in schizophrenia itself (Oertel-Knöchel & Linden, 2011).

Given that hand preference shows some heritability and is established early in development (Ocklenburg et al., 2014), it is reasonable to conclude that mixed-hand preference is a phenotypic marker of a neurodevelopmental course that confers vulnerability to psychosis and schizophrenia. But what does a relationship between mixed-handedness and schizotypy tell us? Can it help us to better understand the genetic and developmental factors that might underlie both cerebral asymmetry and schizotypy? Or the neurological mechanisms that support schizotypal thought?

The answer to the first question lies in part in our understanding of the genetics of hand preference (for a recent review, see Ocklenburg, Beste, & Güntürkün, 2013). Left-handedness runs in families; the incidence of left-handedness in children with right-handed parents is about 8 per cent. It rises to 22 per cent when one parent is left-handed and to 36 per cent when both parents are left-handed. Given the salience of left-handedness in the population, it is not surprising that genetic models of handedness have focused almost exclusively on explaining the incidence of left-handedness, and not mixed-handedness. Early genetic models focused on one or two hypothetical alleles that either conferred dextrality or left lateralisation to chance developmental factors (e.g. Annett, 1998). Thus left-handers (and a subset of chance right-handers) were presumed to be homozygous for the chance alleles. However, contemporary studies using gene-wide association (GWAS) have failed to identify any one gene that accounts for significant phenotypic variance in handedness, and it is currently thought that variability in hand preference arises through multiple genetic and environmental factors and their interactions. Current models estimate that as many as forty different genes may be relevant (McManus, Davison, & Armour, 2013). Research in this area is now focused on identifying genes that play direct roles in establishing the neural correlates of handedness, including those involved in the development of the corpus callosum and those that are asymmetrically expressed in the developing brain.

From a dimensional perspective, association between schizotypy and mixed-handedness is of interest because it may point to some aspect of neuropsychological function or organisation that could underpin some aspects of schizotypal cognition. That is, if we knew how mixed-handers differed from consistent-handers neuropsychologically, we could develop hypotheses regarding similar organisation in schizotypy. Here again the field suffers because the focus of research has been on the left-hander, and less is known about neuropsychological function in mixed handedness. The best understood neuropsychological correlate of hand preference is language lateralisation (Ocklenburg et al., 2014). Although most people have Left-hemisphere specialisation for language processing (particularly for phonological and lexical processes), left-handers are more likely to have bilateral or right-hemisphere language specialisation (rates of up to 25 per cent) and bilateral language is more common in mixed-handers than left-handers (Szaflarski et al., 2002). Structurally, mixed handers have a larger corpus callosum than either left- or right-handers (Luders et al., 2010), which has been associated with decreased lateralisation of function (Westerhausen & Hugdahl, 2008).

Behaviourally, mixed-handers (compared with consistent left- or right-handers) share many cognitive and personality traits with positive schizotypy, including intellectual openness (Bryson, Grimshaw, & Wilson, 2009), creativity (Shobe, Ross & Fleck, 2009) and cognitive flexibility (Prichard et al., 2013). None of these associations is consistent with the idea that mixed handedness is a marker of some deficit in cognitive processing; rather, it appears to be associated with qualitative differences in processing that may reflect better integration of left- and right-hemisphere processing components. These associations of course do not imply causality; a goal in future research should be to examine associations among handedness, schizotypy and these traits, in order to determine patterns of shared and unique variance, and so develop testable models to explain their relationship.

Perceptual asymmetries

Perceptual asymmetries provide a more direct measure of hemispheric differences in cognitive processing than handedness (Bryden, 1982). In the visual modality, stimuli are presented to one visual field. Because input is directed to the contralateral hemisphere, visual half-field tasks typically produce a right visual field advantage (RVFA) for linguistic tasks (reflecting Left-hemisphere specialisation) and a left visual field advantage (LVFA) for visual-spatial or emotion perception tasks (reflecting right-hemisphere specialisation). In dichotic listening tasks, competing auditory stimuli are presented to each ear. Under these conditions, contralateral projections dominate over ipsilateral projections. Dichotic listening tasks typically show a right ear advantage (REA) for linguistic tasks, and a left ear advantage (LEA) for tasks involving perception of emotional prosody or music.

There are some important considerations when interpreting perceptual asymmetry data. The first is that the degree of asymmetry may be affected by overall level of performance. This is particularly problematic when accuracy is the dependent measure because, if performance is near ceiling, the magnitude of the asymmetry is constrained. For this reason, response time may provide a better measure of performance, or an asymmetry index that is not constrained by accuracy (e.g. lambda; Bryden & Sprott, 1981). This limitation is particularly important when comparing asymmetry measures between participant groups (e.g. those high and low in schizotypy) who might vary in overall accuracy. Although perceptual asymmetries are typically taken as measures of trait differences in the processing of various inputs, asymmetry measures are also influenced by top-down executive functions that control the deployment of attention, and by a host of other dynamic, demographic and lifestyle factors, including smoking and drug use (Herzig, Tracy, Munafò, & Mohr, 2010), which may also differ between groups. These factors are rarely assessed or controlled for. Interestingly, one factor that is usually controlled for is hand preference – almost all studies of perceptual asymmetry include only right-handers. Given the relations among schizotypy, hand preference and hemispheric asymmetry, that restriction may well limit the ability of many perceptual asymmetry studies to examine 'typical' schizotypy.

Another consideration in interpreting current research is the potential for studies to capitalise on chance factors through multiple comparisons, compounded by a publication bias for significant effects. A typical perceptual asymmetry study yields a host of dependent measures (accuracy, response time, left and right side performance, an asymmetry measure, and measures of sensitivity and bias), and performance may be correlated with a range of schizotypy dimensions or subscales. Further opportunities for false positive results arise when studies have small samples, or consider subgroups within a sample (e.g. men and women separately). The solution to some of these problems might be meta-analysis, although at present too few studies report sufficient data or use consistent enough methodologies to make that possible. Encouragingly, more recent studies include larger samples, and provide more comprehensive reporting of results, so meta-analysis may become possible in the future. Interestingly, more recent studies are also more likely to report null effects (e.g. Castro & Pearson, 2011; Schofield & Mohr, 2014). Instead we provide a systematic review of existing studies in an effort to identify any consistency. Although asymmetries in a number of cognitive and motor functions have been assessed, most have focused on asymmetries in language and attention, and so we limit our consideration to those. Including assessments of both functions allows us to determine whether atypical asymmetries are specific to language (as suggested by Crow's XY Gene Hypothesis) or reflect increased right-hemisphere function more broadly.

Language studies

Visual half-field studies of language asymmetry are summarised in Table 4.1. Most have used the lexical decision task, which typically produces a RVFA reflecting better/faster lexical access in the left hemisphere. Consistent with hypotheses, the majority of lexical decision studies report schizotypy to be associated with a reduced RVFA. Interpretation of this effect is inconsistent: some attribute it to an 'overactive' right hemisphere, whereas others attribute the result to reduced language lateralisation. However, potential group differences in overall performance make it difficult to interpret any reduction in asymmetry as better right-hemisphere processing or worse Left-hemisphere processing. A small number of studies have used semantic priming tasks instead of lexical decision. Semantic tasks are particularly interesting because the processes involved are less heavily left lateralised than lexical access, and rely instead on complementary left- and right-hemisphere processes. Semantic processes are also more likely to be altered in schizotypy than are lexical processes (Grimshaw, Bryson, Atchley, & Humphrey, 2010), making their assessment more relevant for understanding how hemispheric asymmetry may contribute to schizotypal cognition (Lindell, 2014). Priming studies show reduced lateralisation in schizotypy, particularly for indirect priming tasks (Pizzagalli, Lehmann, & Brugger, 2001) that are most likely to tap diffuse semantic associations that are associated with right-hemisphere processing. Although schizotypal performance on lateralised priming tasks could be interpreted as reduced hemispheric asymmetry, it could also be interpreted as better integration of left- and right-hemisphere processing components, or reduced inhibition of right-hemisphere processes by left-hemisphere processes.

Dichotic listening studies of language asymmetry are summarised in Table 4.2. Findings are less consistent than in visual half-field studies. For linguistic tasks, some studies report that schizotypy is related to reduced lateralisation while others report increased lateralisation, and still others report null effects. Two recent studies are of particular interest here. Castro and Pearson (2011) and Najt and colleagues (Najt, Bayer, & Hausmann, 2012) used the same dichotic task that allows for the assessment of asymmetries in linguistic and prosodic processes with the same stimuli. Participants listened to dichotic words, each spoken in a different tone of voice. In some blocks they listened for a target word (which typically produces an REA), and in others they listened for a target tone of voice (which typically produces an LEA). An important advantage of the task is that it allows for stronger inferences to be made about mechanisms producing asymmetry shifts. If schizotypy is associated with *reduced* language asymmetry, then reduced asymmetry should be seen on both linguistic and prosodic tasks, or at least on one task but not the other. However, if schizotypy is associated with an underactive left hemisphere, or overactive right hemisphere, then asymmetry should shift in the same direction on prosodic and linguistic tasks, producing reduced lateralisation on the linguistic task, but increased lateralisation on the prosodic task. Notably, neither study found associations between schizotypy and lateralisation on the linguistic task. Najt et al. (2012) found schizotypy to be associated with reduced asymmetry on the prosodic

Table 4.1 Visual half-field studies of hemispheric asymmetries in language

Study (year)	Subjects	Schizotypy assessment	Task	Schizotypy effect	Schizotypy dimension
Herzig, Tracy, Munafò, & Mohr, (2010)	N = 40 (Male) Healthy, right handed	O-LIFE	Lexical decision	Less lateralised	Cognitive disorganisation
Leonhard & Brugger (1998)	N = 40 (Male) Healthy, right handed	MI	Lexical decision	Less lateralised	Positive
Mohr, Krummenacher, Landis, Sandor, Fathi, & Brugger (2005)	N = 40 (Male) Healthy, right handed	MI; PAS	Lexical decision	Less lateralised	Positive
Schofield & Mohr (2014)	N = 159 Healthy, right handed	O-LIFE; MI; PAS	Lexical decision	Inconsistent results. More lateralised in one condition.	Negative; cognitive disorganisation
Weinstein & Graves (2001)	N = 32 Healthy	MI; SA; PA	Lexical decision	Less lateralised	Positive; negative
Weinstein & Graves (2002)	N = 60 Healthy	MI; PA; SA	Lexical decision	Less lateralised	Positive
Broks (1984)	N = 36 Healthy, right handed	STQ; EPQ	Read syllables	Less lateralised (males only)	Whole STA scale
Suzuki & Usher (2009)	N = 53 Healthy, right Handed	O-LIFE	Read syllables	Less lateralised	Positive; cognitive disorganisation
Rawlings & Claridge (1984)	N = 20	EPQ; STQ	Letter recognition	Less lateralised	
Kravetz, Faust, & Edelman (1998)	N = 60 (Male) Healthy, right handed	O-LIFE	Semantic priming	Less lateralised	Positive; cognitive disorganisation; impulsive non-conformity
Pizzagalli, Lehmann, & Brugger (2001)	N = 24 (Female) Healthy, right handed	High/low in paranormal belief	Direct/indirect Semantic priming	Less lateralised for indirect targets only	

Note: Schizotypy effect indicates whether schizotypy is associated with less lateralisation or more lateralisation, relative to controls

O-LIFE = Oxford-Liverpool Inventory of Feelings and Experiences; MI = Magical Ideation Scale; PA = Perceptual Aberration Scale; EPQ = Eysenck Personality Questionnaire; STA = Schizotypal Personality Scale; PAS = Physical Anhedonia Scale; SA = Social Anhedonia Scale; SPQ = Schizotypal Personality Questionnaire; PerMag = Perceptual-Aberration-Magical Ideation.

Table 4.2 Dichotic listening studies of hemispheric asymmetries in language

Study (year)	Subjects	Schizotypy assessment	Task	Schizotypy effect	Dimension
Castro & Pearson (2011)	N = 132 Healthy, right handed	SPQ	Linguistic Prosodic	No effects No effects	
Najt, Bayer, & Hausmann (2012)	N = 41 Right handed	Short version of O-Life	Linguistic Prosodic	No effects Less lateralised (males only)	Impulsive non-conformity
Overby (1992)	N = 47 Psychosis prone (N = 20); control (N = 27) Right Handed	PA; MI	Linguistic Tonal contour discrimination	More lateralised Less lateralised	Positive Positive
Poreh, Whitman, & Ross (1993)	N = 85 Right handed	PA, MI; STA (High vs. Low)	Liguistic	Less lateralised	
Rawlings & Borge (1987) Study 1	N = 42 Right handed	EPQ	Linguistic (shadowing)	Less lateralised	Whole STA scale
Rawlings & Borge (1987) Study 2	N = 30 Right handed	STQ;EPQ	Linguistic (shadowing)	Less lateralised* (males only)	Whole STA scale
Voglmaier et al.(2009)	N = 110 Right Handed	Schizotypal personality disorder (N = 42); controls (N = 68)	Linguistic	Less lateralised (males only)	
Weinstein & Graves (2002)	N = 60 Healthy	MI; PA; SA (Revised)	Linguistic	Less lateralised*	Positive

Note: Schizotypy effect indicates whether schizotypy is associated with less lateralisation or more lateralisation, relative to controls

O-LIFE = Oxford-Liverpool Inventory of Feelings and Experiences; MI = Magical Ideation Scale; PA = Perceptual Aberration Scale; EPQ = Eysenck Personality Questionnaire; STA = Schizotypal Personality Scale; PAS = Physical Anhedonia Scale; SA = Social Anhedonia Scale; SPQ = Schizotypal Personality Questionnaire; PerMag = Perceptual-Aberration-Magical Ideation. * = Marginal significance task, but only for the impulsive non-conformity dimension of the Oxford-Liverpool Inventory of Feelings and Experiences (O-LIFE; Mason, Claridge, & Jackson, 1995), and only in the subset of twenty males. Taken together, dichotic listening studies do not provide compelling evidence for altered language asymmetry in schizotypy. This is perhaps not too surprising. The linguistic tasks used in these studies rely heavily on phonological processing that is typically more strongly lateralised to the left hemisphere than lexical access from text (Hickok & Poeppel, 2007). A possible avenue for future research is to use dichotic tasks that have a greater semantic component, and therefore are more likely to tap both left- and right-hemisphere processes. Alternatively, tasks that require the integration of linguistic and prosodic information (e.g. Bulman-Fleming & Bryden, 1994; Grimshaw, 1998) might better assess interhemispheric processing that may be altered in schizotypy.

In sum, there is evidence that schizotypy is associated with reduced language asymmetry, although it is more robust for written text than speech. Of the cited studies, some have included only women or, more commonly, only men. Consistent with the XY Gene Hypothesis, studies that specifically address sex differences are more likely to report findings for men than women. Effects are also more likely to be observed with positive or disorganised than with negative schizotypy, although here results are somewhat mixed, and we note that several studies only assessed positive schizotypy. It is concerning that some reported effects are marginal, or possibly subject to experimenter degrees of freedom. Notably, two very recent studies that have used large samples and well-validated tasks have reported null effects (Castro & Pearson, 2011) or unpredicted effects (Schofield & Mohr, 2014).

Attention studies

The right hemisphere plays an important role in attention. In healthy individuals, this asymmetry can be observed in an attentional bias (or pseudoneglect; Jewell & McCourt, 2000) to the left side of space. These biases are most commonly assessed with chimeric faces or line bisection tasks. Assessing attentional biases in schizotypy allows us to test the global version of the right-hemisphere hypothesis (i.e. that schizotypy is associated with right-hemisphere activation).

Studies of hemi-spatial attention biases are summarised in Table 4.3, where we indicate whether schizotypy was associated with a leftward shift in bias relative to controls (indicating greater right-hemisphere activation) or a rightward shift. There is simply no evidence for a consistent relationship between schizotypy and attentional asymmetry – studies are equally likely to show leftward or rightward attentional shifts, and some show no effects at all. When effects are observed, they may appear in any schizotypal dimension. The lack of a consistent relationship between attentional asymmetry and schizotypy argues against global hemispheric activation accounts of schizotypy (e.g. right-hemisphere overactivation),

Table 4.3 Studies of hemispheric asymmetry in attention

Study (year)	Subjects	Schizotypy assessment	Task	Schizotypy effect	Dimension
Herzig, Tracy, Munafò, & Mohr (2010)	N = 40 (Male) Healthy, right handed	O-LIFE	Facial decision task	No effects	
Mason & Claridge (1999) Study 1	N = 53 Healthy, right-handed	O-LIFE; STA	Chimeric faces	Rightward (males only)	Positive
Mason & Claridge (1999) Study 2	N = 48 Right handed	O-LIFE; STA	Chimeric faces	Rightward (males only)	Positive
Luh & Gooding (1999)	N = 250 High scores MI or PA (N = 98); High scores on SA (N = 40); control (N = 112) Right handed	MI; PA; SA revised	Chimeric faces	Rightward for SA group; Leftward for PerMag group	Negative; positive
Schofield & Mohr (2014)	N = 159 Healthy Right handed	O-LIFE; MI; PAS	Chimeric faces	Inconsistent results. Rightward or leftward (depending on scale)	Negative Schizotypy
Schulter & Papousek (2008)	N = 136 Right handed	Belief in paranormal phenomena questionnaire	Chimeric faces	No effects	
Brugger & Graves (1997)	N = 40 Healthy, right handed	MI	Tactile bisection (rod centering)	Leftward (males only)	Positive
Gooding & Braun (2004)	High positive schizotypy (N = 24), high negative schizotypy (N = 26), control (N = 45) Healthy, right Handed	PA; MI; SA (revised); PAS (revised)	Rey-Osterrieth complex figure	No shift	

Study	Sample	Measure	Task	Bias	Schizotypy effect
Grimshaw, Bryson, Atchley, & Humphrey (2010)	N = 30 High in Positive Schizotypy; N = 30 low in positive schizotypy	SPQ	Manual line bisection	Leftward*	Positive
Liouta, Smith & Mohr (2008)	N = 40 (male) Healthy Right handed	O-LIFE	Manual line bisection	Rightward	Positive
Luh & Gooding (1999)	N = 250, Right handed High scores MI or PA (N = 98); High scores on SA (N = 40); control (N = 112)	MI; PA; SA revised	perceptual line bisection	Rightward	Negative
Mohr, Bracha, & Brugger (2003)	N = 36 Healthy, right handed	MI	Manual line bisection	Leftward	Positive
Ribolsi et al., (2013) S1	N = 205 Healthy	SPQ	Manual line bisection	Rightward	Positive
Ribolsi et al., (2013) S2	N = 80 Healthy	SPQ	Perceptual line bisection	Rightward	Positive
Schulter & Papousek (2008)	N = 136, Right handed	Belief in paranormal phenomena questionnaire	Manual line bisection	No effects	
Taylor, Zäch, & Brugger, (2002)	N = 40 (Male) Healthy, right handed	MI	Implicit line bisection	Leftward	Positive

Note: Schizotypy effect indicates whether schizotypy was associated with a leftward shift or rightward shift in attentional bias, relative to controls.

O-LIFE = Oxford-Liverpool Inventory of Feelings and Experiences; MI = Magical Ideation Scale; PA = Perceptual Aberration Scale; EPQ = Eysenck Personality Questionnaire; STA = Schizotypal Personality Scale; PAS = Physical Anhedonia Scale; SA = Social Anhedonia Scale; SPQ = Schizotypal Personality Questionnaire; PerMag = Perceptual-Aberration-Magical Ideation. * = Marginal significance and is consistent with hypotheses that link atypical asymmetries to specific domains such as language processing.

Conclusions and future directions

The hypotheses that predict altered hemispheric asymmetry in schizotypy have generated a tremendous amount of research. It now seems clear that there is a small but reliable relationship between schizotypy and mixed-hand preference. There has been a recent surge of interest in the genetics and ontogeny of handedness that may contribute to a similar understanding of the genetics and ontogeny of schizotypy and schizophrenia. As we learn more about the neuropsychological correlates of mixed handedness, we may also develop more specific and testable models of neuropsychological organisation in schizotypy.

To understand how altered asymmetry might affect cognition and behaviour in schizotypy, however, it is necessary to examine hemispheric asymmetries for specific processes. Although perceptual asymmetries offer one method for assessing some aspects of lateralisation, the empirical data to date do not offer much clarification. The most robust association observed is between positive (and possibly disorganised) schizotypy and reduced lateralisation for lexical and semantic processing. We suggest that perceptual asymmetry researchers would do well to use tasks that tap the cognitive processes (such as semantic or executive inhibitory processing) that are proposed to be altered in schizotypy.

Future developments may come from neuroimaging studies, which can be used to assess a broader range of processes than perceptual asymmetries. Imaging has been widely used in schizophrenia studies (Oertel-Knöchel & Linden, 2011) but less so in schizotypy. One factor limiting imaging research in schizotypy may be cost, because larger samples are typically necessary than in schizophrenia studies. A recent development in this regard is near-infrared optical imaging, which is a relatively low-cost way to assess asymmetries in blood flow associated with different tasks (e.g. Folley & Park, 2005).

Imaging can be used to study functional asymmetries, but also structural and functional connectivity, which may be particularly useful for studying interhemispheric processing mechanisms. The imaging literature suggests that schizophrenia is marked by a loss of interhemispheric connectivity (Ribolsi et al., 2009) whereas parallels between schizotypy and mixed handedness suggest that high schizotypy might be associated with better interhemispheric connectivity. Patterns of continuity (and discontinuity) between schizotypy and schizophrenia are important for differentiating them and for developing more specific models of their relationship. For now, the clearest conclusion is that there is *some* relationship between hemispheric asymmetry and schizotypy, and so further research on the specific nature of that relationship should lead to better specified models of schizotypal cognition.

References

Annett, M. (1998). Handedness and cerebral dominance: the right shift theory. *Journal of Neuropsychiatry and Clinical Neurosciences, 10*(4), 459–469.

Asai, T., & Tanno, Y. (2009). Schizotypy and handedness in Japanese participants, revisited. *Laterality: asymmetries of body, brain and cognition, 14*(1), 86–94.

Aziz-Zadeh, L., Liew, S. L., & Dandekar, F. (2013). Exploring the neural correlates of visual creativity. *Social Cognitive and Affective Neuroscience, 8*(4), 475–480.

Bishop, D. V. M. (2013). Cerebral asymmetry and language development: cause, correlate, or consequence? *Science, 340*(6138). doi: 10.1126/science.1230531

Boles, D. B., Barth, J. M., & Merrill, E. C. (2008). Asymmetry and performance: toward a neurodevelopmental theory. *Brain and Cognition, 66*(2), 124–139.

Brandler, W. M., & Paracchini, S. (2014). The genetic relationship between handedness and neurodevelopmental disorders. *Trends in Molecular Medicine, 20*(2), 83–90.

Broks, P. (1984). Schizotypy and hemisphere function – II: Performance asymmetry on a verbal divided visual-field task. *Personality and Individual Differences, 5*(6), 649–656.

Brugger, P., & Graves, R. E. (1997). Right hemispatial inattention and magical ideation. *European Archives of Psychiatry and Clinical Neuroscience, 247*(1), 55–57.

Bryden, M. P. (1982). *Laterality: Functional asymmetry in the intact brain.* New York: Academic Press.

Bryden, M. P., & Sprott, D. A. (1981). Statistical determination of degree of laterality. *Neuropsychologia, 19*(4), 571–583.

Bryson, F. M., Grimshaw, G. M., & Wilson, M. S. (2009). The role of intellectual openness in the relationship between hand preference and positive schizotypy. *Laterality, 14*(5), 441–456.

Bulman-Fleming, M. B., & Bryden, M. P. (1994). Simultaneous verbal and affective laterality effects. *Neuropsychologia, 32*(7), 787–797.

Castro, A., & Pearson, R. (2011). Lateralisation of language and emotion in schizotypal personality: evidence from dichotic listening. *Personality and Individual Differences, 51*(6), 726–731.

Chapman, H. L., Grimshaw, G. M., & Nicholls, M. E. R. (2011). Going beyond students: an association between mixed-hand preference and schizotypy subscales in a general population. *Psychiatry Research, 187*(1), 89–93.

Chun, C., Minor, K.S., & Cohen, A.S. (2013). Neurocognition in psychometrically defined college schizotypy samples: we are not measuring the 'right' stuff. *Journal of the International Neuropsychological Society, 19*, 1–14.

Claridge, G. (Ed.). (1997). *Schizotypy: Implications for illness and health.* Oxford University Press.

Corballis, M. C. (2014). Left brain, right brain: facts and fantasies. *PLoS Biology, 12*(1), e1001767.

Crow, T. J. (1990). Temporal lobe asymmetries as the key to the etiology of schizophrenia. *Schizophrenia Bulletin, 16*(3), 433–443.

Crow, T. J. (2013). The XY gene hypothesis of psychosis: origins and current status. *American Journal of Medical Genetics Part B: Neuropsychiatric Genetics, 162*(8), 800–824.

Ettinger, U., Meyhöfer, I., Steffens, M., Wagner, M., & Koutsouleris, N. (2014). Genetics, cognition, and neurobiology of schizotypal personality: a review of the overlap with schizophrenia. *Frontiers in Psychiatry, 5*, 18.

Folley, B. S., & Park, S. (2005). Verbal creativity and schizotypal personality in relation to prefrontal hemispheric laterality: a behavioral and near-infrared optical imaging study. *Schizophrenia Research, 80*(2–3), 271–282.

Friston, K. J. (1998). The disconnection hypothesis. *Schizophrenia Research, 30*(2), 115–125.

Gooding, D. C., & Braun, J. G. (2004). Visuoconstructive performance, implicit hemispatial inattention, and schizotypy. *Schizophrenia Research, 68*(2), 261–269.

Grimshaw, G. M. (1998). Integration and interference in the cerebral hemispheres: relations with hemispheric specialization. *Brain and Cognition, 36*(2), 108–127.

Grimshaw, G. M., Bryson, F. M., Atchley, R. A., & Humphrey, M. K. (2010). Semantic ambiguity resolution in positive schizotypy: a right hemisphere interpretation. *Neuropsychology, 24*(1), 130–138.

Gruzelier, J. H. (1999). Functional neuropsychophysiological asymmetry in schizophrenia: a review and reorientation. *Schizophrenia Bulletin, 25*(1), 91–120.

Guo, S., Kendrick, K. M., Zhang, J., Broome, M., Yu, R., Liu, Z., & Feng, J. (2013). Brain-wide functional inter-hemispheric disconnection is a potential biomarker for schizophrenia and distinguishes it from depression. *NeuroImage: Clinical, 2*, 818–826.

Herzig, D. A., Tracy, J., Munafò, M., & Mohr, C. (2010). The influence of tobacco consumption on the relationship between schizotypy and hemispheric asymmetry. *Journal of Behavior Therapy and Experimental Psychiatry, 41*(4), 397–408.

Hickok, G., & Poeppel, D. (2007). The cortical organization of speech processing. *Nature Reviews Neuroscience, 8*(5), 393–402.

Hirnstein, M., Hugdahl, K., & Hausmann, M. (2014). How brain asymmetry relates to performance: a large-scale dichotic listening study. *Frontiers in Psychology, 4*, 997.

Hirnstein, M., Westerhausen, R., Korsnes, M. S., & Hugdahl, K. (2013). Sex differences in language asymmetry are age-dependent and small: a large-scale, consonant-vowel dichotic listening study with behavioral and fMRI data. *Cortex, 49*(7), 1910–1921.

Homae, F. (2014). A brain of two halves: insights into interhemispheric organization provided by near-infrared spectroscopy. *NeuroImage, 85*(1), 354–362.

Jewell, G., & McCourt, M. E. (2000). Pseudoneglect: a review and meta-analysis of performance factors in line bisection tasks. *Neuropsychologia, 38*(1), 93–110.

Kravetz, S., Faust, M., & Edelman, A. (1998). Dimensions of schizotypy and lexical decision in the two hemispheres. *Personality and Individual Differences, 25*(5), 857–871.

Leonhard, D., & Brugger, P. (1998). Creative, paranormal, and delusional thought: a consequence of right hemisphere semantic activation? *Cognitive and Behavioral Neurology, 11*(4), 177–183.

Lindell, A. K. (2006). In your right mind: right hemisphere contributions to language processing and production. *Neuropsychology Review, 16*(3), 131–148.

Lindell, A K., (2011). Lateral thinkers are not so laterally minded: hemispheric asymmetry, interaction, and creativity. *Laterality, 16*(4), 479–498.

Lindell, A. K. (2014). On the interrelation between reduced lateralization, schizotypy, and creativity. *Frontiers in Psychology, 5*, 813.

Liouta, E., Smith, A. D., & Mohr, C. (2008). Schizotypy and pseudoneglect: a critical update on theories of hemispheric asymmetries. *Cognitive Neuropsychiatry, 13*(2), 112–134.

Luders, E., Cherbuin, N., Thompson, P. M., Gutman, B., Anstey, K. J., Sachdev, P., & Toga, A. W. (2010). When more is less: associations between corpus callosum size and handedness lateralization. *Neuroimage, 52*(1), 43–49.

Luh, K. E., & Gooding, D. C. (1999). Perceptual biases in psychosis-prone individuals. *Journal of Abnormal Psychology, 108*(2), 283–289.

Mason, O., & Claridge, G. (1999). Individual differences in schizotypy and reduced asymmetry using the chimeric faces task. *Cognitive Neuropsychiatry, 4*(4), 289–301.

Mason, O., Claridge, G., & Jackson, M. (1995). New scales for the assessment of schizotypy. *Personality and Individual Differences, 18*, 1, 7–13.

McManus, I. C., Davison, A., & Armour, J. A. L. (2013). Multilocus genetic models of handedness closely resemble single-locus models in explaining family data and are compatible with genome-wide association studies. *Annals of the New York Academy of Sciences, 1288*(1), 48–58.

Mohr, C., Bracha, H. S., & Brugger, P. (2003). Magical ideation modulates spatial behavior. *Journal of Neuropsychiatry and Clinical Neurosciences, 15*(2), 168–174.

Mohr, C., Krummenacher, P., Landis, T., Sandor, P. S., Fathi, M., & Brugger, P. (2005). Psychometric schizotypy modulates levodopa effects on lateralized lexical decision performance. *Journal of Psychiatric Research, 39*(3), 241–250.

Najt, P., Bayer, U., & Hausmann, M. (2012). Atypical lateralisation in emotional prosody in men with schizotypy. *Laterality: Asymmetries of Body, Brain and Cognition, 17*(5), 533–548.

Nielsen, J. A., Zielinski, B. A., Ferguson, M. A., Lainhart, J. E., & Anderson, J. S. (2013). An evaluation of the left-brain vs. right-brain hypothesis with resting state functional connectivity magnetic resonance imaging. *PloS one, 8*(8), e71275.

Ocklenburg, S., Beste, C., & Güntürkün, O. (2013). Handedness: a neurogenetic shift of perspective. *Neuroscience and Biobehavioral Reviews, 37*(10), 2788–2793.

Ocklenburg, S., Beste, C., Arning, L., Peterburs, J., & Güntürkün, O. (2014). The ontogenesis of language lateralization and its relation to handedness. *Neuroscience and Biobehavioral Reviews, 43*, 191–198.

Oertel-Knöchel, V., & Linden, D. E. J. (2011). Cerebral asymmetry in schizophrenia. *The Neuroscientist, 17*(5), 456–467.

Overby, L. A. (1992). Perceptual asymmetry in psychosis-prone college students: evidence for left-hemisphere overactivation. *Journal of Abnormal Psychology, 101*(1), 96–103.

Pizzagalli, D., Lehmann, D., & Brugger, P. (2001). Lateralized direct and indirect semantic priming effects in subjects with paranormal experiences and beliefs. *Psychopathology, 34*(2), 75–80.

Poreh, A. M., Whitman, D. R., & Ross, T. P. (1993). Creative thinking abilities and hemispheric asymmetry in schizotypal college students. *Current Psychology, 12*(4), 344–352.

Prichard, E., Propper, R. E., & Christman, S. D. (2013). Degree of handedness, but not direction, is a systematic predictor of cognitive performance. *Frontiers in Psychology, 4*, 9.

Rawlings, D., & Borge, A. (1987). Personality and hemisphere function: Two experiments using the dichotic shadowing technique. *Personality and Individual Differences, 8*(4), 483–488.

Rawlings, D., & Claridge, G. (1984). Schizotypy and hemisphere function – III: Performance asymmetries on tasks of letter recognition and local-global processing. *Personality and Individual Differences, 5*(6), 657–663.

Ribolsi, M., Lisi, G., di Lorenzo, G., Rociola, G., Niolu, C., & Siracusano, A. (2013). Negative correlation between leftward bias in line bisection and schizotypal features in healthy subjects. *Frontiers in Psychology, 4*, 86.

Ribolsi, M., Koch, G., Magni, V., di Lorenzo, G., Rubino, I. A., Siracusano, A., & Centonze, D. (2009). Abnormal brain lateralization and connectivity in schizophrenia. *Reviews in the Neurosciences, 20*(1), 61–70.

Richardson, A. J., Mason, O., & Claridge, G. (1997). Schizotypy and cerebral lateralization. In G. Claridge (Ed.), *Schizotypy: Implications for illness and health* (pp. 145–168). New York, Oxford University Press.

Rogers, L. J., Vallortigara, G., & Andrew, R. J. (2013). *Divided brains: The biology and behaviour of brain asymmetries*. Cambridge University Press.

Schofield, K., & Mohr, C. (2014). Schizotypy and hemispheric asymmetry: results from two Chapman scales, the O-LIFE questionnaire, and two laterality measures. *Laterality: Asymmetries of Body, Brain and Cognition, 19*(2), 1–23.

Schulter, G., & Papousek, I. (2008). Believing in paranormal phenomena: relations to asymmetry of body and brain. *Cortex, 44*(10), 1326–1335.

Shobe, E. R., Ross, N. M., & Fleck, J. I. (2009). Influence of handedness and bilateral eye movements on creativity. *Brain and Cognition, 71*(3), 204–214.

Somers, M., Sommer, I. E., Boks, M. P., & Kahn, R. S. (2009). Hand-preference and population schizotypy: a meta-analysis. *Schizophrenia Research, 108*(1), 25–32.

Sommer, I. E., Aleman, A., Somers, M., Boks, M. P., & Kahn, R. S. (2008). Sex differences in handedness, asymmetry of the planum temporale and functional language lateralization. *Brain Research, 1206*, 76–88.

Sommer, I., Ramsey, N., Kahn, R., Aleman, A., & Bouma, A. (2001). Handedness, language lateralisation and anatomical asymmetry in schizophrenia: meta-analysis. *British Journal of Psychiatry, 178*(4), 344–351.

Suzuki, A., & Usher, M. (2009). Individual differences in language lateralisation, schizotypy and the remote-associate task. *Personality and Individual Differences, 46*(5), 622–626.

Szaflarski, J. P., Binder, J. R., Possing, E. T., McKiernan, K. A., Ward, B. D., & Hammeke, T. A. (2002). Language lateralization in left-handed and ambidextrous people: fMRI data. *Neurology, 59*(2), 238–244.

Taylor, K. I., Zäch, P., & Brugger, P. (2002). Why is magical ideation related to leftward deviation on an implicit line bisection task? *Cortex, 38*(2), 247–252.

van der Knaap, L. J., & van der Ham, I. J. (2011). How does the corpus callosum mediate interhemispheric transfer? A review. *Behavioural Brain Research, 223*(1), 211–221.

Voglmaier, M. M., Seidman, L. J., Niznikiewicz, M. A., Madan, A., Dickey, C. C., Shenton, M. E., & McCarley, R. W. (2009). Dichotic listening in schizotypal personality disorder: evidence for gender and laterality effects. *Schizophrenia Research, 115*(2), 290–292.

Voyer, D. (2011). Sex differences in dichotic listening. *Brain and cognition, 76*(2), 245–255.

Weinstein, S., & Graves, R. E. (2001). Creativity, schizotypy, and laterality. *Cognitive Neuropsychiatry, 6*(2), 131–146.

Weinstein, S., & Graves, R. E. (2002). Are creativity and schizotypy products of a right hemisphere bias? *Brain and Cognition, 49*(1), 138–151.

Westerhausen, R., & Hugdahl, K. (2008). The corpus callosum in dichotic listening studies of hemispheric asymmetry: a review of clinical and experimental evidence. *Neuroscience and Biobehavioral Reviews, 32*(5), 1044–1054.

Part II
Development and environment

5 Schizotypy
A developmental perspective

Martin Debbané

Introduction

Psychotic disorders typically emerge out of life stories that have not revealed any sure signs of their arrival. Understandably, one of the most frustrating aspects about psychotic disorders, be it for affected individuals, treating clinicians or devoted scientists, is that pathological onset remains largely unpredictable. In the past 20 years, a number of longitudinal studies have provided some hope in this matter, by identifying the pre-clinical, at-risk mental states for the onset of psychosis (McGlashan, 2001; Yung et al., 1998). The tools offered by this preventive approach have benefited early identification strategies and, in many countries, reduced the duration of untreated psychosis (Perkins, Gu, Boteva, & Lieberman, 2005). From a scientific standpoint, investigations into the pre-clinical stages of psychosis have positioned the developmental perspective on the priority list of the scientific agenda in the field of schizophrenia research (Fusar-Poli et al., 2013). In a pioneering fashion, these studies have not only extended to opportunities for early identification and intervention, but they are progressively revolutionising the way we apprehend psychotic disorders by emphasising some of the early signs and developmental mechanisms that increase the *risk* for conversion to an illness state.

While there is reason for hope and enthusiasm, the developmental riddle of psychotic onset still remains quite enigmatic. State-of-the art clinical evaluation protocols, whether assessing the putative psychosis prodromes (McGlashan, Walsh, & Woods, 2010) or basic symptoms of schizophrenia (Schultze-Lutter et al., 2012) will succeed in predicting onset in approximately three cases out of ten who present significant clinical risk, and this over a 2-year period (B. Nelson et al., 2013). These numbers are encouraging, yet prediction still appears to merit further innovative efforts (Schultze-Lutter, Klosterkotter, & Ruhrmann, 2014). Importantly, most high-risk cases will not 'fit' the conversion criteria, but these non-fitting individuals continue to live with psychotic-like phenomena, and can also develop other psychiatric disorders outside the spectrum of psychoses (Kelleher et al., 2013). Schizotypy is traditionally defined as a multidimensional personality trait that confers the *liability* to develop psychotic-spectrum disorders (Claridge, 1997; Lenzenweger, 2010). We note, however, that while the term 'liability' certainly hints towards key developmental processes and trajectories, the personality-based account of schizotypy has to date provided only sparse contributions to the pre-clinical, high-risk movement within schizophrenia research (Raine, 2006).

In this chapter, we will argue that the schizotypy construct can play a critical role in furthering a developmental understanding of psychotic disorders. In the first section, we will proceed to situate the schizotypy construct in the current conception of developing psychotic disorders. This will lead us to formalise a basic developmental model of schizotypy. In the second section, we will provide a rationale for schizotypy research in children and adolescents, articulated around three main arguments. First, that early schizotypy expression currently represents the best distal risk marker for identifying liability to develop psychotic disorders. Second, that early schizotypy may act as a developmental mediator between endogenous childhood risk factors and adult psychotic symptom expression. Third, that an examination of the developmental interactions during the development of trait schizotypy might reveal some of the key mechanisms of symptom exacerbation or remission.

Situating schizotypy: a developmental framework

Most schizotypy researchers would agree that, *at minimum*, the multidimensional structure of the trait includes a triad of dimensions, encompassing a cognitive–perceptual dimension pertaining to such phenomena as magical ideation and perceptual aberrations (positive schizotypy), an interpersonal–affective dimension relating to phenomena such as anhedonia and social isolation (negative schizotypy), and a disorganisation dimension capturing phenomena such as thought problems and odd behaviours (disorganisation schizotypy) (Raine, 2006). It is interesting to note that high-risk studies – whether from an epidemiological standpoint (Poulton et al., 2000), or psychiatric 'prodromal' and 'basic symptoms' perspectives – have proceeded in a kind of de-construction of schizotypy: teasing out and focusing on specific sets of schizotypal experiences (for example, psychotic-like experiences [PLEs] represent positive schizotypy experiences) that hold predictive value for conversion to a psychotic disorder when meeting frequency, severity and (for basic symptoms) subjective rating criteria. However, none of these high-risk accounts provides an integrated view of all the specific schizotypal experiences that carry predictive power. With an impressive amount of data collected by the different high-risk research strategies, it appears somewhat arduous to situate schizotypy and how it would relate developmentally to other accounts of psychosis liability. In order to start situating schizotypy within contemporary perspectives, we suggest a scheme (shown in Figure 5.1) that gathers together the core elements of any developmental model attempting to describe the emergence and development of psychotic disorders.

Theories of psychosis commonly situate the pre-morbid period during childhood and adolescence ('1' in Figure 5.1). Every theory differs according to the elements it puts forward as the putative *necessary but not sufficient* aetiological factors underlying a 'pathological process' at work during early development. Yet all theories posit a kind of seed, a 'schizo seed', which ultimately confers the risk to develop a clinical form of psychosis. Initially operationalising the construct of schizotypy, Paul Meehl formulated a single gene account of schizotypy, where a putative 'schizogene' would be represented as the single aetiological factor leading to 'hypocrisia', a global neural integrative defect underlying basic 'schizotaxia', expressed as subtle deficits encompassing cognitive slippage, anhedonia, interpersonal aversiveness and ambivalence (Meehl, 1962, 1990). This theory inspired the contemporary polygenetic endophenotypical approach to schizotypy (Lenzenweger, 2010) and schizophrenia (Gottesman & Gould, 2003). Before Meehl, psychoanalytical theories had tended to emphasise personality structures and dynamics as the principal scaffolding agents of psychotic psychopathology. Using different methodologies, psychologists including Eysenck and his followers developed the psychology of personality for which one objective was to identify a personality dimension that could be linked to psychotic manifestations. The notion of psychoticism (Eysenck & Eysenck, 1976), and then psychometrically defined schizotypy (Claridge & Beech, 1995), entered the field by emphasising the continuum of schizotypal expression between normal and psychopathological states. Therefore all theories, whether postulating a genetic, neurodevelopmental or personality base to risk for psychosis, effectively postulate

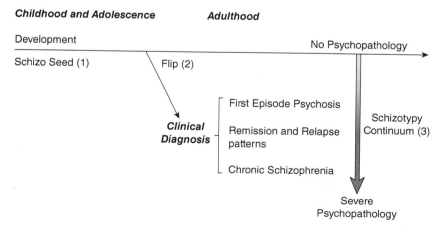

Figure 5.1 Diagram illustrating the developmental core of models accounting for the emergence of psychotic disorders.

an etiological 'schizo seed' that could potentially develop into significant clinical states of psychosis.

The main point of debate between the more medical–biological approach (also called the 'quasi-dimensional approach') and the personality-based, fully dimensional accounts of schizotypy chiefly concerns the transition to a clinical state, or, more precisely, who can be said to be *truly* at risk of 'crossing the line' into psychotic psychopathology (see Mason [2014] for further coverage of this point). During development, a clinically significant modification in psychotic-like or schizotypal manifestations can emerge. This evolution is most often described as an emerging qualitative shift or 'flip' into the individual's first veritable clinical psychotic state ('2' in Figure 5.1). This kind of description is reserved for evolutions that end up meeting the diagnostic criteria of the prevailing diagnostic systems. In essence, quasi-dimensional views argue that such a flip can only occur in a specific subgroup of the population, those 'schizotypes' representing the only individuals at significant risk for developing psychotic disorders. The fully dimensional perspective, on the other hand, would take a more liberal stance on the matter, not restricting the vulnerability of converting strictly to a specific subgroup of the population and thereby widening the population base at significant risk for developing psychotic disorders. The divide between these views sharpens with the specific case of schizophrenia, for which the quasi-dimensionalists firmly defend the existence of a taxon in the general population, limiting the risk base to a maximum of 10 per cent of individuals in the population (Lenzenweger, 2010).

We propose a developmental perspective that could hold the creative tension emanating from the quasi- and fully dimensional debate on schizotypy. Scientific debates are essential to progress, most significantly because both sides seek new evidence and better methodologies to support their claims, which usually makes them transcend their initial positions. Interestingly, development has concretely invited itself to this debate, through the study of Fossati, Raine, Borroni, and Maffei (2007). In this study, the authors employ the Schizotypal Personality Questionnaire (SPQ; Raine, 1991) to investigate the taxonic structure of self-reported schizotypy in a sample of 803 university students (mean age 21.9 years), and compare its structure with that issued from a sample of 929 high school students (mean age 16.4 years). While the authors find evidence for a taxonic structure in the adult group, it is less clear that such a structure can be applied to the data emanating from the adolescent sample (Fossati et al., 2007). This calls into question whether the schizotypy taxon can be observed during adolescent development. Further, it poses somewhat of a conceptual challenge to account for those adolescents at high clinical risk who develop psychotic disorders during the transition between adolescence and adulthood. It is possible that a taxon cannot be adequately observed until the developmental processes of personality traits stabilise, but additional research is needed to reproduce these results.

Amid this debate, we can identify a point of agreement with regards to the 'post-flip' developmental trajectories, where both the quasi- and fully dimensional views posit a continuum of severity in the *clinical* expression of psychosis ('3' in Figure 5.1). As such, the developmental trajectories following first-episode psychosis (FEP) can also be taken as illustrations of the clinical continuum. Here, for heuristic purposes, our developmental model synthesises the trajectories into three possible developmental pathways. A first psychotic episode may constitute an isolated incident in the developmental trajectory of an individual. Indeed, current studies estimate that approximately 20 per cent of first psychotic episodes will go on to represent an isolated life event (Alvarez-Jimenez et al., 2011). Second, a first episode may signal a more or less prolonged period where individuals will go through patterns of remissions and relapses as they try to stabilise their mental health. In a recent meta-analysis of 29 longitudinal studies of FEP covering a minimal interval of 12 months after initial diagnosis, Alvarez-Jimenez et al. (2012) report a relapse rate between 12 and 63 per cent within a 3-year interval after initial diagnosis. The variability of relapse can be accounted for by such moderating factors as medication non-adherence, persistent substance use, criticism on the part of the care provider, as well as poorer premorbid adjustment (Alvarez-Jimenez et al., 2012). A subsequent study on clinical outcome in 153 first-episode patients 13 years after initial diagnosis finds that duration of untreated psychosis significantly reduces the odds of symptomatic remission, as was observed in 47 per cent of that sample of FEP patients (Tang et al., 2014). Finally, a first episode may represent the entry point into a chronic disease; given the variety in treatment services and a number of other factors encompassing but not restricted to those reviewed earlier, it is still unclear how many individuals would evolve from a FEP to chronic schizophrenia. A recent systematic review suggests that, at least for first-episode schizophrenia, around 35 per cent follow a chronic path of illness (AlAqeel & Margolese, 2012).

The developmental core of models accounting for psychosis thus share three characteristics: (1) a *schizo seed* that would represent a causal *necessary but not sufficient* element during development; (2) a developmental point (*flip*) representing the first time an individual's state actually meets diagnostic criteria; and (3) a *continuum of severity* in the clinical expression of the disorder. If one includes the non-clinical states, this continuum is best represented as a *schizotypy continuum*. We now propose to situate the construct of schizotypy among contemporary theories, and to provide a rationale for a developmental account of trait schizotypy.

What is the utility of a developmental framework of schizotypy?

The neurodevelopmental hypothesis of schizophrenia is currently the dominant developmental approach to understanding the emergence of psychotic disorders. While this theory has inspired a great number of studies and provided interesting insights into the cerebral maturational processes that precede and sometimes predict the onset of psychosis (Fusar-Poli et al., 2011), it has to this stage fallen short of bringing substantial change to the fate of at-risk individuals. For patients and treating clinicians, very little clinical yield can be achieved in conceptualising schizophrenia as a brain disorder. Neural markers identified by neuroimaging studies cannot be applied to individual patients and, to date, their predictive value, either in terms of conversion or response to treatment, has not been compared with any structured clinical prediction. The endophenotype approach has suffered from similar shortcomings, and is slowly evolving towards a dimensional systems approach that can gain insight from translational neuroscience (Insel, 2014). It is certainly premature to evaluate the failings of these nascent fields of neuroscientific investigations, especially because the increasing knowledge base they provide will most probably be critical to further understanding the pathological mechanisms at work in psychotic disorders. Concurrently, however, there may be space for a developmental account that helps clinicians and patients understand the progression of risk towards psychosis other than through enigmatic expressions such as 'aberrant brain development', 'cerebral dysconnectivity' or 'accelerated pruning', to which patients either adhere in blind faith, or respond by becoming increasingly distressed about the malfunctions of their brain. Today, leaders in the field of early identification and intervention, indeed those same individuals who pioneered the field of early risk for psychosis research, are now turning to a staging approach in their conceptualisation of developing risk for psychosis (Fusar-Poli, Yung, McGorry, & van Os, 2014). This approach helps discern possible developmental dynamics at every 'stage' of risk, and the potential health choices patients and families could make at each different step. Both scientifically and clinically, it has become necessary to directly address the different developmental stages within the risk period.

My view is that a developmental model of schizotypy holds the necessary ingredients to bring a developmental psychopathology account to psychotic disorders, for three basic reasons. The first is that schizotypy currently represents the best distal risk marker for studying psychosis proneness from childhood to adulthood. Second, schizotypal expression during adolescence is critically linked to childhood risk markers and endophenotypes, which confers a role of a potential *developmental mediator* on the road to psychosis proneness. Finally, by including the ensemble of factors that make up schizotypy (positive, negative, disorganisation dimensions), longitudinal designs can pick up developmental interactions that would more clearly delineate the mechanisms involved in the early stages of symptom appearance, and also focus on mechanisms sustaining spontaneous defusing of clinical risk. We shall elaborate on these three basic points in order to more fully explicate the developmental account of trait schizotypy.

Schizotypy as a distal risk marker

As argued earlier, in the integration of basic research, clinical research and mental health strategies, a developmental account based of trait schizotypy may play an important role in determining both research and clinical targets at every step of development. The construct of schizotypy is the only one that combines PLEs (positive schizotypy), cognitive disorganisation and anhedonia (negative schizotypy), which have all individually been shown to constitute early distal markers of risk to develop psychotic disorders (Debbané et al., in press). Epidemiological studies initially triggered the interest in the longitudinal fate of very early schizotypal signs by demonstrating the (low but significant) predictive value of PLEs in childhood (Fisher et al., 2013). Admittedly, the predictive power of PLEs pales in comparison to more proximal indicators such as at-risk mental states or basic symptoms (Schultze-Lutter et al., 2014). However, the predictive value of these state markers reduces sharply 36 months after their evaluation. Positive schizotypy, on the other hand, carries predictive value over the decades of adolescence and the beginning of adulthood (Poulton et al., 2000). PLEs, for example, can be reliably investigated in children down to 8 years of age, and lend themselves to the examination of developmental dynamics whereby protective factors may come into play and decrease their impact early in development.

The second dimension of schizotypy, the anhedonic-negative phenomena, has also been associated with increased risk for the development of psychotic disorders (Chapman, Chapman, Kwapil, Eckblad, & Zinser, 1994). Over a 10-year period, 24 per cent of individuals scoring high on the Revised Social Anhedonia Scale developed a schizophrenia-spectrum disorder (Kwapil, Chapman, & Chapman, 1999). In a re-analysis of this same sample, negative schizotypy was found to specifically predict schizoid symptoms and social impairment (Kwapil, Gross, Silvia, & Barrantes-Vidal, 2013). Finally, the predictive value of disorganisation schizotypy is currently suggested through somewhat indirect evidence (Debbané et al., in press). For example, a recent epidemiological study measured an index of disorganisation schizotypy combined with negative schizotypy score to provide a disorganisation/negative symptom cluster (Dominguez, Saka, Lieb, Wittchen, & van Os, 2010). In the presence of a positive schizotypy symptom cluster, the disorganisation/negative cluster was shown to significantly augment the need for clinical care during the 5-year study interval.

In the last section of the chapter, we will survey some of the evidence supporting the predictive value of disorganisation schizotypy, while, perhaps more importantly, suggesting potent developmental interactions on the pathway towards need for clinical care. It thus appears that a developmental approach to schizotypy would be relevant to the study of distal risk factors for the emergence of psychotic disorders. Moreover, as suggested in the next section, simultaneously investigating the three dimensions may yield unique sensitivity to important developmental dynamics.

Early schizotypy as a developmental mediator

Poor specificity still stands strong as one of the main challenges to the identification of early risk markers exclusively predicting the emergence of psychotic disorders. A number of studies have already shown that prenatal stress, birth complications, infections and toxic agents are related to the later development of psychotic-spectrum disorders (Dean & Murray, 2005), yet these same factors are also related to increased prevalence of other types of psychopathology during adulthood. From a developmental psychopathology standpoint, this is not surprising. In fact, it represents one of the founding principles of developmental psychopathology – that of *multifinality* (Cicchetti & Rogosch, 2002). A risk factor such as trauma provides a simple illustration of how a factor contributing to the emergence of one psychiatric disorder may also contribute to the unfolding of other disorders. Indeed, trauma has not only been associated with increased risk for the development of schizophrenia (Read, van Os, Morrison, & Ross, 2005), but almost all other psychopathology. This is undoubtedly due to the deleterious effects of early and enduring trauma on the developing hypothalamo-pituary-adrenal (HPA) axis, a key axis in the regulation of developmental stressors, involved in neurobiological accounts of these psychiatric disorders (Gillespie, Phifer, Bradley, & Ressler, 2009). Conversely, a developmental psychopathological account of psychotic disorders must not only acknowledge the multifinal nature of potent risk factors: it must also be equipped to account for the multiple risk factors that yield a number of different possible developmental trajectories towards the equifinal outcome of psychotic-spectrum disorders. Equifinality is a key concept to better embrace the complexity of psychopathological development.

By embracing multifinality and equifinality rather than focusing on 'home-run' markers that decisively predict psychopathology, developmental psychopathology gains sensitivity to distal dynamic interactions that take place during development and effectively play a significant role in the transition to adult clinical states. This leads to structuring longitudinal research designs in such a way as to pick up the intermediate developmental vehicles along the trajectories that evolve into a significant psychiatric disorder. Contemporary research in the developmental psychopathology of borderline personality disorder (BPD) provides abundant examples of such an approach (Sharp & Tackett, 2014). Theories on the development of BPD hypothesise that developmental antecedents such as *early childhood endogenous factors* (maternal medical history, infant motor development, muscle tone, infant activity, emotionality), *early childhood environmental factors* (maltreatment, attachment disorganisation, maternal hostility, maternal boundary dissolution, family disruption, life stress), and *middle childhood to early adolescence factors* (attentional disturbance, emotional instability, behavioural instability, relational disturbance, self-representation disturbance, family disruption, life stress, parent–child relationship disturbance) represent non-specific risk factors, some of which can further mark the development of pathological processes on the way towards adult BPD (Carlson, Egeland, & Sroufe, 2009). In a prototypical longitudinal study of this kind, Carlson et al. (2009) prospectively investigated these developmental antecedents on a sample of 162 first-born children of mothers at high parenting risk because of poverty. In the first step of their analyses, the authors identified those antecedents that best accounted for adult borderline symptoms. They identified early childhood maternal hostility and maternal life stress, as well as middle childhood/adolescent self-representations as significantly related to adult borderline personality symptoms at age 28 years. Thereafter, in an attempt to further investigate the distal dynamic interactions between childhood and adolescence, the authors ran a process analysis specifically testing whether self-representations played the role of a developmental *mediator* between childhood antecedents and adult symptom expression. This led the authors to observe that middle childhood/adolescent self-representations significantly mediated the developmental pathway between childhood attachment disorganisation and adult BPD symptoms. In this way, developmental psychopathology studies illustrate how prospective designs may shed light on developmental mediators (here self-representations) that are construed during development through successive transactions between the individual's endogenous vulnerabilities and environmental risk factors working towards psychopathological outcomes.

At this stage, we would hypothesise that middle childhood/adolescent schizotypy (early schizotypy) could possibly represent such a developmental mediator between early childhood endogenous and exogenous risk factors and future emergence of psychotic disorders. To date, the support for this developmental account comes from two different sources of evidence. First, as described earlier in this chapter, early schizotypal signs of positive, negative or disorganised schizotypy carry the necessary characteristics of a mediator, by virtue of the fact that they significantly correlate with adult symptomatic expression.

The second source of evidence comes from studies relating early schizotypy to early endophenotypes associated with schizophrenia. Indeed, recent research has shown how endophenotypes typically linked to schizophrenia also correlate with schizotypy in sub-clinical samples (for a recent review, see Ettinger, Meyhofer, Steffens, Wagner, & Koutsouleris, 2014). Moreover, early schizotypy has been associated with endophenotypes that can be assessed in infancy or childhood (minor physical anomalies) or that typically mature during childhood neurocognitive development. Barrantes-Vidal et al. (2003) reported on a number of neurocognitive and neurodevelopmental correlates of adolescent schizotypy in a sample of 270 adolescents recruited from the regular school system. The authors found that elevated scores on the Chapman schizotypy scales correlated with a variety of recognised endophenotypes for schizophrenia, most notably dermatoglyphic abnormalities and executive functions (Barrantes-Vidal et al., 2003). Similarly, Hans et al. (2009) found that schizotypal symptoms in adolescents at familial risk for developing schizophrenia were related to minor physical anomalies, fine motor dyscoordination and executive function impairments (Hans et al., 2009). Early schizotypy ratings are also related to visual backward masking (whereby stimulus recognition is reduced by a subsequent masking stimulus), for which adult-like performance is generally acquired by the beginning of adolescence (Macchi et al., 2003). Deterioration in visual backward masking was found to be associated with schizotypy in a sample of late adolescence/early adulthood students (Cappe, Herzog, Herzig, Brand, & Mohr, 2012). Recent scientific reviews have emphasised the overlap in endophenotypical presentation between schizophrenic samples and general population samples recruited on the basis of schizotypal expression (Nelson, Seal, Pantelis, & Phillips, 2013), but developmental evidence suggests that some of these associations might antedate adulthood. It thus appears difficult to deny that the overlap between schizophrenia endophenotypes and psychometrically defined schizotypy can reliably be observed at different levels of analysis (cognition, brain tissue and function, molecular biology), and at varying stages of human development.

Another important reason why early schizotypy might represent a valid developmental mediator is through its association with functional endophenotypes of schizophrenia that typically mature during adolescence, as in the case of mentalising functions such as Theory of Mind. It is now established that mentalising functions continue to mature during adolescence (Dumontheil, Apperly, & Blakemore, 2010) and come to maturation during early adulthood, probably because social cognitive skills rely upon full maturity of long-range cerebral connectivity, which is thought to reach adult-like levels in the early 20s (Supekar et al., 2010). Two functional neuroimaging studies have found that adolescent schizotypal expression is related to atypical brain activation patterns in reality-monitoring and self-appraisal tasks). Another functional magnetic resonance imaging (fMRI) study on perspective taking has found that in both typical adolescents reporting transient auditory verbal hallucinations and adolescents at high genetic risk for schizophrenia, comparable patterns of atypical neural activation could already be observed during first to third person perspective taking (Dahoun et al., 2013). These studies suggest that self-reported schizotypy during adolescence cannot be reduced to mere response biases, but significantly relates to validated endophenotypes associated with increased risk to develop schizophrenia. In our opinion, this emerging body of data on schizotypy begins to address the complex developmental picture relating childhood endogenous risk factors, developmental interactions that give rise to varying degrees of adolescent schizotypal expression, and vulnerability towards the emergence of adult psychotic disorders.

To summarise, the developmental consolidation of schizotypy may confer a 'developmental vehicle' towards psychopathology (Debbané & Barrantes-Vidal, in press). In such a developmental account, a number of endophenotypes would consistently influence the emerging organisation of personality, and each partly consolidating schizotypy. Then, towards middle childhood and through adolescence, significant metacognitive, interpersonal and social experiences may be preferred and consistently selected by the individual as a result of schizotypy (selective appraisals of perceptual aberrations, overt eccentricity in speech and behaviour, decreasing social contact, etc.), thereby initiating developmental transactional influences that may augment the risk for psychopathology. As such, schizotypy may be conceived as a developmental vehicle between early endophenotypes and biomarkers, to selective transactional processes, towards adult risk for psychopathology.

Critical interactions in the developmental course of schizotypy

Recent conceptual developments attempting to account for symptoms of psychosis typically involve the interaction between symptom dimensions. For example, Freeman et al. (2002) describe the interaction between anomalous perceptions and delusional beliefs. From a developmental perspective, their model would suggest that appraisal mechanisms following anomalous perceptions may lead to the genesis of delusional content. Clinically, interactions between the schizotypal dimensions appear inevitable during development (Debbané, Badoud, Balanzin, & Eliez, 2013). For example, it is not rare to see that mild cognitive disorganisation in the form of bizarre or eccentric behaviour and odd speech might put an adolescent at odds with the social practices of their peer group, leading to peer-initiated rejection and/or self-initiated social isolation. In turn, the adolescent can increasingly withdraw from activities with peers, and stay at home for extended periods. Developmental patterns such as these would suggest that interactions between schizotypal dimensions do occur, and that PLEs in youths should be assessed within this developmental context. The question is whether these interactions carry any significance with regard to maintenance or exacerbation of schizotypal manifestations.

Recent longitudinal studies with general population samples as well as help-seeking samples provide evidence suggesting that significant interactions between schizotypal manifestations can take place during development. In a group of 34 non-psychotic help-seeking adolescents, schizotypy dimensions as measured by the SPQ were found to predict each other over a 3-year period. More specifically, baseline negative schizotypy was found to significantly predict positive schizotypy 3 years later, through its mediating relationship with baseline disorganisation (Debbané et al., 2013). In other words, withdrawal and blunted emotion during adolescence, when associated with disorganised speech and behaviour, can significantly predict the maintenance or exacerbation of cognitive–perceptual anomalous perceptions. Importantly, these results were corrected for any influences from internalising and externalising problems in these help-seeking adolescents. Another study investigating a large epidemiological sample of youths, Dominguez et al. (2010) provided a 10-year longitudinal analysis of psychotic-like positive, negative and disorganisation experiences for 3,021 youths aged 14–24 years at baseline. Psychotic-like symptom clusters were evaluated using the Composite International Diagnostic System (CIDI). On the basis of the interview, ratings for a positive symptom cluster and a negative/disorganised symptom cluster were computed, and associated with help-seeking behaviour in relation to symptoms. The authors observed that, during the study interval, between 37 and 39 per cent of those with a significant positive symptom cluster called upon professional help. Help seeking significantly augmented by 16.2 per cent for those individuals with both the positive and negative/disorganised symptom clusters.

It remains unclear, however, whether interactions during development may also significantly influence the emergence of categorically defined psychotic disorders. To the best of our knowledge, there exists only one study testing this hypothesis (Kwapil et al., 2013). In this study, the only interaction tested is between positive and negative schizotypy, in a sample of 503 19-year-old college students followed over a 10-year period. The authors report significant developmental interactions between the positive and negative schizotypy dimension in determining long-term paranoid personality features. A similar – but non-significant – interaction was also found for the development of any psychotic disorders. We note that the disorganisation dimension was not evaluated here, and appears to be critical in other studies examining significant longitudinal change and help-seeking behaviour in relation to schizotypy (Debbané et al., 2013; Dominguez et al., 2010). Future longitudinal studies, encompassing all three dimensions of schizotypy, are needed to investigate the clinical relevance of such interactions. To date, however, the data available do suggest that *mechanisms of change* in schizotypal expression might involve maladaptive dimensional interactions between negative, disorganisation and positive schizotypy. These interactions must be critically studied if promising early identification strategies are to evolve towards empirically based and equally promising early intervention strategies.

Conclusion

In this chapter, we have attempted to draw attention to the developmental perspective in schizotypy research. First, we presented the basic elements that constitute any model for emerging psychotic disorders, and illustrated how the schizotypy continuum may constitute an organising construct for a developmental framework. Second, we presented the rationale for conceptualising schizotypy as a distal risk factor for the development of psychotic disorders. We have emphasised the possible links between the schizotypal account of risk and the contemporary ultra-high risk (UHR) and basic symptoms risk accounts. In essence, schizotypy might be conceived as a developmental *trait risk*, while the other accounts are clearly defined as *state risk* accounts. The schizotypy risk account, we feel, is better suited to a developmental psychopathology perspective, especially in the identification of developmental interactions that *construe* the liability to develop psychotic disorders. As such, the developmental schizotypy account appears to be equipped to face the clinical heterogeneity of developing psychotic disorders, and could significantly help in elaborating developmentally meaningful early intervention strategies.

References

AlAqeel, B., & Margolese, H. C. (2012). Remission in schizophrenia: critical and systematic review. *Harvard Review of Psychiatry, 20*(6), 281–297.

Alvarez-Jimenez, M., Gleeson, J. F., Henry, L. P., Harrigan, S. M., Harris, M. G., Amminger, G. P., . . . McGorry, P. D. (2011). Prediction of a single psychotic episode: a 7.5-year, prospective study in first-episode psychosis. *Schizophrenia Research, 125*(2–3), 236–246.

Alvarez-Jimenez, M., Gleeson, J. F., Henry, L. P., Harrigan, S. M., Harris, M. G., Killackey, E., . . . McGorry, P. D. (2012). Road to full recovery: longitudinal relationship between symptomatic remission and psychosocial recovery in first-episode psychosis over 7.5 years. *Psychological Medicine, 42*(3), 595–606.

Barrantes-Vidal, N., Fananas, L., Rosa, A., Caparros, B., Dolors Riba, M., & Obiols, J. E. (2003). Neurocognitive, behavioural and neurodevelopmental correlates of schizotypy clusters in adolescents from the general population. *Schizophrenia Research, 61*(2–3), 293–302.

Cappe, C., Herzog, M. H., Herzig, D. A., Brand, A., & Mohr, C. (2012). Cognitive disorganisation in schizotypy is associated with deterioration in visual backward masking. *Psychiatry Research, 200*(2–3), 652–659.

Carlson, E. A., Egeland, B., & Sroufe, L. A. (2009). A prospective investigation of the development of borderline personality symptoms. *Development and Psychopathology, 21*(4), 1311–1334.

Chapman, L. J., Chapman, J. P., Kwapil, T. R., Eckblad, M., & Zinser, M. C. (1994). Putatively psychosis-prone subjects 10 years later. *Journal of Abnormal Psychology, 103*(2), 171–183.

Cicchetti, D., & Rogosch, F. A. (2002). A developmental psychopathology perspective on adolescence. *Journal of Consulting and Clinical Psychology 70*(1), 6–20.

Claridge, G. (1997). *Schizotypy: Implications for illness and health.* Oxford University Press.

Claridge, G., & Beech, T. (1995). Fully and quasi-dimensional constructions of schizotypy. In A. Raine, T. Lencz, & S. A. Mednick (Eds.), *Schizotypal personality* (pp. 192–216). Cambridge University Press.

Dahoun, T., Eliez, S., Chen, F., Badoud, D., Schneider, M., Laroi, F., & Debbané, M. (2013). Action simulation in hallucination-prone adolescents. *Frontiers in Human Neuroscience, 7,* 329.

Dean, K., & Murray, R. M. (2005). Environmental risk factors for psychosis. *Dialogues in Clinical Neurosciences, 7*(1), 69–80.

Debbané, M., & Barrantes-Vidal, N. (in press). Schizotypy from a developmental perspective. *Schizophrenia Bulletin.*

Debbané, M., Badoud, D., Balanzin, D., & Eliez, S. (2013). Broadly defined risk mental states during adolescence: disorganization mediates positive schizotypal expression. *Schizophrenia Research, 147*(1), 153–156.

Debbané, M., Eliez, S., Badoud, D., Conus, P., Flückiger, R., & Schultze-Lutter, F. (in press). Developing psychosis and its risk states through the lens of schizotypy. *Schizophrenia Bulletin.*

Debbané, M., Vrticka, P., Lazouret, M., Badoud, D., Sander, D., & Eliez, S. (2014). Self-reflection and positive schizotypy in the adolescent brain. *Schizophrenia Research, 152*(1), 65–72.

Dominguez, M. D., Saka, M. C., Lieb, R., Wittchen, H. U., & van Os, J. (2010). Early expression of negative/disorganized symptoms predicting psychotic experiences and subsequent clinical psychosis: a 10-year study. *American Journal of Psychiatry, 167*(9), 1075–1082.

Dumontheil, I., Apperly, I. A., & Blakemore, S. J. (2010). Online usage of theory of mind continues to develop in late adolescence. *Developmenal Science, 13*(2), 331–338.

Ettinger, U., Meyhofer, I., Steffens, M., Wagner, M., & Koutsouleris, N. (2014). Genetics, cognition, and neurobiology of schizotypal personality: a review of the overlap with schizophrenia. *Front Psychiatry, 5,* 18.

Eysenck, H. J., & Eysenck, S. B. G. (1976). *Psychoticism as a dimension of personality.* London: Hodder & Stoughton.

Fisher, H. L., Caspi, A., Poulton, R., Meier, M. H., Houts, R., Harrington, H., ... Moffitt, T. E. (2013). Specificity of childhood psychotic symptoms for predicting schizophrenia by 38 years of age: a birth cohort study. *Psychological Medicine, 43*(10), 2077–2086.

Fossati, A., Raine, A., Borroni, S., & Maffei, C. (2007). Taxonic structure of schizotypal personality in nonclinical subjects: issues of replicability and age consistency. *Psychiatry Research, 152*(2–3), 103–112.

Freeman, D., Garety, P. A., Kuipers, E., Fowler, D., & Bebbington, P. E. (2002). A cognitive model of persecutory delusions. *British Journal of Clinical Psychology, 41*(4), 331–347.

Fusar-Poli, P., Yung, A. R., McGorry, P., & van Os, J. (2014). Lessons learned from the psychosis high-risk state: towards a general staging model of prodromal intervention. *Psychological Medicine, 44*(1), 17–24.

Fusar-Poli, P., Borgwardt, S., Bechdolf, A., Addington, J., Riecher-Rossler, A., Schultze-Lutter, F., ... Yung, A. (2013). The psychosis high-risk state: a comprehensive state-of-the-art review. *JAMA Psychiatry, 70*(1), 107–120.

Fusar-Poli, P., Borgwardt, S., Crescini, A., Deste, G., Kempton, M. J., Lawrie, S., . . . Sacchetti, E. (2011). Neuroanatomy of vulnerability to psychosis: a voxel-based meta-analysis. *Neuroscience & Biobehavioral Reviews, 35*(5), 1175–1185.

Gillespie, C. F., Phifer, J., Bradley, B., & Ressler, K. J. (2009). Risk and resilience: genetic and environmental influences on development of the stress response. *Depression and Anxiety, 26*(11), 984–992.

Gottesman, I. I., & Gould, T. D. (2003). The endophenotype concept in psychiatry: etymology and strategic intentions. *American Journal of Psychiatry, 160*(4), 636–645.

Hans, S. L., Auerbach, J. G., Nuechterlein, K. H., Asarnow, R. F., Asarnow, J., Styr, B., & Marcus, J. (2009). Neurodevelopmental factors associated with schizotypal symptoms among adolescents at risk for schizophrenia. *Development and Psychopathology, 21*(4), 1195–1210.

Insel, T. R. (2014). The NIMH Research Domain Criteria (RDoC) Project: precision medicine for psychiatry. *American Journal of Psychiatry, 171*(4), 395–397.

Kelleher, I., Devlin, N., Wigman, J. T., Kehoe, A., Murtagh, A., Fitzpatrick, C., & Cannon, M. (2013). Psychotic experiences in a mental health clinic sample: implications for suicidality, multimorbidity and functioning. *Psychological Medicine*, 1–10.

Kwapil, T. R., Chapman, L. J., & Chapman, J. (1999). Validity and usefulness of the Wisconsin Manual for Assessing Psychotic-like Experiences. *Schizophrenia Bulletin, 25*(2), 363–375.

Kwapil, T. R., Gross, G. M., Silvia, P. J., & Barrantes-Vidal, N. (2013). Prediction of psychopathology and functional impairment by positive and negative schizotypy in the Chapmans' ten-year longitudinal study. *Journal of Abnormal Psychology, 122*(3), 807–815.

Lagioia, A., Eliez, S., Schneider, M., Simons, J. S., Van der Linden, M., & Debbane, M. (2011). Neural correlates of reality monitoring during adolescence. *Neuroimage, 55*(3), 1393–1400.

Lenzenweger, M. F. (2010). *Schizotypy and schizophrenia: the view from experimental psychology*. New York: Guilford Press.

Macchi, M., Rossi, L. N., Cortinovis, I., Menegazzo, L., Burri, S. M., Piller, M., . . . Vassella, F. (2003). Development of visual perception and attention, assessed by backward masking and application in children with epilepsy. *Developmental Medicine and Child Neurology, 45*(8), 562–567.

Mason, O. J. (2014). The duality of schizotypy: is it both dimensional and categorical?. *Frontiers in psychiatry, 5*.

McGlashan, T. (2001). *Structured interview for prodromal syndromes (SIPS)*. New Haven: Springer.

McGlashan, T. H., Walsh, B. C., & Woods, S. W. (2010). *The psychosis-risk prodrome: handbook for diagnosis and follow-up*. New York: Oxford University Press.

Meehl, P. E. (1962). Schizotaxia, schizotypy, schizophrenia. *American Psychologist, 17*, 827–838.

Meehl, P. E. (1990). Toward an integrated theory of schizotaxia, schizotypy, and schizophrenia. *Journal of Personality Disorders, 4*, 1–99.

Nelson, B., Yuen, H. P., Wood, S. J., Lin, A., Spiliotacopoulos, D., Bruxner, A., . . . Yung, A. R. (2013). Long-term follow-up of a group at ultra high risk ('prodromal') for psychosis: the PACE 400 study. *JAMA Psychiatry, 70*(8), 793–802.

Nelson, M. T., Seal, M. L., Pantelis, C., & Phillips, L. J. (2013). Evidence of a dimensional relationship between schizotypy and schizophrenia: a systematic review. *Neuroscience & Biobehavioral Reviews, 37*(3), 317–327.

Perkins, D. O., Gu, H., Boteva, K., & Lieberman, J. A. (2005). Relationship between duration of untreated psychosis and outcome in first-episode schizophrenia: a critical review and meta-analysis. *American Journal of Psychiatry, 162*(10), 1785–1804.

Poulton, R., Caspi, A., Moffitt, T. E., Cannon, M., Murray, R., & Harrington, H. (2000). Children's self-reported psychotic symptoms and adult schizophreniform disorder: a 15-year longitudinal study. *Archives of General Psychiatry, 57*(11), 1053–1058.

Raine, A. (1991). The SPQ: a scale for the assessment of schizotypal personality based on DSM-III-R criteria. *Schizophrenia Bulletin, 17*(4), 555–564.

Raine, A. (2006). Schizotypal personality: neurodevelopmental and psychosocial trajectories. *Annual Review of Clinical Psychology, 2,* 291–326.

Read, J., van Os, J., Morrison, A. P., & Ross, C. A. (2005). Childhood trauma, psychosis and schizophrenia: a literature review with theoretical and clinical implications. *Acta Psychiatrica Scandinavica, 112*(5), 330–350.

Schultze-Lutter, F., Klosterkotter, J., & Ruhrmann, S. (2014). Improving the clinical prediction of psychosis by combining ultra-high risk criteria and cognitive basic symptoms. *Schizophrenia Research, 154*(1–3), 100–106. doi: 10.1016/j.schres.2014.02.010

Schultze-Lutter, F., Ruhrmann, S., Fusar-Poli, P., Bechdolf, A., Schimmelmann, B. G., & Klosterkotter, J. (2012). Basic symptoms and the prediction of first-episode psychosis. *Current Pharmaceutical Design, 18*(4), 351–357.

Sharp, C., & Tackett, J. L. (2014). *Borderline personality disorder in children and adolescents.* New York: Springer.

Supekar, K., Uddin, L. Q., Prater, K., Amin, H., Greicius, M. D., & Menon, V. (2010). Development of functional and structural connectivity within the default mode network in young children. *Neuroimage, 52*(1), 290–301.

Tang, J. Y., Chang, W. C., Hui, C. L., Wong, G. H., Chan, S. K., Lee, E. H., . . . Chen, E. Y. (2014). Prospective relationship between duration of untreated psychosis and 13-year clinical outcome: a first-episode psychosis study. *Schizophrenia Research, 153*(1–3), 1–8.

Yung, A. R., Phillips, L. J., McGorry, P. D., McFarlane, C. A., Francey, S., Harrigan, S., . . . Jackson, H. J. (1998). Prediction of psychosis. A step towards indicated prevention of schizophrenia. *British Journal of Psychiatry – Supplements, 172*(33), 14–20.

6 Childhood trauma and schizotypy
A systematic review

Tjasa Velikonja, Oliver J. Mason and Helen L. Fisher

Schizotypal traits are believed to be moderately heritable (see Chapter 3 for review) with evidence for a genetic component from the elevated schizotypal characteristics observed in relatives of patients with schizophrenia (Battaglia, Bernardeschi, Franchini, Bellodi, & Smeraldi, 1995). However, studies of identical twins have found that the heritability of schizotypal personality characteristics is far from 100 per cent (estimated at around 60 per cent, Torgersen et al., 2000), leaving a strong role for environmental factors. Indeed, the combined effect of genetic and environmental factors on all three schizotypal dimensions has been supported (Linney et al., 2003): specifically the interaction of genetic risk for schizophrenia and environmental factors (van Os, Rutten, & Poulton, 2008), with childhood trauma having an especially prominent role (Fisher & Craig, 2008).

Relationship between childhood trauma and schizotypy

Childhood trauma encompasses a range of adverse experiences that occur before 18 years of age. These include sexual, physical and emotional abuse by caregivers or other adults, parental neglect of a child's physical or emotional needs, bullying by peers or siblings, witnessing domestic or community violence, and exposure to war or natural disasters. This chapter will focus on maltreatment, parental loss and bullying, because these are the types of trauma most often studied in relation to schizotypy. A national survey recently conducted in the UK found that one in four children were maltreated by their parents before the age of 17, mainly through neglect, while nearly two-thirds were victimised by their peers (Radford, Corral, Bradley, & Fisher, 2013). Figures from other parts of the world also suggest that a substantial minority of children are exposed to these forms of victimisation (Kessler et al., 2010), indicating that childhood trauma remains a global problem.

Traumatic childhood experiences have been linked to a range of psychopathologies, including depression (Bifulco, Brown, & Adler, 1991), post-traumatic stress disorder (PTSD; Gearon, Kaltman, Brown, & Bellack, 2003), anxiety and bipolar disorder (Fisher & Hosang, 2010), substance misuse (Jonas et al., 2011), eating disorders (Rorty, Yager, & Rossotto, 1994) and personality disorders (Afifi et al., 2011). Moreover, a growing body of evidence is emerging showing a robust association between childhood trauma and both subclinical psychosis and psychotic disorders (Varese et al., 2012), including increased schizotypy (Waxman, Fenton, Skodol, Grant, & Hasin, 2014). Indeed, multiple studies have reported increased rates of childhood trauma reported by schizotypal individuals in comparison with controls (Afifi et al., 2011). Overall, the individuals showed approximately a 2- (Afifi et al., 2011) to 4-fold (Lentz, Robinson, & Bolton, 2010) increase in levels of schizotypy if they also reported childhood trauma. Similar evidence is observed in non-clinical samples where childhood maltreatment and bullying are associated with increased psychotic-like experiences (Kelleher et al., 2008), as occur within the positive dimension of schizotypy. Furthermore, childhood traumatic experiences have been shown to predict schizotypal symptomatology in a dose-response manner (Berenbaum, Thompson, Milanak, Boden, & Bredemeier, 2008), tentatively suggesting that there might be a causal relationship between early trauma and schizotypy.

A systematic review of the literature

A systematic review of the empirical literature was completed using four search databases (PsycInfo, PubMed, EMBASE, Web of Science) and the following search terms: trauma* OR maltreat* OR abuse OR advers* OR neglect OR bully* OR victim* OR parental loss OR separat* AND adolescen* OR child* AND schizoty* OR psychos* OR psychotic OR illusion OR hallucination OR delusion OR derealisation OR depersonalisation OR social isolation OR hypersensitivity OR magical ideation OR introversion OR referential thinking OR suspiciousness OR restricted affect.

This produced thirty studies exploring the association between childhood trauma (defined as either abuse, maltreatment, neglect, bullying, victimisation, parental loss or parental separation) and schizotypal traits (including schizotypal personality disorder [SPD] and dissociative disorder) in community samples. We included original research papers written in English from 1806 to 31 October 2014. Table 6.1 includes the methodologically most robust studies (scoring seven or above out of fourteen points on a quality assessment tool). The quality indicators were the method of sample selection, the percentage of individuals approached who agreed to participate, the size of the sample, the type of assessment tools used, whether different types of trauma were considered separately in the analysis and whether analyses were adjusted for confounding factors (e.g. demographic information, genetic risk, substance use and depression). A copy of the tool can be obtained from the authors.

Table 6.1 Summary of studies on childhood trauma and schizotypal traits (ordered by weight [W])

Authors	Study design	Sample	Measure of trauma	Measure of schizotypy	Measure of effect	W
Waxman et al. 2014 (USA)	Cross-sectional	40093	CTQ, AUDADIS-IV	DSM-IV	Sexual abuse and SPD (OR=2.15***), Emotional abuse (OR=1.40**), Physical neglect (OR=1.48***)	14
Afifi et al. 2011 (Canada)	Cross-sectional	34653	CTQ	AUDADIS-IV	Physical abuse and SPD (OR=1.62**), Emotional abuse (OR=1.76**), Sexual abuse (OR=2.05**), Physical neglect (OR=1.61**), Emotional neglect (OR=1.35**)	12
Lentz et al. 2010 (USA)	Cross-sectional	34653	5 childhood events	AUDADIS-IV	Physical and SPD (adj. OR=4.43***), Neglect by parent (adj. OR=4.57***), Sexual assault (adj. OR=4.15***)	12
Powers, Thomas, Ressler, & Bradley, 2011 (USA)	Cross-sectional	541	CTQ, Early Trauma Interview	SNAP, The Personality Disorder Diagnostic scales	Childhood physical and emotional abuse and SPD (r=0.15***) Physical abuse and unusual perceptions (r=0.11**), eccentric behaviour (r=0.15***) and social anxiety (r=0.12**)	10
Rossler, Hengartner, Ajacic-Gross, Haker, & Angst, 2014 (Switzerland)	Longitudinal study	335	SPIKE	SCL90-R/ adapted subscales	Family problems and schizotypal signs (b=0.044, sig.), conflict between parents (b=0.062, sig.), disliked/ rejected (b=0.057, sig.)	10
Lobbestael, Arntz, & Bernstein, 2010 (Netherlands)	Cross-sectional	409	Interview for Traumatic events in childhood	SCID-II	Sexual abuse and SPD (ρ=0.19**), Physical abuse (ρ=0.25**), Emotional abuse (ρ=0.29**), Emotional neglect (ρ=0.21**), Physical neglect (ρ=0.11**)	10
Berenbaum, Thompson, Milanak, Boden, & Bredemeier, 2008, Study 1 (USA)	Cross-sectional	1510	Telephone interview	Telephone interview on SPD	Childhood maltreatment and schizotypal symptoms (for men: β=.33**, women: β=.29**)	10

(continued)

Table 6.1 (continued)

Authors	Study design	Sample	Measure of trauma	Measure of schizotypy	Measure of effect	W
Berenbaum, Thompson, Milanak, Boden, & Bredemeier, 2008, Study 2 (USA)	Cross-sectional	303	Self-report of physical abuse, Childhood trauma Interview	SCID-II	Emotional abused and schizotypal symptoms (β=.28**), Childhood maltreatment and schizotypal symptoms for men (β=.46**) for women (β=.19*)	10
Rossler et al. 2007 (Switzerland)	Prospective study	372	Life events list Holmes/Rahe scale	SPIKE, SCL90-R	Parental neglect and schizotypal load (OR=6.7***) Conflict among parents (OR=3.5**), punishment (OR=3.1*)	10
Battle et al. 2004 (USA)	Longitudinal study	51 PD 83 MDD	CEQ-Revised	SCID-II	SPD vs MDD: Emotional abuse (x^2=15.74***), Verbal abuse (x^2=8.26**), Physical abuse (x^2=8.62**), Sexual abuse (x^2=5.85*), Neglect (x^2=9.76*)	10
Johnson et al. 1999 (USA), 2001 (USA)	Longitudinal study	793	Official data – New York State Central registry	DISC, Personality Diagnostic Questionnaire	Childhood abuse/neglect and SPD (adj. F=26.44**)	10
Berenz et al. 2013 (Norway)	Cross-sectional	449 (twin pairs)	MCIDI	SIDP-IV	Childhood trauma and schizotypal PD (β=0.08, t=4.37***)	8
Hengartner, Ajdacid-Gross, Rodgers, Muller, & Rossler, 2013 (Switzerland)	Cross-sectional	512	CTQ	ADP-IV	Victim of bullying and SPD (β=0.08), Emotional abuse (β=0.182) Emotional neglect (β=0.173) Physical abuse (β=0.116) Physical neglect (β=0.129) Sexual abuse (β=0.081)	8
Myin-Germeys et al. 2011 (Netherlands)	Cross-sectional	272 cases 227 controls	CTQ	PANSS, SIS-R	Trauma and positive schizotypy (OR=4.82***), Abuse and positive schizotypy (OR=5.53***), Neglect and positive schizotypy (OR=3.67***)	8
Anglin, Cohen, & Chen, 2008 (USA)	Longitudinal study	776	Maternal separation–reported by mothers	SPD symptom scale	Separation before age 5 and SPD symptoms (b=2.03*)	8

Study	Design	N	Measure of abuse	Measure of psychosis	Results	Quality score
Sommer et al. 2010 (The Netherlands)	Cross-sectional	103 AVH 60 controls	CTQ	SCID-II	Trauma and delusional tendency inventory (r=0.3**), Schizotypal personality questionnaire (r=0.54***)	7
Tyrka, Wyche, Kelly, Price, & Carpenter, 2009 (USA)	Cross-sectional	105	CTQ	SCID-II	Emotional abuse/neglect group differed from No abuse for Cluster A PD (and B,C) U-test** Physical/Sexual differed from control group for clusters A PD (and B,C) U-test***	7
Elliott, Cunningham, Linder, Colangelo, & Gross 2005 (USA)	Cross-sectional	1725	Child Physical Abuse	Social isolation – 11 items	Physical abuse and social isolation (R²=1.95***)	7
Gibb, Wheeler, Alloy, & Abramson, 2001 (USA)	Cross-sectional	272	The life experiences questionnaire	PD dimensions	Physical maltreatment and Paranoid PD dimensional scores (t(263)=2.93***, β=.33). Emotional maltreatment and SPD dimensional scores (t(263)=3.38***, β=.43)	7
Irwin, 2001 (Australia)	Cross-sectional	116	CTQ	SPQ-B, DES	PA/EA and Cognitive perceptual traits (r=.44**), EN (r=.36***), PN (r=.34***), SA (r=.21*). PA/EA and Interpersonal perceptual traits (r=.28**), EN (r=.28**), PN (r=.26**). PA/EA and disorganised dimension (r=.39***), EN (r=.32**), PN (r=.31***), SA (r=.20*)	7
Simeon, Guralnik, Schmeidler, Sirof, & Knutelska, 2001 (USA)	Cross-sectional	75	The Childhood Trauma Interview	SCID-II, DES	Emotional abuse alone predicted diagnosis (x²=17.95**). Total trauma scores predicted the total score on DES (R=0.42, R²=0.18, F=2.41*), depersonalisation score (R=0.50, R²=0.25, F=3.81**)	7
Berenbaum, 1999 (USA)	Cross-sectional	458	Physical punishment scale, Sexual abuse scale, CEQ	Perceptual aberration Magical ideation	Childhood maltreatment = 10.5 times more likely to have high perceptual aberration scores	7

Note: significance * p<0.05, ** p<0.01, *** p<0.001 Abbreviations: CTQ, Childhood Trauma Questionnaire. AUDADIS-IV, Alcohol Use Disorder and Associated Disabilities Interview Schedule –IV. OR, odd ratio. SPD, Schizotypal personality disorder. Adj., adjusted. SNAP, The Schedule for Nonadaptive and Adaptive Personality. r, Pearson correlation coefficient. SCID-II, Structured clinical Interview for Personality Disorder. ρ, Spearman'r rank correlation coefficient. β, Beta regression coefficient. SPIKE, Semi-structured Psychopathological Interview. SCL90-R, Symptoms Checklist. CEQ Childhood Experiences Questionnaire. DES, Dissociative Experiences Scale. MDD, major depression without PD. x², Chi-squared test. DISC – Diagnostic Interview Schedule for Children. F, F-ratio. PANSS, The Positive and Negative Syndrome Scale. SIS-R, The Structured Interview for Schizotypy – Revised. b, regression coefficient. AVH, Auditory Verbal Hallucinations. PD, Personality Disorder. U-test, Mann Whitney test. R, multiple correlation coefficient. t, T-test. SPQ-B, Schizotypal Personality Questionnaire – Brief. PA, Physical Abuse. EA, Emotional Abuse. PN, Physical Neglect. SA, Sexual Abuse.

Specificity of the trauma-schizotypy association

While some have argued that there are no differential effects of specific trauma types on schizotypal symptoms (Tyrka, Wyche, Kelly, Price, & Carpenter, 2009), others have suggested that the greatest risk is conferred by either neglect (Johnson, Smailes, Cohen, Brown, & Bernstein, 2000), emotional abuse (Berenbaum et al., 2008), physical abuse (Martinez-Taboas, Canino, Wang, Garcia, & Bravo, 2006) or sexual trauma (Waxman et al. 2014) and in an ultra-high risk for psychosis group (Bechdolf et al., 2010). Emotional abuse, however, has been shown to be most consistently associated with schizotypy even after adjusting for different types of trauma, with a reported approximately two- (Afifi et al., 2011) to six-times (Martinez-Taboas et al., 2006) increase in schizotypal load. Furthermore, emotional abuse has not only been shown to predict general schizotypy, but, focusing on individuals with SPD, has also demonstrated a link to some specific traits, such as ideas of reference, excessive social anxiety, a lack of close friends, unusual perceptual experiences and eccentric behaviour or appearance (Powers, Thomas, Ressler, & Bradley, 2011).

In terms of schizotypal dimensions, a recent study (Myin-Germeys et al., 2011) found that childhood abuse (emotional, physical and general) showed stronger associations with the positive schizotypy dimension (5.5-fold increase), while neglect was associated with both positive (to a lesser degree, with 3.7-fold increase) and negative schizotypy (4.0-fold increase). The particularly robust ties between childhood abuse and especially positive schizotypal symptomatology have been further supported by evidence that paranoia (Steel, Marzillier, Fearon, & Ruddle, 2009), unusual perceptions (Powers, Thomas, Ressler, & Bradley, 2011), dissociation (Simeon, Guralnik, Schmeidler, Sirof, & Knutelska, 2001), depersonalisation scores (Simeon et al., 2001), levels of precognition, spiritualism, witchcraft, superstition (Berkowski & MacDonald, 2014; Perkins & Allen, 2006) and unusual beliefs or experiences (Berenbaum, Valera, & Kerns, 2003), including paranormal beliefs (Berkowski & MacDonald, 2014), are all more likely to be increased if an individual reported childhood trauma. There is also evidence for increased negative (Myin-Germeys et al., 2011; Sheinbaum, Kwapil, & Barrantes-Vidal, 2014) and disorganised schizotypal dimensions (Irwin, 2001) in abused or neglected individuals, such as social anxiety (Powers et al. 2011). Additionally, physical or emotional abuse or neglect (Irwin, 2001) have been shown to be associated with the disorganised schizotypy dimension, particularly eccentric behaviour (Powers et al., 2011) and elevated levels of peculiarity (Berenbaum, 1999).

Bullying is another form of victimisation associated with positive, negative and disorganised dimensions (Raine, Fung, & Lam, 2011). Interestingly, there is emerging evidence that being a victim of bullying and a perpetrator of bullying at the same time (bully–victim) results in even higher psychoticism scores than for those who were only victims (Mynard & Joseph, 1997).

Furthermore, being a bully meant an almost ten times increased risk for psychotic-like experiences (Kelleher et al., 2008) and has been linked to psychotic disorders (Trotta et al., 2013). However, there is limited research available on bullying so caution is required in interpreting these results.

Stepping away from schizotypy defined in a personality/dimensional framework to more specific psychosis-like symptomatology, similar associations with childhood trauma can be found. Empirical literature has linked childhood trauma to predispositions to auditory hallucinations (Whitfield, Dube, Felitti, & Anda, 2005), tactile hallucinations (Shevlin, Dorahy, & Adamson, 2007) and visual hallucinations (Shevlin et al., 2007), including beliefs about voices being more malevolent, omnipotent and benevolent (Andrew, Gray, & Snowden, 2008). Likewise, childhood trauma has been shown to predict delusional experiences in the community (Scott, Chant, Andrews, Martin, & McGrath, 2007).

Methodological considerations

Sample characteristics and study designs

A major limitation to study comparison in this area is the massive age range from 6 to 95 years, with some of the studies restricted to only children or adolescent populations (e.g. Johnson, Cohen, Brown, Smailes, & Bernstein, 1999). The age of the participants is important because it has been found to be associated with the prevalence of certain schizotypal personality traits (Mason & Claridge, 2006; Rawlings, Claridge, & Freeman, 2001), and using young samples may result in underestimating associations because the participants will not yet have passed through the critical period for developing schizotypal traits. Another factor prompting caution when comparing the empirical evidence is the major difference in study designs and discrepancies in sample sizes, which range from 43 (Merckelbach & Jelicic, 2004) to 40,093 (Waxman et al., 2014). With 90 per cent of the studies conducted in the US or Europe, it is also difficult to generalise conclusions to other contexts, with some schizotypal traits (e.g. magical ideation) found to be especially culturally dependent (Sharpley & Peters, 1999).

Most studies used cross-sectional retrospective designs, yet the few prospective and longitudinal studies (Battle et al., 2004; Rossler, Hengartner, Ajadic-Gross, Haker, & Angst, 2014) suggested similar childhood trauma-schizotypy associations. This provides some evidence against the possibility of 'reverse causality'. Despite concerns that individuals with more schizotypal traits (as well as psychotic-like experiences) might be more likely to be exposed to traumatic experiences, the dose-response effect of trauma on schizotypal levels and the differential effect of certain trauma types on particular symptoms would be difficult to justify if schizotypy preceded the traumatic experiences. Moreover, a study by Kelleher et al. (2013) found that maltreatment and bullying still predicted the occurrence of new psychotic-like experiences even when previous psychotic-like experiences were taken into account, thus providing further evidence that reverse causality cannot fully explain the trauma-schizotypy association. Furthermore, additional evidence of directionality was found in the observation that cessation of trauma predicted cessation of psychotic experiences (Kelleher et al., 2013).

Definition of exposure and outcome

Aside from discrepancies in the definitions of childhood trauma used across the globe (Giovanni & Beccerra, 1979), attempts to measure trauma also vary considerably. Some of the studies discussed earlier in this chapter were limited to inclusion of one trauma type (e.g. Raine et al., 2011); others have used broader conceptualisations of childhood trauma and included, for instance, any life-threatening event or conflicts between parents (Berenbaum et al., 2008; Rossler et al., 2014). Similarly, the age threshold as to what was considered childhood trauma was limited to the age of 16 and below in some cases (e.g. Lentz, Robinson, & Bolton, 2010), with many more expanding the age range of trauma occurrence up to 18 years (e.g. Afifi et al., 2011). The timing of exposure to adversity has also been suggested to play a significant role (Fisher et al., 2010) because earlier exposure to trauma has been associated with more severe and persistent adult psychopathology (Blaauw, Arensman, Kraaij, Winkel, & Bout, 2002), but unfortunately most schizotypal studies have not assessed age of exposure.

Additionally, schizotypy has been shown to consist of many sub-factors (Vollema & Vandenbosch, 1995) and an extensive range of assessment tools has claimed to assess its multidimensionality. The studies looking at the relationship between childhood trauma and schizotypy have either used standardised measures administrated by clinicians or more unstandardised methods and self-reports that are limited in the reliability of some key schizotypal traits like oddness (Kendler, Thacker, & Walsh, 1996). This further limits the ability to compare findings between studies.

Childhood trauma assessment

When measuring childhood trauma, many studies relied on crude measurements, such as brief self-report questionnaires or checklist formats with yes/no responses. Such tools do not allow for any clarification or details to be obtained about the traumatic experiences, and also raise the possibility of under- or over-reporting and recall bias (McFarland & Buehler, 1998). Furthermore, those measures do not assess the frequency and severity of abuse, previously shown to have an important impact on trauma and psychotic disorder associations (e.g. Fisher et al., 2010).

There has been a lot of controversy about the validity of retrospectively obtained information, particularly concerning child abuse reporting (Briere &

Conte, 1993; Williams, 1994). Relative instability and low reliability of young people's reports were, for example, indicated for childhood sexual abuse, and parental physical punishment (Fergusson, Horwood, & Woodward, 2000), as well as neglect (Widom, 1996). Therefore, some caution is necessary regarding the interpretation of data obtained via retrospective techniques. Besides the possibility of childhood amnesia for extremely early events (Loftus, 1993), there is also a tendency for individuals to distort or reconstruct past events to enhance positive affect (Yarrow, Campbell, & Burton, 1970), for social desirability reasons (Widom, 1996), a general tendency to seek meaning in memories (Fivush, 1995), embarrassment or inclination to protect parents/abuser, feelings of deserving the abuse or even a conscious wish to forget the experiences (Della, Yeager, & Lewis, 1990). Individuals can have false beliefs that an event has occurred when in reality it never has (Loftus & Ketcham, 1994); this might be expected to be particularly problematic in schizotypal individuals with delusional beliefs. However, individuals have been found to be more likely to fail to report abuse than falsely claim it occurred (Hardt & Rutter, 2004). Furthermore, people can only recall what they were aware of at the time and thus some forms of potential trauma – for example, domestic violence – may not be reported if the individual did not witness them (Robins et al., 1985). Additionally, individuals scoring high on schizotypy might suffer from more trauma-related intrusions (Marzillier & Steel, 2007) because the information is not contextually integrated but based on perceptual information during the traumatic event (Jones & Steel, 2012). Consequently, the voluntary recall of trauma-related experiences is weakened, but at the same time the fragments of trauma can be involuntarily re-experienced (Holmes, Grey, & Young, 2005). Nevertheless, a recent study that compared low and high schizotypy groups showed no significant difference in frequency of deliberately retrieved memories (Jones & Steel, 2012).

However, despite all the concerns about the reliability of retrospective reporting, there is some encouraging evidence that childhood trauma reports are reasonably reliable and stable over a long period of time, even among clinically psychotic patients (Fisher et al., 2011). Also, because of economical and ethical considerations about prospective assessment of childhood maltreatment in sufficiently large numbers to yield statistical power to detect associations with schizotypy, the retrospective reporting approach still stands as an appropriate and satisfactorily reliable technique (Maughan, 1997). However, the accuracy (validity) of retrospectively obtained reports is still somewhat questionable.

Potential mechanisms underlying the childhood trauma-schizotypy association

The biological pathophysiology of psychotic disorders has been widely supported, with childhood trauma influencing the development of the hypothalamic-pituitary-adrenal (HPA) axis and leading to an acquired vulnerability or enhanced sensitivity to stress (e.g. Read, Perry, Moskowitz, & Connolly, 2001). The overactivity of the HPA axis has not only been demonstrated in psychotic patients but also in individuals at ultra-high risk for psychosis and individuals with SPD (Walker & Diforio, 1997). Similarly, dysregulation of dopaminergic pathways has been advocated as one of the underlying mechanisms of the childhood trauma and psychosis link (Selten & Cantor-Graae, 2005). More research is required to test these potential mechanisms.

An affective pathway to psychosis has also been hypothesised (Garety, Kuipers, Fowler, Freeman, & Bebbington, 2001). According to this model, early adverse experiences lead to negative thoughts and beliefs, and these faulty perceptions of self and/or others may lead to misinterpretations of social situations and negative affect that in turn result in psychotic symptoms developing. Negative beliefs may be further fuelled by negative emotions (especially anxiety, mistrust and suspiciousness) (Fowler et al., 2006), which have been shown to play a role in the relationship between trauma and paranoia (Gracie et al., 2007). Moreover, interpersonal forms of trauma are specifically considered to predispose to a paranoid view of the world (Lovatt, Mason, Brett, & Peters, 2010). Indeed, Fisher et al. (2013) found that the association between harsh parenting or bullying in childhood and psychotic-like experiences in early adolescence was partly explained by increased levels of anxiety and depression in the intervening period. Also consistent with the 'affective pathway' hypothesis, a recent study showed that social defeat might be a direct and exclusive mediator of the association between childhood trauma and psychosis (van Nierop et al., 2014).

Additionally, exposure to childhood trauma may predispose an individual to have dysfunctional responses or maladaptive coping strategies to subsequent stressors (Cohen et al., 1996), possibly resulting in psychotic symptom formation (Garety et al., 2001). For example, abused individuals are more likely to misuse substances such as cannabis (Lo & Cheng, 2007) and this in turn may trigger the development of psychotic-like phenomena (Di Forti et al., 2009). Equally, traumatic childhood experiences might severely disrupt the ability to trust and form attachments with others (Liem & Boudewyn, 1999) that can also be linked to low self-esteem (Mullen, Martin, Anderson, Romans, & Herbison, 1996), as well as feelings of guilt or self-blame (Liem & Boudewyn, 1999). Low self-esteem has also been shown to partially account for associations between childhood trauma and psychotic-like experiences (Fisher et al., 2013). Further replication of these findings is required though, along with exploration for other schizotypal symptoms.

The sociodevelopmental–cognitive model attempted to incorporate these various hypothesised theories linking childhood trauma to psychosis. The model proposes that childhood trauma (early stress) leads to dopamine dysregulation, causing the aberrant assignment of salience to stimuli. It is then the cognitive interpretations (biased cognitive schemas) of these stimuli that consequently result in psychotic symptoms (and more psychosocial stress – thus creating a vicious cycle) (Howes & Murray, 2014). Theories also suggest a mediating role of PTSD or dissociation symptoms between traumatic experiences and psychosis (psychosis-like symptoms), especially hallucinations and paranoia (e.g. Gaudiano & Zimmerman, 2010; Kilcommons & Morrison, 2005). Moreover, there is a lot of evidence suggesting the importance of adulthood adversity on psychotic and subclinical psychotic experiences (Beards et al., 2013), including the synergistic effects of childhood and adulthood trauma in pathways to psychosis (Morgan et al., 2013). Similarly, the interaction between early trauma and cannabis use was also documented with 'more than additive' effects (e.g. Harley et al. 2010). Literature stipulates that cannabis either has direct pharmacological effects on psychotic symptoms (especially the positive domain) via increased dopaminergic hyperactivity, or indirectly by affecting mood states (e.g. anxiety, depression; Kapur, 2003). Further replication of these findings is required though, along with exploration of symptom-specific pathways between childhood trauma and schizotypy.

Conclusions

The empirical literature provides support for an association between childhood maltreatment and schizotypy. Nonetheless, further research is needed to improve on the methodological limitations of previous studies, by going beyond crude self-report measurements, using more homogeneous samples and including the contextual aspects of childhood trauma in relation to schizotypy symptom load. Also, further investigation of the possible underlying mechanisms supporting this association (e.g. familial risk of psychosis, affective states and cannabis use) would provide valuable clues regarding the aetiology of schizotypy, and potentially psychotic disorders. Elucidation of such mechanisms has important implications for clinical practice through suggesting useful targets for preventative interventions.

References

Afifi, T. O., Mather, A., Boman, J., Fleisher, W., Enns, M. W., MacMillan, H., . . . Sareen, J. (2011). Childhood adversity and personality disorders: results from a nationally representative population-based study. *Journal of Psychiatric Research, 45*, 814–822.

Andrew, E. M., Gray, N. S., & Snowden, R. J. (2008). The relationship between trauma and beliefs about hearing voices: a study of psychiatric and non-psychiatric voice hearers. *Psychological Medicine, 38*, 1409–1417.

Anglin, D. M., Cohen, P. R., & Chen, H. (2008). Duration of early maternal separation and prediction of schizotypal symptoms from early adolescence to midlife. *Schizophrenia Research, 103*, 143–150.

Battaglia, M., Bernardeschi, L., Franchini, L., Bellodi, L., & Smeraldi, E. (1995). A family study of schizotypal disorder. *Schizophrenia Bulletin, 21*, 33–45.

Battle, C. L., Shea, M. T., Johnson, D. M., Yen, S., Zlotnick, C., Zanarini, M. C., . . . Morey, L. C. (2004). Childhood maltreatment associated with adult personality disorders:

findings from the Collaborative Longitudinal Personality Disorders Study. *Journal of Personality Disorders, 18*, 193–211.

Beards, S., Gayer-Anderson, C., Borges, S., Dewey, M. E., Fisher, H. L. & Morgan, C. (2013). Life events and psychosis: a review and meta-analysis. *Schizophrenia Bulletin, 39*, 740–747.

Bechdolf, A., Thompson, A., Nelson, B., Cotton, S., Leicester, S., Francey, S., . . . Yung, R. (2010). Experience of trauma and conversion to psychotic disorder in individuals at ultra high risk ('prodromal') of developing first episode psychosis. *Schizophrenia Research, 117*, 529–530.

Berenbaum, H. (1999). Peculiarity and reported childhood maltreatment. *Psychiatry: Interpersonal and Biological Processes, 62*, 21–35.

Berenbaum, H., Valera, E. M., & Kerns, J. G. (2003). Psychological trauma and schizotypal symptoms. *Schizophrenia Bulletin, 29*, 143–152.

Berenbaum, H., Thompson, R. J., Milanak, M. E., Boden, M. T., & Bredemeier, K. (2008). Psychological trauma and schizotypal personality disorder. *Journal of Abnormal Psychology, 117*, 502–519.

Berenz, E. C., Amstadter, A. B., Aggen, S. H., Knudsen, G. P., Reichborn-Kjennerud, T., Gardner, C. O., . . . Kendler, K. S. (2013). Childhood trauma and personality disorder criterion counts: a co-twin control analysis. *Journal of Abnormal Psychology, 122*, 1070–1076.

Berkowski, M., & MacDonald, D. A. (2014). Childhood trauma and the development of paranormal beliefs. *Journal of Nervous and Mental Disease, 202*, 305–312.

Bifulco, A., Brown, G. W., & Adler, Z. (1991). Early sexual abuse and clinical depression in adult life. *British Journal of Psychiatry, 159*, 115–122.

Blaauw, E., Arensman, E., Kraaij, V., Winkel, F. W., & Bout, R. (2002). Traumatic life events and suicide risk among jail inmates: the influence of types of events, time period and significant others. *Journal of Traumatic Stress, 15*, 9–16.

Briere, J., & Conte, J. (1993). Self-reported amnesia for abuse in adults molested as children. *Journal of Traumatic Stress, 6*, 21–31.

Cohen, Y., Spirito, A., Sterling, C., Donaldson, D., Seifer, R., Plummer, B., . . . Ferrer, K. (1996). Physical and sexual abuse and their relation to psychiatric disorder and suicidal behavior among adolescents who are psychiatrically hospitalized. *Journal of Child Psychology and Psychiatry, 37*, 989–993.

Della, F. D., Yeager, C. A., & Lewis, D. O. (1990). Child abuse: adolescent records vs. adult recall. *Child Abuse & Neglect, 14*, 227–231.

Di Forti, M., Morgan, C., Dazzan, P., Pariante, C., Mondelli, V., Marques, T. R., . . . Murray, R. M. (2009). High-potency cannabis and the risk of psychosis. *British Journal of Psychiatry, 195*, 488–491.

Elliott, G. C., Cunningham, S. M., Linder, M., Colangelo, M., & Gross, M. (2005). Child physical abuse and self-perceived social isolation among adolescents. *Journal of Interpersonal Violence, 20*, 1663–1684.

Fergusson, D. M., Horwood, L. J., & Woodward, L. J. (2000). The stability of child abuse reports: a longitudinal study of the reporting behaviour of young adults. *Psychological Medicine, 30*, 529–544.

Fisher, H., & Craig, T. (2008). Childhood adversity and psychosis. In C. Morgan, K. Mckenzie, & P. Fearon (Eds.), *Society and psychosis* (pp. 95–111). Cambridge University Press.

Fisher, H., Craig, T. K., Fearon, P., Morgan, K., Dazzan, P., Lappin, J., . . . Morgan, C. (2011). Reliability and comparability of psychosis patients' retrospective reports of childhood abuse. *Schizophrenia Bulletin, 37*, 546–553.

Fisher, H. L., & Hosang, G. M. (2010). Childhood maltreatment and bipolar disorder: a critical review of the evidence. *Mind & Brain, the Journal of Psychiatry, 1,* 75–85.

Fisher, H. L., Jones, P. B., Fearon, P., Craig, T. K., Dazzan, P., Morgan, K., ... Morgan, C. (2010). The varying impact of type, timing and frequency of exposure to childhood adversity on its association with adult psychotic disorder. *Psychological Medicine, 40,* 1967–1978.

Fisher, H. L., Schreier, A., Zammit, S., Maughan, B., Munafo, M. R., Lewis, G., ... Wolke, D. (2013). Pathways between childhood victimization and psychosis-like symptoms in the ALSPAC birth cohort. *Schizophrenia Bulletin, 39,* 1045–1055.

Fivush, R. (1995). Language, narrative, and autobiography. *Consciousness and Cognition, 4,* 100–103.

Fowler, D., Freeman, D., Smith, B., Kuipers, E., Bebbington, P., Bashforth, H., ... Garety, P. (2006). The Brief Core Schema Scales (BCSS): psychometric properties and associations with paranoia and grandiosity in non-clinical and psychosis samples. *Psychological Medicine, 36,* 749–759.

Garety, P. A., Kuipers, E., Fowler, D., Freeman, D., & Bebbington, P. E. (2001). A cognitive model of the positive symptoms of psychosis. *Psychological Medicine, 31,* 189–195.

Gaudiano, B. A., & Zimmerman, M. (2010). The relationship between childhood trauma history and the psychotic subtype of major depression. *Acta Psychiatrica Scandinavica, 121*(6), 462–470.

Gearon, J. S., Kaltman, S. I., Brown, C., & Bellack, A. S. (2003). Traumatic life events and PTSD among women with substance use disorders and schizophrenia. *Psychiatric Services, 54,* 523–528.

Gibb, B. E., Wheeler, R., Alloy, L. B., & Abramson, L. Y. (2001). Emotional, physical, and sexual maltreatment in childhood versus adolescence and personality dysfunction in young adulthood. *Journal of Personality Disorders, 15,* 505–511.

Giovanni, J. M., & Beccerra, R. M. (1979). *Defining child abuse.* New York: The Free Press.

Gracie, A., Freeman, D., Green, S., Garety, P. A., Kuipers, E., Hardy, A., ... Fowler, D. (2007). The association between traumatic experience, paranoia and hallucinations: a test of the predictions of psychological models. *Acta Psychiatrica Scandinavica, 116,* 280–289.

Hardt, J., & Rutter, M. (2004). Validity of adult retrospective reports of adverse childhood experiences: review of the evidence. *Journal of Child Psychology and Psychiatry, 45,* 260–273.

Harley, M., Kelleher, I., Clarke, M., Lynch, F., Arseneault, L., Connor, D., ... Cannon, M. (2010). Cannabis use and childhood trauma interact additively to increase the risk of psychotic symptoms in adolescence. *Psychological Medicine, 40,* 1627–1634.

Hengartner, M. P., Ajdacic-Gross, V., Rodgers, S., Muller, M., & Rossler, W. (2013). Childhood adversity in association with personality disorder dimensions: new findings in an old debate. *European Psychiatry, 28,* 476–482.

Holmes, E. A., Grey, N., & Young, K. A. (2005). Intrusive images and 'hotspots' of trauma memories in posttraumatic stress disorder: an exploratory investigation of emotions and cognitive themes. *Journal of Behavior Therapy and Experimental Psychiatry, 36,* 3–17.

Howes, O. D., & Murray, R. M. (2014). Schizophrenia: an integrated sociodevelopmental-cognitive model. *Lancet, 383,* 1677–1687.

Irwin, H. J. (2001). The relationship between dissociative tendencies and schizotypy: an artifact of childhood trauma? *Journal of Clinical Psychology, 57,* 331–342.

Johnson, J. G., Cohen, P., Brown, J., Smailes, E. M., & Bernstein, D. P. (1999). Childhood maltreatment increases risk for personality disorders during early adulthood. *Archives in General Psychiatry, 56*, 600–606.

Johnson, J. G., Smailes, E. M., Cohen, P., Brown, J., & Bernstein, D. P. (2000). Associations between four types of childhood neglect and personality disorder symptoms during adolescence and early adulthood: findings of a community-based longitudinal study. *Journal of Personality Disorders, 14*, 171–187.

Johnson, J. G., Cohen, P., Smailes, E. M., Skodol, A. E., Brown, J., & Oldham, J. M. (2001). Childhood verbal abuse and risk for personality disorders during adolescence and early adulthood. *Comprehensive Psychiatry, 42*, 16–23.

Jonas, S., Bebbington, P., McManus, S., Meltzer, H., Jenkins, R., Kuipers, E., . . . Brugha, T. (2011). Sexual abuse and psychiatric disorder in England: results from the 2007 Adult Psychiatric Morbidity Survey. *Psychological Medicine, 41*, 709–719.

Jones, V., & Steel, C. (2012). Schizotypal personality and vulnerability to involuntary autobiographical memories. *Journal of Behavior Therapy and Experimental Psychiatry, 43*, 871–876.

Kapur, S. (2003). Psychosis as a state of aberrant salience: a framework linking biology, phenomenology, and pharmacology in schizophrenia. *American Journal of Psychiatry, 160*(1), 13–23.

Kelleher, I., Harley, M., Lynch, F., Arseneault, L., Fitzpatrick, C., & Cannon, M. (2008). Associations between childhood trauma, bullying and psychotic symptoms among a school-based adolescent sample. *British Journal of Psychiatry, 193*, 378–382.

Kelleher, I., Keeley, H., Corcoran, P., Ramsay, H., Wasserman, C., Carli, V., . . . Cannon, M. (2013). Childhood trauma and psychosis in a prospective cohort study: cause, effect, and directionality. *American Journal of Psychiatry, 170*, 734–741.

Kendler, K. S., Thacker, L., & Walsh, D. (1996). Self-report measures of schizotypy as indices of familial vulnerability to schizophrenia. *Schizophrenia Bulletin, 22*, 511–520.

Kessler, R. C., McLaughlin, K. A., Green, J. G., Gruber, M. J., Sampson, N. A., Zaslavsky, A. M., . . . Williams, D. R. (2010). Childhood adversities and adult psychopathology in the WHO World Mental Health Surveys. *British Journal of Psychiatry, 197*, 378–385.

Kilcommons, A. M., & Morrison, A. P. (2005). Relationships between trauma and psychosis: an exploration of cognitive and dissociative factors. *Acta Psychiatrica Scandinavica, 112*(5), 351–359.

Lentz, V., Robinson, J., & Bolton, J. M. (2010). Childhood adversity, mental disorder comorbidity, and suicidal behavior in schizotypal personality disorder. *Journal of Nervous and Mental Disease, 198*, 795–801.

Liem, J. H., & Boudewyn, A. C. (1999). Contextualizing the effects of childhood sexual abuse on adult self- and social functioning: an attachment theory perspective. *Child Abuse & Neglect, 23*, 1141–1157.

Linney, Y. M., Murray, R. M., Peters, E. R., MacDonald, A. M., Rijsdijk, F., & Sham, P. C. (2003). A quantitative genetic analysis of schizotypal personality traits. *Psychological Medicine, 33*, 803–816.

Lo, C. C., & Cheng, T. C. (2007). The impact of childhood maltreatment on young adults' substance abuse. *American Journal of Alcohol and Alcohol and Drug Abuse, 33*, 139–146.

Lobbestael, J., Arntz, A., & Bernstein, D. P. (2010). Disentangling the relationship between different types of childhood maltreatment and personality disorders. *Journal of Personality Disorders, 24*, 285–295.

Loftus, E. F. (1993). Desperately seeking memories of the first few years of childhood: the reality of early memories. *Journal of Experimental Psychology: General, 122*, 274–277.

Loftus, E. F., & Ketcham, K. (1994). *The myth of repressed memory*. New York: St Martin's Press.

Lovatt, A., Mason, O., Brett, C., & Peters, E. (2010). Psychotic-like experiences, appraisals, and trauma. *Journal of Nervous and Mental Disease, 198*, 813–819.

Martinez-Taboas, A., Canino, G., Wang, M. Q., Garcia, P., & Bravo, M. (2006). Prevalence and victimization correlates of pathological dissociation in a community sample of youths. *Journal of Traumatic Stress, 19*, 439–448.

Marzillier, S. L., & Steel, C. (2007). Positive schizotypy and trauma-related intrusions. *Journal of Nervous and Mental Disease, 195*, 60–64.

Mason, O., & Claridge, G. (2006). The Oxford-Liverpool Inventory of Feelings and Experiences (O-LIFE): further description and extended norms. *Schizophrenia Research, 82*, 203–211.

Maughan, B. R. M. (1997). Retrospective reporting of childhood adversity: issues in assessing long-term recall. *Journal of Personality Disorders, 11*, 19–33.

Mcfarland C., & Buehler, R. (1998). The impact of negative affect on autobiographical memory: the role of self-focused attention to moods. *Journal of Personality and Social Psychology, 75*, 1424–1440.

Merckelbach, H., & Jelicic, M. (2004). Dissociative symptoms are related to endorsement of vague trauma items. *Comprehensive Psychiatry, 45*, 70–75.

Morgan, C., Reininghaus, U., Fearon, P., Hutchinson, G., Morgan, K., Dazzan, P., ... Craig, T. (2013). Modelling the interplay between childhood and adult adversity in pathways to psychosis: initial evidence from the AESOP study. *Psychological Medicine, 44*, 407–419.

Mullen, P. E., Martin, J. L., Anderson, J. C., Romans, S. E., & Herbison, G. P. (1996). The long-term impact of the physical, emotional, and sexual abuse of children: a community study. *Child Abuse & Neglect, 20*, 7–21.

Myin-Germeys, I., Heins, M., Simons, C., Lataster, T., Delespaul, P., & Krabbendam, L. (2011). Childhood trauma and psychosis: a case-control and case-sibling control comparison across different levels of genetic liability, psychopathology and type of trauma. *Schizophrenia Bulletin, 37*, 58–59.

Mynard, H., & Joseph, S. (1997). Bully/victim problems and their association with Eysenck's personality dimensions in 8 to 13 year-olds. *British Journal of Educational Psychology, 67*, 51–54.

Perkins, S. F. L., & Allen, R. (2006). Childhood physical abuse and differential development of paranormal belief systems. *Journal of Nervous and Mental Disease, 194*, 349–355.

Powers, A. D., Thomas, K. M., Ressler, K. J., & Bradley, B. (2011). The differential effects of child abuse and posttraumatic stress disorder on schizotypal personality disorder. *Comprehensive Psychiatry, 52*, 438–445.

Radford, L., Corral, S., Bradley, C., & Fisher, H. L. (2013). The prevalence and impact of child maltreatment and other types of victimization in the UK: findings from a population survey of caregivers, children and young people and young adults, *Child Abuse & Neglect, 37*, 801–813.

Raine, A., Fung, A. L. C., & Lam, B. Y. H. (2011). Peer victimization partially mediates the schizotypy-aggression relationship in children and adolescents. *Schizophrenia Bulletin, 37*, 937–945.

Rawlings, D., Claridge, G., & Freeman, J. L. (2001). Principal components analysis of the Schizotypal Personality Scale (STA) and the Borderline Personality Scale (STB). *Personality and Individual Differences, 31*, 409–419.

Read, J., Perry, B. D., Moskowitz, A., & Connolly, J. (2001). The contribution of early traumatic events to schizophrenia in some patients: a traumagenic neurodevelopmental model. *Psychiatry, 64*, 319–345.

Robins, L. M., Schoenberg, S. P., Holmes, S. J., Ratcliff, K. S., Benham, A., & Works, J. (1985). Early home environment and retrospective recall: a test for concordance between siblings with and without psychiatric disorders. *American Journal of Orthopsychiatry, 55*, 27–41.

Rorty, M., Yager, J., & Rossotto, E. (1994). Childhood sexual, physical, and psychological abuse in bulimia nervosa. *American Journal of Psychiatry, 151*, 1122–1126.

Rossler, W., Hengartner, M. P., Ajadic-Gross, V., Haker, H., & Angst, J. (2014). Impact of childhood adversity on the onset and course of subclinical psychosis symptoms – results from a 30-year prospective community study. *Schizophrenia Research, 153*, 189–195.

Rossler, W., Riecher-Rossler, A., Angst, J., Murray, R., Gamma, A., Eich, D., . . . Gross V. A. (2007). Psychotic experiences in the general population: a twenty-year prospective community study. *Schizophrenia Research, 92*, 1–14.

Scott, J., Chant, D., Andrews, G., Martin, G., & McGrath, J. (2007). Association between trauma exposure and delusional experiences in a large community-based sample. *British Journal of Psychiatry, 190*, 339–343.

Selten, J. P., & Cantor-Graae, E. (2005). Social defeat: risk factor for schizophrenia? *British Journal of Psychiatry, 187*, 101–102.

Sharpley, M. S., & Peters, E. R. (1999). Ethnicity, class and schizotypy. *Social Psychiatry and Psychiatric Epidemiology, 34*, 507–512.

Sheinbaum, T., Kwapil, R. K., & Barrantes-Vidal, N. (2014). Fearful attachment mediates the association of childhood trauma with schizotypy and psychosis-like experiences. *Psychiatry Research, 220*, 691–693.

Shevlin, M., Dorahy, M., & Adamson, G. (2007). Childhood traumas and hallucinations: an analysis of the National Comorbidity Survey. *Journal of Psychiatric Research, 41*, 222–228.

Simeon, D., Guralnik, O., Schmeidler, J., Sirof, B., & Knutelska, M. (2001). The role of childhood interpersonal trauma in depersonalization disorder. *American Journal of Psychiatry, 158*, 1027–1033.

Sommer, I. E. C., Daalman, K., Rietkerk, T., Diederen, K. M., Bakker, S., Wijkstra, J., . . . Boks, M. P. (2010). Healthy individuals with auditory verbal hallucinations; who are they? Psychiatric assessments of a selected sample of 103 subjects. *Schizophrenia Bulletin, 36*, 633–641.

Steel, C., Marzillier, S., Fearon, P., & Ruddle, A. (2009). Childhood abuse and schizotypal personality. *Social Psychiatry and Psychiatric Epidemiology, 44*, 917–923.

Torgersen, S., Lygren, S., Oien, P. A., Skre, I., Onstad, S., Edvardsen, J., . . . Kringlen, E. (2000). A twin study of personality disorders. *Comprehensive Psychiatry, 41*, 416–425.

Trotta, A., Di Forti, M., Mondelli, V., Dazzan, P., Pariante, C., David, A., . . . Fisher, H.L. (2013). Prevalence of bullying victimisation amongst first-episode psychosis patients and unaffected controls. *Schizophrenia Research, 150*, 169–175.

Tyrka, A. R., Wyche, M. C., Kelly, M. M., Price, L. H., & Carpenter, L. L. (2009). Childhood maltreatment and adult personality disorder symptoms: influence of maltreatment type. *Psychiatry Research, 165*, 281–287.

van Nierop, M., van Os, J., Gunther, N., van Zelst, C., de Graaf, R., ten Have, M., . . . van Winkel, R. (2014). Does social defeat mediate the association between childhood trauma and psychosis? Evidence from the NEMESIS-2 Study. *Acta Psychiatrica Scandinavica, 129*, 467–476.

van Os, J., Rutten, B. P., & Poulton, R. (2008). Gene-enviroment interactions in schizophrenia: review of epidemiological findings and future directions. *Schizophrenia Bulletin, 34*, 1066–1082.

Varese, F., Smeets, F., Drukker, M., Lieverse, R., Lataster, T., Viechtbauer, W., Read., van Os, J., . . . Bentall, R. P. (2012). Childhood adversities increase the risk of psychosis: a meta-analysis of patient-control, prospective- and cross-sectional cohort studies. *Schizophrenia Bulletin, 38*, 661–671.

Vollema, M. G., & Vandenbosch, R. J. (1995). The multidimensionality of schizotypy. *Schizophrenia Bulletin, 21*, 19–31.

Walker, E. F., & Diforio, D. (1997). Schizophrenia: a neural diathesis-stress model. *Psychological Review, 104*, 667–685.

Waxman, R., Fenton, M. C., Skodol, A. E., Grant, B. F. & Hasin, D. (2014). Childhood maltreatment and personality disorders in the USA: specificity of effects and the impact of gender. *Personality and Mental Health, 8*, 30–41.

Whitfield, C. L., Dube, S. R., Felitti, V. J., & Anda, R. F. (2005). Adverse childhood experiences and hallucinations. *Child Abuse & Neglect, 29*, 797–810.

Widom, C. S., and Shepard, R. L. (1996). Accuracy of adult recollections of childhood victimization: Part 1. Childhood physical abuse. *Psychological Assessment, 8*, 412–421.

Williams, L. M. (1994). Recall of childhood trauma: a prospective study of women's memories of child sexual abuse. *Journal of Consulting and Clinical Psychology, 62*, 1167–1176.

Yarrow, M. R., Campbell, J. D., & Burton, R. V. (1970). Recollections of childhood. A study of the retrospective method. *Monographs of the Society for Research in Child Development, 35*, 1–83.

7 Mechanisms mediating the pathway from environmental adversity to psychosis proneness

Tamara Sheinbaum and Neus Barrantes-Vidal

Introduction

A fast-growing field of research investigating the effects of psychosocial adversity on the brain is challenging the view that the endophenotypic abnormalities found in schizotypy and schizotypal personality disorder (SPD) only derive from genetic and biological insults – for instance, early life maltreatment impairs brain structure and physiology (e.g. Teicher, Anderson, Ohashi, & Polcari, 2013). Notably, animal models (e.g. of maternal separation) suggest that these exposures cause brain and behavioural phenotypes that are analagous to those observed in individuals with schizophrenia (Brown, 2011).

Epidemiological research has recently shown an association of psychosocial factors both at macro (i.e. social) and micro (i.e. personal) environmental levels with clinical and non-clinical psychosis, particularly for the dimension of reality distortion (reviews in Bentall & Fernyhough, 2008; Brown, 2011). Some studies are conflicting, but there is an increasing consensus that psychosocial adversity is not merely a trigger of a genetically based "psychosis proneness", but rather a co-participating factor in the make-up of the diathesis to psychosis. Velikonja, Mason, & Fisher (Chapter 6 in this volume) have reviewed in depth the relation of schizotypy with maltreatment, parental loss and bullying. In this chapter, we will first provide a brief overview of the array of candidate psychosocial factors that have been associated with schizotypy, and then focus on the mediating mechanisms that have received most attention in accounting for the adversity–schizotypy connection.

Macro-environmental risk factors

Urbanicity

An increasing body of evidence indicates that early exposure to an urban environment is associated with both subclinical and clinical psychosis (Krabbendam & van Os, 2005). Studies have demonstrated a dose-response effect of urbanicity on psychotic-like experiences (PLEs) (van Os, Hanssen,

Bijl, & Vollebergh, 2001) and that the persistence of PLEs is greater among those living in an urban as opposed to a rural area (Spauwen, Krabbendam, Lieb, Wittchen, & van Os, 2006).

Poverty

Poverty seems to be more strongly related to psychosis than to other psychiatric conditions (Read, 2010). A Swiss general population survey that assessed all *DSM-IV* (American Psychiatric Association, 2000) personality disorders found that poverty was uniquely associated with SPD ratings (Hengartner, Ajdacic-Gross, Rodgers, Müller, & Rössler, 2013). Additionally, other general population studies have provided evidence that socio-economic disadvantage (variously defined) is associated with a greater likelihood of reporting PLEs (e.g. Saha, Scott, Varghese, & McGrath, 2013).

Minority status

Evidence suggests that both first- and second-generation immigrants have an increased risk for developing psychosis (Bourque, van der Ven, & Malla, 2011), and that migrant status is associated with a greater prevalence of PLEs (van Os, Linscott, Myin-Germeys, Delespaul, & Krabbendam, 2009). According to van Os (2012), several pieces of evidence (including the fact that the risk for psychosis persists into the second generation and is also found in ethnic minorities without recent history of migration) suggest that it is not migration in itself that elevates psychosis proneness, but rather certain features of the greater social context in the host country, particularly the situation of being in a minority group position. In this respect, research examining the rates of psychotic disorders among ethnic minority individuals has shown that the rates increase as the proportion of the own ethnic group in the neighbourhood of residence decreases (e.g. Boydell et al., 2001). Although studies focusing on ethnic density and psychosis proneness are scarce, a nationally representative study in the UK indicated that, as a whole, ethnic minorities living in a lower own-group density neighbourhood were more likely to endorse PLEs (Das-Munshi et al., 2012).

Micro-environmental risk factors

Family environment

There is evidence linking family environment variables, such as parental communication deviance and expressed emotion, with the risk and course of psychotic disorders. Certain aspects of the family milieu have been associated with PLEs. For example, children with psychotic symptoms are more likely to have mothers with negative expressed emotion, but not decreased warmth (Polanczyk et al., 2010), and individuals high on social anhedonia report less cohesive and more conflictive family environments than controls (Blanchard, Collins, Aghevli, Leung, & Cohen, 2011).

Childhood interpersonal adversity: abuse and neglect, bullying, parental separation

Childhood interpersonal adversity shows associations with clinical and non-clinical psychotic phenomena (e.g. Varese et al., 2012). Different types of abuse and/or neglect have been linked to PLEs and to both the positive and negative dimensions of schizotypy, with evidence appearing to be stronger for the positive dimension (see Velikonja et al., this volume). Bullying has also been associated with PLEs. For example, a recent prospective study found that, after controlling for a range of potential confounders, experiences of bullying in childhood were associated with PLEs at age 18 years (Wolke, Lereya, Fisher, Lewis, & Zammit, 2013). Additionally, the duration of early maternal separation has been associated with elevated levels of SPD symptoms later in life in children with an angry temperament (Anglin, Cohen, & Chen, 2008).

Mediating mechanisms

Overall, the meta-analytic evidence available for psychosis and the systematic review conducted in schizotypy by Velikonja et al. (this volume) seems to indicate that there is a robust association between adversity and non-clinical and clinical psychosis. However, such *statistical association* does not necessarily involve *causation*, a demonstration that remains a critical challenge in the field. The accumulating evidence, though, favours the interpretation of a causal link: the magnitude of the association in psychosis is considerable (odds ratio [OR] = 2.8) and actually comparable to that of most genetic risk factors; furthermore, several population studies indicate a dose-response relationship (Varese et al., 2012).

A critical issue is whether adversity is the cause *or* the consequence of schizotypy. Although prospective studies have shown that the risk factor (adversity) temporally precedes the outcome (PLEs or psychosis), there is still the possibility that schizotypy or PLEs might be present before the adversity and increase the likelihood of trauma exposure, what is known as reverse causation. A likely possibility would be a complex scenario of bidirectional effects. In this regard, a prospective population sample study with early adolescents showed that trauma predicted PLEs over time and vice versa and, importantly, that trauma predicted new incident PLEs even when controlling for the presence of baseline PLEs (Kelleher et al., 2013). Another possible, non-mutually exclusive, explanation for the association between trauma and schizotypy might be genetic confounding or gene-environment correlation, which proposes that a genetic diathesis is responsible for both schizotypy traits and increased probability of trauma exposure, meaning that trauma does not participate in the genesis of schizotypy (van Winkel, van Nierop, Myin-Germeys, & van Os, 2013). This seems to be particularly relevant when considering the potentially causal role of adversity in the development of schizotypy, probably even more so than when considering psychosis as an outcome; given the trait-like nature of schizotypy features, these would be expected to be present early in life (e.g. social awkwardness, cognitive peculiarities) and to condition the odds of exposure to a differential treatment in the family and social environment. The investigation of this possibility is challenging; however, the fact that the association between trauma and PLEs remains significant when controlling for familial liability to psychosis seems to support that exposure to trauma in itself further enhances psychosis proneness, suggesting a partial genetic mediation of environmental effects (van Winkel et al., 2013).

Another critical point for assuming causality is the existence of plausible mechanisms to account for the statistical association. Nowadays there are promising biological and psychosocial models, even though empirical research testing the validity of candidate mediators is still scarce. Some of these models favour the search for unifying mechanisms underlying the wide array of disparate psychosocial risk factors. They assume that psychosocial factors present in very different forms but eventually converge on exerting their pathogenic effect through dysregulation of the stress-regulating systems, which in turn hits both unspecific and schizotypy-relevant psychobiological mechanisms – such as dopamine dysregulation (e.g. Collip, Myin-Germeys, & van Os, 2008). Meanwhile, other models focus on the specific impact that diverse adversity exposures may have. For instance, Bentall, Wickham, Shevlin, and Varese (2012) have argued that different forms of adversity may exert differential influences upon cognitive and emotional processes and, as such, a certain degree of symptom specificity would be expected. They suggest that disrupted attachment and experiences of victimisation are more likely to give rise to paranoid thinking, whereas severe early-life trauma, particularly sexual abuse, is more likely to lead to hallucinatory experiences. Indeed, their study found that, once the co-occurrence of paranoia and hallucinations had been controlled for, sexual abuse was specifically associated with hallucinatory experiences, whereas institutional care (as a proxy for attachment disruptions) was associated with paranoia. It is likely that both approaches are necessary to satisfactorily account for both the unspecific effects of adversity on cognitive and emotional development, and the relatively specific impact of certain experiences in shaping particular traits or yielding the need for certain maladaptive strategies that pave the risk for psychosis. The remainder of this section will present a summary of such models.

Traumagenic neurodevelopment and sensitisation hypotheses

The accumulating knowledge of the neurobiology of childhood trauma, and the appreciation of its significant overlap with neurochemical and neuroanatomical impairments in schizophrenia, have fuelled the suggestion of a causal role of childhood adversity in the development of spectrum disorders. Studies of early trauma have shown that stress exposure during critical developmental stages may result in structural and functional changes within the brain and a lowered threshold for neurobiological stress responses (e.g. Teicher et al., 2003). The traumagenic neurodevelopmental model of psychosis draws on these and other research findings, and postulates that the increased stress sensitivity found in people with psychotic disorders may result from the neurodevelopmental brain changes caused by prolonged or severe early-life adversity exposure (Read, Fosse, Moskowitz, & Perry, 2014). Thus, vulnerability to spectrum disorders could be acquired through developmental experience and not only inherited; both acquired (biological and psychosocial) and genetic risks would interact to potentiate the vulnerability towards psychotic features. Support for this model comes from evidence of shared biological alterations between childhood trauma and psychosis (e.g. over-reactivity of the hypothalamic-pituitary-adrenal (HPA) axis, hippocampal damage, alterations in dopaminergic and glucocorticoid release), and animal and human studies indicating that severe early social adversity may trigger long-term disturbances of the HPA system and an increased dopaminergic response to stress (Read et al., 2014).

There is increasing acceptance that these disparate neurobiological factors related to psychosocial adversity exposure may act via a final common pathway of impaired stress-regulation mechanisms that would sensitise the dopaminergic system (e.g. van Winkel, Stefanis, & Myin-Germeys, 2008). Such sensitisation would entail an exaggerated dopaminergic response in advance of exposure to subsequent environmental stressors. Some findings at the behavioural level are compatible with the notion of increased stress sensitivity in individuals exposed to early trauma. Using experience sampling methodology (ESM: a diary method to assess symptoms, thoughts, emotions and context in the flow of daily life), Barrantes-Vidal et al. (unpublished findings) found that childhood trauma and daily-life momentary stress interacted to predict paranoid ideation (but not PLEs) in everyday life in non-clinical young adults. Furthermore, consistent with the hypothesis that stress-sensitivity would be a relevant pathway specifically for reality distortion, Barrantes-Vidal, Chun, Myin-Germeys, and Kwapil (2013) found that daily-life stressful situations and social stress were associated with momentary PLEs and paranoia for those high in positive schizotypy, and that the experience of stress temporally preceded the onset of PLEs only for those with high positive schizotypy (whereas stress preceded the onset of paranoid symptoms in general).

The mesolimbic dopaminergic system is critical in the attribution of salience, a process whereby thoughts and events are motivationally invested and influence goal-directed behaviour given their association with punishment or reward (Berridge & Robinson, 1998). Hyperdopaminergia, which has long been linked to reality distortion, might alter the attribution of emotional or incentive salience to internal representations and external stimuli at a mind level, which would lead to cognitive and perceptual oddities (Kapur, 2003). Also, the increased levels of tonic mesolimbic dopamine might increase the noise in the reward system, 'drowning out' dopaminergic signals associated with stimuli indicating reward, resulting in a reduced motivational drive and thus in the negative features of withdrawal and avolition (Howes & Kapur, 2009; Roiser et al., 2009). On the other hand, Raine (2006) suggests that physical and emotional neglect may result in environmental deprivation, which is also known to affect brain development (e.g. Teicher et al., 2013).

The social defeat hypothesis

The social defeat (SD) hypothesis holds that a wide range of environmental factors share a common feature of exclusion from the majority group – that is, a subordinate or outsider position – and induce decreased self-value (Selten, van der Ven, Rutten, & Cantor-Graae, 2013). Drawing on findings from animal studies indicating that SD stress (e.g. repeated attacks of a stronger intruding animal) induce dopaminergic abnormalities, Selten et al. suggested that enduring exposure to SD might induce sensitisation of the mesolimbic dopaminergic system, thereby resulting in a greater vulnerability for developing psychosis. The authors propose that SD may serve as a unifying explanatory mechanism linking some of the established psychosocial risk factors with the psychosis phenotype. A recent review concluded that the evidence that a state of SD contributes to dopamine dysregulation in humans is still scarce, but that the evidence for SD as a 'common denominator' of the risk-conferring effects of certain psychosocial factors supports a causal effect, especially for migrant status and childhood trauma (Selten et al., 2013). Related to SD is the concept of social capital, which has been associated with incidence of psychotic disorders (Brown, 2011), but whether social capital mediates the effects of macro-environmental factors on schizotypy and psychosis has been scarcely investigated.

In relation to the non-clinical phenotype, there is preliminary evidence consistent with the SD hypothesis. Das-Munshi et al. (2012) found that, in general, ethnic minorities residing in neighbourhoods of lower own-group density were more likely to report social adversity factors such as increased discrimination and decreased practical social support – both regarded as potential markers of SD according to Selten et al. (2013), which in turn were related to endorsement of PLEs. In addition, a Dutch general population study found that SD (operationalised as feelings of worthlessness, hopelessness and self-devaluation), as well as affective dysregulation, mediated the association between childhood trauma and PLEs (van Nierop et al., 2013). Interestingly, SD uniquely explained the association between trauma and symptoms in the subgroup of individuals with psychotic disorder, suggesting that SD may be more crucially involved in the trajectory leading to core clinical psychosis (van Nierop et al., 2013).

Psychological mechanisms

Negative cognitive schemas, insecure attachment styles and impaired social cognition are interrelated psychological constructs that have been proposed to be involved in the developmental trajectory from childhood adversity to psychotic phenomena. The literature in this area is at a nascent stage and, therefore, the conceptual boundaries between these constructs, as well as the incremental value that each one can offer to our understanding of the development of schizotypy, are not yet clear and require further elucidation.

Negative cognitive schemas

Cognitive accounts of psychosis implicate enduring negative schemas of oneself (e.g. as worthless or vulnerable) and others (e.g. as untrustworthy or devious) in the pathway from adversity to positive symptoms (e.g. Garety, Bebbington, Fowler, Freeman, & Kuipers, 2007). Such negative schemas built upon negative interpersonal experiences are thought to convey vulnerability to psychotic features by shaping (or biasing) the subsequent interpretation of anomalous or unusual experiences in a schema-consistent manner. In support of the notion that negative schemas are specifically relevant to positive psychotic phenomena, Barrantes-Vidal et al. (2013) showed that increased negative self- and other-schemas were associated with positive, but not negative, psychometric schizotypy.

It has been proposed that negative schematic beliefs may be particularly involved in the pathway to paranoia following childhood adversity, and a few cross-sectional studies have tested this prediction in non-clinical samples. Fisher, Appiah-Kusi, and Grant (2012) found that negative self-schemas and anxiety levels were mediators of the association of physical or emotional abuse with paranoia. Ashford, Ashcroft, and Maguire (2012) tested potential mediators of an association between forms of bullying and paranoia. They found that the association of indirect aggression with paranoia was mediated by negative self-schemas and depression, whereas the association of direct verbal aggression with paranoia was mediated by negative other-schemas. The authors reasoned that different forms of aggression (i.e. direct/overt versus indirect/covert) might be differentially attributed to the self and others and thereby lead to specific negative beliefs. The study by Freeman and Fowler (2009) did not find support for mediation by negative self-schemas (only anxiety emerged as a mediator); this study did not include negative other-schemas and the measure of trauma was not restricted to childhood. It may be that negative self- and other-schemas operate differently as a function of type or timing of trauma. Although not yet conclusive, the evidence appears to support cognitive models regarding the interplay between negative schemas and emotional factors in the development of paranoid thinking.

Insecure attachment

Attachment theory stands as an integrative framework of several of the hypothesised psychological mechanisms through which early interpersonal adversity may confer risk for developing schizotypy and psychosis (Read & Gumley, 2008). The theory suggests that early caregiving experiences provide the building blocks for the formation of cognitive/affective representations of the self and others (or 'internal working models') and characteristic affect regulation strategies – which are reflected in a person's attachment style (Mikulincer & Shaver, 2007). Individual differences in attachment style have been broadly conceptualised as being of a secure or insecure nature, and different forms of attachment insecurity have been identified.

Previous research has provided support for an association of insecure attachment styles with positive and negative features across the psychosis continuum (Korver-Nieberg, Berry, Meijer, & de Haan, 2013; Sheinbaum, Bedoya, Ros-Morente, Kwapil, & Barrantes-Vidal, 2013); however, the mediating effect of insecure attachment in the association of trauma with the psychosis phenotype has been scarcely investigated. Preliminary evidence comes from a cross-sectional study from our group in which fearful attachment, a style characterised by negative self and other views as well as high anxiety and avoidance in relationships, mediated the association of physical/emotional childhood trauma with positive and negative schizotypy, suspiciousness and PLEs (Sheinbaum, Kwapil, & Barrantes-Vidal, 2014). Current evidence suggests that insecure attachment may be more strongly linked to paranoia than to other psychotic traits. Although this may be the case, our findings would seem to suggest that, if relational adversity is internalised in the form of fearful attachment, this might contribute nonspecifically to psychosis proneness. Insecure attachment as a mediating mechanism requires replication and should be investigated in the context of longitudinal research designs. In addition, it is unclear to what extent it may act as a mediating and/or moderating factor in the face of adversity.

Social cognition

Social cognition is a multifaceted concept referring to a range of mental operations that are important in navigating social interactions, including, among others, attributional processes and mentalising/Theory of Mind (ToM) skills. As regards attributional processes, it has been suggested that adverse experiences could result in a tendency to appraise negative experiences as externally caused (an external attributional style), potentially facilitating positive symptoms (Garety et al., 2007). Bentall and Fernyhough (2008) proposed a model of paranoia in which experiences of victimisation (particularly in insecurely attached people) would lead to diminished self-esteem and increased likelihood of externalising explanatory biases, thereby resulting in greater social threat anticipation and consequently paranoid thinking. The authors suggest that diminished ToM capacities may contribute to an external explanatory style, because this would further complicate attributing negative actions of other people to situational factors. In the non-clinical domain, evidence for the role of external attributions comes from a recent prospective study in the UK that measured the related construct of external locus of control (LoC). This study found that external LoC (as well as depression, anxiety and low self-esteem) mediated the pathway from three forms of childhood adversity (bullying, harsh parenting and domestic violence) to PLEs (Fisher et al., 2013).

As regards mentalising, we are not aware of research examining its mediating effects in the link between adversity and schizotypy. It has been suggested, however, that exposure to early adversity/deprivation could result in mentalising deficits that in turn would confer risk for psychotic symptoms (van Os, Kenis, & Rutten, 2010). This is supported by independent strands of work showing an association between childhood maltreatment and diminished ToM abilities (e.g. Pears & Fisher, 2005), and between diminished ToM abilities and schizotypy (e.g. Morrison, Brown, & Cohen, 2013). Given that the capacity for mentalising is thought to develop within the context of early attachment relationships (Fonagy & Target, 2006), the interplay between attachment and mentalisation, and how this has an impact on schizotypy, looks to be a fruitful avenue for future investigation.

Dissociation

Dissociation involves a disruption in certain mental functions that are usually integrated, such as memory, identity and consciousness. Early traumatic experiences have been consistently linked to dissociation (Carlson, Yates, & Sroufe, 2009) and research has shown that dissociation is associated with psychotic symptoms, particularly hallucinations (Moskowitz & Corstens, 2007) and schizotypy (Moskowitz, Barker-Collo, & Ellson, 2005). It has been proposed that dissociative tendencies that result from overwhelming negative experiences could be involved in the pathway to hallucinatory experiences (e.g. Moskowitz & Corstens, 2007).

In a sample of individuals with psychosis, Perona-Garcelán et al. (2012) found that dissociation (specifically depersonalisation) mediated the link between childhood trauma and hallucinations, but not the link between trauma and delusions. Similarly, Varese, Barkus, and Bentall (2012) showed that the association of childhood trauma with hallucination proneness was mediated by dissociation in both a subgroup of people with psychotic disorders and in the aggregated sample comprising clinical and non-clinical participants. In a sample of university students, Perona-Garcelán et al. (2014) reported that dissociative experiences of depersonalisation and absorption mediated the link between childhood trauma and hallucination proneness. Taken together, the evidence seems to support a role of dissociative tendencies in the route to hallucinatory experiences. It will be the task of longitudinal studies to provide clues as to whether and how dissociative tendencies, which may begin as an adaptive or protective response to trauma, interact with other vulnerabilities (such as source-monitoring deficits) in leading to hallucinatory experiences.

Conclusions and future directions

The present chapter has provided an overview of some of the environmental factors that have been associated with schizotypy as well as some of the plausible mechanisms that may account for such observed associations. The accumulating work on these risk factors and mediators seems to support the suggested aetiological continuity between schizotypy and schizophrenia. However, it should be highlighted that, in most cases, the empirical evidence regarding mediators remains scarce (and is mostly cross-sectional) and therefore cannot yet provide conclusive answers as to whether the mechanisms reviewed here contribute to explaining the putative causal links.

It should be noted that, although each of the potential mediators has been presented separately, the processes whereby environmental exposures contribute to psychosis proneness are likely to be mediated by multiple mechanisms acting at different levels and, in many cases, interacting with each other. As such, the field has much to gain by investigating the dynamic interplay of these mechanisms from a developmental psychopathology framework. This would provide insights into the trajectories through which potentially initiating conditions (e.g. trauma) may move the individual along a path of atypical biological, psychological and/or social development that eventually leads to schizotypal features. Equally, this would allow for the appreciation of the processes underpinning resilient adaptation over the life course.

Another important issue that merits attention is that of specificity, because some of the environmental factors reviewed in this chapter, as well as the potential mediators, are not specific to schizotypy. Although this may be considered a downside of this line of enquiry, the lack of narrowly defined pathways between specific risk factors, mechanisms and phenotypes in the realm of psychology and psychiatry seems to be the norm rather than the exception. It is likely that future research conducted from a broader conceptualisation of the continuity from personality to psychopathology and across seemingly distinct disorders may be better able to delineate the commonalities and specificities of environmental factors.

A major challenge in this field concerns the fact that environmental exposures do not necessarily lead to schizotypal traits or psychosis, which suggests that they are neither necessary nor sufficient causes of psychosis proneness. Current research aims at identifying the plethora of factors contributing to determine the outcome of such exposures. Psychosocial factors, such as the developmental timing of the exposure, severity, duration, presence of support and qualitative aspects of the trauma (e.g. intra- versus extra-familial abuse), are likely to greatly influence the impact of adversity (Read et al., 2014). In addition, genetic vulnerability to psychosis may be a critical moderating factor in shaping whether these exposures translate into a schizotypy phenotype.

Genetic variation entails differences in biological functionality that may be problematic or advantageous in particular environments; gene–environment interaction can enable a combined effect that is greater than the sum of its parts (van Winkel et al., 2010). So far very few studies have tested gene–environment interaction in schizotypy, particularly with molecular studies. For instance, Savitz, van der Merwe, Newman, Stein, & Ramesar (2010) reported that the COMT Val allele was associated with positive schizotypy only in individuals exposed to high levels of childhood trauma, suggesting that genetically driven variation in COMT-Val1 may interact with trauma in the causal pathway to schizotypal traits. More recently, epigenetic mechanisms have been proposed as another pathway by which gene-environment interaction may occur. Epigenetics refers to the reversible regulation of various genomic functions by means of changes in DNA methylation and chromatin structure, which take place independently of DNA sequence (van Winkel et al., 2013). Epigenetic mechanisms might mediate environmental effects on gene function by 'switching' on and off gene transcription throughout development. Many enzymatic, hormonal and second-messenger cascades connect the external environment with the chromatin to modulate gene activity in front of psychosocial exposures. Therefore, epigenetic regulation of DNA activity in response to changes or pathogens in the environment constitutes a mechanism for rapid genome adaptations to the environment; at the same time, it also entails that adverse environments can have an adverse impact on the genome by altering epigenetic states that can impair biological functions (Svrakic, Zorumski, Svrakic, Zwir, & Cloninger, 2013).

Another line of endeavour is the refinement of environmental measures. Currently, there is a growing focus on the micro-environment of real life by means of momentary assessment techniques, such as ESM. The repeated assessment of the person–environment interplay unravels dynamic processes and variability over time, as well as identifying contextual determinants and patterns of reactivity of experiences. Therefore, this approach is a valuable addition to conventional cross-sectional measurements (Myin-Germeys et al., 2009), and it has already been shown that it is a feasible method to study the phenomenology and environmental stress-reactivity dynamics of the schizotypy dimensions (Barrantes-Vidal, Gross et al., 2013). Furthermore, the mixed nomothetic and idiographic nature of ESM can empower the challenging empirical study of subjective phenomenology. It would be very useful to ascertain what specific qualities of environmental stressors, beyond the recollection of their occurrence, may be specifically relevant for or have causal efficiency in schizotypy. For instance, the appraisal of intentionality in interpersonal trauma seems to be a critical pathogenic element, but it is still poorly understood how this element of subjective meaning translates into the fuelling of, for instance, paranoid attributions. In this sense, the richness of intense idiographic and qualitative studies would probably have more explanatory power than large-scale quantitative studies to examine such a meaning system, but these approaches have been traditionally overlooked as methodologically weak and unreliable, even if they could offer good explanations. (Barrantes-Vidal, 2013). Finally, ESM is beginning to prove a useful tool in the field of gene-environment interaction studies. Unlike retrospective measures of distal exposures, it prospectively collects repeated measures of proximal environmental factors; this allows the detection of subtle and varied common environmental pathogens, their possible cumulative effects, and chains of effects rather than the impact of a single factor in one exposure (Myin-Germeys et al., 2009). These features should increase the chances of our understanding how genes amplify the likelihood of displaying specific psychological responses to the environment.

Acknowledgements

N. Barrantes-Vidal is supported by the ICREA Acadèmia Research Award (Institució Catalana de Recerca i Estudis Avançats), Suport als Grups de Recerca (2009SGR672), La Marató de TV3 (091110) and Ministerio de Economía y Competitividad (PSI2011-30321-C02-01). T. Sheinbaum is supported by a fellowship from CONACYT, Mexico (212581).

References

American Psychiatric Association. (2000). *Diagnostic and statistical manual of mental disorders (DSM-IV)* (4th ed., rev.). Washington, DC: Author.

Anglin, D. M., Cohen, P. R., & Chen, H. (2008). Duration of early maternal separation and prediction of schizotypal symptoms from early adolescence to midlife. *Schizophrenia Research, 103,* 143–150.

Ashford, C. D., Ashcroft, K., & Maguire, N. (2012). Emotions, traits and negative beliefs as possible mediators in the relationship between childhood experiences of being bullied and paranoid thinking in a non-clinical sample. *Journal of Experimental Psychopathology, 3,* 624–638.

Barrantes-Vidal, N. (2013). Trauma and psychosis: is it easier to study quarks than subjective meaning? *Acta Psychiatrica Scandinavica.* doi: 10.1111/acps.12218

Barrantes-Vidal, N., Chun, C., Myin-Germeys, I., & Kwapil, T. R. (2013). Psychometric schizotypy predicts psychotic-like, paranoid, and negative symptoms in daily life. *Journal of Abnormal Psychology, 122,* 1077–1087.

Barrantes-Vidal, N., Gross, G. M., Sheinbaum, T., Mitjavila, M., Ballespí, S., & Kwapil, T. R. (2013). Positive and negative schizotypy are associated with prodromal and schizophrenia-spectrum symptoms. *Schizophrenia Research, 145,* 50–55.

Bentall, R. P., & Fernyhough, C. (2008). Social predictors of psychotic experiences: specificity and psychological mechanisms. *Schizophrenia Bulletin, 34,* 1012–1020.

Bentall, R. P., Wickham, S., Shevlin, M., & Varese, F. (2012). Do specific early-life adversities lead to specific symptoms of psychosis? A study from the 2007 Adult Psychiatric Morbidity Survey. *Schizophrenia Bulletin, 38,* 734–740.

Berridge, K. C, & Robinson, T. E. (1998). What is the role of dopamine in reward: hedonic impact, reward learning, or incentive salience? *Brain Research Reviews, 28,* 309–369.

Blanchard, J. J., Collins, L. M., Aghevli, M., Leung, W. W., & Cohen, A. S. (2011). Social anhedonia and schizotypy in a community sample: The Maryland Longitudinal Study of Schizotypy. *Schizophrenia Bulletin, 37,* 587–602.

Bourque, F., van der Ven, E., & Malla, A. (2011). A meta-analysis of the risk for psychotic disorders among first- and second-generation immigrants. *Psychological Medicine, 41,* 897–910.

Boydell, J., van Os, J., McKenzie, K., Allardyce, J., Goel, R., McCreadie, R.G., & Murray, R. M. (2001). Incidence of schizophrenia in ethnic minorities in London: ecological study into interactions with environment. *British Medical Journal, 323,* 1336–1338.

Brown, A. S. (2011). The environment and susceptibility to schizophrenia. *Progress in Neurobiology, 93,* 23–58.

Carlson, E. A., Yates, T. M., & Sroufe, L. A. (2009). Dissociation and development of the self. In P. F. Dell, & J. A. O'Neil (Eds.), *Dissociation and the dissociative disorders: DSM-V and beyond* (pp. 39–52). New York: Routledge.

Collip, D., Myin-Germeys, I., & van Os, J. (2008). Does the concept of 'sensitization' provide a plausible mechanism for the putative link between the environment and schizophrenia? *Schizophrenia Bulletin, 34,* 220–225.

Das-Munshi, J., Bécares, L, Boydell, J. E., Dewey, M. E., Morgan, C., Stansfeld, S. A., & Prince, M. J. (2012). Ethnic density as a buffer for psychotic experiences: findings from a national survey (EMPIRIC). *British Journal of Psychiatry, 201,* 282–290.

Fisher, H. L., Appiah-Kusi, E., & Grant, C. (2012). Anxiety and negative self-schemas mediate the association between childhood maltreatment and paranoia. *Psychiatry Research, 196,* 323–324.

Fisher, H. L, Schreier, A., Zammit, S., Maughan, B., Munafò, M. R., Lewis, G., & Wolke, D. (2013). Pathways between childhood victimization and psychosis-like symptoms in the ALSPAC birth cohort. *Schizophrenia Bulletin, 39,* 1045–1055.

Fonagy, P., & Target, M. (2006). The mentalization-focused approach to self pathology. *Journal of Personality Disorders, 20,* 544–576.

Freeman, D., & Fowler, D. (2009). Routes to psychotic symptoms: trauma, anxiety and psychosis-like experiences. *Psychiatry Research, 169,* 107–112.

Garety, P. A., Bebbington, P., Fowler, D., Freeman, D., & Kuipers, E. (2007). Implications for neurobiological research of cognitive models of psychosis: a theoretical paper. *Psychological Medicine, 37,* 1377–1391.

Hengartner, M.P., Ajdacic-Gross, V., Rodgers, S., Müller, M., & Rössler, W. (2013). Childhood adversity in association with personality disorder dimensions: new findings in an old debate. *European Psychiatry, 28,* 476–482.

Howes, O.D., & Kapur, S. (2009). The dopamine hypothesis of schizophrenia: version III – the final common pathway. *Schizophrenia Bulletin, 35,* 549–562.

Kapur, S. (2003). Psychosis as a state of aberrant salience: a framework linking biology, phenomenology, and pharmacology in schizophrenia. *American Journal of Psychiatry, 160,* 13–23.

Kelleher, I., Keeley, H., Corcoran, P., Ramsay, H., Wasserman, C., Carli, V., . . . Cannon, M. (2013). Childhood trauma and psychosis in a prospective cohort study: cause, effect, and directionality. *American Journal of Psychiatry, 170,* 734–741.

Korver-Nieberg, N., Berry, K., Meijer, C. J., & de Haan, L. (2013). Adult attachment and psychotic phenomenology in clinical and non-clinical samples: a systematic review. *Psychology and Psychotherapy: Theory, Research and Practice.* doi: 10.1111/papt.12010

Krabbendam, L., & van Os, J. (2005). Schizophrenia and urbanicity: a major environmental influence – conditional on genetic risk. *Schizophrenia Bulletin, 31,* 795–799.

Mikulincer, M., & Shaver, P. R. (2007). *Attachment in adulthood: Structure, dynamics, and change.* New York: Guilford Press.

Morrison, S. C., Brown, L. A., & Cohen, A. S. (2013). A multidimensional assessment of social cognition in psychometrically defined schizotypy. *Psychiatry Research, 210,* 1014–1019.

Moskowitz, A., & Corstens, D. (2007). Auditory hallucinations: psychotic symptom or dissociative experience? *Journal of Psychological Trauma, 6,* 35–63.

Moskowitz, A., Barker-Collo, S., & Ellson, L. (2005). Replication of dissociation-psychosis link in New Zealand students and inmates. *Journal of Nervous and Mental Disease, 193,* 722–727.

Myin-Germeys, I., Ooschort, M., Collip, D., Lataster, J., Delespaul, P., & van Os, J. (2009). Experience sampling research in psychopathology: opening the black box of daily life. *Psychological Medicine, 39,* 1533–1547.

Pears, K. C., & Fisher, P. A. (2005). Emotion understanding and theory of mind among maltreated children in foster care: evidence of deficits. *Development and Psychopathology, 17,* 47–65.

Perona-Garcelán, S., Carrascoso-López, F., García-Montes, J. M., Ductor-Recuerda, M. J., López-Jiménez, A. M., Vallina-Fernández, O., . . . Gómez-Gómez, M. T. (2012). Dissociative experiences as mediators between childhood trauma and auditory hallucinations. *Journal of Traumatic Stress, 25,* 323–329.

Perona-Garcelán, S., García-Montes, J. M., Rodríguez-Testal, J. F., López-Jiménez, A. M., Ruiz-Veguilla, M., Ductor-Recuerda, M. J., . . .Pérez-Álvarez, M. (2014). Relationship between childhood trauma, mindfulness, and dissociation in subjects with and without hallucination proneness. *Journal of Trauma & Dissociation, 15,* 35–51.

Polanczyk, G., Moffitt, T. E., Arseneault, L., Cannon, M., Ambler, A., Keefe, R. S. E, & Caspi, A. (2010). Etiological and clinical features of childhood psychotic symptoms: results from a birth cohort. *Archives of General Psychiatry, 67,* 328–338.

Raine, A. (2006). Schizotypal personality: neurodevelopmental and psychosocial trajectories. *Annual Review of Clinical Psychology, 2,* 291–326.

Read, J. (2010). Can poverty drive you mad? 'Schizophrenia', socio-economic status and the case for primary prevention. *New Zealand Journal of Psychology, 39,* 7–19.

Read, J., & Gumley, A. (2008). Can attachment theory help explain the relationship between childhood adversity and psychosis? *Attachment: New Directions in Psychotherapy and Relational Psychoanalysis, 2,* 1–35.

Read, J., Fosse, R., Moskowitz, A., & Perry, B. (2014). The traumagenic neurodevelopmental model of psychosis revisited. *Neuropsychiatry, 4,* 65–79.

Roiser, J. P., Stephan, K. E., den Ouden, H. E., Barnes, T. R., Friston, K. J., & Joyce, E. M. (2009). Do patients with schizophrenia exhibit aberrant salience? *Psychological Medicine, 39*, 199–209.

Saha, S., Scott, J. G., Varghese, D., & McGrath, J. J. (2013). Socio-economic disadvantage and delusional-like experiences: a nationwide population-based study. *European Psychiatry, 28*, 59–63.

Savitz, J., van der Merwe, L., Newman, T. K., Stein, D. J., & Ramesar, R. (2010). Catechol-o-methyltransferase genotype and childhood trauma may interact to impact schizotypal personality traits. *Behavior genetics, 40*(3), 415–423.

Selten, J. P., van der Ven, E., Rutten, B. P. F., & Cantor-Graae, E. (2013). The social defeat hypothesis of schizophrenia: an update. *Schizophrenia Bulletin, 39*, 1180–1186.

Sheinbaum, T., Kwapil, T. R., & Barrantes-Vidal, N. (2014). Fearful attachment mediates the association of childhood trauma with schizotypy and psychotic-like experiences. *Psychiatry Research, 220*(1–2), 691–193.

Sheinbaum, T., Bedoya, E., Ros-Morente, A., Kwapil, T. R., & Barrantes-Vidal, N. (2013). Association between attachment prototypes and schizotypy dimensions in two independent nonclinical samples of Spanish and American young adults. *Psychiatry Research, 210*, 408–413.

Spauwen, J., Krabbendam, L., Lieb, R., Wittchen, H.-U., & van Os, J. (2006). Evidence that the outcome of developmental expression of psychosis is worse for adolescents growing up in an urban environment. *Psychological Medicine, 36*, 407–415.

Svrakic, D. M., Zorumski, C. F., Svrakic, N. M., Zwir, I., & Cloninger, C. R. (2013). Risk architecture of schizophrenia: the role of epigenetics. *Current Opinion in Psychiatry, 26*, 188–195.

Teicher, M. H., Anderson, C. M., Ohashi, K., & Polcari, A. (2013). Childhood maltreatment: altered network centrality of cingulate, precuneus, temporal pole and insula. *Biological Psychiatry*. doi: 10.1016/j.biopsych.2013.09.016

Teicher, M. H., Andersen, S. L., Polcari, A., Anderson, C. M., Navalta, C. P., & Kim, D. M. (2003). The neurobiological consequences of early stress and childhood maltreatment. *Neuroscience and Biobehavioral Reviews, 27*, 33–44.

van Nierop, M., van Os, J., Gunther, N., van Zelst, C., de Graaf, R., ten Have, M, . . . van Winkel, R. (2013). Does social defeat mediate the association between childhood trauma and psychosis? Evidence from the NEMESIS-2 study. *Acta Psychiatrica Scandinavica.* doi: 10.1111/acps.12212

van Os, J. (2012). Psychotic experiences: disadvantaged and different from the norm. *British Journal of Psychiatry, 201*, 258–259.

van Os, J., Kenis, G., & Rutten, B. P. F. (2010). The environment and schizophrenia. *Nature, 468*, 203–212.

van Os, J., Hanssen, M., Bijl, R. V., & Vollebergh, W. (2001). Prevalence of psychotic disorder and community level of psychotic symptoms: an urban–rural comparison. *Archives of General Psychiatry, 58*, 663–668.

van Os, J., Linscott, R. J., Myin-Germeys, I., Delespaul, P., & Krabbendam, L. (2009). A systematic review and meta-analysis of the psychosis continuum: evidence for a psychosis proneness–persistence–impairment model of psychotic disorder. *Psychological Medicine, 39*, 179–195.

van Winkel, R., Stefanis, N. C., & Myin-Germeys, I. (2008). Psychosocial stress and psychosis. A review of the neurobiological mechanisms and the evidence for gene-stress interaction. *Schizophrenia Bulletin, 34*, 1095–1105.

van Winkel, R., van Nierop, M., Myin-Germeys, I., & van Os, J. (2013). Childhood trauma as a cause of psychosis: linking genes, psychology, and biology. *Canadian Journal of Psychiatry, 58,* 44–51.

van Winkel, R., Esquivel G., Kenis, G., Wichers, M., Collip, D., Peerbooms, O., . . . van Os, J. (2010). Genome-wide findings in schizophrenia and the role of gene-environment interplay. *CNS Neuroscience and Therapeutics, 16,* 185–192.

Varese, F., Barkus, E., & Bentall, R. P. (2012). Dissociation mediates the relationship between childhood trauma and hallucination-proneness. *Psychological Medicine, 42,* 1025–1036.

Varese, F., Smeets, F., Drukker, M., Lieverse, R., Lataster, T., Viechtbauer, W., & Bentall, R. P. (2012). Childhood adversities increase the risk of psychosis: a meta-analysis of patient-control, prospective- and cross-sectional cohort studies. *Schizophrenia Bulletin, 38,* 661–671.

Wolke, D., Lereya, S. T., Fisher, H. L., Lewis, G., & Zammit, S. (2013). Bullying in elementary school and psychotic experiences at 18 years: a longitudinal, population-based cohort study. *Psychological Medicine.* doi: 10.1017/S0033291713002912

8 Schizotypy and substance use

Emma Barkus

Introduction

The relationship between substance use and psychotic disorders has produced much controversy in clinical, public policy and research domains. Given the role of regulators in determining the legality of substances of abuse, the relationship between substance use and psychosis has been a matter for contentious debate. Counter to these discussions, however, is the indication that the most commonly used substances in patients with schizophrenia, and those who express schizotypal traits, are alcohol and nicotine. There is evidence that substance use patterns are established before the onset of illness. Therefore, consideration of substance use in relation to schizotypy may help to elucidate the nature of the relationship between risk and substance use. Ross and Peselow (2012) provide a classification system for the potential relationships between psychotic and addictive disorders, which is equally relevant to schizotypy. The diagnostic formulation has been adapted to reflect schizotypy here. There are two possible causal models:

- *Co-occurring* – the existence of both schizotypy and substance use, with separate and distinct causal factors leading to each; or
- *Common factor* – where causal factors are common to both schizotypy and substance use.

The co-occurring model suggests separate causal models (and treatments) are required for schizotypy and substance use, thereby creating a highly complex situation where two distinct sets of behaviours necessitate explanatory mechanisms. However, the common factor model would assume that there were overlapping aetiological factors for both schizotypy and substance use. While the selection of one model would provide a clear-cut framework within which to consider aetiological factors underpinning schizotypy and substance use, the situation seems more likely to be a combination of the two: with the existence of some causal factors that are common to both schizotypy and substance use. However, given that these two behavioural outcomes are expressed independently from one another, causal factors may also exist that are unique to each.

In addition, the nature of the relationship between schizotypy and substance may occur in one of two directions:

- *Secondary substance use* – schizotypal traits increase the likelihood that substance use occurs; or
- *Secondary psychopathology* – schizotypal traits are caused by substance use.

One hypothesis captured by secondary substance use is that of self-medication. While this hypothesis has received much attention in clinical patients, particularly in relation to cigarette use (caffeine use has also been considered), it has received little attention in the schizotypy literature. While schizotypy is considered subclinical, self-medication may still take place. For instance, alcohol may be used to facilitate social interactions. It is also worth noting that the presence of schizotypal traits in the general population has been reported to be associated with receiving disability benefits (Knudsen et al., 2012). Two other points from the latter publication are worth mentioning. The association between subclinical personality disorders as a whole and disability benefits was substantially reduced through the inclusion of common mental health disorders as a covariate. However, the inclusion of substance use did not further reduce the association between these two variables. The authors concluded that common mental health disorders may be a contributory cause to people receiving disability benefits, while their intractable presence was dependent upon the presence of the personality difficulties. Substance use, at least in this sample, did not appear to contribute to the reduced capacity of these individuals to be part of the workforce.

The alternative relationship of secondary psychopathology proposes that substance use causes schizotypal traits. This of course is highly relevant to the diagnoses of substance-induced psychoses, where, in its strictest definition, the symptoms should abate once the substance has been cleared from the body. This could hold true for an episodic disorder, such as a brief limited intermittent psychosis; however, parallels with stable traits such as schizotypy may be more difficult to test. On the other hand, a number of studies are now emerging that point to the fact that a substantial percentage of patients who present with substance-induced psychosis go on to gain a diagnosis of schizophrenia within 2 years (Niemi-Pynttäri et al., 2013). This suggests a situation that may be much less clear-cut from a causal perspective. However, it allows for stable risk factors, such as schizotypy, underpinning the experiences individuals have after taking substances, and the likelihood of subsequent psychopathology.

Three of these four models come with an assumption that the treatment of the primary difficulty will relieve the symptoms associated with the secondary concern. This is heavily reliant upon a causal relationship between schizotypy and substance use, regardless of the assumed direction. The co-occurring model highlights that these two behaviours coexist and therefore require tailored interventions. The stability of schizotypy implies that substance use behaviours may be more amenable to intervention. However, only the environmentally reactive components of schizotypy, directly related to the substance use, would be relieved by such an intervention. The application of such clinical models to the relationship between substance use and schizotypy allows for the separation of stable and episodic factors associated with psychosis proneness. This may assist in our understanding of underlying risk for psychosis and the consequences of this risk interacting with environmental factors such as substance use. Rather than considering substance use in a global manner, the evidence for individual substances will be considered in line with the approach of Ross & Peselow (2012). The substances most frequently considered are nicotine and cannabis, with some limited consideration given to alcohol. The other substances for which there is a small amount of literature in relation to schizotypy will also be reviewed.

Is there an association between substance use and schizotypy?

Cannabis

Cannabis use has been ubiquitously linked with psychosis in the minds of the general public, legislators and social policy developers (e.g. Gage, Zammit, & Hickman, 2013). However clinicians and researchers acknowledge that, while many young people smoke cannabis, only a few go on to develop psychosis (e.g. Buadze et al., 2012; Castle, 2013). Existing evidence in the literature suggests that cannabis use may equally predate depression, anxiety and panic attacks as well as the well-publicised psychotic disorders (e.g. Rubino, Zamberletti, & Parolaro, 2012). Given that underlying liability to a disorder probably has a role to play in responses to cannabis, schizotypy becomes an important predictor and/or mediator of outcomes.

Some studies suggest that those who have smoked cannabis have higher schizotypy scores (e.g. Mason et al., 2009); however, these results are not consistent (e.g. Cohen, Buckner, Najolia, & Stewart, 2011). The association between cannabis use and positive schizotypy appears to be stronger in young adolescence (van Gastel et al., 2012). In turn, regular cannabis use (rather than poly-drug or alcohol use) in adolescence is associated with persistent schizotypal traits in adulthood (Rössler, Hengartner, Angst, & Ajdacic-Gross 2012; Wigman et al., 2011). Collectively these studies could lead some people to conclude that smoking cannabis increases schizotypy scores: a causal hypothesis. However, removal of even one item on a schizotypy scale that cannabis users misinterpret removes statistically significant differences between current and past users (Earleywine, 2006). Further, poly-substance use may explain the relationship between cannabis and schizotypy (Van Dam, Earleywine, & DiGiacomo, 2008) or anxiety and depressive symptoms

(Najolia, Buckner, & Cohen, 2012). In addition, schizotypal traits appear to predate the onset of cannabis use (Schiffman, Nakamura, Earleywine, & LaBrie, 2005), although this requires replication. Given the degree to which cannabis dominates the literature on substance use and schizotypy, if there were a clear causal relationship between cannabis and psychosis risk, it would have been unequivocally supported. It is likely that multiple factors combine to underpin the association between schizotypy and cannabis use. These could be (but are not limited to) openness to experiences and the appealing nature of 'alternative' lifestyle choices to high schizotypes, as well as self-medication of the anxiety associated with schizotypy. Existing studies point to a complex picture that requires further investigation led by scientific questions rather than legislative and media scaremongering.

Nicotine

Health-targeted campaigns appear to have worked to reduce the rates of nicotine smoking in the general population; however, rates are still high for those with mental health problems (Aubin, Rollema, Svensson, & Winterer, 2012). For patients with schizophrenia, studies suggested that approximately 90 per cent of patients smoke (de Leon and Diaz, 2005). In addition, they are more likely to display nicotine dependence, which is more difficult to reduce than in general population smokers (Lasser et al., 2000). Rates of smoking are higher in patients with schizophrenia than in other psychiatric groups. Patients with schizophrenia who smoke have the expectation that smoking will reduce negative affect, medication side effects and negative symptoms (de Leon, Diaz, Aguilar, Jurado, & Gupergui, 2006; Esterberg and Compton, 2005). However, many patients with schizophrenia start smoking before the onset of the disorder (Riala, Hakko, Isohanni, Pouta, & Räsänen et al., 2004). Consequently, there may be shared biological vulnerability for smoking and schizophrenia.

Indeed, rates of smoking have been found to be higher in relatives of patients with schizophrenia (Esterberg, Jones, Compton, & Walker, 2007; Smith, Barch, Wolf, Mamah, & Csernansky, 2008). However, only some studies (e.g. Esterberg et al., 2007) report a relationship between schizotypy and smoking in relatives of patients with schizophrenia (Ferchiou et al., 2012). Race is one variable that needs consideration (Ferchiou et al., 2012): given racial differences in nicotine metabolism, it is a possible mediating variable. Furthermore, defensive responding to schizotypy scales confounds studies in relatives (Calkins, Curtis, Grove, & Iacono, 2004). In general population studies, rates of smoking nicotine are twice as high in those who express schizotypy (Stewart, Cohen, & Copeland, 2010). Higher schizotypy scores are associated with smoking status (Wiles et al., 2006), number of cigarettes smoked per day and greater dependence in some studies (e.g. Stewart, Vinci, Adams, Cohen, & Copeland, 2013), but not others (e.g. Esterberg et al., 2007). The reasons for such elevated and persistent nicotine use in those who express schizotypy are as yet unknown. There are many biological explanations for the role of nicotine in facilitating cognition and in the pathogenesis of schizophrenia; however, the relationship between nicotine and psychosis risk is as yet unclear.

Understanding the reasons for nicotine use could begin to point to which biological systems we should be concerned with. Within the substance use literature, drug expectancies are used to indicate reasons for use through self-reported expected drug effects. High schizotypes who have smoked nicotine have more positive and fewer negative expectancies about smoking than control smokers (Stewart et al., 2013). Therefore, they view nicotine as having beneficial effects over and above those endorsed by controls. This could point to high schizotypes being more sensitive to nicotine. Substance use expectancies are derived from a learning theory model. Therefore environmental factors – such as peers and family acceptability of smoking – need to be kept in mind. Selection of peer group within a school setting would not only determine the acceptability of nicotine use for a high schizotypal young person but also the use of other illicit substances. This requires further investigation.

Given that the rates of nicotine use are relatively high in the general population, compared with other (illegal) substances considered, it is unlikely that nicotine has a causal role in shaping schizotypy scores. However, of the substances considered here, the literature on nicotine use provides the strongest evidence for a co-occurring relationship that is even delineated by genetic proximity to schizophrenia. Certainly, there appear to be overlapping neurobiological vulnerabilities to psychosis and nicotine use. These are worthy of investigation for elucidating the neurobiological profile of schizotypy and may point to factors underpinning cognitive deficits.

Alcohol

Next to nicotine, alcohol is the most readily available substance of abuse for young people. Its social acceptability often means it is viewed as harmless by young people and the increase in a binge-drinking culture has normalised drinking to excess. However, for patients with schizophrenia, there is evidence that alcohol is used to self-medicate. Additionally, some studies have reported that alcohol consumption actually increases before the onset of psychosis. Certainly, while for many, excess alcohol use is merely youthful angst, for a significant subset of individuals it reflects a reduction in well-being and increases in depression and anxiety.

There is much literature concerning antisocial personality disorder and alcohol use; however, schizotypal traits have received less attention. These have been associated with alcohol dependence (Pulay et al., 2009) and lifetime alcohol dependence in older (average age 60 years) individuals (Agrawal, Narayanan, & Oltmanns, 2013) from the general population. Hasin et al. (2011) reported an association between persistent alcohol dependence and schizotypal traits. This result occurred after controlling for gender, education, race, age at initial assessment, family history of substance use problems, treatment at baseline for drug and alcohol abuse, cannabis and nicotine use, and current Axis I disorders. The level of statistical rigour applied suggests that many confounds were taken into account. Using a 30-year community sample, Rössler et al. (2012) devised two groups of characteristics that reflected 'schizotypal signs' and 'schizophrenia nuclear symptoms'. Given that no one in their sample met the criteria for a psychotic disorder, these categories reflect differing severities of schizotypal traits. In the analysis conducted, the authors assessed what predicted an individual's score to 'shift' so that they were in the upper 85th percentile for the two groups of characteristics. Alcohol misuse in adulthood was a significant predictor for high 'schizotypal signs', while frequent alcohol intoxication in adolescence was predictive of high 'schizophrenia nuclear symptoms'. Again, these associations were tested with similar covariates to those used in Hasin et al. (2011). Taken together, the Hassin et al. and Rössler et al. data suggest that there may be two differing trajectories for those who express higher schizotypy. There may be persistent but attenuated schizotypy that is associated with long-term alcohol use, in a manner consistent with the self-medication hypothesis. But there is also a group who use alcohol heavily during adolescence and will have a more severe expression of schizotypy. There may be meaningful information in the heterogeneity of schizotypy that is largely unconsidered and may provide clinically relevant data. Of course at this point we can only speculate, given that it is not possible to conclusively determine causality in these studies.

Other substances

There are a number of other substances, such as amphetamines and ketamine, which in acute administration, at least, are associated with psychotic-like experiences. Many of these substances are used as pre-clinical models of schizophrenia in both animals and healthy human volunteers. However, the association between schizotypy and such substances has rarely been investigated. Whether or not these substances represent a valid model for schizophrenia (e.g. Barkus & Murray, 2010), they are worthy of investigation for association with schizotypy given their relevance to the pathophysiology of schizophrenia. Ketamine is a N-methyl-D-aspartate receptor (NMDA) antagonist, which has been reported to produce psychosis-like effects in healthy volunteers when administered acutely (e.g. Krystal et al., 1994), and to exacerbate psychotic symptoms in recovered patients with schizophrenia (Lahti, Weiler, Tamara, Parwani, & Tamminga, 2001). Stirling and McCoy (2010) reported that current ketamine users scored significantly higher than past users on positive schizotypy. Additionally, while Stefanovic et al. (2009) did not report an association between ketamine and schizotypy, positive schizotypy did positively correlate with automatic semantic priming in only ketamine users. This suggests that those with schizotypal traits may be prone to schizophrenia-like cognitive performance when their system is perturbed by substances such as ketamine.

Cocaine is a substance that should be considered closely related to psychosis, given that it increases dopamine when administered acutely and can also lead to sensitisation of dopamine systems (as demonstrated in animal studies [Addy, Daberkow, Ford, Garris, & Wightman 2010]). This would make it of interest in association with schizotypy – not only for exacerbating underlying propensities in the immediate response, but also for the possibility that dopamine release could be more likely in those exposed to cocaine after other dopamine-releasing events such as environmental stressors. Higher schizotypy scores have been associated with cocaine use (Montes et al., 2013) but not consistently (Compton, Chien, & Bollini, 2009). Indeed, relatives of patients with schizophrenia may be less likely than controls to use cocaine (Compton, Chien, & Bollini, 2009). That cocaine has received little attention in the schizotypy research is not a reflection of its potential as a risk factor for schizophrenia (see Giordano, Ohlsson, Sundquist, K., Sundquist, J., and Kendler, 2014, for population risk associated with schizophrenia). Rather, it may reflect the fact that cocaine use varies internationally and, unlike cannabis, the message of cocaine's potential causative role in schizophrenia is yet to reach the ears of the press and legislators.

Drug distributors are becoming ever inventive in producing compounds that fall outside the regulations defining substances as 'illegal'. This has led to an increasing number of legal highs. One such substance – mephedrone – has received some interest in the psychosis literature because of its biochemical similarity to amphetamine. This drug has been associated with higher schizotypy scores (Freeman et al., 2012; Herzig, Brooks, & Mohr, 2013). There is an insufficient accumulation of evidence on the other substances considered here to determine whether the relationship between their use and schizotypy could be considered either causative or co-occurring. The lack of consideration given to substances besides cannabis highlights a substantial gap that needs addressing.

Do the subjective effects of substances relate to schizotypal traits?

While association and experimental studies provide statistically rigorous indications of the nature of the relationship between schizotypy and substance use, they address the question at a surface level. These studies do little to inform about the effects these substances have subjectively. Nor do they provide tangible evidence that can be used in a therapeutic situation to advise people about their individual risk. Consideration of the subjective effects of substances takes into account the complex interplay between an individual's biological vulnerability and the pharmacology of substances of abuse. Investigation of individual differences in experiences after using psychoactive substances has primarily been considered for cannabis, although one study discussed later investigated ketamine.

Existing literature provides a framework that suggests that certain personality types may be prone to seek out substances such as cannabis (Barkus, 2008); therefore, personality traits may provide a clue to inherent psychological vulnerabilities. Anecdotal evidence for individual differences in the experiences people report after cannabis use has existed for as long as cannabis has been smoked by humans. It is possible that the diversity in subjective experiences is related to individual differences and both may be biologically driven. Given this, the same biological predispositions that underpin vulnerability to expressing personality traits may also underpin the subjective experiences people report after cannabis. Genetic polymorphisms associated with schizophrenia have also been found to be related to schizotypy (e.g. Docherty & Sponheim, 2008; Grant et al., 2013). Previously, it has been demonstrated that those who score highly on schizotypy are more likely to have psychotic-like immediate experiences and increased after-effects from cannabis use (Barkus and Lewis, 2008; Stirling et al., 2008). A small functional magnetic resonance imaging study has demonstrated that males who had a psychotic response to orally administered delta-9-tetrahydrocannabinol (THC) had a differential (reduced) pattern of activation in the right middle temporal gyrus and cerebellum compared with those who did not report psychotic experiences after THC; these areas of reduced activation were independent of the effects of the drug (Atakan et al., 2012). Collectively, these papers suggest that individual differences in responses to cannabinoids may be related to schizotypy and could be underpinned by biological differences.

There is some evidence for genetic factors that mediate subjective experiences after cannabis and schizotypy. A number of studies have investigated the role of a functional single nucleotide polymorphism (SNP) in the gene coding for catechol-o-methyl transferase (COMT). COMT is an enzyme that breaks down dopamine at the synapse and is particularly important for the efficiency of the prefrontal cortex, where dopamine is not produced (Akil et al., 2003). The polymorphism coding for highly active COMT is associated with schizotypy (e.g. Smyrnis et al., 2007) and schizophrenia. It is hypothesised that high dopamine turnover leads to an inefficient prefrontal cortex that reduces cognitive performance (e.g. Smyrnis et al., 2007). The high-activity SNP has been reported to interact with cannabis use and a history of child abuse to predict psychotic-like experiences in healthy volunteers (Alemany et al., 2013). In an experimental study where participants were exposed to THC, those who had the high-active enzyme were more likely to report psychotomimetic effects if they had high scores on psychometrically assessed psychosis proneness (Henquet et al., 2006). Additionally, those participants carrying the SNP for the high-activity COMT demonstrated greater sensitivity to the deleterious effects of THC on memory and attention. However, as with many genetic studies, the relationship between COMT and psychotic-like experiences after cannabis is not consistently replicated and there may be other variables interacting with this SNP to determine experiences after cannabis use (Zammit, Owen, Evans, Heron, & Lewis, 2011).

Stirling and McCoy (2010) are the only authors to consider subjective experiences reported after recreational ketamine use. They found those who scored higher on positive and interpersonal schizotypy were more likely to endorse 'k-hole' experiences. These included 'a sense of floating', 'marked confusion' and 'dissociation of mind/body'. This one study tentatively suggests that schizotypy may be involved in mediating the intensity of drug experiences other than cannabis.

Are schizotypal individuals more likely to engage in substance use?

In the literature on substance use and dependence in the general population, a number of factors have been highlighted to predict likelihood of substance use and also problematic use. One explanation for elevated rates of substance use in individuals who score highly on schizotypy, or those with schizotypal personality disorder, could be an over-representation of these factors in this group of individuals. This has three implications:

1   Increased difficulty in changing patterns of substance use. Schizotypal traits have been associated with elevated dropouts from substance abuse treatment (e.g. Ravndal & Vaglum, 1991).
2   Help seeking may be more problematic. Some schizotypal traits, such as social withdrawal and anxiety, may mean help seeking may be less likely to occur without the intervention of others.
3   Styles of drug intervention to not be a good 'fit' for schizotypal individuals. Schizotypal traits such as social anxiety and suspiciousness may mean group interventions (often used in a substance use setting) are less appealing.

The two demographic factors of male sex and younger age are predictive of substance use engagement. The literature on sex differences in schizotypy is mixed, with some studies reporting sex differences in keeping with those reported in patients with schizophrenia, while more recent studies do not replicate these findings. Males scoring higher on the more negative features of schizotypy could see substance use as an attractive coping and self-medication mechanism. Further investigation could be required to determine whether male and female high schizotypes have different reasons for substance use as well as differential involvement. However, it seems unlikely that sex could be a strong driver explaining the association between substance use and schizotypy. Younger age is associated with both substance use and higher schizotypy scores in the general population. This is an area that is worthy of additional investigation, given the potential for substance use against the background of the young adolescent vulnerable brain. Emotional distress and substance use have been reported to cluster in high school students (Stuart, 2006). Further investigation is required to determine the trajectories of schizotypal traits, tracking individuals from adolescence to adulthood and the role substance use has to play in defining these trajectories. Hasin et al. (2011) provide evidence that there is a persistence of nicotine use and a decrease in alcohol problems with age in the general population. This suggests that substance use trajectories themselves still require further investigation, with care taken to investigate each substance independently. Given that both substance use problems and schizotypy decrease with age, there is a need to be mindful of substance use issues when working clinically with young people.

Lower educational attainment is associated with both schizotypy and substance use (e.g. King, Meehan, Trim, & Chassin, 2006). However, the relationship between these three variables has not been tested, although they are likely to be strongly related. There are multiple variables that may be involved in mediating the relationship between schizotypy, substance use and educational attainment; it is a complex picture. However, a clear message is that remaining in education for longer and gaining good marks are protective factors against both future high levels of schizotypy and substance use. These may be variables that co-occur rather than having a reciprocal causal relationship with one another: mere indicators of other underlying difficulties. There are a number of other similar factors – such as being single, family history of substance abuse, childhood trauma – which co-occur with both schizotypy and substance use. It seems for many demographic variables associated with substance use engagement that there are corresponding studies demonstrating a relationship with schizotypy. These two bodies of work now need to be married in larger, more comprehensive studies in which demographic variables associated with substance use are taken into account when investigating drug associations with schizotypy. Given that demographic variables associated with substance use risk are related to schizotypy, they act to increase the likelihood of substance abuse taking place.

Genetic factors shape risk for both schizotypy and heavy substance use. Additionally there is some overlap, through GABA and dopamine systems, in the neurotransmitters conferring risk. While family studies are not ideal (because they conflate both biological and learning factors), they would provide the ideal environment to start to tease apart the complex associations between substance use and schizotypy. Until plausible common biological mechanisms are put forward, genetic association studies will be underpowered, untargeted investigations. While dopamine seems an attractive candidate (see Chapter 2), linked to both addictive substances and psychotic symptoms, the many other characteristics (such as depression and withdrawal) in schizotypy are not so readily explained by this neurotransmitter system alone. Additionally, not all substances of abuse are predicated by manipulation of dopaminergic transmission. An intriguing thought, of course, is that there are different biological mechanisms underpinning schizotypy and substance use. It does raise an important question about heritability: why should inheriting schizotypal traits co-occur with inheriting substance use genes?

Given that we are considering the expression of a personality trait, the genetic story becomes complicated. Additional personality factors, such as impulsivity, are both components of schizotypy and predictive of substance use (e.g. Stautz and Cooper, 2013). Schizotypy is a heterogeneous personality trait and varies in presentation. The exploration of personality variables that modify the presentation of schizotypy has hardly begun. Schizotypy is a clinical risk for depression, anxiety, psychosis and bipolar disorder. It is possible that personality traits shape the clinical outcomes for which schizotypy provides a background risk. It could be hypothesised that the expression of these more normal personality traits will shape emotional responses and coping styles, and increase the likelihood that certain behaviours, such as substance abuse, will occur.

Conclusions and future directions

The reasons for, and consequences of, substance use in an otherwise psychologically healthy group are complex. Coupled with additional factors, such as mental health vulnerabilities and extreme personality traits, the triggering, maintenance and consequences of substances use became more inseparable. Currently there are two streams of literature considering these issues: substance use/abuse and psychiatry. From a service delivery perspective, there is what seems like an impassable gap between these two. Psychiatry views substance-induced conditions as divorced from other mental health difficulties, while substance use clinicians view mental health difficulties as a major complication to successful treatment outcomes, but outside their sphere of influence. This ideological and governance separation is reflected in the current literature. While cannabis use is considered a component cause in the aetiology of schizophrenia, the same level of rigour has not been applied to other substances in the psychiatric literature. The relationship between schizotypy and substance use is just fundamentally more complex than we are currently giving it credit for.

Of course one area of research that is grossly under-represented in the psychosis literature, as a whole, is the role of emotional regulation. In relation to substance use and schizotypy, there are a number of points that are pertinent. First, the degree of emotional response following a stressor (stress reactivity) may mediate the likelihood of substance use. Links between stress and substance use exist and may be more potent for those vulnerable to extreme emotional changes following a stressor. Second, affect regulation in general has a role to play in the initiation and maintenance of substance use. The avoidance of negative emotional states is certainly associated with substance abuse – in particular, alcohol abuse. Substance abuse clinicians often see young adults using illicit substances as an escape from negative emotions. Negative affect is also an area of recognised under-treatment in patients with schizophrenia. Patients often report using alcohol and cannabis to avoid negative affect. Emotional factors in schizotypy can be viewed as additive risk factors for substance use. Again, other personality factors may be involved in shaping emotional reactions. However, a point to note concerning emotional regulation is that it is a factor more amenable to change than genetics and/or personality. As a means of reducing risk behaviours for progression to more serious mental health difficulties, it may be an excellent target for reducing substance use and improving well-being.

References

Addy, N. A., Daberkow, D. P., Ford, J. N., Garris, P. A., & Wightman, R. M. (2010). Sensitization of rapid dopamine signaling in the nucleus accumbens core and shell after repeated cocaine in rats. *Journal of Neurophysiology, 104*, 922–931.

Agrawal, A., Narayanan, G., & Oltmanns, T.F. (2013). Personality pathology and alcohol dependence in midlife in a community sample. *Personality Disorders, 4*(1), 55–61.

Akil, M., Kolachana, B. S., Rothmond, D. A., Hyde, T. M., Weinberger, D. R., & Kleinman, J. E. (2003). Catechol-O-methyltransferase genotype and dopamine regulation in the human brain. *Journal of Neuroscience, 23*(6), 2008–13.

Alemany, S., Arias, B., Fatjó-Vilas, M., Villa, H., Moya, J., Ibáñez, M. I., Ortet, G., . . . Fañanás, L. (2013). Psychosis-inducing effects of cannabis are related to both childhood abuse and COMT genotypes. *Acta Psychiatrica Scandinavica.* doi: 10.1111/acps.12108

American Psychiatric Association. (2013). *Diagnostic and statistical manual of mental disorders (DSM-V)* (5th ed.). Arlington, VA: Author.

Atakan, Z., Bhattacharyya, S., Allen, P., Martín-Santos, R., Crippa, J. A., Borgwardt, S. J., McGuire, P. (2012). Cannabis affects people differently: inter-subject variation in the psychotogenic effects of Δ9-tetrahydrocannabinol: a functional magnetic resonance imaging study with healthy volunteers. *Psychological Medicine, 1*, 1–13.

Aubin, H. J., Rollema, H., Svensson, T. H., & Winterer, G. (2012). Smoking, quitting, and psychiatric disease: a review. *Neuroscience and Biobehavioral Reviews, 36*, 271–284.

Barkus, E. (2008). Personality and cannabis use. *Advances in Schizophrenia and Clinical Psychiatry, 3*(3), 84–9.

Barkus, E., & Lewis, S. (2008). Schizotypy and psychosis-like experiences from recreational cannabis in a non-clinical sample. *Psychological Medicine, 38*(9), 1267–76.

Barkus, E., & Murray, R. M. (2010). Substance use in adolescence and psychosis: clarifying the relationship. *Annual Review of Clinical Psychology, 6*, 365–389.

Buadze, A., Kaiser, S., Stohler, R., Roessler, W., Seifritz, E., Liebrenz, M. (2012). Patient's perceptions of the cannabis-psychosis link – a systematic review. *Current Pharmacology Designs, 18*(32), 5105–12.

Calkins, M. E., Curtis, C. E., Grove, W. M., & Iacono, W.G. (2004). Multiple dimensions of schizotypy in first-degree biological relatives of schizophrenia patients. *Schizophrenia Bulletin, 30*, 317–325.

Castle, D. J. (2013). Cannabis and psychosis: what causes what? *F1000 Medical Reports*, 5, 1.

Cohen, A. S., Buckner, J. D., Najolia, G. M., & Stewart, D. W. (2011). Cannabis and psychometrically-defined schizotypy: use, problems and treatment considerations. *Journal of Psychiatric Research*, 45, 548–54.

Compton, M. T., Chien, V. H., & Bollini, A. M. (2009). Associations between past alcohol, cannabis, and cocaine use and current schizotypy among first-degree relatives of patients with schizophrenia and non-psychiatric controls. *Psychiatry Quarterly*, 80, 143–54.

de Leon, J., & Diaz, F. J. (2005). A meta-analysis of worldwide studies demonstrates an association between schizophrenia and tobacco smoking behaviors. *Schizophrenia Research*, 76, 135–157.

de Leon, J., Diaz, F. J., Aguilar, M. C., Jurado, D., & Gupergui, M. (2006). Does smoking reduce akathisia? Testing a narrow version of the self-medication hypothesis. *Schizophrenia Research*, 86, 256–268.

Docherty, A. R., & Sponheim, S. R. (2008). Anhedonia as a phenotype for the Val158Met COMT polymorphism in relatives of patients with schizophrenia. *Journal of Abnormal Psychology*, 117, 788–98.

Earleywine, M. (2006). Schizotypy, marijuana, and differential item functioning. *Human Psychopharmacology*, 21, 455–61.

Esterberg, M. L., & Compton, M.T. (2005). Smoking behaviour in persons with a schizophrenia-spectrum disorder: a qualitative investigation of the trans-theoretical model. *Social Science and Medicine*, 61, 293–303.

Esterberg, M. L., Jones, E. M., Compton, M. T., & Walker. E. F. (2007). Nicotine consumption and schizotypy in first degree relatives of individuals with schizophrenia and non-psychiatric controls. *Schizophrenia Research*, 97, 6–13.

Ferchiou, A., Szöke, A., Laguerre, A., Méary, A., Leboyer, M., & Schürhoff, F. (2012). Exploring the relationships between tobacco smoking and schizophrenia in first-degree relatives. *Psychiatry Research*, 200(2), 674–678.

Freeman, T. P., Morgan, C. J., Vaughn-Jones, J., Hussain, N., Karimi, K. & Curran H.V. (2012). Cognitive and subjective effects of mephedrone and factors influencing use of a 'new legal high'. *Addiction*, 107(4), 792–800.

Gage, S. H., Zammit, S., & Hickman, M. (2013). Stronger evidence is needed before accepting that cannabis plays an important role in the aetiology of schizophrenia in the population. *F1000 Medical Reports*, 5, 2.

Grant, P., Kuepper, Y., Mueller, E. A., Wielpuetz, C., Mason, O., & Hennig, J. (2013). Dopaminergic foundations of schizotypy as measured by the German version of the Oxford-Liverpool Inventory of Feelings and Experiences (O-LIFE) – a suitable endophenotype of schizophrenia. *Frontiers of Human Neuroscience*, 7: 1.

Giordano, G. N., Ohlsson, H., Sundquist, K., Sundquist, J., & Kendler, K. S. (2014). The association between cannabis abuse and subsequent schizophrenia: a Swedish national co-relative control study. *Psychological Medicine*, 3, 1–8.

Hasin, D., Fenton, M. C., Skodol, A., Krueger, R., Keyes, K., Geier, T., . . . Grant, B. (2011) Personality disorders and the 3-year course of alcohol, drug and nicotine use disorders. *Archives of General Psychiatry*, 68(11), 1158–1167.

Henquet, C., Rosa, A., Krabbendam, L., Papiol, S., Fananás, L., Drukker. M., . . . van Os, J. (2006). An experimental study of catechol-o-methyltransferase Val158Met moderation of delta-9-tetrahydrocannabinol-induced effects on psychosis and cognition. *Neuropsychopharmacology*, 31, 2748–57.

Herzig, D. A., Brooks, R., & Mohr, C. (2013). Inferring about individual drug and schizotypy effects on cognitive functioning in polydrug using mephedrone users before and after clubbing. *Human Psychopharmacology, 28*, 168–82.

King, K. M., Meehan, B. T., Trim, R. S., & Chassin L. (2006). Marker or mediator? The effects of adolescent substance use on young adult educational attainment. *Addiction, 101*, 1730–40.

Knudsen, A. K., Skogen, J. C., Harvey, S. B., Stewart, R., Hotopf, M., & Moran P. (2012). Personality disorders, common mental disorders and receipt of disability benefits: evidence from the British National Survey of Psychiatric Morbidity. *Psychological Medicine, 42*, 2631–2640.

Krystal, J. H., Karper, L. P., Seibyl, J. P., Freeman, G. K., Delaney, R., Bremner, J. D., & Charney, D. S. (1994). Subanesthetic effects of the noncompetitive NMDA antagonist, ketamine, in humans: psychotomimetic, perceptual, cognitive, and neuroendocrine responses. *Archives of General Psychiatry, 51*(3), 199–214.

Lahti, A. C., Weiler, M. A., Tamara, M., Parwani, A., & Tamminga, C. A. (2001). Effects of ketamine in normal and schizophrenic volunteers. *Neuropsychopharmacology, 25*(4), 455-467.

Lasser, K., Boyd, J. W., Wollhandler, S., Himmelstein, D. U., McCormick, D., & Bor, D. H. (2000). Smoking and mental illness: a population-based prevalence study. *Journal of the American Medical Association, 284*, 2602–2610.

Mason, O., Morgan, C. J., Dhiman, S. K., Patel, A., Parti, N., Patel, A., & Curran, H. V. (2009). Acute cannabis use causes increased psychotomimetic experiences in individuals prone to psychosis. *Psychological Medicine, 39*, 951–956.

Montes, J. M. G., Basurto, F. Z., Montoya, M. M., & Cubos, P. F. (2013). Relationship between drug use and psychopathological variables of risk in university students. *Psicothema, 25*(4), 433–439.

Najolia, G. M., Buckner, J. D., & Cohen, A. S. (2012). Cannabis use and schizotypy: the role of social anxiety and other negative affective states. *Psychiatry Research, 200*, 660–668.

Niemi-Pynttäri, J. A., Sund, R., Putkonen, H., Vorma, H., Wahlbeck, K., & Pirkola, S. P. (2013). Substance-induced psychoses converting into schizophrenia: a register-based study of 18,478 Finnish inpatient cases. *Journal of Clinical Psychiatry, 74*(1):e94–99.

Pulay, A. J., Stinson, F. S., Dawson, D. A., Goldstein, R. B., Chou, S. P., Huang, B., . . . Grant, B. F. (2009). Prevalence, correlates, disability and comorbidity of DSM-IV schizotypal personality disorder: results from wave 2 national epidemiologic survey on alcohol and related conditions. *Primary Care Companion Journal of Clinical Psychiatry, 11*(2), 53–67.

Ravndal, E., & Vaglum P. (1991). Psychopathology and substance abuse as predictors of program completion in a therapeutic community for drug abusers: a prospective study. *Acta Psychiatrica Scandinavica, 83*(3), 217–222.

Riala, K., Hakko, H., Isohanni, M., Pouta, A., & Räsänen, P. (2004). Is initiation of smoking associated with the prodromal phase of schizophrenia? *Journal of Psychiatric Neuroscience, 30*, 26–32.

Ross, S., & Peselow, E. (2012). Co-occurring psychotic and addictive disorders: neurobiology and diagnosis. *Clinical Neuropharmacology, 35*(5), 235–243.

Rössler, W., Hengartner, M. P., Angst, J., & Ajdacic-Gross, V. (2012). Linking substance use with symptoms of subclinical psychosis in a community cohort over 30 years. *Addiction, 107*(6), 1174–1184.

Rubino, T., Zamberletti, E., & Parolaro D. (2012). Adolescent exposure to cannabis as a risk factor for psychiatric disorders. *Journal of Psychopharmacology, 26*, 177–188.

Schiffman, J., Nakamura, B., Earleywine, M., & LaBrie, J. (2005). Symptoms of schizotypy precede cannabis use. *Psychiatry Research, 134*(1), 37–42.

Smith, M. J., Barch, D. M., Wolf, T. J., Mamah, D., & Csernansky, J. G. (2008). Elevated rates of substance use disorders in non-psychotic siblings of individuals with schizophrenia. *Schizophrenia Research, 106*, 294–299.

Smyrnis, N., Avramopoulos, D., Evdokimidis, I., Stefanis, C. N., Tsekou, H., & Stefanis, N. C. (2007). Effect of schizotypy on cognitive performance and its tuning by COMT val158 met genotype variations in a large population of young men. *Biological Psychiatry, 61*, 845–853.

Stautz, K., & Cooper, A. (2013). Impulsivity-related personality traits and adolescent alcohol use: a meta-analytic review. *Clinical Psychology Review, 33*, 574–92.

Stefanovic, A., Brandner, B., Klaassen, E., Cregg, R., Nagaratnam, M., Bromley, ... Curran, H. V. (2009). Acute and chronic effects of ketamine on semantic priming: modeling schizophrenia? *Journal of Clinical Psychopharmacology, 29*, 124–33.

Stewart, D. W., Cohen, A. S., & Copeland, A. L. (2010). Smoking across the schizotypy spectrum. *Psychiatry Research, 179*, 113–115.

Stewart, D. W., Vinci, C., Adams, C. E., Cohen, A. S., & Copeland, A. L. (2013). Smoking topography and outcome expectancies among individuals with schizotypy. *Psychiatry Research, 205*, 205–12.

Stirling, J., & McCoy, L. (2010). Quantifying the psychological effects of ketamine: from euphoria to the k-Hole. *Substance Use & Misuse, 45*(14), 2428–2443. doi: 10.3109/10826081003793912.

Stirling, J., Barkus, E. J., Nabosi, L., Irshad, S., Roemer, G., Schreudergoidheijt, B., & Lewis, S. (2008). Cannabis-induced psychotic-like experiences are predicted by high schizotypy: confirmation of preliminary results in a large cohort. *Psychopathology, 41*, 371–378.

Stuart, H. (2006). Psychosocial risk clustering in high school students. *Social Psychiatry and Psychiatric Epidemiology, 41*(6), 498–507.

Van Dam, N. T., Earleywine, M., & DiGiacomo, G. (2008). Polydrug use, cannabis, and psychosis-like symptoms. *Human Psychopharmacology, 23*(6), 475–85.

van Gastel, W. A., Wigman, J. T., Monshouwer, K., Kahn, R. S., van Os, J., Boks, M. P., & Vollebergh, W. A. (2012). Cannabis use and subclinical positive psychotic experiences in early adolescence: findings from a Dutch survey. *Addiction, 107*, 381–387.

Wigman, J. T., van Winkel, R., Raaijmakers, Q. A., Ormel, J., Verhulst, F. C., Reijneveld, S. A., ... Vollebergh, W A. (2011) Evidence for a persistent, environment-dependent and deteriorating subtype of subclinical psychotic experiences: a 6-year longitudinal general population study. *Psychological Medicine, 41*, 2317–2329.

Wiles, N. J., Zammit, S., Bebbington, P., Singleton, N., Meltzer, H.,& Lewis G. (2006). Self-reported psychotic symptoms in the general population. Results from the longitudinal study of the British National Psychiatric Morbidity Study. *British Journal of Psychiatry, 188*, 519–526.

Zammit, S., Owen, M. J., Evans, J., Heron, J., Lewis, G. (2011). Cannabis, COMT and psychotic experiences. *British Journal of Psychiatry, 199*, 380–385.

9 Inducing psychotic-like experiences

The role of schizotypy

Christina Daniel and Oliver J. Mason

Introduction

Although most commonly associated with psychiatric disorders, it is now acknowledged that, during their lifetime, about 28 per cent of the general population may have quasi-psychotic experiences, at least as detected by screening questions in the US National Comorbidity Survey (Kendler, Thacker, & Walsh, 1996; for review, see Johns & van Os 2011): These may include hallucinations, passivity phenomena, and overvalued or delusional ideas. Other experiences phenomenologically more distal to psychosis, such as 'psychic' or paranormal experiences (e.g. telepathy, extrasensory perception [ESP], telekinesis, 'out-of-body'), synaesthesia, lucid dreaming and hypnopompic/hypnagogic states, occur even more widely in the population. These have variously been associated with schizotypy, and thus may form part of the broader constellation of quasi-psychotic phenomena. This chapter outlines a range of non-pharmacological research strategies to provoke such experiences, or what we term here quasi-psychotic 'states of consciousness', with a view to studying their relevance to schizotypy.

There is a long history of experimental paradigms attempting to induce anomalous experiences in healthy individuals, much of it taking place back in the 1950s and 1960s. Many of these studies employed sensory deprivation of various kinds as the method for inducing anomalous experiences. The findings were inconsistent, possibly due to an inadequate recognition of the complexity of the variables that enter into the situation of sensory restriction (Ziskind, 1964). Prolonged periods of deprivation were found to produce a range of psychotic phenomena in many, if not all, participants. However, experiences at shorter durations varied, depending on the nature of the deprivation and the characteristics of the participants involved. Researchers subsequently lost interest in the field of inducing anomalous experiences, many dismissing the phenomena as imaginary and not a true parallel of the hallucinations and other positive symptoms seen in psychosis.

With the potential utility for studying anomalous experiences in the normal population now clearly re-established as part of the psychosis continuum (Johns & van Os 2011) and schizotypy rubrics, researchers have taken a fresh look at methods to experimentally induce such experiences, with perhaps the most widely studied relating to the induction of auditory-verbal hallucinations. Many of these methods have been informed by recent theoretical accounts of 'voice hearing', such as increased impact of top-down processing (Aleman, Bocker, & Hijman, 2003; Grossberg, 2000); reality discrimination failure (Bentall, 1990); and increased sensitivity to internally generated percepts (Blakemore, Smith, Steel, Johnstone, & Frith 2000). We aim to provide a critical synopsis of the variety of experimental techniques available for the induction of anomalous experiences in the normal population and to report their relationship with schizotypal traits. As studies using auditory paradigms form a relatively homogenous group, Table 9.1 provides an overview of their characteristics and major findings. The remainder are relatively heterogeneous, containing various forms of sensory restriction or deprivation together with other 'unusual' perceptual conditions (see Table 9.2).

Ambiguous auditory environments

In response to the claim that ambiguity in the environment is implicated in the experience of hallucinations (Jakes & Hemsley, 1986), Feelgood and Rantzen (1994) tested the hypothesis that hallucination-prone individuals would experience significantly more verbal hallucinations during a jumbled voice task than non-prone. Participants listened to a 5-minute recording of a male voice consisting of randomly spliced 1-second sections played backwards via headphones. They were instructed that, at certain points in the recording, words and phrases would appear. They were then asked to write these down when they heard them. As predicted, high scorers on the Launay-Slade Hallucination Scale (LSHS; Launay & Slade, 1981) reported significantly more verbal hallucinations than low scorers. In a subsequent replication study, Pearson et al. (2001) researched a large group of children aged between 9 and 11 years. The children were also asked whether they had a current imaginary friend, and this was used as a proxy for high and low hallucination proneness. As predicted, children who reported a current imaginary friend were more likely to report hearing a higher number of words than those children who had never experienced an imaginary companion.

Both Pearson's and Feelgood and Rantzen's results suggest that scrambled voice paradigms are effective in inducing false auditory experiences in both normal adult and child populations. However, neither study collected data regarding the certainty with which participants heard the words, nor whether participants thought they could have imagined their experiences. However, Pearson et al. (2001) did attempt to control for the effect of speech illusions by removing from the scoring any word that was reported by 10 per cent of any class or by 10 per cent of the whole group. It is also possible that demand characteristics could account for the findings:

Table 9.1 Auditory paradigms

Study	Design/ Participants/Method	Psychometric measures	Schizotypy relationships
Feelgood & Rantzen (1994)	Low LSHS (n=10) vs. high LSHS (n=12). 5 minute audio recording consisting of randomly spliced 1 second sections of a male voice played backwards.	LSHS.	High scorers reported significantly more verbal hallucinations than low scorers.
Merckelbach & van de Ven (2001)	44 healthy undergraduate students. White noise presented while instructed to press a button when they believed hearing a recording of Bing Crosby's 'White Christmas' (without the record actually being presented).	Social Desirability Scale, LSHS, Questionnaire upon Mental Imagery (Sheenan 1976); Creative Experiences Questionnaire.	Participants reporting hearing the song were found to have higher score on both the LSHS and the fantasy proneness scale.
Vercammen & Aleman (2010)	High and low LSHS groups were presented with two word recognition tasks (using a combination of speech and white noise bursts). Top-down influences on perceptions were manipulated through sentence context (semantic tasks) or auditory imagery (phonological task).	LSHS.	Hallucination proneness was associated with an increased false word perception. Higher levels of hallucination proneness were not related to specific error types in the phonological task.
Galdos, Simons, & Fernandez-Rivas (2011)	30 psychosis patients, 28 siblings and 307 controls. All experienced white noise only and mixtures of white noise and neutral speech at different volumes.	Structured Interview for Schizotypy-Revised.	Speech illusions were strongly associated with positive schizotypy and with increasing level of familial risk.
Randell, Goyal, & Saunders (2011)	41 non-clinical participants scoring high or low on the Oxford-Liverpool Inventory of Feelings and Experiences (brief version). Asked to report heard words during 10 1-minute recordings of white noise, some of which contained embedded concrete or abstract words.	Oxford-Liverpool Inventory of Feelings and Experiences (brief) (Mason et al. 2005)	High scorers on the unusual experiences scale reported hearing more words (not actually present), and showed a bias toward making hallucinatory reports of an abstract type over a concrete type

Note: LSHS – Launay-Slade Hallucination Scale (LSHS; Launay & Slade, 1981).

Table 9.2 Sensory deprivation and other paradigms

Study	Design/ Participants/Method	Psychometric measures	Schizotypy relationships
Lloyd, Lewis, Payne, & Wilson (2012)	Analysed participants' real-time descriptions of their experiences during 30 minutes of combined auditory and visual perceptual deprivation (white noise through headphones and the wearing of white Ganzfeld field goggles).	LSHS-R. State Trait Anxiety Inventory (Spielberger, Gorsuch, Lushene, Vagg, & Jacobs, 1983); Marlow-Crowne Social Desirability Scale (Strahan & Gerbasi, 1972).	A range of sensory phenomena from simple precepts to the feeling of immersion in a complex multisensory environment. Exploratory behaviour was also prominent.
Mason & Brady (2009)	High and low LSHS-R scorers placed in sensory deprivation conditions.	The Psychotomimetic States Inventory (Mason, Morgan, Stefanovic, & Curran, 2008); LSHS-R.	High scorers experienced more perceptual disturbances.
McCreery and Claridge (1996a, 1996b)	20 participants with out-of-body experience (OBE; mean age 41) were matched with control participants. Used pink noise and ganzfeld field goggles. Participants also followed a progressive relaxation exercise.	Abbreviated form of the Combined Schizotypal Traits Questionnaire (Bentall et al. 1999).	Reporters of previous OBEs scored higher on the measure of schizotypy than the controls, and showed greater responsiveness to the procedure.
Polito, Langdon, & and Brown (2012)	55 attendees (29 male, 26 female) in a shamanic sweat lodge ceremony.	The Altered State of Consciousness Scale (APZ: Dittrich 1998); The paranormal belief scale (Tobacyk, 1988); Profile of Mood States; Toronto Alexithymia Scale (Bagby et al. 1994).	No measures of paranormal beliefs were related to overall APZ scores. There was a positive relationship between alexithymia and intensity of the altered state of consciousness.

French, Haque, & Bunton-Stasyshyn (2009)	79 healthy participants each in one of four conditions: electromagnetic fields either present or absent, and infrasound either present or absent. Participants spent 50 minutes in the room and reported any anomalous sensations they experienced.	EXIT scale (measuring specific anomalous sensations); Australian Sheep-Goat Scale (Thalbourne and Delin, 1993). Personal Philosophy Inventory (Makarec & Persinger, 1990).	Many reported experiencing mildly anomalous sensations. However, the degree to which these anomalous sensations were reported was unrelated to the experimental conditions employed or to PPI.
Terhune and Smith (2006)	40 healthy participants were randomly allocated to either a control or suggestion condition. Participants spent 45 minutes gazing into a mirror, and were also played white noise. They were then asked to report any anomalous experiences.	Hyperesthesia Scale; Intrusive Thoughts subscale of the White Bear Supression Inventory (Blumberg 2000); Revised Paranormal Belief Scale (Tobacyk, 1988); Visual Style of Processing Scale; Haunt Experience Checklist; Phenomenology of Consciousness Inventory (Pekala 1991).	Participants in both groups reported anomalous experiences while mirror gazing. Those in the suggestion condition reported a significantly greater number of visual apparitions and a greater number of vocal apparitions than those allocated to the control condition.
Caputo et al. (2012)	16 patients with schizophrenia and 21 healthy controls. Mirror gazing as above.	Cardiff Anomalous Perceptions Scale.	Apparitions of strange faces were significantly more intense in schizophrenic patients than in controls.

Note: LSHS – Launay-Slade Hallucination Scale (Launay & Slade, 1981). LSHS-R Launay-Slade Hallucination Scale-Revised (Morrison et al. 2001).

it may be that high hallucination-prone participants responded more to the demands of the task and were therefore predisposed to report hearing words while being aware that their reports were untrue.

Auditory stimuli with no apparent voice characteristics are perhaps the most commonly used: 'white noise' has been employed in a variety of contexts. Merckelbach and van de Ven (2001) attempted to account for the potential impact of demand characteristics in their white noise study by incorporating the Social Desirability Scale (Crowne & Marlow, 1964), a commonly used measure of tendency to provide socially desirable responses across many situations. In this study, forty-four healthy undergraduate students were asked to listen to white noise and instructed to press a button when they believed they were hearing a recording of Bing Crosby's 'White Christmas' (without the record actually being presented). Fourteen participants (32 per cent) pressed the button at least once. Interestingly, reports of hallucinatory experiences were not found to be associated with a heightened sensitivity to situational demand, indicating that suggestibility or compliance to demand characteristics is not able to account for hallucinatory findings. Imagery ability was similarly not related. Participants reporting hearing the song were found to have higher scores on both the LSHS and the fantasy-proneness scale. Follow-up logistic regression analysis suggested that the contribution of fantasy proneness to the 'White Christmas' phenomenon was more substantial than that of hallucinatory disposition. However, this is inconsistent with previous research showing that, as a rule, fantasy-prone individuals do not have 'life-like' hallucinations. Specifically, Lynn and Rhue (1988) suggest that fantasy-prone people adopt lax criteria when they classify internal experiences as hallucinations. However, it may be that fantasy proneness mediates the process by which highly prone individuals experience hallucinations. For example, Bentall (1990) has suggested that fantasy proneness drives a specific response bias reflecting impaired reality testing, which in turn leads to reports of hallucinations.

Better evidence in support of the normal population experiencing true hallucinatory experiences during ambiguous auditory paradigms (as opposed to merely endorsing them via adoption of 'lax' response criteria) comes from experimental studies using random noise to induce hallucinations in groups with increasing familial risk for psychosis (Galdos, Simons, & Fernandez-Rivas, 2011). Following a white noise task (consisting of white noise only; white noise and clearly audible neutral speech; or white noise and barely audible neutral speech), participants were asked to press buttons to indicate whether they had heard speech, and also whether this had been positive, negative or neutral. There was also an option, to reduce the likelihood of guessing, for participants to report that they were unsure of what they had heard. Results showed a significant trend across groups for hearing speech illusions (with 9 per cent of controls, 14 per cent of siblings of patients, and 30 per cent of clinical patients hearing any speech illusion), thus indicating that the experience of speech illusion during the task mirrors the continuum of psychosis across clinical and normal populations. In controls, positive (but not negative) schizotypy also strongly predicted the effect. The findings of this study are of particular interest because it has several design strengths, particularly the large sample of controls (n = 307), interview-based measures of schizotypy and statistical control for IQ, executive control of attention and auditory verbal episodic memory.

Lastly, Randell, Goyal, and Saunders (2011) embedded words in white noise to examine the occurrence and content of auditory hallucinatory experiences in forty-one participants split into two groups based on the Unusual Experiences scale. They listened to ten 1-minute recordings of white noise: two of these contained concrete words (embedded at an average of 9-second intervals); two contained abstract words; the remaining six recordings were white noise only. The sets of concrete words (e.g. desk, arm, letter), and abstract words (e.g. myth, abyss, sorrow) were randomly chosen from a pool for each participant (so no two participants received the same combination). Participants were asked to write down any words they had heard during each recording. Participants were asked not to guess what they believed a word to be if they were unsure, but simply just to tick that they had heard a word. Consistent with previous studies, participants high in positive schizotypy made more false reports than low unusual experience scorers, a finding that was accentuated for falsely reporting abstract words.

Sensory deprivation

Five studies identified from the recent schizotypy literature have used a range of sensory deprivation contexts to attempt to induce hallucinations. Lloyd, Lewis, Payne, & Wilson (2012) subjected thirty-one participants to a 30-minute period of combined auditory and visual perceptual deprivation, achieved by playing white noise through headphones and the wearing of white ganzfeld field goggles. Hayashi, Morikawa, and Hori (1992) demonstrated that hallucinations during a prolonged period of 72 hours in sensory deprivation were associated with changes in EEG wave alpha activity (activity associated with vivid dream-like states). Mason and Brady (2009) explored whether perceptual disturbances could be elicited by only a brief period (15 minutes) of complete isolation from sound and vision in an anechoic chamber (a chamber constructed as a room within a room lined with glass fibre wedges and metallic acoustic panels). McCreery and Claridge (1996a, 1996b) combined sensory deprivation with the use of physical relaxation techniques in an attempt to induce out-of-body experiences (OBEs). All studies were successful in inducing hallucinations of varying complexity in many of the participants.

Lloyd et al. (2012) used a variant of interpretative phenomenological analysis to analyse participants' real-time descriptions of their experiences during a 30-minute period in sensory deprivation. Participants spontaneously reported a large number of visual, auditory and bodily sensations.

A correlational analysis revealed a positive correlation between the number of percepts reported and hallucinatory tendencies (LSHS-revised [-R]): this relationship was not mediated by high anxiety or suggestibility. Qualitative data revealed two main themes. The first was sensory phenomena with a range of spatial characteristics from simple percepts to the feeling of immersion in a complex multisensory environment. The most basic reports described noticing variation within the audiovisual environment (e.g. hearing a beep or seeing flashes of light). The more complex reports incorporated descriptions of a percept's cause, location, direction of movement and effects of the environment. The second major theme was the prominence of exploratory behaviour: participants interacted with their perceptions through their degree of attention or focus, or through moving their body to explore the qualities of the perception. This theme is of particular interest, because the fact that participants attempted to interrogate their perceptions argues against the suggestion that experiences in sensory deprivation are purely imaginary phenomena.

Mason and Brady (2009) selected both a high hallucination-prone and a low hallucination-prone group using the LSHS-R. The sensory deprivation conditions were created using an anechoic chamber (a chamber constructed as a room within a room lined with glass fibre wedges and metallic acoustic panels) that resulted in a soundproof environment. The room was also sealed to light, creating conditions of total darkness. After spending 15 minutes in the anechoic chamber, participants completed the Psychotomimetic States Inventory (Mason, Morgan, Stefanovic, & Curran, 2008). Psychosis-like experiences, taking the form of perceptual disturbances, paranoia and anhedonia, were found across both groups in sensory deprivation. However, the hallucination-prone group experienced more perceptual disturbances than the low-scoring group. The study was very small scale, failed to control for anxiety and its experimental set-up was criticised for using a 'panic' button (Bell 2010), which may alter the effects of sensory deprivation (Orne & Scheibe, 1964). However, this study has recently been replicated in a larger sample using an amended design (Daniel, Lovatt, & Mason, 2014).

McCreery and Claridge (1996a; 1996b) were particularly interested in inducing OBEs in a group with prior OBE experience and in closely matched controls. Participants were asked to lie on a sun-lounger, set in a nearly horizontal position, in a sound-shielded cubicle. They were then fitted with 'ping-pong ball' goggles (producing a ganzfeld visual field), and earphones through which was played a 20-minute exercise based on the 'progressive relaxation' technique of Jacobson (1929). Participants were then instructed to imagine themselves floating up to the ceiling and looking down on their physical body. Ten minutes of pink noise then followed (similar to white noise, but of a different frequency). Afterwards, participants completed questions regarding their state of relaxation during the experiment. The experiment confirmed that reporters of previous OBEs scored higher on the measure of schizotypy than controls, and showed greater responsiveness to the procedure. A significant proportion of the OBE group reported imagery experiences (fifteen versus eight in the control group). One participant in the OBE group reported a clear OBE during the procedure. Examination of EEG data from the participants (McCreery & Claridge, 1996b) revealed some differences between groups. Median frequency of EEG signals across both hemispheres started off approximately equal in both groups, declined substantially in both hemispheres by the end of the experiment in the control group, but declined less markedly in the left hemisphere of the 'OBErs' and actually increased over the course of the experiment in their right hemisphere.

'Naturalistic' experiments

In contrast to drug studies, only one 'naturalistic' experiment was identified in the literature. Polito, Langdon, and Brown (2010) examined the top-down influence of pre-existing beliefs and affective factors in shaping an individual's characterisation of anomalous sensory experiences. They investigated the effects of paranormal beliefs and alexithymia in determining the intensity and quality of an altered state of consciousness (ASC) achieved during a shamanic sweat lodge ceremony. A sweat lodge is a small dome-shaped structure, consisting of bent wooden poles or sticks covered with thick hides and blankets. Inside, participants sit silently in near total darkness, surrounding a small pit in which heated rocks are placed. The ceremony is led by a shaman who pours water over the rocks; this water then evaporates, creating heat like a sauna. The shaman sings songs, tells stories, chants and plays rhythmic, repetitive drumbeats. The sweat lodge ceremony has previously been shown by several researchers to induce an altered state of consciousness (Bucko, 1999; Eliade, 1972; McWhorter, 1994; Price-Williams & Hughes, 1994). Participants completed questionnaires before and after the ceremony. At baseline, participants completed the profile of mood states questionnaire (McNair, Lorr, & Droppleman, 1971), rating their emotions during the previous week; the APZ questionnaire (altered state of consciousness scale; Dittrich, 1998), rating their state of consciousness in the preceding few hours; and the paranormal belief scale (Tobacyk & Milford, 1983). Following the ceremony, participants again completed the profile of mood states and APZ questionnaires, with instructions to base response on their experiences during the sweat lodge. As predicted, participation in the sweat lodge ceremony induced higher ratings on measures of altered state experience compared with baseline. Specifically, there were significantly higher scores on the subscale dimensions of 'oceanic boundlessness' (referring to experiences of heightened mood, well-being, loss of boundaries and intense feelings of connectedness) and 'visionary restructuralisation' (referring to sensory illusions, altered sense of meaning, synaesthesias and ideas of reference). There were also marked changes in the profile of mood state questionnaire scores after the ceremony, with participants reporting reductions in tension, depression, anger, fatigue and confusion. No measures of paranormal beliefs were related to overall altered state scores, although three specific paranormal beliefs (psi, spiritualism and precognition) were associated with higher 'oceanic boundlessness' scores. There was a positive relationship between alexithymia and intensity of the altered state of consciousness, and this was found to be the only significant predictor of altered state experience.

Polito et al.'s (2010) research suggests that affective factors may have a facilitatory impact on altered states of consciousness. The authors hypothesise that alexithymia may lead to an enhanced ability to detach from personal experience, increasing the intensity with which altered states may be experienced. The relationship between paranormal beliefs (the best proxy for positive schizotypy here) and overall intensity of altered states was less clear. Given that this was a naturalistic study, the participants had arranged to attend the sweat lodge event of their own volition, rather than being recruited directly into the study. Therefore, it seems likely that the sample was self-selecting to some extent for holding unusual beliefs.

Manipulating electromagnetic fields and infrasound

It has long been argued that certain environmental factors associated with particular locations may directly cause susceptible individuals to experience anomalous sensations. In particular, 'haunting' phenomena (such as perceived sudden changes in temperature, unusual odours, a sense of presence or full-blown apparitions) have been suggested to be induced by exposure to unusual geomagnetic and electromagnetic fields (EMFs) (Braithwaite, 2004; Persinger and Koren, 2001). Another suggested cause of haunting-like anomalous experiences is the presence of infrasound – that is, sounds of such a low frequency that they are outside the audible range for human beings (Tandy & Lawrence, 1998). In light of these suggestions, French, Haque, & Bunton-Stasyshyn (2009) conducted the 'Haunt' project, in which they attempted to construct an artificial 'haunted' room by systematically varying environmental EMFs and infrasound.

In French et al.'s (2009) experiment, participants were asked to spend 50 minutes in an empty, white, circular room that was dimly lit and cool in temperature. The study employed a 2×2 design (EMF present versus EMF absent) and (infrasound present versus infrasound absent). Seventy-nine healthy participants were randomly allocated to one of the four conditions. Participants were asked to spend 50 minutes in the room and to record on a floor plan a brief description of any anomalous sensations they experienced, where they were when the experience occurred and the time at which it occurred. The EXIT scale (a scale containing twenty items asking about specific anomalous sensations) was given to participants to complete once they had left the room. Participants also completed the Australian

Sheep-Goat Scale (a widely used measure of belief in and experience of the paranormal (Thalbourne & Delin, 1993) and items from the temporal lobe sign (TLS) subsection of Persinger's Personal Philosophy Inventory (measuring psychological experiences thought to be associated with temporal lobe epilepsy but normally distributed throughout the normal population (Makarec & Persinger, 1990). Both these are to some extent proxies for positive schizotypy. Many of the participants in the experiment reported experiencing mildly anomalous sensations. However, the degree to which the anomalous sensations were reported was unrelated to the experimental conditions employed. The authors conclude that, given that all participants were informed in advance that they might experience unusual sensations while in the room (in line with ethical requirements), the most parsimonious explanation of the findings is in terms of participant suggestibility. The explanation is also supported by the fact that TLS scores, known to correlate with suggestibility (Granqvist, Fredikson, & Unge, 2005) significantly predicted the total number of anomalous experiences reported on the floor plan and the scores on the EXIT scale.

Mirror gazing

A technique known as 'scrying', involving gazing into a reflective surface to facilitate the appearance of apparitions, was popular in the late nineteenth century and has recently resurfaced in the context of bereavement therapy with the use of a mirror-gazing chamber (Moody, 1992; Moody & Perry, 1993). Although there is evidence to suggest that mirror gazing provides a suitable environment for apparitions (Moody, 1994), many of the reported experiences have not been formally studied. Terhune and Smith (2006) sought to investigate the variables involved in the induction of mirror-gazing hallucinations, particularly focusing on the role of suggestion. Forty participants were randomly allocated to either a control or suggestion condition, wherein they received different suggestions about the types of experiences they might expect to have. Participants then sat down in a comfortable chair in front of a mirror in an environment that was otherwise draped in black velvet. They spent 45 minutes gazing into the mirror while white noise was played. Participants in both groups reported anomalous experiences while those in the suggestion condition reported a significantly greater number of both visual and vocal apparitions. A range of trait measures including paranormal belief traits (a proxy for positive schizotypy) were not found to predict mirror-gazing hallucinations. More recently, Caputo et al. (2012) have used the paradigm with both schizophrenia patients and controls. While patients reported more frequent and intense apparitions, the Cardiff Anomalous Perceptions Scale did not predict apparitions in the control subjects. Although rather few data pertain to this task at present, it would appear to be producing effects due to suggestibility, and not schizotypy per se, in common with the haunt experiences discussed earlier.

Comparative effectiveness

A variety of ambiguous auditory environments and perceptually ambiguous visual paradigms have proved successful in inducing hallucinations (for an overview, see Table 9.1). The type of hallucinations induced has generally been shown to be restricted to the sensory modality being experimentally manipulated. In sensory deprivation conditions, where several sensory modalities are restricted simultaneously, more complex hallucinations involving tactile, visual and auditory experiences have been reported. While it has previously been demonstrated that such experiences occur following prolonged periods of deprivation, this has also been shown with a relatively brief exposure of 15 minutes (Mason & Brady, 2009). The most common confounds of studies in this area are relatedly probably trait suggestibility on the part of participants, and 'leading' instructional sets on the part of experimenters. For instance, although only a small number of studies have investigated manipulation of EMFs or infrasound, no evidence has been found to suggest that these methods are successful in inducing hallucinations above and beyond suggestion. It remains unclear whether mirror gazing can be considered an effective method for inducing hallucinations because of the methodological limitations of the current research. The complete absence of the use of suggestion in studies using white noise, ganzfeld or sensory deprivation would suggest that these paradigms are preferable in schizotypy research.

Methodological issues and future directions

While there is mounting evidence to suggest that experimentally induced hallucinations are not purely the product of demand characteristics and suggestibility, a number of studies that have measured these variables report that they are associated with increased likelihood of anomalous experiences. It remains unclear whether suggestibility or fantasy proneness is associated with increased reports of hallucinations through direct causality, or whether these traits are associated with high schizotypy and it is schizotypal tendencies that drive the experience of hallucinations, perhaps with fantasy proneness exacerbating reporting tendencies. Studies that have directly compared high and low schizotypal groups have not generally incorporated measures of suggestibility and fantasy proneness, and there is a need for future studies to do so. More studies that have adopted double-blind procedures are also necessary to confirm that current data are not affected by experimenter bias. In its broadest sense, the term 'hallucination' can apply to any non-voluntary perception that does not match external stimulation (Lloyd et al. 2012). From an experimental perspective, there remains an important need to establish whether some of the more fleeting misperceptions reported are truly on the same continuum as hallucinations.

References

Aleman, A., Bocker, K. B., & Hijman, R. (2003). Cognitive basis of hallucinations in schizophrenia: role of top-down information processing. *Schizophrenia Research, 64*(2–3), 175–185.

Bagby, R. M., Parker, J. D. A., & Taylor, G. J. (1994). The twenty-item Toronto Alexithymia scale-1. Item selection and cross-validation of the factor structure. *Journal of Psychosomatic Research, 38*(1), 23–32.

Bell, V. (2010). An alternative interpretation of 'The psychotomimetic effects of short-term sensory deprivation'. *Journal of Nervous and Mental Disease, 198*(2), 166.

Bentall, R. P. (1990). The illusion of reality: a review and integration of psychological research on hallucinations. *Psychological Bulletin, 107*(1), 82–95.

Blakemore, S. J., Smith, J., Steel, R., Johnstone, E. C., & Frith, C. D. (2000). The perception of self-produced sensory stimuli in patients with auditory hallucinations and passivity experiences: evidence for a breakdown in self-monitoring. *Psychological Medicine, 30*, 1131–1139.

Blumberg, S. J. (2000). The white bear suppression inventory: revisiting its factor structure. *Personality and Individual Differences, 29*, 943–950.

Braithwaite, J. J. (2004). Magnetic variances associates with 'haunt-type-experiences: a comparison using time-synchronised baseline measurements. *European Journal of Parapsychology, 19*, 3–28.

Bucko, R. A. (1999). *The Lakota ritual of the sweat lodge: History and contemporary practice*. Lincoln, NE: Bison Books.

Caputo, G. B., Ferrucci, R., Bortolomasi, M., Giacopuzzi, M., Priori, A., & Zago, S. (2012). Visual perception during mirror gazing at one's own face in schizophrenia. *Schizophrenia Research, 140*(1), 46–50.

Crowne, D., & Marlow, D. (1964). *The approval motive*. New York: Wiley.

Daniel, C., Lovatt, A., & Mason, O. J. (2014). Psychotic-like experiences and their cognitive appraisal under short-term sensory deprivation. *Frontiers in Psychiatry, 5*.

Dittrich, A. (1998). The standardized psychometric assessment of altered states of consciousness (ASCs) in humans. *Pharmacopsychiatry, 31*(Suppl. 2), 80–84.

Eliade, M. (1972). *Shamanism: Archaic techniques of ecstacy*. Princeton, NJ: Bollingen.

Feelgood, S. R., & Rantzen, A. J. (1994). Auditory and visual hallucinations in university students. *Personality and Individual Differences, 17*(2), 293–296.

French, C. C., Haque, U., & Bunton-Stasyshyn, R. (2009). The 'Haunt' project: an attempt to build a 'haunted' room by manipulating complex electromagnetic fields and infrasound. *Cortex, 45*, 619–629.

Galdos, M., Simons, C., & Fernandez-Rivas, A. (2011). Affectively salient meaning in random noise: a task sensitive to psychosis liability. *Schizophrenia Bulletin, 37*(6), 1179–1186.

Granqvist, P., Fredikson, M., & Unge, P. (2005). Sensed presence and mystical experiences are predicted by suggestibility, not by the application of transcranial weak complex magnetic fields. *Neuroscience Letters, 375*, 69–74.

Grossberg, S. (2000). How hallucinations may arise from brain mechanisms of learning, attention, and volition. *Journal of the International Neuropsychological Society, 6*(5), 583–592.

Hayashi, M., Morikawa, T., & Hori, T. (1992). EEG alpha activity and hallucinatory experience during sensory deprivation. *Perceptual and Motor Skills, 75*(2), 403–412.

Jacobson, E. (1929). *Progressive relaxation*. University of Chicago Press.

Jakes, S., & Hemsley, D.,R. (1986). Individual differences in reaction to brief exposure to unpatterned visual stimulation. *Personality and Individual Differences, 7*, 121–123.

Johns, L. C., & van Os, J. (2011). The continuity of psychotic experiences in the general population. *Clinical Psychology Review, 21*(8), 1123–1141.

Kendler, K. S., Thacker, L., & Walsh, D. (1996). Self-report measures of schizotypy as indices of familial vulnerability to schizophrenia. *Schizophrenia Bulletin, 22*(3), 511–520.

Launay, G., & Slade, P. D. (1981). The measurement of hallucinatory predisposition in male and female prisoners. *Personality and Individual Differences, 2*, 221–234.

Lloyd, D. M, Lewis, E., Payne, J., & Wilson, L. (2012). A qualitative analysis of sensory phenomena induced by perceptual deprivation. *Phenomenology and Cognitive Science, 11*, 95–112.

Lynn, S. J., & Rhue, J.W. (1988). Fantasy proneness and paranormal beliefs. *Psychological Reports, 66*, 655–658.

Makarec, K., & Persinger, M. A. (1990). Electroencephalographic validation of a temporal lobe signs inventory. *Journal of Research in Personality, 24*, 323–337.

Mason, O. J., & Brady, F. (2009). The psychotomimetic effects of short-term sensory deprivation. *Journal of Nervous and Mental Disease, 197*(10), 783–785.

Mason, O. J., Morgan, C. J. A, Stefanovic, A., & Curran, H. V. (2008). The Psychotomimetic States Inventory (PSI): measuring psychotic-type experiences from ketamine and cannabis. *Schizophrenia Research, 103*(1–3), 138–142.

McCreery, C., & Claridge, G. (1996a). A study of hallucination in normal subjects – I. Self-report data. *Personality and Individual Differences, 21*(5), 739–747.

McCreery, C., & Claridge, G. (1996b). A study of hallucination in normal subjects – II. Electrophysiological data. *Personality and Individual Differences, 21*(5), 749–758.

McNair, D. M., Lorr, M., & Droppleman, L. F. (1971). *Manual for the profile of mood states*. San Diego, CA: Educational and Industrial Testing Service.

McWhorter, P. J. (1994). *Native spiritual practice in contemporary mainstream life: A qualitative study of spirituality and well-being*. University of Utah: Department of Educational Psychology.

Merckelbach, H., & van de Ven, V. (2001). Another white Christmas: fantasy proneness and reports of hallucinatory experiences in undergraduate students. *Journal of Behavior Therapy and Experimental Psychiatry, 32*, 137–144.

Moody, R. A. (1992). Family reunions: visionary encounters with the depated in a modern-day psychomanteum. *Journal of Near Death Studies, 11*, 83–121.

Moody, R. A. (1994). A latter-day psychomanteum. *Proceedings of the 37th Annual Convention of the Parapsychological Association* (pp. 335–336).

Moody, R. A., & Perry, P. (1993). *Reunions: Visionary Encounters with Departed Loved Ones*. New York: Villard Books.

Orne, M. T., & Scheibe, K. E. (1964). The contribution of nondeprivation factors in the production of sensory deprivation effects: the psychology of the 'panic button'. *Journal of Abnormal Social Psychology, 68*: 3–12.

Pearson, D., Burrow, A., FitzGerald, C., Green, K., Lee, G., & Wise N. (2001). Auditory hallucinations in normal child populations. *Personality and Individual Differences, 31*, 401–407.

Pekala, R. J. (1991). *The Phenomenology of Consciousness Inventory*. West Chester, PA: Mid-Atlantic Educational Institute, Inc.

Persinger, M. A., & Koren, S. A. (2001). Predicting the characteristics of haunt phenomena from geomagnetic factors and brain sensitivity. In J. Houran, &

Lange, R. (Eds), *Hauntings and poltergeists: Multidisciplinary perspectives* (pp. 179–194). Jefferson, NC: McFarland.

Polito, V., Langdon, R., & Brown, J. (2010). The experience of altered states of consciousness in shamanic ritual: the role of pre-existing beliefs and affective factors. *Consciousness and Cognition, 19*, 918–925.

Price-Williams, D., & Hughes, D. J. (1994). Shamanism and altered states of consciousness. *Anthropology of Consciousness, 5*(2), 1–15.

Randell, J., Goyal, M., & Saunders, J. (2011). Effect of a context of concrete and abstract words on hallucinatory content in individuals scoring high in schizotypy. *Journal of Behavior Therapy and Experimental Psychiatry, 42*, 149–153.

Strahan, R., & Gerbasi, K. C. (1972). Short, homogeneous versions of the Marlowe-Crowne Social Desirability Scale. *Journal of Clinical Psychology, 28*, 191–193.

Tandy, V., & Lawrence, T. R. (1998). The ghost in the machine. *Journal of the Society for Psychical Research, 62*, 360–364.

Terhune, D. B., & Smith, M. (2006). The induction of anomalous experiences in a mirror-gazing facility. Suggestion, cognitive perceptual personality traits and phenomenological state effects. *The Journal of Nervous and Mental Disease, 194*(6), 415–421.

Thalbourne, M. A., & Delin, P. S. (1993). A new instrument for measuring the sheep-goat variable: its psychometric properties and factor structure. *Journal of the Society for Psychical Research, 59*, 172–186.

Tobacyk, J. J. (1988). A revised paranormal belief scale. Unpublished manuscript. Ruston, LA: Louisiana Tech University.

Tobacyk, J. J., & Milford, G. (1983). Belief in paranormal phenomena: assessment instrument development and implications for personality functioning. *Journal of Personality and Social Psychology, 44*(5), 1029–1037.

Vercammen, A., & Aleman, A. (2010). Semantic expectations can induce false perceptions in hallucination-prone individuals. *Schizophrenia Bulletin, 36*(1), 151–156.

Ziskind, E. (1964). A second look at sensory deprivation. *Journal of Nervous and Mental Disease, 138*, 223–232.

Part III
Consequences and outcomes

10 Dimensional approaches to delusional beliefs

Charlie Heriot-Maitland and Emmanuelle Peters

Psychiatric definitions of delusions

Classic psychiatry, following the Jasperian tradition (Jaspers, 1913), has long assumed that the delusions of patients diagnosed with psychotic conditions are qualitatively different from the beliefs of the general population. Qualitative difference implies that one or more factors are categorically distinct – supposedly attributable to their pathological origin. The fifth edition of *the Diagnostic and statistical manual of mental disorders (DSM-5*; American Psychiatric Association, 2013) brought about some subtle, but important, changes to the way delusions are defined in mainstream Western psychiatry. Because these changes are reflective of the broader advancement in psychological viewpoints of delusions over the past 20 years, we consider shifting psychiatric definitions before exploring dimensionality in more detail – discussing how dimensional approaches have characterised and influenced the psychological understanding, measurement, study of, and psychological interventions for, delusional beliefs.

In *DSM-IV* (American Psychiatric Association, 2000), the predecessor to *DSM-5*, delusions were defined as follows:

> A false belief based on incorrect inference about external reality that is firmly sustained despite what almost everyone else believes and despite what constitutes incontrovertible and obvious proof or evidence to the contrary. The belief is not one ordinarily accepted by other members of the person's culture or subculture (e.g. it is not an article of religious faith). When a false belief involves a value judgment, it is regarded as a delusion only when the judgment is so extreme as to defy credibility. (American Psychiatric Association, 2000, p. 765)

And now, in the recent *DSM-5*:

> Delusions are fixed beliefs that are not amenable to change in light of conflicting evidence . . . . Delusions are deemed bizarre if they are clearly implausible and not understandable to same-culture peers and do not derive from ordinary life experiences. . . . The distinction

between a delusion and a strongly held idea is sometimes difficult to make and depends in part on the degree of conviction with which the belief is held despite clear or reasonable contradictory evidence regarding its veracity. (American Psychiatric Association, 2013, p. 87)

The first noteworthy change between the two editions is that falsity is no longer central to the definition of delusional beliefs. Also, the changing language from 'incontrovertible and obvious proof or evidence to the contrary' (*DSM-IV*) to 'clear or reasonable contradictory evidence' (*DSM-5*) recognises that we may indeed never have proof against the truth of a belief. This reflects a shift from the belief content having a defining and diagnostic importance, towards even 'bizarre' content being seen as just one dimension of a delusional belief. In *DSM-5*, more emphasis is placed on the other dimensions of certainty and resistance to counter-evidence. So, while there seems to be a narrowing gap between delusions and everyday beliefs in terms of *content*, and an explicit recognition of the similarities between delusions and other strongly held ideas, the current psychiatric definition still posits that delusional beliefs can be distinguished from other beliefs in qualities of conviction and incorrigibility.

Psychological models of delusions: multiple interacting continua of belief dimensions

Psychological models view delusions as (i) on a continuum with normal beliefs; (ii) multidimensional; (iii) attempts to make sense of anomalous experiences; (iv) mediated by maladaptive appraisals; (v) involving reasoning and cognitive biases; and (vi) influenced by emotional processes.

Delusions on a continuum with normal beliefs

Psychological approaches to delusions have typically adopted a 'continuum' model, which denies categorical distinctions between delusional and everyday beliefs, and, in doing so, challenges the traditional notion that having a diagnosed psychotic condition is qualitatively different from normal human experience. The idea that psychotic symptoms, such as delusions, lie on a continuous distribution from normal to pathological has been around for many years (Strauss, 1969). We first outline a dimensional understanding of delusions and measurement thereof.

Delusional themes generally reflect the types of beliefs held in the general population (Peters, Joseph, Day, & Garety, 2004), and this resemblance extends across their factor structure. People who are high on the delusional ideation continuum also share the same epidemiological patterns of variation and risk factors (Johns & van Os, 2001). In two recent systematic reviews and meta-analyses of the psychosis continuum, van Os and colleagues gathered comprehensive evidence for a continuity in psychotic experiences, their associated psychopathology, and correlations in positive, negative and affective dimensions (Linscott & van Os, 2013; van Os, Linscott, Myin-Germeys, Delespaul, & Krabbendam, 2009). With respect to delusions specifically, 10 per cent to 15 per cent of the non-clinical population had fairly regular delusional ideation, with a further 1–3 per cent with delusions of a level of severity comparable to clinical cases of psychosis, and 5–6 per cent with less severe beliefs nevertheless associated with a range of social and emotional difficulties (Freeman, 2006). van Os et al. (2009) conclude that while non-clinical expressions of psychosis are predictive of a higher risk of clinical psychotic disorder, they are 'mostly self-limiting and of good outcome' (p. 190). The most widely used measure of delusional ideation in the general population is the Peters et al. Delusions Inventory (PDI; Peters et al., 2004; Peters, Joseph, & Garety, 1999), which assesses a range of delusional ideation themes. Other measures, such as the Green et al. Paranoid Thoughts Scale (Green et al., 2008), have concentrated specifically on paranoid beliefs in the general population (see Bell & Peters, 2014, for a review of delusion scales).

Continuum of belief content

Bizarre or unfounded content

In the clinical population with delusions, there is clear variability among individuals in the bizarreness and/or impossibility of their beliefs. In some delusions, there is an element (or kernel) of truth – for example, when an individual has been the victim of a violent mugging, and subsequently believes they are now in danger of being attacked. On the other hand, some delusions are clearly impossible – for example, when an individual believes that there are spiders crawling under their skin. However, even in the most bizarre or unfounded delusions, there is often still a thread of validity, even if it is not a literal truth. While, on the surface, delusional content may seem irrational or false to the onlooker, psychological formulations have increasingly recognised the personal significance of delusions in relation to an individual's unique circumstances and experiences (Janssen et al., 2003). For example, Johns et al. (2004) showed that paranoid thoughts were significantly associated with victimisation experiences and stressful life events.

In the same way that clinical delusions can express or convey truth, the beliefs of non-clinical populations can, of course, be false – or, at least, not grounded in objective evidence. For instance, in a large random sample of American adults, Newport and Strausberg (2001) found that 42 per cent believed in haunted houses, and 33 per cent believed that extra-terrestrial beings had visited earth. Clearly, belief content is neither necessary nor sufficient to define a delusion, and bizarre or unfounded content is distributed throughout the range of 'normal' belief.

Personal reference of content

This key characteristic was originally identified by Oltmanns (1988) to help distinguish between delusional and other firmly held beliefs, such as religious, scientific or political. One account of the personal reference dimension that has received much attention is the dopamine-salience hypothesis (Kapur, 2003), which stems from earlier models seeking to integrate the neural and cognitive aspects of psychosis (Gray, Feldon, Rawlins, Smith, & Hemsley, 1991). This model suggests that dysregulated firing and/or release of dopamine leads to the assignment of inappropriate salience to internal and external events, inducing a sense of exaggerated personal importance, potentially leading to the emergence of ideas of personal reference. While Kapur's model, by citing a pathological (biological) cause, only seeks to explain this phenomenon in clinical populations, a more fully dimensional account of personal reference, as occurring on a continuum with normality, may be provided by psychological models emphasising the role of emotional processes in beliefs, such as anticipation of threat (Freeman, 2007; Gumley, Braehler, Laithwaite, MacBeth, & Gilbert, 2010) and relationship to self-esteem (Bentall, Corcoran, Howard, Blackwood, & Kinderman, 2001). These emotional experiences, which involve personal salience, may, of course, still be correlated with dopamine release, without necessarily implying pathological causation. As with bizarre content, the degree of personal reference in delusions varies considerably, from 'I am being specifically targeted' to 'We are all doomed'. As with other types of delusions, proneness to ideas of reference can also be assessed in the general population psychometrically, with a number of studies employing the Referential Thinking Scale (Lenzenweger, Bennett, & Lilenfeld, 1997).

Multidimensionality of delusions

The view that delusions are multi-dimensional, and the notion of multiple interacting continua, is also not new (Garety & Hemsley, 1987; Kendler, Glazer, & Morgenstern, 1983). Oltmanns (1988) suggested that a definition of delusion should incorporate a list of defining characteristics, and, while none is sufficient or necessary, the more characteristics that are indicated, the more a consensus should be reached on the delusional nature of a belief. This body of work marked an important move towards recognising individual variability in the characteristics or dimensions of delusional experience. Also, Oltmanns' view that no single dimension is sufficient or necessary to define a delusion implies that the individual variability or distribution of a single dimension may be continuous with normality. We now outline the dimensions of delusions that are most commonly acknowledged in the literature (conviction, incorrigibility, interference with functioning, distress and preoccupation; Freeman, 2007). For each belief dimension, the individual variability among clinical populations will be explored, as well as its continuum with normal ideation.

Belief dimension of conviction

There is evidence that many delusions do not show absolute conviction, with approximately 50 per cent of people with delusions acknowledging they may be mistaken (Garety et al., 2005). Conviction not only fluctuates between individuals in the clinical population, but also within individuals on a moment-to-moment basis (Peters et al., 2012) and from one environment to the next (Myin-Germeys, Nicolson, & Delespaul, 2001). Delusions can vary from being held with full conviction to only occasionally being activated (e.g. when someone is stressed or in specific social situations). Likewise, in the non-clinical population, there is great variability in the degree to which beliefs are firmly held, with beliefs that are highly meaningful and significant to the person, such as religious beliefs, being held with conviction levels equal to delusions (Jones & Watson, 1997). Studies using the PDI (Peters et al., 2004), which assesses the three key delusional dimensions of conviction, preoccupation and distress, have also demonstrated that conviction is not the best dimension to differentiate between individuals with and without a 'need for care' (Peters, Day, McKenna, & Orbach 1999). Therefore, despite its central importance to current psychiatric definitions of delusions (*DSM-5*), conviction cannot be established on its own as a defining characteristic of delusional beliefs.

Belief dimension of incorrigibility

The incorrigibility, or resistance to change, of delusions is also a key feature of the *DSM-5* definition. There is, however, evidence of variability of this dimension in the clinical population, with small case series research showing individual differences in accommodation of contradictory evidence (Brett-Jones, Garety, & Hemsley, 1987). Clinical trials of psychological interventions also demonstrate that delusions can, in fact, be 'corrigible', using a process of re-evaluating evidence and changing thinking style (Wykes, Steel, Everitt, & Tarrier, 2008). Furthermore, similar to high conviction, incorrigibility is not a hallmark of delusions per se, but characteristic of all personally meaningful beliefs: Colbert, Peters, and Garety (2010) found that personally meaningful beliefs, whether delusions or idiosyncratic, were held with equal conviction and belief flexibility between groups with current and remitted delusions, and a non-clinical group. 'Normal' cognitive biases, such as attentional and confirmation biases (discussed further later), operate across the spectrum of personally significant beliefs, allowing them to be impervious to contradictory evidence. However, Colbert and colleagues found that there were differences between groups in control beliefs (that is, standard, non-personal beliefs), with the clinical groups showing less belief flexibility than the non-clinical groups, suggesting that belief inflexibility may be more a characteristic of the thinking styles of individuals with delusions, than delusions themselves being incorrigible.

Belief dimension of interference with functioning

Many delusions can interfere significantly with social and occupational functioning, leading people to isolate themselves and disengage from hobbies, activities and interests. It is understandable how, for example, paranoid ideation can have an impact on social involvement, and interference with functioning is central to developing a 'need for care'. It is closely related to the dimensions of distress and preoccupation, but, interestingly, less so with delusional conviction (Peters et al., 2012). On the other hand, some people with delusions can still function at a high level, effectively maintaining jobs, activities and social relationships. In the non-clinical population, the influence of beliefs on behaviour and functioning is widely apparent, and particularly highlighted around religious rituals, such as solitude, abstinence and fasting.

Belief dimensions of distress and preoccupation

Some people can be extremely distressed and preoccupied by their beliefs, particularly if they are paranoid or hold persecutory beliefs, or if they believe that the threats/criticisms/taunts of their voices belong to a powerful being and therefore must be taken seriously. However, some beliefs are less distressing and preoccupying, and some (e.g. grandiose delusions) can be positively fulfilling. Although belief content is, to some degree, inevitably linked to these two dimensions (David, 2010), nevertheless they have been shown to be more predictive than content alone in distinguishing between healthy and clinical populations (Lincoln, 2007; Peters, Day et al., 1999).

In psychological approaches, distress is often regarded to be the defining feature of a psychological problem; in other words, if a psychotic symptom is not distressing, then it is not a problem, and there is no rationale for psychological therapy (Chadwick & Trower, 1996). As such, psychological interventions often aim to facilitate change along this belief dimension. The studies that have monitored distress and preoccupation have shown that these dimensions are highly variable on a moment-to-moment basis (Peters et al., 2012), and can change independently of others in response to both psychological (Chadwick & Lowe, 1994) and pharmacological (So, Peters, Swendsen, Garety, & Kapur, 2014) interventions.

Psychological models of delusions: other key aspects

Delusions are attempts to make sense of anomalous experiences

The relationship between experiences and beliefs in delusions has been a topic of much interest, particularly the question of which comes first: are delusions unusual convictions that alter one's way of experiencing the world, or are they hypotheses formulated to make sense of unusual experiences, which are then endorsed as beliefs? In most cognitive accounts, an anomalous experience or event is thought to be primary. For instance, Maher (1974) proposed that delusions are interpretations of altered perceptual phenomena, so essentially normal responses to anomalous experiences. Chadwick, Birchwood, and Tower's (1996) ABC-analysis model of delusions also emphasises the importance of experiences in driving delusions, whereby 'A's constitute activating events or experiences, 'B's are evaluative beliefs about the event, and 'C's are the emotional and behavioural consequences of the beliefs. Biological models implicating dopamine in the development of psychotic symptoms also suggest that delusions are attempts to make sense of experiences of 'aberrant salience' (Gray et al., 1991; Kapur, 2003). The 'delusions as explanations of experience' view is supported in a number of sources; for instance, Freeman et al. (2004) found that three-quarters of his deluded sample had no alternative explanation for their experiences. Those individuals who did have alternatives did not stick to their delusions because they were less distressing, but because they were more plausible.

Delusions are mediated by maladaptive appraisals

More recent cognitive accounts have conceived a more complex interaction between anomalous experiences and biased reasoning/cognitive processes (Garety, Kuipers, Fowler, Freeman, & Bebbington, 2001), or between aberrant perceptual experiences and evaluative biases (Langdon & Coltheart, 2000). Bentall et al. (2001) have also highlighted that the relationship between delusions and hallucinations (common forms of anomalous perceptual experience) is reciprocal: for example, not only can hallucinations provoke delusional interpretations, but beliefs can also influence the source-monitoring judgements of hallucinating patients. This circular influence may help to explain the co-occurrence of hallucinations and delusions in people with psychotic conditions and in the general population (Altman, Collins, & Mundy, 1997), indicating the continuum of a 'hallucinatory–delusional syndrome', independent of disorder (Smeets et al., 2012).

Psychological models all have in common that they regard individuals' appraisals as key mediators in determining the outcome of anomalous experience or arousal (Bentall et al., 2001; Garety et al., 2001; Morrison, 2001). Thus, the experience of hearing a voice, for instance, does not necessarily become a full-blown psychotic symptom unless it is appraised in a maladaptive way. They have, however, differed slightly in what they conceive to be the main aspects of a maladaptive appraisal: Garety et al. (2001) focus on appraisals of experiences as externally caused and personally significant, while Morrison (2001) focuses on appraisals of experiences as culturally unacceptable. Cognitive models further emphasise that appraisals are aligned to the individual's previous experiences, knowledge, memories and decision-making processes, as well as to their emotional, social and cultural context.

A challenge for research in this field has been to disentangle experiences, appraisals and outcomes. One strategy has been to control a social environment experimentally using virtual reality, and to study participants' appraisals about virtual situations and characters (Freeman, 2008). Freeman and his colleagues have been able to demonstrate that individuals diverge markedly in their appraisals of the same virtual reality environment, and that paranoid interpretations are predicted by emotional and cognitive factors, in addition to the presence of perceptual anomalies.

Another approach has been to recruit people in the general population who report anomalous experiences of an equivalent nature to those with psychosis, but whose lives have not been negatively affected in terms of functioning and well-being (Heriot-Maitland, Knight, & Peters, 2012). Recruiting this population, alongside clinical populations, allows insight into the appraisals that may be mediating these different outcomes. Empirical studies seeking to identify the specific appraisals that mediate a transition from experiences to psychotic symptoms, either using retrospective interviews or responses to experimental analogues of anomalous experiences, have implicated appraisals that experiences are caused by 'other people' (Brett et al., 2007; Lovatt, Mason, Brett, & Peters, 2010), which themselves are predictive of more distress (Brett, Heriot-Maitland, McGuire, & Peters, 2013), and appraisals of experiences as personally salient, threatening and uncontrollable (Brett et al., 2007; Ward et al., 2013).

Delusions involve reasoning and cognitive biases

The process by which a particular appraisal reaches a delusional level is regarded, in psychological models, as depending upon cognitive biases, such as attributional style, theory of mind (understanding others' mental states) deficits, and 'jumping to conclusions' (Bentall et al., 2009; Garety et al., 2001). The literature on attributional style has typically focused on the tendency to appraise experiences as externally caused, and so functioning as a self-serving bias (Bentall et al., 2001) with a dynamic relationship between fluctuations in self-esteem and paranoid appraisals (Thewissen, Bentall, Lecomte, van Os, & Myin-Germeys, 2008). 'Jumping to conclusions' is the best evidenced cognitive bias in clinical populations with delusions (Garety & Freeman, 2013), and it is also present in healthy but delusion-prone (van Dael et al., 2006) and prodromal (Broome et al, 2007) individuals, suggesting that a tendency to make premature judgements on the basis of limited evidence may have a causal role in delusion formation. Dudley and Over (2003) propose that 'jumping to conclusions' is a normal threat-related reasoning process, which is increased among people with delusions/delusional ideation because they perceive threat in objectively non-threatening situations.

Although these biases are often presented (rightly or wrongly) as cognitive abnormalities or deficits that increase vulnerability to delusions, psychological models of delusion formation also highlight the influence of both 'Beckian' (after Aaron Beck) cognitive distortions seen in emotional disorders (Peters et al., 2014), and normal cognitive biases. The 'confirmation bias', for instance, is the well-known propensity for people to notice, gather, and process information that confirms their beliefs, while discarding information that disconfirms them. This processing bias operates to influence belief conviction and incorrigibility, regardless of whether or not an individual is experiencing clinically diagnosable delusions.

Delusions are influenced by emotional processes

The role of emotions in delusion formation is gathering increasing attention in the psychological literature (Garety & Freeman, 2013), with empirical evidence that negative emotions drive paranoid appraisals, rather than the other way round (Fowler et al., 2012; Thewissen et al., 2011). Of particular interest has been the role of anxiety in threat anticipation and paranoid thinking (Freeman, Garety, Kuipers, Fowler, & Bebbington, 2002), the role of depression and self-esteem (Bentall et al., 2009; Udachina, Varese, Oorschot, Myin-Germeys, & Bentall, 2012), and the role of social rank, power differentials, attachment and emotional schema in distressing beliefs about interpersonal experiences, including voice hearing (Mayhew & Gilbert, 2008). Emotions and affect-based schema will drive cognitive processes such as attention and memory, and will also influence the kinds of responses elicited, thus providing the driving force for circular patterns of emotion, thinking and behaviour. In the case of anxiety, the activation of the brain's threat-protection systems will increase vigilance towards threatening information and elicit responses such as dissociation and avoidance (Gumley et al., 2010). Not only will this increase the likelihood of threat beliefs developing, it will also restrict access to information and situations that could provide disconfirmatory evidence. The psychological concept of mood-congruent processing is relevant here; in other words, the idea that, in a state of emotional arousal, information processing will favour emotion-relevant material, similar to how the confirmation bias operates with beliefs. A detailed theoretical account of how the brain orientates in line with dominant motives and emotions is provided in the evolutionary model of social mentalities (Gilbert, 1989).

Clinical implications of dimensional approaches to delusions

The increasing evidence for the continuum and multi-dimensionality of delusions has important implications for how delusions are understood, assessed and addressed in therapy. Although *DSM-5* has moved further than *DSM-IV* towards recognising the complexity in distinguishing delusions from everyday beliefs, the evidence reviewed here suggests that it could still go further, and indeed raises questions as to the validity of making categorical distinctions at all. This section will explore the implications of dimensional approaches to delusions in terms of psychological formulation and interventions.

Understanding delusions

The main practical implication of a dimensional approach is that, in order to understand delusions, we need to understand each dimension of delusional experience. So, rather than asking 'What causes a delusion?', we should instead be asking 'What predicts the degree of conviction?'; 'What maintains preoccupation?'; 'How does personal reference interact with other dimensions?', 'Which psychological factors are related to delusional distress?', etc. (Freeman, 2007). In the words of Delespaul and van Os (2003):

> The process of delusion formation is not irreducible but instead can be traced to a multi-factorial aetiology involving an interaction, over the course of development, between a range of cognitive and emotional vulnerabilities, social circumstances, and somatic factors, all of which are distributed in the general population and all of which may impact independently on one or more belief dimensions. (p. 286).

This is the essence of psychological models, as outlined at the start of this chapter, and, as we have seen, this explanatory framework is becoming increasingly supported by empirical evidence.

The implications for future research are to investigate specifically the causes of different dimensions of delusions. The assessment of delusions has been facilitated in recent years by the development of both questionnaire (PDI; Peters et al., 2004) and interview (Psychotic Symptom Rating Scales [PSYRATS]; Haddock et al 1999) multidimensional measures of delusional beliefs. There is already some research on predictors of delusional conviction (Garety et al., 2005), distress (Startup, Freeman, & Garety, 2007) and belief flexibility (So et al., 2012); however, more is needed on the other dimensions, as well as studies that look at the interactions between dimensions, their relationships with other variables and whether there are common or different factors influencing each dimension. Research in delusions should be carried out within the context of what we know about 'normal' belief formation and processes (Bentall, 1994), and the field will benefit from more studies of non-clinical populations who report unusual or bizarre beliefs, but without associated distress and interference with functioning. Such research may provide insight into the protective, as well as risk, factors associated with dimensions of beliefs across the psychosis continuum.

Psychological interventions for delusions

There is increasing evidence that psychological therapy can modify some dimensions of delusions, irrespective of others (Chadwick & Lowe, 1994;

Sharp et al., 1996). This implies that therapists can identify specific goals with clients regarding which aspect of their experience they are hoping to change (e.g. to lower distress or improve functioning). Formulations can then identify the barriers or blocks to these goals (e.g. by highlighting that distress is maintained because of secondary appraisals about the authority of a persecutor [Freeman, Garety, & Kuipers, 2001]). The implication for therapy trials is mainly regarding which outcomes are investigated. As argued by Birchwood and Trower (2006), future trials of cognitive behaviour therapy for psychosis (CBTp) should primarily target emotional, cognitive and behavioural outcomes, with possible secondary effects on psychotic phenomena. Freeman (2011) also points to the development and testing of different factor-specific interventions as crucial for the future of CBTp. Recent studies have targeted specific aspects of delusion with promising results, such as reasoning biases (Moritz et al., 2011) and worry (Foster, Startup, Potts, & Freeman, 2010). Dimensional approaches to delusions have not only helped identify the outcome targets of psychological interventions, but also helped to 'normalise' these dimensions as continuous, which importantly cultivates hope and motivation for recovery. The wider treatment implications, at the level of services, are to work towards normalising people's unusual experiences and beliefs, deconstructing illness labels, and encouraging a culture of acceptance and hope, as opposed to the current culture aimed at increasing insight into illness.

Conclusions

The evidence is now converging for a multifaceted psychological model, which places delusions on a continuum with normal beliefs, and which views the range of delusional ideation as representing multiple interacting 'continua', each altering propensity to perceive and interpret the world in different ways. The psychiatric manual, *DSM-5*, has recently started to narrow the gap between delusions and everyday beliefs, and dimensional approaches offer a promising way forward for future understandings and interventions for delusional experience.

References

Altman, H., Collins, M., & Mundy, P. (1997). Subclinical hallucinations and delusions in nonpsychotic adolescents. *Journal of Child Psychology and Psychiatry and Allied Disciplines*, 38(4), 413–420.

American Psychiatric Association. (2000). *Diagnostic and statistical manual of mental disorders (DSM-IV)* (4th ed., rev.). Washington, DC: Author.

American Psychiatric Association. (2013). *Diagnostic and statistical manual of mental disorders (DSM-V)* (5th ed.). Arlington, VA: Author.

Bell, V., & Peters, E. R. (2014). Delusions. In F. Waters, & M. Stephane (Eds.), *The Assessment of psychosis: A compendium of assessment scales for psychotic symptoms*. New York: Routledge.

Bentall, R. P. (1994). Cognitive biases and abnormal beliefs – towards a model of persecutory delusions. *Neuropsychology of Schizophrenia*, 337–360.

Bentall, R. P., Corcoran, R., Howard, R., Blackwood, N., & Kinderman, P. (2001). Persecutory delusions: a review and theoretical integration. *Clinical Psychology Review*, 21(8), 1143–1192.

Bentall, R. P., Rowse, G., Shryane, N., Kinderman, P., Howard, R., Blackwood, N., ... Corcoran, R. (2009). The cognitive and affective structure of paranoid delusions: a transdiagnostic investigation of patients with schizophrenia spectrum disorders and depression. *Archives of General Psychiatry*, 66(3), 236–247.

Birchwood, M., & Trower, P. (2006). The future of cognitive-behavioural therapy for psychosis: not a quasi-neuroleptic. *British Journal of Psychiatry*, 188, 107–108.

Brett, C., Heriot-Maitland, C., McGuire, P., & Peters, E. (2013). Predictors of distress associated with psychotic-like anomalous experiences in clinical and non-clinical populations. *British Journal of Clinical Psychology*. doi: 10.1111/bjc.12036

Brett, C. M. C., Peters, E. P., Johns, L. C., Tabraham, P., Valmaggia, L. R., & McGuire, P. (2007). Appraisals of Anomalous Experiences Interview (AANEX): a multidimensional measure of psychological responses to anomalies associated with psychosis. *British Journal of Psychiatry*, 191, S23–S30.

Brett-Jones, J., Garety, P., & Hemsley, D. (1987). Measuring delusional experiences: a method and its application. *British Journal of Clinical Psychology*, 26, 257–265.

Broome, M. R., Johns, L. C., Valli, I., Wolley, J. B., Tabraham, P., Brett, C., ... McGuire, P.K. (2007). *British Journal of Psychiatry*, 191, S38–S42.

Chadwick, P., Birchwood M., & Tower, P. (1996). *Cognitive Therapy for Delusions, Voices and Paranoia*. Chichester: Wiley.

Chadwick, P., & Trower, P. (1996). Cognitive therapy for punishment paranoia: a single case experiment. *Behavioral Research and Therapy*, 34(4), 351–356.

Chadwick, P. D., & Lowe, C. F. (1994). A cognitive approach to measuring and modifying delusions. *Behavioral Research and Therapy*, 32(3), 355–367.

Colbert, S. M., Peters, E., & Garety, P. (2010). Jumping to conclusions and perceptions in early psychosis: relationship with delusional beliefs. *Cognitive Neuropsychiatry*, 15(4), 422–440.

David, A. S. (2010). Why we need more debate on whether psychotic symptoms lie on a continuum with normality. *Psychological Medicine*, 40(12), 1935–1942.

Delespaul, P., & van Os, J. (2003). In debate: Jaspers was right after all – delusions are distinct from normal beliefs. *British Journal of Psychiatry*, 183, 285–286.

Dudley, R. E. J., & Over, D. E. (2003). People with delusions jump to conclusions: A theoretical account of research findings on the reasoning of people with delusions. *Clinical Psychology & Psychotherapy*, 10(5), 263–274.

Foster, C., Startup, H., Potts, L., & Freeman, D. (2010). A randomised controlled trial of a worry intervention for individuals with persistent persecutory delusions. *Journal of Behavior Therapy and Experimental Psychiatry*, 41(1), 45–51.

Fowler, D., Hodgekins, J., Garety, P., Freeman, D., Kuipers, E., Dunn, G., ... Bebbington, P. E. (2012). Negative cognition, depressed mood, and paranoia: a longitudinal pathway analysis using structural equation modeling. *Schizophrenia Bulletin*, 38(5), 1063–1073.

Freeman, D. (2006). Delusions in the nonclinical population. *Current Psychiatry Reports*, 8, 191–204.

Freeman, D. (2007). Suspicious minds: the psychology of persecutory delusions. *Clinical Psychology Review*, 27(4), 425–457.

Freeman, D. (2008). Studying and treating schizophrenia using virtual reality: a new paradigm. *Schizophrenia Bulletin, 34(4)*, 605–610.
Freeman, D. (2011). Improving cognitive treatments for delusions. *Schizophrenia Research, 132*(2–3), 135–139.
Freeman, D., Garety, P. A., & Kuipers, E. (2001). Persecutory delusions: developing the understanding of belief maintenance and emotional distress. *Psychological Medicine, 31*(7), 1293–1306.
Freeman, D., Garety, P. A., Kuipers, E., Fowler, D., & Bebbington, P. E. (2002). A cognitive model of persecutory delusions. *British Journal of Clinical Psychology, 41*, 331–347.
Freeman, D., Garety, P. A., Fowler, D., Kuipers, E., Bebbington, P. E., & Dunn, G. (2004). Why do people with delusions fail to choose more realistic explanations for their experiences? An empirical investigation. *Journal of Consulting and Clinical Psychology, 72*(4), 671–680.
Garety, P. A. & Freeman, D. (2013). The past and future of delusions research: from the inexplicable to the treatable. *British Journal of Psychiatry, 203*, 327–33. doi: 10.1192/bjp.bp.113.126953
Garety, P. A., & Hemsley, D. R. (1987). Characteristics of delusional experience. *European Archives of Psychiatry and Clinical Neuroscience, 236*(5), 294–298. doi: 10.1007/Bf00380955
Garety, P. A., Freeman, D., Jolley, S., Dunn, G., Bebbington, P. E., Fowler, D. G., . . . Dudley, R. (2005). Reasoning, emotions, and delusional conviction in psychosis. *Journal of Abnormal Psychology, 114*(3), 373–384.
Garety, P. A., Kuipers, E., Fowler, D., Freeman, D., & Bebbington, P. E. (2001). A cognitive model of the positive symptoms of psychosis. *Psychological Medicine, 31*(2), 189–195.
Gilbert, P. (1989). *Human nature and suffering*. Hove: Lawrence Erlbaum Associates.
Gray, J. A., Feldon, J., Rawlins, J. N. P., Smith, A. D., & Hemsley, D. R. (1991). The neuropsychology of schizophrenia. *Behavioral and Brain Sciences, 14*(1), 1–19.
Green, C. E., Freeman, D., Kuipers, E., Bebbington, P., Fowler, D., Dunn, G., & Garety, P. A. (2008). Measuring ideas of persecution and social reference: the Green et al. Paranoid Thought Scales (GPTS). *Psychological Medicine, 38*(1), 101–111.
Gumley, A., Braehler, C., Laithwaite, H., MacBeth, A., & Gilbert, P. (2010). A compassion focused model of recovery after psychosis. *International Journal of Cognitive Therapy, 3*(2), 186–201.
Haddock, G., McCarron, J., Tarrier, N., & Faragher, E.B. (1999). Scales to measure dimensions of hallucinations and delusions: the psychotic symptom rating scale (PSYRATS). *Psychological Medicine, 29*(4), 879–889.
Heriot-Maitland, C., Knight, M., & Peters, E. (2012). A qualitative comparison of psychotic-like phenomena in clinical and non-clinical populations. *British Journal of Clinical Psychology, 51*, 37–53.
Janssen, I., Hanssen, M., Bak, M., Bijl, R. V., de Graaf, R., Vollebergh, W., . . . van Os, J. (2003). Discrimination and delusional ideation. *British Journal of Psychiatry, 182*, 71–76.
Jaspers, K. (1913). Causal and coherent connections between fortune and psychosis in dementia praecox (schizophrenia). *Zeitschrift Fur Die Gesamte Neurologie Und Psychiatrie, 14*, 158–263.
Johns, L. C., & van Os, J. (2001). The continuity of psychotic experiences in the general population. *Clinical Psychology Review, 21*(8), 1125–1141.
Johns, L. C., Cannon, M., Singleton, N., Murray, R. M., Farrell, M., Brugha, T., . . . Meltzer, H. (2004). Prevalence and correlates of self-reported psychotic symptoms in the British population. *British Journal of Psychiatry, 185*, 298–305.

Jones, E., & Watson, J. P. (1997). Delusion, the overvalued idea and religious beliefs: a comparative analysis of their characteristics. *British Journal of Psychiatry, 170*, 381–386.

Kapur, S. (2003). Linking neurochemistry, emotions, and therapeutics – a feasible project or just a delusion. *Brain and Cognition, 51*(2), 160.

Kendler, K. S., Glazer, W. M., & Morgenstern, H. (1983). Dimensions of delusional experience. *American Journal of Psychiatry, 140*(4), 466–469.

Langdon, R., & Coltheart, M. (2000). The cognitive neuropsychology of delusions. *Mind & Language, 15*(1), 184–218.

Lenzenweger, M. F., Bennett, M. E., & Lilenfeld, L. R. (1997). The Referential Thinking Scale as a measure of schizotypy: scale development and initial construct validation. *Psychological Assessment, 9*, 452–463.

Lincoln, T. M. (2007). Relevant dimensions of delusions: continuing the continuum versus category debate. *Schizophrenia Research, 93*(1–3), 211–220.

Linscott, R. J., & van Os, J. (2013). An updated and conservative systematic review and meta-analysis of epidemiological evidence on psychotic experiences in children and adults: on the pathway from proneness to persistence to dimensional expression across mental disorders. *Psychological Medicine, 43*(6), 1133–1149.

Lovatt, A., Mason, O., Brett, C., & Peters, E. (2010). Psychotic-like experiences, appraisals, and trauma. *Journal of Nervous and Mental Disease, 198*(11), 813–819.

Maher, B. A. (1974). Delusional thinking and perceptual disorder. *Journal of Individual Psychology, 30*(1), 98–113.

Mayhew, S. L., & Gilbert, P. (2008). Compassionate mind training with people who hear malevolent voices: a case series report. *Clinical Psychology & Psychotherapy, 15*(2), 113–138.

Moritz, S., Schilling, L., Wingenfeld, K., Kother, U., Wittekind, C., Terfehr, K., & Spitzer, C. (2011). Psychotic-like cognitive biases in borderline personality disorder. *Journal of Behavior Therapy and Experimental Psychiatry, 42*(3), 349–354.

Morrison, A. P. (2001). The interpretation of intrusions in psychosis: an integrative cognitive approach to hallucinations and delusions. *Behavioural and Cognitive Psychotherapy, 29*(3), 257–276.

Myin-Germeys, I., Nicolson, N. A., & Delespaul, P. A. E. G. (2001). The context of delusional experiences in the daily life of patients with schizophrenia. *Psychological Medicine, 31*(3), 489–498.

Newport, F., & Strausberg, M. (2001). Americans' belief in psychic and paranormal phenomena is up over last decade. Available online at http://www.gallup.com/poll/4483/americans-belief-psychic-paranormal-phenomena-over-last-decade.aspx (accessed 7 March 2015).

Oltmanns, T. F. (1988). Approaches to the definition and study of delusions. In T. F. Oltmanns, & B. A. Maher (Ed.), *Delusional Beliefs*. New York: Wiley.

Peters, E., Day, S., McKenna, J., & Orbach, G. (1999). Delusional ideation in religious and psychotic populations. *British Journal of Clinical Psychology, 38*, 83–96.

Peters, E., Joseph, S., Day, S., & Garety, P. (2004). Measuring delusional ideation: the 21-item Peters et al. Delusions Inventory (PDI). *Schizophrenia Bulletin, 30*(4), 1005–1022.

Peters, E., Lataster, T., Greenwood, K., Kuipers, E., Scott, J., Williams, S., . . . Myin-Germeys, I. (2012). Appraisals, psychotic symptoms and affect in daily life. *Psychological Medicine, 42*(5), 1013–1023.

Peters, E. R., Joseph, S. A., & Garety, P. A. (1999). Measurement of delusional ideation in the normal population: introducing the PDI (Peters et al. Delusions

Inventory). *Schizophrenia Bulletin, 25*(3), 553–576. check refs Move re 1999a and 1999b Check refs – et al etc. correct

Peters, E. R., Moritz, S., Schwannauer, M., Wiseman, Z., Greenwood, K. E., Scott, J., ... Garety, P. A. (2014). Cognitive biases questionnaire for psychosis. *Schizophrenia Bulletin, 40*(2), 300–314.

Sharp, H. M., Fear, C. F., Williams, J. M., Healy, D., Lowe, C. F., Yeadon, H., & Holden, R. (1996). Delusional phenomenology – dimensions of change. *Behaviour Research and Therapy, 34*(2), 123–142.

Smeets, F., Lataster, T., Dominguez, M., Hommes, J., Lieb, R., Wittchen, H. U., & van Os, J. (2012). Evidence that onset of psychosis in the population reflects early hallucinatory experiences that through environmental risks and affective dysregulation become complicated by delusions. *Schizophrenia Bulletin, 38*(3), 531–542.

So, S., Peters, E. R., Swendsen, J., Garety, P. A., & Kapur, S. (2014). Changes in delusions in the early phase of antipsychotic treatment – an experience sampling study. *Psychiatry Research, 215*(3), 568–573.

So, S. H., Freeman, D., Dunn, G., Kapur, S., Kuipers, E., Bebbington, P., ... Garety, P. A. (2012). Jumping to conclusions, a lack of belief flexibility and delusional conviction in psychosis: a longitudinal investigation of the structure, frequency, and relatedness of reasoning biases. *Journal of Abnormal Psychology, 121*(1), 129–139.

Startup, H., Freeman, D., & Garety, P. A. (2007). Persecutory delusions and catastrophic worry in psychosis: developing the understanding of delusion distress and persistence. *Behavioral Research and Therapy, 45*(3), 523–537.

Strauss, J. S. (1969). Hallucinations and delusions as points on continua function – rating scale evidence. *Archives of General Psychiatry, 21*(5), 581.

Thewissen, V., Bentall, R. P., Lecomte, T., van Os, J., & Myin-Germeys, I. (2008). Fluctuations in self-esteem and paranoia in the context of daily life. *Journal of Abnormal Psychology, 117*(1), 143–153.

Thewissen, V., Bentall, R. P., Oorschot, M., Campo, J. A., van Lierop, T., van Os, J., & Myin-Germeys, I. (2011). Emotions, self-esteem, and paranoid episodes: an experience sampling study. *British Journal of Clinical Psychology, 50*, 178–195.

Udachina, A., Varese, F., Oorschot, M., Myin-Germeys, I., & Bentall, R. P. (2012). Dynamics of self-esteem in 'poor-me' and 'bad-me' paranoia. *Journal of Nervous and Mental Disease, 200*(9), 777–783.

Van Dael, F., Vermissen, D., Janssen, I., Myin-Germeys, I., van Os, J., & Krabbendam, L. (2006). Data gathering: biased in psychosis? *Schizophrenia Bulletin, 32*(2), 341–351.

van Os, J., Linscott, R. J., Myin-Germeys, I., Delespaul, P., & Krabbendam, L. (2009). A systematic review and meta-analysis of the psychosis continuum: evidence for a psychosis proneness-persistence-impairment model of psychotic disorder. *Psychological Medicine, 39*(2), 179–195.

Ward, T. A., Gaynor, K. J., Hunter, M. D., Woodruff, P. W., Garety, P. A., & Peters, E. R. (2013). Appraisals and responses to experimental symptom analogues in clinical and nonclinical individuals with psychotic experiences. *Schizophrenia Bulletin.* doi: 10.1093/schbul/sbt094

Wykes, T., Steel, C., Everitt, B., & Tarrier, N. (2008). Cognitive behavior therapy for schizophrenia: effect sizes, clinical models, and methodological rigor. *Schizophrenia Bulletin, 34*(3), 523–537.

11 Schizotypy and psychopathology

Jo Hodgekins

Introduction and overview

This chapter reviews the literature examining links between schizotypal phenomena and psychopathology. It will begin by discussing literature linking schizotypal traits to psychosis and will also consider the utility of assessing schizotypal symptoms following transition in relation to adaptation to and recovery from a psychotic episode. Following this, links between schizotypy and other forms of psychopathology will be discussed. Finally, clinical implications will be considered, including issues relating to assessment and treatment.

Defining terms: schizotypy versus at-risk mental state

Over recent years, there has been a move towards assessing psychotic-like experiences (PLEs) as opposed to psychometrically defined schizotypy using traditional scales. This has resulted in the development of at-risk mental state (ARMS) criteria, referring to the identification of individuals who may be at risk of developing psychotic illness in the future, either because of family history of psychosis or the presence of PLEs (Yung et al., 1998). A defining feature of ARMS criteria, which delineates that definition from the notion of 'high risk' defined using psychometric schizotypy scales, is that individuals are help seeking in relation to their experiences. ARMS status is often defined using a semi-structured interview, such as the Comprehensive Assessment of At-Risk Mental States (CAARMS; Yung et al., 2002).

The terms 'schizotypy', 'PLEs' and 'subclinical psychotic symptoms' are often used interchangeably, and many studies have suggested that they are tapping into the same underlying construct. For example, Morrison et al. (2002) have demonstrated that individuals defined as being high risk for future development of psychosis using ARMS criteria also scored higher on the Oxford-Liverpool Inventory of Feelings and Experiences (O-LIFE; Mason, Claridge, & Jackson, 1995) than non-clinical controls. Similarly, individuals scoring highly on schizotypy have been found to display metacognitive processes similar to those seen in individuals meeting ARMS criteria, suggesting similar underlying mechanisms (Barkus et al., 2010). Therefore, for the purposes of this chapter, the terms 'schizotypy', 'PLEs' and 'ARMS' will be used interchangeably to refer to experiences occurring towards the non-clinical end of the psychosis continuum.

Schizotypy and psychotic disorders

There is a wealth of literature examining links between schizotypy and psychotic disorders. This mostly relates to schizotypy as a risk factor for psychosis and examines relationships between premorbid schizotypy and psychotic illness. However, schizotypy may also play an important role following transition to psychotic illness.

Schizotypy before the onset of psychosis

Many studies have identified common risk factors in individuals scoring high on trait schizotypy and individuals with diagnosable psychotic illness (Nelson, Seal, Pantelis, & Phillips, 2013). For example, first-degree relatives of individuals diagnosed with psychotic disorders are found to score higher on psychometric measures of schizotypy than control groups with no family history of psychosis, suggesting a common genetic origin (Fanous et al., 2007). In addition to the presence of common risk factors, there is longitudinal evidence to suggest that individuals scoring high on trait schizotypy may be at increased risk of developing psychosis. In the Edinburgh High-Risk Study, individuals with increased genetic risk of psychosis reported higher levels of schizotypy than a control group (Miller et al., 2002). Furthermore, within the high-risk group, baseline levels of schizotypal symptoms – particularly items from the Social Withdrawal factor – were accurate at predicting which individuals went on to develop psychosis at a later time point (Johnstone, Ebmeier, Miller, Owens, & Lawrie, 2005). This suggests that schizotypy confers some risk for the later development of psychosis. A review of longitudinal studies assessing PLEs as opposed to trait schizotypy have suggested a 16- to 60-fold increase in risk of transition to psychosis in individuals reporting PLEs in childhood and adolescence (van Os, Linscott, Myin-Germeys, Delespaul, & Krabbendam, 2009). For example, in the Dunedin birth cohort study, Poulton et al. (2000) report that 25 per cent of children with self-reported PLEs aged 11 had developed schizophreniform disorder at age 26. Thus, it is suggested that high schizotypy may be *both* a risk factor for psychosis *and* represent a prodromal phase of illness.

Schizotypy after psychosis

Schizotypy is generally considered as premorbid to psychosis and is not usually assessed after transition has been made. However, assessing state schizotypy in individuals already diagnosed with psychotic disorders may be informative in relation to monitoring adaptation to and recovery from a psychotic episode (Hodgekins et al., 2012). Although schizotypy is currently thought of as a *prodromal* phenomenon, it may also feature in the psychotic *postdrome*, and influence how individuals adapt to a first episode of psychosis as well as the recovery process.

Adaptation to psychosis

Research suggests that individuals with first-episode psychosis and premorbid schizotypal traits display less insight into their illness than individuals without such traits (Campos et al., 2011). Although retrospective, these findings suggest that premorbid personality may be an important factor to consider in the early stages of psychosis in relation to adaptation to the psychotic episode. Moreover, as schizotypy has been linked with increased vulnerability to other non-psychotic mental illness (Rossler et al., 2011), it could be the case that individuals experiencing schizotypal features after transition to psychosis may experience higher levels of comorbidity that may result in a more complex and severe illness presentation.

Recovery

Although clinically definable psychotic symptoms dissipate following an episode of psychosis, individuals may still experience residual psychotic symptoms of a subclinical nature, similar to those experienced in the prodromal phases of the disorder. There is evidence to suggest a relationship between residual and prodromal symptomatology via the 'rollback phenomenon' (Detre & Jarecki, 1971). This suggests that individuals may inhabit a postdromal phase following the remission of an acute episode of illness, and supports the suggestion that it is possible to move up and down different points on the psychosis continuum over time (Yung et al., 2006). The postdrome may reflect both underlying vulnerability and an individual's response to the experience of the psychotic episode itself. It is important that low-level symptoms are measured during the recovery phase because they may have implications for future relapse. In addition, particular types of low-level psychotic, or schizotypal, symptoms (e.g. extreme social anxiety) may be directly related to impairments in social functioning, thus influencing longer-term recovery from psychosis. However, because of their subclinical nature, such symptoms may not be detected using traditional psychiatric assessment tools for psychosis. A measure of current schizotypal symptoms may be more appropriate in the assessment of these phenomena.

A measure developed to assess state schizotypal symptoms is the Schizotypal Symptoms Inventory (SSI; Hodgekins et al., 2012). This is an adaptation of Raine's Schizotypal Personality Questionnaire (Raine, 1991) and has been shown to have good psychometric properties in both clinical and non-clinical samples. Hodgekins et al. (2012) highlighted high levels of current schizotypal symptoms present in individuals who had been defined as recovered from their acute psychotic episode, suggesting that residual psychotic symptoms may be being missed with the use of traditional psychotic symptoms scales.

Schizotypy and other clinical disorders

Although schizotypy has traditionally been linked to psychosis and schizophrenia, elevated levels of schizotypy have been highlighted in other mental health difficulties, including anxiety and mood disorders (Hanssen et al., 2003), and with increased psychotic features in Alzheimer's disease (Eror, Lopez, Dekosky, & Sweet, 2005). As such, schizotypy may confer a generalised vulnerability to common mental health conditions. In a longitudinal study conducted over 30 years, individuals reporting schizotypal signs at age 20 were more likely to develop common mental health problems (including dysthymia, bipolar disorder, social phobia, and obsessive–compulsive disorder [OCD]) at age 50 (Rossler et al., 2011). These findings are consistent with high levels of comorbidity in individuals experiencing psychotic illness. Indeed, as identified by Lewandowski et al. (2006), many of the symptom features of schizophrenia-spectrum disorders overlap with symptom features of depression (e.g. social withdrawal, anhedonia) and anxiety (e.g. worry, concentration difficulties), and thus there may be common underlying mechanisms.

The literature suggests that schizotypal individuals who do not go on to develop psychosis do not necessarily experience a positive outcome. A study by Lin et al. (2011) demonstrated that individuals rated as being at risk for psychosis who did not make transition over a 2–13-year period experienced poor functional outcomes and neurocognitive deficits. Moreover, Addington et al. (2011) found that at-risk individuals who had not made transition to psychosis after 2 years still experienced attenuated psychotic symptoms and had poorer social and role functioning compared with a non-clinical group. Links between schizotypy and other mental health difficulties will now be discussed.

Obsessive–compulsive disorder

Although OCD is classified as an anxiety disorder, it has been argued that it may be more closely aligned to the schizophrenia spectrum (Norman, Davies, Malla, Cortese, & Nicholson, 1996). OCD-type symptoms have also been noted in individuals with schizophrenia (Berman, Kalinowski, Berman, Lengua, & Green, 1995). Several studies suggest that schizotypal features are common in OCD (Stanley, Turner, & Borden, 1990) and have been associated with poor insight (Catapano et al., 2010), lower functioning (Poyurovsky et al., 2008) and treatment resistance (Moritz et al., 2004). A schizotypy subtype of OCD has been proposed (Sobin et al., 2000), which includes endorsement of superstitious beliefs and beliefs about unusual methods of causation, such as the ability of thoughts or feelings to be passed into other people or objects. It is argued that individuals with OCD and schizotypal features may experience increased perceptual aberrations and more intrusive thoughts and obsessions (Moritz et al., 2004; Yamamoto et al., 2012). This may result in increased distress and compulsion. Cognitive processing styles found in schizotypy, such as reduced cognitive inhibition, have also been highlighted in individuals with OCD (Chamberlain, Blackwell, Fineberg, Robbins, & Sahakian, 2005) and may explain the overlap in observed symptoms. Schizotypal magical thinking has also been linked with thought–action fusion, such that individuals with OCD and high schizotypy have increased conviction that having a thought will result in the thought occurring in reality (Lee, Cougle, & Telch, 2005).

Anxiety

Lewandowski et al. (2006) assessed self-reported symptoms of anxiety in a non-clinical sample of college students who also completed a measure of schizotypy. Higher levels of anxiety were associated with increased scores on the positive dimension of the schizotypy scale, suggesting a potential overlap between the two phenomena. However, because of the cross-sectional design of this study, it is difficult to interpret the direction of these findings. Indeed, anxiety may be a cause and/or a consequence of schizotypy. It may also be that items on the schizotypy scale tap into features of anxiety and are thus measuring a similar underlying construct. For example, the Unusual Experiences subscale of the O-LIFE contains the item: 'Do you ever have a sense of vague danger or sudden dread for reasons that you do not understand?' (Mason, Linney, & Claridge, 2005). This is likely to be endorsed by individuals experiencing high levels of anxiety. There is also an established overlap between neuroticism and schizotypy (Ettinger et al., 2005), potentially explaining relationships between anxiety and schizotypal traits.

In relation to subtypes of anxiety, there is arguably a conceptual overlap between symptoms of social anxiety and schizotypal traits. For example, the items 'I feel very uncomfortable in social situations involving unfamiliar people' and 'I tend to keep in the background on social occasions' are included in the Schizotypal Personality Questionnaire (SPQ) (Raine, 1991) and reflect core symptoms of social anxiety (Clark & Wells, 1995), which have also been found to overlap with paranoia (Freeman, 2007). Studies have identified social anxiety as a central component of the underlying factor structure of schizotypy, suggesting anxiety may be an intrinsic part of the schizotypy construct (Brown, Silvia, Myin-Germeys, Lewandowski, & Kwapil, 2008). Social anxiety is often present in individuals with psychotic illness, and has also been identified in the prodromal phase, providing further evidence for this argument.

Depression

As with anxiety, a cross-sectional association has been highlighted between self-reported positive schizotypy and symptoms of depression in a non-clinical sample (Lewandowski et al., 2006). Consistent with these findings, a 10-year longitudinal study has demonstrated that positive schizotypal symptoms predict future mood disorders (Kwapil, Gross, Silvia, & Barrantes-Vidal, 2013). Furthermore, in a study using experience sampling methodology (ESM) to examine daily fluctuations in symptomatology, non-clinical individuals scoring high on positive dimensions of schizotypy were found to experience increased negative affect, negative beliefs about current activities and feelings of rejection (Kwapil, Brown, Silvia, Myin-Germeys, & Barrantes-Vidal, 2012). Taken together, these studies suggest that increased schizotypal personality traits may reflect a vulnerability to mood fluctuations and possible mood disorder. It is also plausible that anomalous experiences may result in distress, leading to low mood.

It has also been hypothesised that negative schizotypy, and particularly social or introvertive anhedonia, may be linked to increased trait negative affectivity (NA). Trait NA reflects an increased tendency to experience negative affect (Watson & Clark, 1984) and thus it is unsurprising that anhedonic individuals may be more vulnerable to experiencing low mood. Social anhedonia has also been linked with poor affective control (Martin, Cicero, & Kerns, 2012). Similarly, Blanchard, Collins, Aghevli, Leung, and Cohen (2011) found that individuals scoring high on the social anhedonia subscale of a measure of schizotypy reported higher rates of mood disorder, less positive affect, less social support and more interpersonal conflict.

Bipolar disorder

The presence of schizotypal traits in relation to bipolar disorder have particular relevance when psychotic features are a part of the presentation. For example, Schurhoff, Laguerre, Szoke, Meary, and Leboyer (2005) examined schizotypy in the first-degree relatives of individuals with schizophrenia, bipolar disorder with psychotic features and bipolar disorder without psychotic features. Symptoms on the disorganisation dimension of the SPQ were common to first-degree relatives of individuals with schizophrenia and bipolar disorder with psychotic features, but were not found to be present in relatives of individuals with bipolar disorder without psychotic features. However, negative schizotypal symptoms were present in all three groups. Similarly, Heron et al. (2003) found that individuals with bipolar disorder had increased schizotypy compared with healthy controls, but lower than the schizophrenia group. Unlike the study by Schurhoff et al. (2005), levels of schizotypy in the bipolar group were unrelated to the presence of psychotic symptoms.

Rossi and Daneluzzo (2002) compared scores on the SPQ across clinical samples of individuals with a range of psychiatric diagnoses, including bipolar disorder. Individuals with bipolar disorder reported elevated schizotypy scores compared with individuals with OCD and unipolar depression, but had a similar SPQ profile to a sample of individuals diagnosed with schizophrenia. However, the bipolar group scored higher on the disorganisation subscale of the SPQ compared with the schizophrenia group.

These studies suggest that schizotypal phenomena are common in individuals with bipolar disorder, especially symptoms relating to the disorganisation dimension. This is perhaps unsurprising when considering that bipolar disorder is often included under the umbrella of the schizophrenia-spectrum disorders, and studies have identified similar susceptibility factors (e.g. Bramon & Sham, 2001). The presence of schizotypal symptoms in individuals with bipolar disorder and those at genetic risk further confirms hypotheses about similar underlying mechanisms between bipolar disorder and psychosis.

Post-traumatic stress disorder

Schizotypy has been implicated as having a potential influence on how individuals process information – specifically, how information is integrated into meaningful context. It has been hypothesised that this may result in schizotypal individuals being more prone to developing post-traumatic stress disorder (PTSD) (Steel, Fowler, & Holmes, 2005). Holmes and Steel (2004) showed that individuals scoring high on a measure of schizotypy were more likely to report intrusions following an analogue trauma experience. Moreover, individuals with high positive schizotypy scores who were seeking psychological help following a real-life trauma were more likely to experience intrusions and other PTSD symptomatology, including avoidance, hypervigilance and low mood (Marzillier & Steel, 2007). As well as schizotypy potentially predisposing individuals to the development of PTSD, individuals with a trauma history have been found to have elevated scores on the SPQ, with the suggestion that schizotypal phenomena may develop as part of the sequelae of trauma exposure (Berenbaum, Valera, & Kerns, 2003). This mirrors research and theories suggesting that trauma may play a role in the development of psychosis.

Autistic-spectrum disorders

An overlap between schizophrenia-like phenomena and autistic-spectrum disorders (ASD) has been hypothesised for some time, particularly in relation to negative symptoms (e.g. withdrawal). Indeed, the term 'autism' was adopted by Kanner (1943) from Bleuler's (1908) description of the withdrawn behaviours characteristic in adults with schizophrenia. However, others have argued that ASD and schizophrenia are diametrically opposing disorders (Crespi & Badcock, 2008). Studies examining the overlap between schizotypal and autistic-spectrum symptoms in typically developing young adults (Russell-Smith, Maybery, & Bayliss, 2011; Wakabayashi, Baron-Cohen, & Ashwin, 2012) have found correlations between self-reported ASD-type symptoms and self-reported schizotypy, as well as some overlap with OCD-type symptoms. The largest overlap was in relation to interpersonal and socio-emotional symptoms, whereas cognitive–perceptual aspects of schizotypy did not predict the presence of autistic-spectrum symptoms.

Similar research has been conducted with clinical samples. Barneveld et al. (2011) assessed for schizotypal symptoms in adolescents with ASD, compared with normally developing controls. They found elevated levels of schizotypal traits in the ASD group, and specific associations between autistic symptoms and negative, disorganised and positive schizotypal symptoms within individuals, particularly in relation to attention switching. Moreover, in a study by Sprong et al. (2008), 78 per cent of children diagnosed with multiple complex developmental disorder (a pervasive developmental disorder subtype) were found to meet at-risk mental state criteria, further suggesting a link between ASD-type symptoms and schizophrenia-like phenomena. Esterberg, Trotman, Brasfield, Compton, and Walker (2008) examined the presence of ASD symptoms in adolescents diagnosed with schizotypal personality disorder (SPD) compared with healthy controls, and found higher levels of unusual interests and behaviours and more impairment in childhood social functioning in the SPD group. However, these features were not predictive of a later transition to psychosis.

There has been some discussion about whether the shared features between schizophrenia-spectrum disorders and ASD are the result of overlapping or separate processes. A potential candidate for an overlapping process is a social competence impairment, which has also been found to be related to ASD and OCD-type symptoms (Chasson et al., 2011). Indeed, as outlined earlier in this chapter, schizotypal phenomena have also been found to be common in individuals with OCD.

Epilepsy

In addition to an overlap between ASD and schizotypy, schizotypal traits and symptoms have also been noted in individuals with epilepsy, particularly in relation to temporal lobe epilepsy and the cognitive–perceptual factor of the SPQ (Mula et al., 2008). The same authors identified that an earlier age of onset of seizures was associated with increased trait schizotypy. Temporal lobe epilepsy has been defined as a 'mock-up' of schizophrenia, with schizophrenia-like psychoses occurring more frequently than expected in individuals with this diagnosis (Roberts, Done, Bruton, & Crow, 1990). Rates of negative psychotic-like symptoms have also been found to be elevated in individuals with temporal lobe epilepsy (Getz et al., 2003).

Bell, Halligan and Ellis (2006) suggest that a particular subtype of anomalous experiences may be linked to temporal lobe epilepsy, such as perceptual experiences with an absence of semantic content (e.g. hearing music rather than verbal utterances) and feelings of familiarity (e.g. 'Do you ever sense the presence of another being, despite being unable to see any evidence?). These phenomena have been linked with the onset of temporal lobe seizures (Gloor, 1990) and may shed light on the pathophysiology underlying some PLEs. However, more research is needed regarding the relationship between schizotypy and epilepsy in order to further understand how this can inform knowledge about psychotic illness (Kanemoto, Tadokoro, & Oshima, 2012).

Conclusions

The studies reviewed here suggest that the presence of schizotypy overlaps with several different forms of psychopathology, both within and outside the schizophrenia spectrum. The exact reasons for this are unknown. It may be that other forms of psychopathology (e.g. anxiety, depression) are a consequence of distress associated with the experience of schizotypal phenomena (e.g. low-level paranoid beliefs, social withdrawal, anomalous experience), or it could be that schizotypy reflects a generic vulnerability to psychological difficulties. Evidence suggesting common underlying cognitive mechanisms, such as reduced cognitive inhibition (Chamberlain et al., 2005), alludes to the latter.

Schizotypal subtypes and outcome

It may be the case that particular subtypes of schizotypy confer different levels of risk for future psychopathology. The interpersonal or 'negative' dimension of schizotypy has been found to be particularly associated with poorer functioning and quality of life, suggesting that this may indicate a need for care in relation to psychotic illness (Lin et al., 2013). In addition, cross-sectional baseline data from the Maryland Longitudinal Study of Schizotypy (Blanchard et al., 2011), identified a group scoring high on social anhedonia who experienced greater trait (NA), higher levels of mood disorders and lower global functioning than a group scoring low on social anhedonia. Moreover, Tabak and Weisman de Mamani's (2013) latent profile analysis of schizotypal experiences in a non-clinical sample identified a 'high introvertive anhedonia/cognitive disorganisation' subgroup who scored lowest on quality of life and functioning compared with all other subtypes. These findings are consistent with higher levels of schizoid personality accentuations in individuals who make transition to psychosis (Schultze-Lutter, Klosterkotter, Michel, Winkler, & Ruhrmann, 2012), suggesting that a persistence of social deficits may be important when considering risk. According to cognitive models of psychosis, social withdrawal may play a role in the development of psychosis because of reduced opportunities for collecting disconfirmatory evidence in relation to paranoid beliefs or anomalous experiences (Garety, Kuipers, Fowler, Freeman, & Bebbington, 2001).

Persistence, distress and functional impairment

Studies assessing schizotypal traits do not always take into account the frequency of schizotypal phenomena experienced. Thus, within a high schizotypy group, some people may have experienced schizotypal symptoms on only a few occasions some time ago, whereas others' experiences may be more persistent and current. It is arguably the latter group who are at higher risk of future psychopathology. This is the argument proposed by the psychosis-proneness-persistence-impairment model (van Os et al., 2009). It is hypothesised that exposure to a range of environmental risk factors, combined with underlying vulnerability (i.e. schizotypal traits) has an impact on behavioural and neurotransmitter sensitisation, thus increasing both the persistence of schizotypal experiences and the need for care. Indeed, although the presence of PLEs is common, particularly in adolescence, only a minority of individuals experience persistent symptoms over time (Wigman et al., 2011). The theory is further supported by evidence from longitudinal studies, which have identified that it is individuals with persistent PLEs who are most likely to develop psychosis over an 8-year period (Dominguez, Wichers, Lieb, Wittchen, & van Os, 2011).

Persistence of symptoms may result in increased distress and help seeking in response to experiences. It may also result in functional impairments, because persistent PLEs may have a negative impact on sleep and the completion of day-to-day tasks. Functional impairments in conjunction with schizotypal symptoms are thought to increase the likelihood of making transition to psychosis (Mason et al., 2004; Valmaggia et al., 2013). It is argued that withdrawing from activity and social relationships may reduce opportunities for normalising anomalous experiences (French & Morrison, 2004). Moreover, reductions in functioning may result in low mood due to fewer experiences of pleasure and achievement, further increasing the likelihood of mental ill health.

Cognitive factors and individual differences

Individual differences in perceived stress, trait NA, temperament and coping style have been identified as potential explanatory variables in understanding why only some people with schizotypal traits go on to develop psychosis or other mental health difficulties (Hori et al., 2014). These factors may influence how schizotypal experiences are responded to or appraised, and thus the level of distress experienced. In a study by Lovatt et al. (2010), individuals with PLEs who had a need for care had more externalising and personalising appraisals of their experiences than a group who were also experiencing PLEs but who did not need care. Metacognitive beliefs have also been highlighted as being important, with maladaptive metacognitive beliefs being linked with elevated levels of psychopathology in at-risk samples (Brett, Johns, Peters, & McGuire, 2009). Furthermore, the type of coping an individual uses in response to unusual experiences has been found to moderate risk, with individuals using 'symptomatic coping' (i.e. responding to symptoms) being at increased risk of needing care, and reporting less control over their symptoms (Bak et al., 2003).

Clinical implications: assessment and interventions

The findings of literature reviewed in this chapter suggest that it may be important to assess schizotypal features in all individuals with mental health difficulties. When occurring in conjunction with psychopathology, schizotypy may complicate the illness presentation and have a negative impact on recovery and long-term outcome. This has been demonstrated in OCD, when the presence of schizotypal symptoms has been shown to be associated with reduced treatment response (Moritz et al., 2004). Moreover, if schizotypy or the presence of PLEs increases an individual's risk of making transition to psychosis, early intervention could play a prophylactic role. Assessment and intervention are thus important areas to consider in the conclusion of this chapter.

Interventions for schizotypal symptoms

The literature reviewed earlier highlights the potential for schizotypal symptoms to have clinical consequences both before and after the onset of symptoms. Therefore, it could be argued that interventions should be developed to target schizotypal phenomena. A few studies have examined interventions for individuals with elevated trait schizotypy. For example, Liberman and Robertson (2005) piloted a social skills training intervention with high school students scoring high on trait schizotypy. The intervention was found to reduce schizotypal symptoms and to improve social competence and self-esteem. However, it could be argued that interventions should be targeted towards those who are distressed by their experiences and are thus help seeking. Indeed, the majority of recent intervention studies have focused on individuals meeting ARMS criteria, using cognitive–behavioural techniques to address negative appraisals attached to anomalous experiences. This has proved effective in reducing transitions to psychotic illness over a 24-month period (see Hutton & Taylor, 2014, for a review).

Following the onset of psychosis, schizotypal experiences should arguably continue to be considered as a potential treatment target because they may reflect residual psychotic symptoms or be misinterpreted as signs of relapse (Hodgekins et al., 2012). Recent studies assessing the efficacy of recovery-focused interventions in first-episode psychosis have suggested interventions for residual psychotic experiences as one element of an intervention package (Fowler et al., 2012). This may involve psychoeducation about low-level psychotic symptoms with the aim of reducing catastrophising in relation to those experiences. Indeed, as outlined earlier, some individuals may return to an ARMS presentation following a psychotic episode and thus experience continued heightened sensitivity to stress or increased experiences of salience in response to certain environmental cues. Avoidance may thus be used to cope with experiences of information overload. Encouraging individuals to engage in recovery-focused activity in spite of this sensitivity can challenge negative appraisals about one's vulnerability, thus reducing avoidance and improving recovery.

References

Addington, J., Cornblatt, B. A., Cadenhead, K. S., Cannon, T. D., McGlashan, T. H., Perkins, D. O., & Heinssen, R. (2011). At clinical high risk for psychosis: outcome for nonconverters. *American Journal of Psychiatry, 168,* 800–805.

Bak, M., Myin-Germeys, I., Hanssen, M., Bijl, R., Vollebergh, W., Delespaul, P., & van Os, J. (2003). When does experience of psychosis result in a need for care? A prospective general population study. *Schizophrenia Bulletin, 29,* 349–358.

Barkus, E., Stirling, J., French, P., Morrison, A., Bentall, R., & Lewis, S. (2010). Distress and metacognition in psychosis prone individuals comparing high schizotypy to the at-risk mental state. *Journal of Nervous and Mental Disease, 198,* 99–104.

Barneveld, P. S., Pieterse, J., de Sonneville, L., van Rijn, S., Lahuis, B., van Engeland, H., & Swaab, H. (2011). Overlap of autistic and schizotypal traits in adolescents with autism spectrum disorders. *Schizophrenia research, 126,* 231–236.

Bell, V., Halligan, P. W., & Ellis, H. D. (2006). The Cardiff Anomalous Perceptions Scale (CAPS): a new validated measure of anomalous perceptual experience. *Schizophrenia Bulletin, 32,* 366–377.

Berenbaum, H., Valera, E. M., & Kerns, J. G. (2003). Psychological trauma and schizotypal symptoms. *Schizophrenia Bulletin, 29,* 143–152.

Berman, I., Kalinowski, A., Berman, S. M., Lengua, J., & Green, A. I. (1995). Obsessive and compulsive symptoms in chronic schizophrenia. *Comprehensive Psychiatry, 36,* 6–10.

Blanchard, J. J., Collins, L. M., Aghevli, M., Leung, W. W., & Cohen, A. S. (2011). Social anhedonia and schizotypy in a community sample: the Maryland longitudinal study of schizotypy. *Schizophrenia Bulletin, 37,* 587–602.

Bleuler, E. (1908). Die Prognose der Dementia Praecox – Schizophreniegruppe. *Allgemeine Zeitschrift für Psychiatrie, 65,* 436–464.

Bramon, E., & Sham, P. C. (2001). The common genetic liability between schizophrenia and bipolar disorder: a review. *Current Psychiatry Reports, 3,* 332–337.

Brett, C. M., Johns, L. C., Peters, E. P., & McGuire, P. K. (2009). The role of metacognitive beliefs in determining the impact of anomalous experiences: a comparison of help-seeking and non-help-seeking groups of people experiencing psychotic-like anomalies. *Psychological Medicine, 39,* 939–950.

Brown, L. H., Silvia, P. J., Myin-Germeys, I., Lewandowski, K. E., & Kwapil, T. R. (2008). The relationship of social anxiety and social anhedonia to psychometrically identified schizotypy. *Journal of Social and Clinical Psychology, 27,* 127–149.

Campos, M. S., Garcia-Jalon, E., Gilleen, J. K., David, A. S., Peralta, V. M., & Cuesta, M. J. (2011). Premorbid personality and insight in first-episode psychosis. *Schizophrenia Bulletin, 37*, 52–60.

Catapano, F., Perris, F., Fabrazzo, M., Cioffi, V., Giacco, D., De Santis, V., & Maj, M. (2010). Obsessive-compulsive disorder with poor insight: a three-year prospective study. *Progress in Neuropsychopharmacology and Biological Psychiatry, 34*, 323–330.

Chamberlain, S. R., Blackwell, A. D., Fineberg, N. A., Robbins, T. W., & Sahakian, B. J. (2005). The neuropsychology of obsessive compulsive disorder: the importance of failures in cognitive and behavioural inhibition as candidate endophenotypic markers. *Neuroscience & Biobehavioral Reviews, 29*, 399–419.

Chasson, G. S., Timpano, K. R., Greenberg, J. L., Shaw, A., Singer, T., & Wilhelm, S. (2011). Shared social competence impairment: another link between the obsessive-compulsive and autism spectrums? *Clinical Psychology Review, 31*, 653–662.

Clark, D. M., & Wells, A. (1995). A cognitive model of social phobia. In R. G. Heimberg, M. R. Liebowitz, D. A. Hope, & F. R. Schneier (Eds.), *Social Phobia: Diagnosis, Assessment and Treatment*. New York: Guilford Press.

Crespi, B., & Badcock, C. (2008). Psychosis and autism as diametrical disorders of the social brain. *Behavioral and Brain Sciences, 31*, 241–261.

Detre, T. P., & Jarecki, H. (1971). *Modern Psychiatric Treatment*. Philadelphia, PA: Lippincott.

Dominguez, M. D. G., Wichers, M., Lieb, R., Wittchen, H. U., & van Os, J. (2011). Evidence that onset of clinical psychosis is an outcome of progressively more persistent subclinical psychotic experiences: an 8-year cohort study. *Schizophrenia Bulletin, 37*, 84–93.

Eror, E. A., Lopez, O. L., Dekosky, S. T., & Sweet, R. A. (2005). Alzheimer disease subjects with psychosis have increased schizotypal symptoms before dementia onset. *Biological Psychiatry, 58*, 325–330.

Esterberg, M. L., Trotman, H. D., Brasfield, J. L., Compton, M. T., & Walker, E. F. (2008). Childhood and current autistic features in adolescents with schizotypal personality disorder. *Schizophrenia Research, 104*, 265–273.

Ettinger, U., Kumari, V., Crawford, T. J., Flak, V., Sharma, T., Davis, R. E., & Corr, P. J. (2005). Saccadic eye movements, schizotypy, and the role of neuroticism. *Biological Psychology, 68*, 61–78.

Fanous, A. H., Neale, M. C., Gardner, C. O., Webb, B. T., Straub, R. E., O'Neill, F. A., . . . Kendler, K. S. (2007). Significant correlation in linkage signals from genome-wide scans of schizophrenia and schizotypy. *Molecular Psychiatry, 12*, 958–965.

Fowler, D., French, P., Hodgekins, J., Lower, R., Turner, R., Burton, S., & Wilson, J. (2012). CBT to address and prevent social disability in early and emerging psychosis. In C. Steel (Ed.), *CBT for Schizophrenia: Evidence Based Interventions and Future Directions*: John Wiley & Sons.

Freeman, D. (2007). Suspicious minds: the psychology of persecutory delusions. *Clinical Psychology Review, 27*, 425–457.

French, P., & Morrison, A. P. (2004). *Early Detection and Cognitive Therapy for People at High Risk of Developing Psychosis: A Treatment Approach*. New York: Wiley.

Garety, P. A., Kuipers, E., Fowler, D., Freeman, D., & Bebbington, P. E. (2001). A cognitive model of the positive symptoms of psychosis. *Psychological Medicine, 31*, 189–195.

Getz, K., Hermann, B., Seidenberg, M., Bell, B., Dow, C., Jones, J., & Woodard, A. (2003). Negative symptoms and psychosocial status in temporal lobe epilepsy. *Epilepsy Research, 53*, 240–244.

Gloor, P. (1990). Experiential phenomena of temporal lobe epilepsy: facts and hypotheses. *Brain, 113*, 1673–1694.

Hanssen, M., Peeters, F., Krabbendam, L., Radstake, S., Verdoux, H., & van Os, J. (2003). How psychotic are individuals with non-psychotic disorders? *Social Psychiatry and Psychiatric Epidemiology, 38*, 149–154.

Heron, J., Jones, I., Williams, J., Owen, M. J., Craddock, N., & Jones, L. A. (2003). Self-reported schizotypy and bipolar disorder: demonstration of a lack of specificity of the Kings Schizotypy Questionnaire. *Schizophrenia Research, 65*, 153–158.

Hodgekins, J., Coker, S., Freeman, D., Ray-Glover, K., Bebbington, P., Garety, P., . . . Fowler, D. (2012). Assessing levels of subthreshold psychotic symptoms in the recovery phase: the Schizotypal Symptoms Inventory (SSI). *Journal of Experimental Psychopathology, 3*, 582–593.

Holmes, E. A., & Steel, C. (2004). Schizotypy: a vulnerability factor for traumatic intrusions. *Journal of Nervous and Mental Disease, 192*, 28–34.

Hori, H., Teraishi, T., Sasayama, D., Matsuo, J., Kinoshita, Y., Ota, M., . . . Kunugi, H. (2014). A latent profile analysis of schizotypy, temperament and character in a nonclinical population: association with neurocognition. *Journal of Psychiatric Research, 48*, 56–64.

Hutton, P., & Taylor, P. J. (2014). Cognitive behavioural therapy for psychosis prevention: a systematic review and meta-analysis. *Psychological Medicine, 44*, 449–468.

Johnstone, E. C., Ebmeier, K. P., Miller, P., Owens, D. G., & Lawrie, S. M. (2005). Predicting schizophrenia: findings from the Edinburgh High-Risk Study. *British Journal of Psychiatry, 186*, 18–25.

Kanemoto, K., Tadokoro, Y., & Oshima, T. (2012). Psychotic illness in patients with epilepsy. *Therapeutic Advances in Neurological Disorders, 5*, 321–334.

Kanner, L. (1943). Autistic disturbances of affect content. *Nervous Child, 2*, 217–250.

Kwapil, T. R., Gross, G. M., Silvia, P. J., & Barrantes-Vidal, N. (2013). Prediction of psychopathology and functional impairment by positive and negative schizotypy in the Chapmans' ten-year longitudinal study. *Journal of Abnormal Psychology, 122*, 807–815.

Kwapil, T. R., Brown, L. H., Silvia, P. J., Myin-Germeys, I., & Barrantes-Vidal, N. (2012). The expression of positive and negative schizotypy in daily life: an experience sampling study. *Psychological Medicine, 42*, 2555–2566.

Lee, H. J., Cougle, J. R., & Telch, M. J. (2005). Thought-action fusion and its relationship to schizotypy and OCD symptoms. *Behaviour Research and Therapy, 43*, 29–41.

Lewandowski, K. E., Barrantes-Vidal, N., Nelson-Gray, R. O., Clancy, C., Kepley, H. O., & Kwapil, T. R. (2006). Anxiety and depression symptoms in psychometrically identified schizotypy. *Schizophrenia Research, 83*, 225–235.

Liberman, R., & Robertson, M. (2005). A pilot controlled skills training study of schizotypal high school students. *Verhaltenstherapie, 15*, 176–180.

Lin, A., Wigman, J. T., Nelson, B., Wood, S. J., Vollebergh, W. A., van Os, J., & Yung, A. R. (2013). Follow-up factor structure of schizotypy and its clinical associations in a help-seeking sample meeting ultra-high risk for psychosis criteria at baseline. *Comprehensive Psychiatry, 54*, 173–180.

Lin, A., Wood, S. J., Nelson, B., Brewer, W. J., Spiliotacopoulos, D., Bruxner, A., . . . Yung, A. R. (2011). Neurocognitive predictors of functional outcome two to 13 years after identification as ultra-high risk for psychosis. *Schizophrenia Research, 132*, 1–7.

Lovatt, A., Mason, O., Brett, C., & Peters, E. (2010). Psychotic-like experiences, appraisals, and trauma. *Journal of Nervous and Mental Disease, 198,* 813–819.

Martin, E. A., Cicero, D. C., & Kerns, J. G. (2012). Social anhedonia, but not positive schizotypy, is associated with poor affective control. *Personality Disorders: Theory, Research and Treatment, 3*(3), 263–272.

Marzillier, S. L., & Steel, C. (2007). Positive schizotypy and trauma-related intrusions. *Journal of Nervous and Mental Disease, 195,* 60–64.

Mason, O., Claridge, G., & Jackson, M. (1995) New scales for the assessment of schizotypy. *Personality and Individual Differences, 18,* 7–13.

Mason, O., Linney, Y., & Claridge, G. (2005). Short scales for measuring schizotypy. *Schizophrenia Research, 78,* 293–296.

Mason, O., Startup, M., Halpin, S., Schall, U., Conrad, A., & Carr, V. (2004). Risk factors for transition to first episode psychosis among individuals with 'at-risk mental states'. *Schizophrenia Research, 71,* 227–237.

Miller, P., Byrne, M., Hodges, A., Lawrie, S. M., Owens, D. G. C., & Johnstone, E. C. (2002). Schizotypal components in people at high risk of developing schizophrenia: early findings from the Edinburgh High-Risk Study. *British Journal of Psychiatry, 180,* 179–184.

Moritz, S., Fricke, S., Jacobsen, D., Kloss, M., Wein, C., Rufer, M., . . . Hand, I. (2004). Positive schizotypal symptoms predict treatment outcome in obsessive-compulsive disorder. *Behaviour Research and Therapy, 42,* 217–227.

Morrison, A. P., Bentall, R. P., French, P., Kilcommons, A., Knight, A., Kreutz, M., & Lewis, S. W. (2002). Randomised controlled trial of early detection and cognitive therapy for preventing transition to psychosis in high risk individuals. Study design and interim analysis of transition rate and psychological risk factors. *British Journal of Psychiatry, 181,* 78–84.

Mula, M., Cavanna, A., Collimedaglia, L., Viana, M., Barbagli, D., Tota, G., . . . Monaco, F. (2008). Clinical correlates of schizotypy in patients with epilepsy. *Journal of Neuropsychiatry and Clinical Neurosciences, 20,* 441–446.

Nelson, M. T., Seal, M. L., Pantelis, C., & Phillips, L. J. (2013). Evidence of a dimensional relationship between schizotypy and schizophrenia: a systematic review. *Neuroscience and Biobehavioral Reviews, 37,* 317–327.

Norman, R. M., Davies, F., Malla, A. K., Cortese, L., & Nicholson, I. R. (1996). Relationship of obsessive-compulsive symptomatology to anxiety, depression and schizotypy in a clinical population. *British Journal of Clinical Psychology, 35,* 553–566.

Poulton, R., Caspi, A., Moffitt, T. E., Cannon, M., Murray, R., & Harrington, H. (2000). Children's self-reported psychotic symptoms and adult schizophreniform disorder: a 15-year longitudinal study. *Archives of General Psychiatry, 57,* 1053–1058.

Poyurovsky, M., Faragian, S., Pashinian, A., Heidrach, L., Fuchs, C., Weizman, R., & Koran, L. (2008). Clinical characteristics of schizotypal-related obsessive-compulsive disorder. *Psychiatry Research, 159,* 254–258.

Raine, A. (1991). The SPQ: a scale for the assessment of schizotypal personality based on *DSM-III-R* criteria. *Schizophrenia Bulletin, 17,* 555–564.

Roberts, G. W., Done, D. J., Bruton, C., & Crow, T. J. (1990). A 'mock up' of schizophrenia: temporal lobe epilepsy and schizophrenia-like psychosis. *Biological Psychiatry, 28*(2), 127–143.

Rossi, A., & Daneluzzo, E. (2002). Schizotypal dimensions in normals and schizophrenic patients: a comparison with other clinical samples. *Schizophrenia Research, 54,* 67–75.

Rossler, W., Hengartner, M. P., Ajdacic-Gross, V., Haker, H., Gamma, A., & Angst, J. (2011). Sub-clinical psychosis symptoms in young adults are risk factors for subsequent common mental disorders. *Schizophrenia Research, 131,* 18–23.

Russell-Smith, S. N., Maybery, M. T., & Bayliss, D. M. (2011). Relationships between autistic-like and schizotypy traits: an analysis using the Autism Spectrum Quotient and Oxford-Liverpool Inventory of Feelings and Experiences. *Personality and Individual Differences, 51,* 128–132.

Schultze-Lutter, F., Klosterkotter, J., Michel, C., Winkler, K., & Ruhrmann, S. (2012). Personality disorders and accentuations in at-risk persons with and without conversion to first-episode psychosis. *Early Intervention in Psychiatry, 6,* 389–398.

Schurhoff, F., Laguerre, A., Szoke, A., Meary, A., & Leboyer, M. (2005). Schizotypal dimensions: continuity between schizophrenia and bipolar disorders. *Schizophrenia Research, 80,* 235–242.

Sobin, C., Blundell, M. L., Weiller, F., Gavigan, C., Haiman, C., & Karayiorgou, M. (2000). Evidence of a schizotypy subtype in OCD. *Journal of Psychiatric Research, 34,* 15–24.

Sprong, M., Becker, H. E., Schothorst, P. F., Swaab, H., Ziermans, T. B., Dingemans, P. M., . . . van Engeland, H. (2008). Pathways to psychosis: a comparison of the pervasive developmental disorder subtype Multiple Complex Developmental Disorder and the "At Risk Mental State". *Schizophrenia Research, 99,* 38–47.

Stanley, M. A., Turner, S. M., & Borden, J. W. (1990). Schizotypal features in obsessive-compulsive disorder. *Comprehensive Psychiatry, 31,* 511–518.

Steel, C., Fowler, D., & Holmes, E. A. (2005). Trauma-related intrusions and psychosis: an information processing account. *Behavioural and Cognitive Psychotherapy, 33,* 139–152.

Tabak, N. T., & Weisman de Mamani, A. G. (2013). Latent profile analysis of healthy schizotypy within the extended psychosis phenotype. *Psychiatry Research, 210,* 1008–1013.

Valmaggia, L. R., Stahl, D., Yung, A. R., Nelson, B., Fusar-Poli, P., McGorry, P. D., & McGuire, P. K. (2013). Negative psychotic symptoms and impaired role functioning predict transition outcomes in the at-risk mental state: a latent class cluster analysis study. *Psychological Medicine, 43,* 2311–2325.

van Os, J., Linscott, R. J., Myin-Germeys, I., Delespaul, P., & Krabbendam, L. (2009). A systematic review and meta-analysis of the psychosis continuum: evidence for a psychosis proneness-persistence-impairment model of psychotic disorder. *Psychological Medicine, 39,* 179–195.

Wakabayashi, A., Baron-Cohen, S., & Ashwin, C. (2012). Do the traits of autism-spectrum overlap with those of schizophrenia or obsessive-compulsive disorder in the general population? *Research in Autism Spectrum Disorders, 6,* 717–725.

Watson, D., & Clark, L. A. (1984). Negative affectivity: the disposition to experience aversive emotional states. *Psychological Bulletin, 96,* 465–490.

Wigman, J. T., van Winkel, R., Raaijmakers, Q. A., Ormel, J., Verhulst, F. C., Reijneveld, S. A., . . . Vollebergh, W. A. (2011). Evidence for a persistent, environment-dependent and deteriorating subtype of subclinical psychotic experiences: a 6-year longitudinal general population study. *Psychological Medicine, 41,* 2317–2329.

Yamamoto, H., Tsuchida, H., Nakamae, T., Nishida, S., Sakai, Y., Fujimori, A., . . . Fukui, K. (2012). Relationship between severity of obsessive-compulsive symptoms and schizotypy in obsessive-compulsive disorder. *Journal of Neuropsychiatric Disease and Treatment, 8,* 579–583.

Yung, A. R., Phillips, L., McGorry, P., Ward, J., Donovan, K., & Thompson, K. (2002). *Comprehensive Assessment of At Risk Mental State (CAARMS)*. Melbourne: PACE Clinic, Department of Psychiatry, University of Melbourne.

Yung, A. R., Phillips, L. J., McGorry, P. D., McFarlane, C. A., Francey, S., Harrigan, S., . . . Jackson, H. J. (1998). Prediction of psychosis – a step towards indicated prevention of schizophrenia. *British Journal of Psychiatry, 172,* 14–20.

Yung, A. R., Stanford, C., Cosgrave, E., Killackey, E., Phillips, L., Nelson, B., & McGorry, P. D. (2006). Testing the ultra high risk (prodromal) criteria for the prediction of psychosis in a clinical sample of young people. *Schizophrenia Research, 84,* 57–66.

12 Schizotypy
A creative advantage?

Nicola J. Holt

Introduction

The notion of the 'mad, creative genius' is a well-established one, with both a rich historical and contemporary context, from Aristotle's well-known assertion that 'there was never a genius without a tincture of madness' (although by 'madness' he meant a form of 'divine inspiration') to biographies of modern poets, comedians and writers who struggled with mental health issues (Claridge, Pryor, & Watkins, 1998; Kottler, 2006). Nevertheless, there is a range of perspectives in this contentious area, from arguments that 'madness' enables creativity (Jamison, 1993), critiques of the evidence base for such claims (Weisberg, 2006), warnings that interpretations of research findings may be biased in favour of the 'mad-genius stereotype' (Silvia & Kaufman, 2010) and proponents of the therapeutic benefits of creative involvement (Camic, 2008).

Further complexities include the componential nature of both psychopathology and creativity, as well as the apparently paradoxical findings that creativity has been associated with indices of both psychopathology and well-being (Barron, 1993). First, the relationship between creativity and mental illness may be confined to certain domains or levels of creativity (e.g. to the arts but not to entrepreneurship, or to eminent but not 'everyday' levels of creativity), and limited to certain forms or levels of psychopathology (e.g. to bipolar but not anxiety disorders, or to subclinical symptoms only). Second, while parallels have been drawn between creative and clinical populations (e.g. between creative cognition and thought disorder), there are also disjunctions where the populations differ (e.g. in executive control), suggesting that any relationship between psychopathology and creativity is not a straightforward one (Merton & Fischer, 1999). In this chapter, such complexities will be considered and a review will be made of the empirical and theoretical associations between creativity, schizotypy and well-being. Because of space restrictions, only the briefest of reviews will be made of the literature on psychopathology and creativity; for a broader review, see Silvia and Kaufman (2010).

Defining terms: creativity and schizotypy

> ... the madman who, in Russell's apt phrase, believes himself to be a poached egg may very well be uttering a novel thought, but few of us, I imagine, would want to say that he was producing a creative one. (Briskman, 1980, cited in Isaksen, 1987, p. 13)

Why might 'uttering a novel thought' not necessarily be creative? Creativity is commonly defined in terms of 'adaptive novelty', when a creative process results in originality – originality that can be usefully applied in some context, whether this is solving a problem in everyday life or producing an aesthetically pleasing performance (Eysenck, 1993). As such, mere remoteness, idiosyncrasy or bizarreness is not sufficient – any creative product must also be 'valuable' or 'appropriate', at an individual, social or cultural level (as difficult to determine in some cases as this might be). However, this abstract definition of creativity is not typically applied at an operational level, in part because it belies the heterogeneity of the construct. Creativity is conceptualised as having four components: the creative process (e.g. neurocognitive mechanisms); the creative person (e.g. traits and behaviours); the creative product (e.g. dance, inventions); and the creative 'press' (social influences, judgements and support). As such, diverse measures of creativity exist that attempt to measure these different components. Included are measures of 'creative cognition', such as the widely used tests of divergent thinking (DT; Guilford, 1967), which, in a given time frame, assess the ability to produce original (rare) responses to a stimulus, as well as the number of responses produced (fluency) and the number of switches from one idea to a different one (flexibility). In addition, there exist trait measures, such as the Creative Personality Scale (CPS; Gough, 1979), assessing characteristics and beliefs commonly reported by creative professionals (e.g. that one is imaginative and independent). A further type of test has asked people about their involvement in a range of activities presumed to be creative (e.g. the Creative Achievement Questionnaire; Carson, Peterson, & Higgins, 2005). While these three forms of test (cognitive, trait and behavioural) are the most commonly used measures of creativity, yet more tests exist, such as the preference for complex visual stimuli, prevalent among visual artists (Barron, 1972), and self, peer and expert ratings of an individual's creativity and productivity.

All these methods have been used in the research on schizotypy that is discussed in the following sections. What is important is to consider the impact this diversity has on understanding the relationship between creativity and schizotypy. For example, each measure of creativity has its own unique flaws, with interpretative implications. For instance, scores on DT tests do not assess an individual's ability to evaluate the relevance of ideas for creative use, and involvement in particular activities does not equate to creativity in that area (one can be a talented technical painter without painting anything original). Different measures might tap into different stages of the creative process (e.g. idea generation versus idea development) or different creativity constructs, such as eminent or professional achievement (requiring ambition, determination and confidence) versus 'everyday' creativity or potential (Eysenck, 1993).

Although there is debate as to whether or not schizotypy is a continuum or a categorical variable, the construct can be defined as the presence, at a subclinical level, of experiences and behaviours that are analogous with those of schizophrenia, including positive, negative and disorganised symptoms. As such, schizotypy is a set of traits (see Chapter 1). Various measures of schizotypy have been used in the creativity literature. Again, these have different implications when considering outcomes: for example, some scales (e.g. the Chapman scales) have been designed with a categorical construct in mind and measure more extreme experiences than others (e.g. the Oxford-Liverpool Inventory of Feelings and Experiences [O-LIFE]; Mason, Claridge, & Jackson, 1995). Some scales are global, rather than multidimensional, measures of schizotypy. This adds further obfuscation to the interpretation of the literature, because creativity may relate differentially to both sub-dimensions and levels of schizotypy.

Creativity and psychopathology

Does creativity come at the cost of 'madness'? Are creative minds more vulnerable, labile or chaotic? Evidence for a link between creativity and mental illness comes from several strands, including (1) historiographical studies that have diagnosed well-known artistic figures (such as Lord Byron and Sylvia Plath) as having bipolar disorder, schizoaffective disorder or personality disorders (e.g. Jamison, 1993); and (2) studies of living professional and eminent artists that have found a higher incidence of psychopathology among them in comparison to control groups (e.g. Andreasen, 1987). This body of research can be taken to support the 'mad genius hypothesis'. However, critics have argued that the similarity between 'madness' and creativity is more apparent than real, illustrating a number of methodological problems with this work, including difficulties with posthumous diagnosis and the potentially unrepresentative characteristics of creative samples (e.g. those at a workshop for 'burnt out' writers in Andreasen's [1987] study) (Schlesinger, 2009; Weisberg, 2006).

Overall, research appears to better support a 'weak' rather than a 'strong' link between creativity and psychopathology. Bipolar disorder and schizophrenia are debilitating and in their worse expressions do not enable creative functioning (Richards, Kinney, Lunde, Benet, & Merzel, 1988; Rubinstein, 2008). Focusing on the schizophrenic spectrum, peak creativity has been observed for moderate (rather than low or high) levels of schizotypal symptoms (Kinney et al., 2001) and in *non-diagnosed* relatives of schizophrenics (Kyaga et al., 2013). Further, schizophrenic patients have scored poorly on measures of creative cognition compared with controls, as well as poorly on tests of executive functioning (Abraham, Windmann, McKenna, & Güntürkün, 2007; Jaracz, Patrzala, & Rybakowski, 2012; Rubinstein, 2008). This suggests that executive dysfunction in schizophrenia might inhibit creative idea production. An inverted 'U' model has been proposed, whereby schizophrenic-like symptoms facilitate creativity up to a point, but inhibit it when too severe (Kinney et al., 2001). This model has been theoretically important in seeking to explain why schizophrenia is still prevalent, conveying a creative advantage in its 'milder forms' (Kyaga et al., 2013). Such curvilinear models, then, would hypothesise that subclinical schizotypal symptoms predict creativity.

Creativity and schizotypy: overview of the literature

Several studies have reported relationships between global measures of schizotypy and creativity. However, creativity has been operationalised in diverse ways, with few studies replicating the same method. As such, it is difficult to obtain a clear picture of how creativity and schizotypy might be related. Nevertheless, positive relationships have been reported – for example, between schizotypy and originality on DT tasks (Green & Williams, 1999) and inhibiting the 'constraints of examples' (here high schizotypes were better at ignoring exemplar features in order to invent original products) (Abraham & Windmann, 2008). However, non-significant results have also been reported (e.g. Rawlings, Twomey, Burns, & Morris, 1998; Wuthrich & Bates, 2001).

The sub-dimensions of schizotypy do not always correlate significantly with each other, indicating that they are distinct constructs (Claridge & McDonald, 2009; Dinn et al., 2002). Further, they may have different neurocognitive correlates and differential implications for functioning and well-being (Barrantes-Vidal et al., 2002; Barrantes-Vidal, Lewandowski, & Kwapil, 2010; Cicero & Kerns, 2010). As such, they may also have different implications for creative functioning. Indeed, in a recent meta-analysis of the relationship between creativity and schizotypy, Acar and Sen (2013) reported that 'positive and impulsive' dimensions were significant positive predictors of schizotypy (mean $r = .14$, $p < .001$), while 'negative and disorganised' dimensions were significant negative predictors of schizotypy (mean $r = -.09$, $p < .001$). In the following sections, the import of sub-dimensions of schizotypy for creativity will be considered separately in order to evaluate their relative contribution in more depth.

Creativity and positive symptoms: Perceptual–cognitive aberrations and magical thinking

Much emphasis has been placed on the role that positive features of schizotypy might play in creativity. For example, parallels have been drawn between 'creative inspiration' and hallucinations, drawing on the anecdotal reports of famous scientists and artists, such as Henri Poincaré and Samuel Taylor Coleridge (Holt, 2012). Consider the poet Theodore Roethke who experienced a sensed presence after writing his poem 'The Dance' in 1952.

> I felt, I knew, that I had hit it. I walked around, and I wept; and I knelt down – I always do after I've written what I know is a good piece. But at the same time I had, as God is my witness, the actual sense of a Presence – as if Yeats himself were in that room. The experience was in a way terrifying, for it lasted for at least half an hour. That house, I repeat, was charged with a psychic presence: the very walls seemed to shimmer. I wept for joy . . . He, they – the poets dead – were with me. (Cited by Smith, 2007, p. 114)

Most research in this area has focused on cognitive measures of creativity. Theoretically, it draws upon associative models, where creative thinking is defined as 'the forming of associative elements into new combinations', constrained by goals and selection criteria, where 'the more mutually remote the elements of the new combination, the more creative the process' (Mednick, 1962, p. 221). The making of 'remote associations' has been compared to 'thought disorder', apophenia and magical ideation, where loose connections are made that may seem 'aberrantly' meaningful (Eysenck, 1993; Mohr, Graves, Gianotti, Pizzagalli, & Brugger, 2001). As such, several studies have compared the positive symptoms of schizotypy to the capacity to make or perceive remote associations. Using a variety of approaches, some studies have reported significant effects (e.g. Miller & Chapman, 1983; Mohr et al., 2001) and others non-significant outcomes (e.g. Gibson, Folley, & Park, 2009; Schuldberg, 1990). The most successful approach appears to be based on free-response word association tasks. For example, Miller and Chapman (1983) asked participants to make as many associations to a stimulus word as they could in one minute. Responses were analysed for commonality, as well as for idiosyncratic words (producing a word that no-one else did) that were considered to be either deviant (did not relate to the stimulus word, e.g. clanging or neologisms), or non-deviant (unique but appropriate). High scorers on positive schizotypy produced significantly fewer common word associations and more 'deviant' idiosyncratic responses than controls. However, one may question whether the ability to make remote and 'inappropriate' word associations is indicative of creativity defined as 'adaptive novelty'.

It is notable that most of the non-significant studies discussed used the Remote Associates Test (Mednick & Mednick, 1967), where creativity is judged by the ability to select a response that solves a specific problem. This suggests that positive schizotypy is associated with the ability to make unusual responses, but not necessarily in a way that meets Mednick's (1962) criteria for creativity. Further support for this comes from studies that collectively imply that DT is not a robust predictor of positive schizotypy, most reporting null outcomes (e.g. Batey & Furnham, 2009; Claridge & Blakey, 2009). While the appropriateness of responses is not assessed in these tests, the context, where participants are aware that their creativity is being measured and are asked to select and develop their most original ideas, conceivably requires more sustained attention and evaluative cognition than word association tasks. Word association tasks might better tap into the ability to make uninhibited and original responses.

Outcomes are more promising for perceptual and behavioural creativity, indicative of involvement in the arts. Significant positive correlations have been reported between positive schizotypy and a preference for complex imagery, indicating some overlap between the unusual perceptual experiences of schizotypy and the perceptual preferences of artistic individuals (e.g. Schuldberg, 2000–2001). However, it may be that some factor other than creativity (such as attraction to the unusual) underlies this relationship. Further research has compared populations drawn from 'creative' domains with controls. These studies consistently report that artists score higher than non-artists on positive symptoms (Burch, Pavelis, Hemsley, & Corr, 2006; Gibson et al., 2009; Nettle, 2006; Rawlings & Locarnini, 2008). For example, Nettle (2006) compared levels of schizotypy across poets, visual artists, mathematicians and controls. He reported that both artistic groups had significantly higher levels of positive schizotypy, and that professional mathematicians had significantly lower levels of positive schizotypy than non-mathematicians, suggesting that positive schizotypy is only associated with the arts. This was supported in a conceptual replication by Rawlings and Locarnini (2008) who, interestingly, also observed that making remote word associations was a shared feature of both positive schizotypy and being an artist.

In summary, there appears to be a relationship between the positive features of schizotypy and creativity. However, this is limited to particular types of creativity, originality on word association tasks, figural preference and creative involvement, especially in the arts. The latter finding seems to be particularly robust, and is further supported by studies that have found high levels of anomalous experiences (e.g. mystical experiences) in artistic populations (Holt, 2012).

Creativity and impulsive non-conformity: risk taking and norm breaking

Impulsive non-conformity has been theoretically linked to creativity through risk taking and a lack of censorship of ideas, widening the range of possible responses and behaviours (Rawlings & Toogood, 1997). Further links relate to its overlap with hypomania (Claridge et al., 1996); see also Chapter 13, this volume): the 'flight of ideas' typically found in that disorder has been associated with creative production (Schuldberg, 1990).

Overall, the research on this dimension of schizotypy is mixed, for both student and creative populations (e.g. Rawlings & Locarnini, 2008). For example, three of the studies that used DT reported significant effects indicating a positive relationship with positive schizotypy (Batey & Furnham, 2009; Burch, Hemsley, Corr, & Pavelis, 2005; O'Reilly, Dunbar, & Bentall, 2001) and two reported null outcomes (Claridge & McDonald, 2009; Claridge & Blakey, 2009). However, in a subsequent regression analysis, Claridge and Blakey (2009) found that originality was predicted by cyclothymia, hyperthymia, low anxiety and impulsive non-conformity (while the same facets, without impulsive non-conformity, predicted fluency). This suggests that 'mood factors' facilitated the number of ideas produced, but that impulsivity added to the originality of these ideas.

Impulsive individuals may be more likely to 'blurt out' their thoughts, having less concern with taboo, leading to higher scores on measures of originality. Indeed, Rawlings and Toogood's (1997) study partially supports this hypothesis, but with a global measure of schizotypy. Here, schizotypes were more likely to make responses that were both original *and* taboo. Interestingly, Miller and Chapman (1983), in a *post hoc* analysis, reported that the most remote word associations were obtained by high scorers on positive schizotypy who *also* scored highly on impulsive non-conformity, suggesting an interaction between these two dimensions in the creation of original responses (impulsive non-conformity was not a significant predictor on its own). Thus, impulsive non-conformity may moderate the expression of ideas.

Creativity and negative symptoms: Social withdrawal and physical anhedonia

If creativity were universally associated with psychopathology, then we would expect to find significant positive correlations between negative symptoms and creativity. However, on the whole this is not the case. Although Schuldberg (1990) suggests that negative symptoms in the cyclical pattern of creative work might play an adaptive role in the creative process (e.g. temporarily withdrawing into one's own world to focus on creative pursuits), most of the research finds that negative symptoms inhibit or play no role in creative functioning (e.g. Batey & Furnham, 2009; Claridge & McDonald, 2009). For instance, with creative populations, Nettle (2006) found no significant difference between poets and non-poets, or mathematicians and non-mathematicians, on levels of negative schizotypy, but did report that those who were involved with the visual arts reported lower levels than those who were not.

Negative symptoms have been associated with low levels of openness-to-experience, reduced verbal fluency, executive dysfunction, apathy and decreased positive affect in everyday life (Dinn et al., 2002; Howanitz, Cicalese, & Harvey, 2000; Kwapil, Brown, Silvia, Myin-Germeys, & Barrantes-Vidal, 2012;

Ross, Lutz, & Bailey, 2002). An inverse relationship between negative schizotypy and schizotypy, then, may be due to behavioural factors (diminished attraction to novelty and exploration), social factors (withdrawing from social influences that might support or inspire), cognitive constriction (Shrira & Tsakanikos, 2009), or affective factors, such as infrequent positive moods that facilitate DT (Davis, 2009).

Creativity and cognitive disorganisation: Distractibility and anxiety

Cognitive disorganisation has been correlated with poor executive control, emotional confusion and reduced conscientiousness (Cicero & Kerns, 2010). It is indicated by social anxiety, distractibility and, conceptually, with cognitive looseness. Theoretically, it might increase originality through the making of 'cognitive leaps', but, on the other hand, it may limit creative achievement through reduced determination, focus and confidence, traits that identify individuals who are creative at a professional level (Gough, 1979).

An evaluation of the empirical literature yields mixed, but mostly null, outcomes across all components of creativity, rendering the role of cognitive disorganisation in creativity weak (e.g. Batey & Furnham, 2009, Claridge & McDonald, 2009). Studies that have compared the schizotypal traits of 'creative populations' fare better, but still have mixed outcomes (e.g. Rawlings & Locarnini, 2008). Collectively, these studies suggest that cognitive disorganisation is not a successful predictor of cognitive or trait creativity, but may be elevated in particular artistic domains, such as music, and lower among scientists.

Summary

Creativity and schizotypy have different relationships with each other depending on the components that are measured. Positive schizotypy, for example, appears to be associated with involvement in the arts and remote word associations, but not with tests that involve the selection of appropriate responses, suggesting that schizotypy might play a role in generative but not evaluative creative cognition (a hypothesis that deserves further exploration). Negative schizotypy appears to be inversely correlated with creativity, but its potential function in the evaluation and development of ideas has not been fully explored (Claridge & McDonald, 2009). However, it must be noted that the effect sizes in these studies tend to be small, suggesting that factors other than schizotypy are responsible for much of the variance in creativity scores. Further, a number of limitations must be considered when evaluating outcomes, such as small sample sizes and potentially masked curvilinear effects, which might contribute to the mixed results obtained. An additional problem is that of potential reporting artefacts. Schizotypy questionnaires are sensitive to defensive responding (Mohr & Leonards, 2005), and artists may be more likely to remember or report unusual or taboo experiences, thereby providing one explanation for their inflated scores. As this work is largely correlational or observational, we cannot infer causality from it, such as whether positive schizotypy leads to creativity, or vice versa, or indeed whether some third variable is responsible for any relationships, such as novelty seeking. This issue will be explored in the following section where explanations for the link between schizotypy and creativity are briefly reviewed.

Potential underlying mechanisms

A number of models have been proposed to explain the relationship between creativity and psychopathology. These include models of cognitive disinhibition, affect, motivation and personality. Most models have focused on the positive symptoms of schizotypy in relation to creativity, but some attempt will be made here to consider 'bidirectional' models that also consider negative schizotypy.

Neurocognitive models

The notion that a continuum of cognitive disinhibition links creativity and psychopathology has been commonly propounded (Mohr et al., 2001; Prentky, 2000–2001). Eysenck (1993) deemed both creative and psychotic cognition to be 'overinclusive', indirect support for which came from idiosyncratic responses of creatives on object-sorting tasks, and word association tasks, as discussed earlier. He proposed latent inhibition (LI) as a potential mechanism for overinclusive thinking, enabling remote or irrelevant information to enter awareness.

LI has been defined as 'the capacity to screen from conscious awareness stimuli previously experienced as irrelevant' (Carson, Peterson, & Higgins, 2003, p. 499), an unconscious process that adaptively reduces the load on working memory (Wuthrich & Bates, 2001). Positive schizotypy is thought to be underpinned by less efficient LI (Gray, Fernandez, Williams, Ruddle, & Snowden, 2002), whereas negative schizotypy has been found to accentuate the LI effect, leading to more focused attention (Shrira & Tsakanikos, 2009). Shrira and Tsakanikos (2009) thus propose a bidirectional model in which negative and positive symptoms affect LI in opposing directions. Such a model is in accord with findings that (1) positive schizotypy is associated with creativity (because latent disinhibition would facilitate remote associations); and (2) that negative symptoms are potentially inhibitive (because robust LI would screen remote associations from attention).

A number of studies have tested whether creativity is related to LI. Carson et al. (2003) reported that high creative achievers had significantly lower LI scores than low creative achievers (as did high scorers on both DT and creative personality). Kéri (2011) replicated this for creative achievement, and Fink, Slamar-Haldbedl, Unterrainer and Weiss (2012) for verbal (but not figural) originality. However, further studies have found either no relationship between LI and cognitive and trait measures of creativity, or a relationship in the opposite direction (whereby creative people were better at screening out irrelevant information!) (Burch, Hemsley, Corr, & Pavelis, 2005; Wuthrich & Bates, 2001). Outcomes may depend in part upon the samples chosen. Carson et al. (2005) used a 'high IQ' sample, and both Kéri (2011) and Carson et al. reported that creative achievement was best predicted by low LI and high IQ. Perhaps latent disinhibition only leads to creative achievement in participants with high levels of intellectual ability.

A related approach has suggested that creative people are 'ambicognitive' (Brod, 1997). Here, rather than being prone to cognitive disinhibition per se, they functionally shift between focused and defocused attentional states (characterised by low and high cortical arousal, respectively) as is appropriate to task demands (Fink & Neubauer, 2006; Martindale, 1999). For example, while thinking of ideas for a story (requiring originality), participants whose subsequent stories were rated as creative had low arousal (indicated by alpha rhythm levels), but then high arousal when writing out the final version (elaborating and selecting the best ideas) (Martindale & Hasenfus, 1978). Martindale's (1999) model accords with biphasic models of creativity, in which both divergent and convergent cognition are needed to produce a creative product. However, the precise neurological mechanisms of how this might occur are as yet unclear and perhaps oversimplified (Kaufman, Kornilov, Bristol, Tan, & Grigorenko, 2010).

An alternative model for a link between schizotypy and creativity is the right hemisphere preference model (Weinstein & Graves, 2001). Reduced hemispheric asymmetry has been found among high schizotypals (e.g. Broks, Claridge, Matheson, & Hargreaves, 1984; see Chapter 4, this volume). Further, right-hemispheric activation is associated with improved performance on creativity tasks, especially when these tasks are figural and involve global processing (Mihov, Denzler, & Förster, 2011). Such findings support the idea that remote associations might involve right hemispheric networks. However, the activation of *both* hemispheres is likely to be important for creative ideation (Atchley, Keeney, & Burgess, 1999), so creativity may be associated with increased hemispheric interaction (Kaufman et al., 2010). Prentky (2000–2001) proposed that hemispheric dysregulation underlies a continuum of 'constricted' to 'overinclusive' cognition upon which mild deviancies, in either direction, facilitate creativity and, in extreme deviancies, psychopathology. Such an approach might serve as the basis of a model that links the negative and positive symptoms of schizotypy to convergent and divergent creativity – where global and holistic versus sequential and analytical processes predominate in each (Kaufman et al., 2010).

In summary, various neurocognitive parallels have been drawn between creativity and schizotypy that require further refinement and development.

These models are not necessarily incompatible. Thus brain-imaging studies have associated creative cognition with increases in alpha power in the posterior cortex of the right hemisphere with concurrent alpha synchronisation in the prefrontal circuits, suggesting the involvement of a frontal-right-parietal network in original ideation (Fink et al., 2006; Howard-Jones, Blakemore, Samuel, Summers, & Claxton, 2005). However, the models do have different implications for well-being. Martindale's (1999) hypothesis suggests that, in the case of creativity, 'schizotypal' states are temporary and functional – generating originality in pursuit of a goal.

Affect and motivation

Affect has been proposed to be involved in creativity in a number of ways. Strong emotion may increase the motivation to produce, through catharsis or excitement (Averill, 2005). Further, moods appear to affect DT (Davis, 2009). Both motivational and cognitive elements of affect may help us to further understand the links between creativity and schizotypy.

Rather than sharing a cognitive mechanism, O'Reilly et al. (2001) propose a motivational model, where schizotypal experiences predispose one to an interest in the arts because they allow idiosyncratic and subjective accounts to be expressed. This model was thought to better explain their finding that degree subject of participants (creative arts versus humanities) explained the variance between schizotypy and DT. Indeed, the more subjective and emotional a domain is (within both the arts and sciences), the higher the rates of psychopathology (Ludwig, 1998), and both artists and positive schizotypes have been characterised as attending to emotions (Feist, 1998; Kerns, 2005). Collectively, this provides *indirect* support for the hypothesis that the arts provide an arena where affective and unusual experiences can be explored or used creatively, which may even play a therapeutic role (Camic, 2008).

Alternatively, the hedonic valence of moods has been proposed to modulate creative cognition. Moderate positive moods have been reported to increase creativity (especially positive and 'approach' emotions, such as joy), and negative and 'avoidant' emotions, such as anxiety, to inhibit creativity (Baas, De Dreu, & Nijstad, 2008; Davis, 2009). Positive affect may trigger cognitive flexibility and a broad associative network, and negative affect cognitive constriction (Fredrickson, 2002). Both hedonic valence and motivational components of affect may contribute to creative performance, modulating both attention and persistence at a creative task (Baas et al., 2008). Because of its overlap with cyclothymia (Claridge & Blakey, 2009), positive schizotypy might involve positive 'approach' moods that increase creative ideation and/or perseverance. Conversely, both motivational (avolition) and affective factors of negative schizotypy (decreased positive moods in daily life) may lead to reduced performance on creativity tasks. Dopaminergic models of affect have been extended to account for such findings. Higher levels of baseline dopamine have been implicated in DT, latent disinhibition and schizophrenia, and low levels in convergent thinking (Chermahini & Hommel, 2010; Davis, Kahn, Ko, & Davidson, 1991; Gray et al., 1992). However, Chermahini and Hommel (2010) report that indicators of both low and high levels of dopamine inhibited DT, proposing an inverted 'U-curve' relationship, where *moderate* baseline dopamine levels facilitate creativity. This supports curvilinear models, as previously discussed, where non-clinical symptomatology is associated with creativity.

Personality: experience seeking

In personality models it is proposed that schizotypy does not play a causal role in creativity, but that the two are indirectly related via shared behavioural tendencies, subsumed within traits such as openness-to-experience and sensation seeking. These involve curiosity, exploring novel or unusual ideas and experiences. Again, a bidirectional relationship with schizotypy dimensions has been reported, whereby positive schizotypy is associated with increased, and negative schizotypy with decreased, openness-to-experience (Kwapil, Barrantes-Vidal, & Silvia, 2008).

Creative people score highly on openness-to-experience (Feist, 1998), being curious about 'both inner and outer worlds' and 'willing to entertain novel ideas and unconventional values' (Costa & McCrae, 1992, p. 15). Miller & Tal (2007) propose that *curiosity*, rather than analogues of mental illness, is more appropriate for modelling creativity, based on their finding that openness-to-experience explained the variance between creativity and schizotypy. In a related vein, Rawlings et al. (1998) reported that 'experience seeking' was a better predictor of creativity than schizotypy. One route by which experience seeking might lead to positive schizotypy is by seeking drug-induced experiences. Indeed, Preti and Vellante (2007) found professional artists to score significantly higher than controls on both magical thinking and experimentation with illicit psychotropic drugs. Further, drug use was a significant mediator between group membership and magical thinking scores. This suggests, then, that positive schizotypy among artists may be a by-product of experience seeking.

However, among artists, positive schizotypy has shared unique variance with experiences in the creative process that openness-to-experience could not explain, such as the 'flow state' (Nelson & Rawlings, 2008). 'Flow', which Csikszentmihalyi (1996) observed was a common component of the creative work of eminent artists and scientists, involves a loss of self-awareness in a state of intense concentration, which may be described as a 'healthy state of dissociation'. Thus, there may be a variety of links between positive schizotypy and creativity, some explained by experience seeking (e.g. drug-induced experiences) and others not (e.g. being prone to dissociative states that facilitate creative involvement).

Implications for health and well-being

> You must also be able to handle what is apt to come out of the bottle. (Smith & van der Meer, 1994, p. 162).

Thus far the focus has been on similarities between schizotypy and creativity and potential explanations for these. However, dissimilarities have also been proposed, which will be briefly considered here. Creativity has been associated with indicators of healthy functioning, such as happiness and good working memory capacity (De Dreu, Nijstad, Baas, Wolsink, & Roskes, 2012; Panells & Claxton, 2008). Dual-factor models propose that creative and clinical populations may share traits indicative of a predisposition for psychopathology, but in creatives the additional presence of 'healthy' factors (e.g. social support, resilience, intelligence, executive functioning, cognitive flexibility) leads to their expression in an adaptive form (Barron, 1993; Carson et al. 2003; Martindale, 1999; Schuldberg, 1990). For example, Barron (1993, p. 183) described creativity as 'controllable oddness', where 'oddness of thought or feeling, when coupled with an ability to reconsider and reformulate' is a resource for creativity. A number of studies support this model, in which the highest creativity scores have been found in profiles characterised by psychosis proneness and resilience (Fodor, 1995); latent disinhibition and intelligence (Carson et al., 2003; Kéri, 2011); idiosyncratic word associations plus cognitive inhibition when required (to censor inappropriate responses) (Merton & Fischer, 1999); and high positive schizotypy, along with the *absence* of debilitating factors such as confused thinking and anhedonia (Holt, Simmonds-Moore, & Moore, 2008). Dual-factor models have implications for the perceived health status of positive schizotypy. Schuldberg (1990) suggests that being healthy is a heterogeneous construct. Creativity, which has correlated with 'healthy' and 'non-healthy' constructs, might be a particular form of 'health', and as such this suggests that subclinical expressions of positive schizotypy may be adaptive and part of a healthy profile.

Conclusion and future directions

Overall, research supports an inverted 'U' model, in which moderate features on the schizophrenia spectrum are associated with creativity, and perhaps buffered, and channelled into creative pursuits, with the assistance of adaptive factors (such as high intelligence or resilience). However, there are numerous potential pathways between creativity and schizotypy, some of which are direct (e.g. shared neurocognitive mechanisms broadening attention) and some of which are indirect (e.g. novelty seeking, independently leading to both creative and schizotypal experiences). Further, different components of schizotypy relate differentially to different types of creativity (e.g. positive schizotypy with artistic, but not scientific, creative behaviour). A complex interaction between neurocognitive, affective, motivational and self-regulatory factors may be required to best model the relationships between 'creativities' and 'schizotypies'. However, more research is required to synthesise, understand and extend findings and models. For example, *why* does positive schizotypy relate to some forms of creativity and not to others? *How* might affective and neurocognitive models be reconciled? *What* variables in dual-factor models are most important for creativity, and does this apply across domains and subdomains of creative endeavour? Better understanding of such factors may help to clarify whether, and how, schizotypy can be expressed 'creatively' and, thus, be adaptive in certain contexts.

References

Abraham, A., & Windmann, S. (2008). Selective information processing advantages in creative cognition as a function of schizotypy. *Creativity Research Journal, 20*, 1–6.

Abraham, A., Windmann, S., McKenna, P., & Güntürkün, O. (2007). Creative thinking in schizophrenia: the role of executive dysfunction and symptom severity. *Cognitive Neuropsychiatry, 12*, 235–258.

Acar, S., & Sen, S. (2013). A multilevel meta-analysis of the relationship between creativity and schizotypy. *Psychology of Aesthetics, Creativity, and the Arts, 7*, 214–228.

Andreasen, N. (1987). Creativity and mental illness: prevalence rates in writers and their first-degree relatives. *American Journal of Psychiatry, 144*, 1288–1292.

Atchley, R., Keeney, M., & Burgess, C. (1999). Cerebral hemispheric mechanisms linking ambiguous word meaning retrieval and creativity. *Brain and Cognition, 40*, 479–499.

Averill, J. (2005). Emotions as mediators and as products of creative activity. In J. Kaufman, & J. Baer (Eds.), *Creativity across domains: Faces of the muse* (pp. 225–243). Mahwah, NJ: Erlbaum.

Baas, M., de Dreu, C. K. W., & Nijstad, B. A. (2008). A meta-analysis of 25 years of mood-creativity research: hedonic tone, activation, or regulatory focus? *Psychological Bulletin, 134*, 779–806.

Barrantes-Vidal, N., Fañanás, L., Rosa, A., Caparrós, B., Riba, M., & Obiols, J. (2002). Neurocognitive, behavioural and neurodevelopmental correlates of schizotypy clusters in adolescents from the general population. *Schizophrenia Research, 61*, 293–302.

Barrantes-Vidal, N., Lewandowski, K. E., & Kwapil, T. R. (2010). Psychopathy, social adjustment and personality correlates of schizotypy clusters in a large nonclinical sample. *Schizophrenia Research, 122*, 219–225.

Barron, F. (1972). *Artists in the making*. New York: Seminar Press.

Barron, F. (1993). Controllable oddness as a resource in creativity. *Psychological Inquiry, 4*, 182–184.

Batey, M., & Furnham, A. (2009). The relationship between creativity, schizotypy and intelligence. *Individual Differences Research, 7*, 272–284.

Brod, J. (1997). Creativity and schizotypy. In G. Claridge (Ed.), *Schizotypy: Implications for illness and health* (pp. 274–298). New York: Oxford University Press.

Broks, P., Claridge, G., Matheson, J., & Hargreaves, J. (1984). Schizotypy and hemispheric function – IV story comprehension under binaural and monoaural listening conditions. *Personality and Individual Differences, 5*, 649–656.

Burch, G., Hemsley, D., Corr, P., & Pavelis, C. (2005). Personality, creativity and latent inhibition. *European Journal of Personality, 19*, 1–16.

Burch, G., Pavelis, C., Hemsley, D., & Corr, P. (2006). Schizotypy and creativity in visual artists. *British Journal of Psychology, 97*, 177–190.

Camic, P. (2008). Playing in the mud: health psychology, the arts and creative approaches to health care. *Journal of Health Psychology, 13*, 287–298.

Carson, S., Peterson, J., & Higgins, D. (2003). Decreased latent inhibition is associated with increased achievement in high-functioning individuals. *Personality and Individual Differences, 85*, 499–506.

Carson, S., Peterson, J., & Higgins, D. (2005). Reliability, validity and factor structure of the Creative Achievement Questionnaire. *Creativity Research Journal, 17*, 37–50.

Chermahini, A. S., & Hommel, B. (2010). The (b)link between creativity and dopamine: spontaneous eye blink rates predict and dissociate divergent and convergent thinking. *Cognition, 115*, 458–465.

Cicero, D., & Kerns, J. (2010). Can disorganized and positive schizotypy be discriminated from dissociation? *Journal of Personality, 78*, 1239–1270.

Claridge, G., & Blakey, S. (2009). Schizotypy and affective temperament: relationships with divergent thinking and creativity styles. *Personality and Individual Differences, 46*, 820–826.

Claridge, G., & McDonald, A. (2009). An investigation into the relationships between convergent and divergent thinking, schizotypy and autistic traits. *Personality and Individual Differences, 46*, 794–799.

Claridge, G., Pryor, R., & Watkins, G. (1998). *Sounds from the bell jar: Ten psychotic authors*. Cambridge, MA: Malor Books.

Claridge, G., McCreery, C., Mason, O., Bentall, R., Boyle, G., Slade, P., & Popplewell, D. (1996). The factor structure of 'schizotypal' traits: a large replication study. *British Journal of Clinical Psychology, 35*, 103–115.

Costa, P., & McCrae, R. (1992). *Professional manual: Revised NEO personality inventory (NEO PI-R) and NEO five-factor inventory (FFI)*. Florida: Psychological Assessment Resources.

Csikszentmihalyi, M. (1996). *Creativity: Flow and the psychology of discovery and invention*. New York: HarperCollins.

Davis, K. L., Kahn, R. S., Ko, G., & Davidson, M. (1991). Dopamine in schizophrenia: a review and reconceptualization. *American Journal of Psychiatry, 148*, 1474–1486.

Davis, M. (2009). Understanding the relationship between mood and creativity: a meta-analysis. *Organizational Behaviour and Human Decision Processes, 108*, 25–38.

De Dreu, C., Nijstad, B., Baas, M., Wolsink, I., & Roskes, M. (2012). Working memory benefits creative insight, musical improvisation, and original ideation through maintained task-focused attention. *Personality and Social Psychology Bulletin, 38*, 656–669.

Dinn, W., Harris, C., Ayciegi, A., Greene, P., & Andover, M. (2002). Positive and negative schizotypy in a student sample: neurocognitive and clinical correlates. *Schizophrenia Research, 56*, 171–185.

Eysenck, H. (1993). Creativity and personality: suggestions for a theory. *Psychological Inquiry, 4*, 147–178.

Feist, G. (1998). A meta-analysis of personality in scientific and artistic creativity. *Personality and Social Psychology Review, 2*, 290–390.

Fink, A., & Neubauer, A. (2006). EEG alpha oscillations during the performance of verbal creativity tasks: differential effects of sex and verbal intelligence. *International Journal of Psychophysiology, 62*, 46–53.

Fink, A., Grabner, A., Benedek, M., & Neubauer, A. (2006). Divergent thinking training is linked to frontal electroencephalogram alpha synchronization. *European Journal of Neuroscience, 23*, 2241.

Fink, A., Slamar-Haldbedl, M., Unterrainer, H., & Weiss, E. (2012). Creativity: genius, madness or a combination of both? *Psychology of Aesthetics, Creativity and the Arts, 6*, 11–18.

Fodor, E. (1995). Subclinical manifestations of psychosis-proneness, ego strength, and creativity. *Personality and Individual Differences, 18*, 635–642.

Fredrickson, B. (2002). Positive emotions. In C. Snyder, & S. Lopez (Eds.), *Handbook of positive psychology* (pp. 120–134). New York: Oxford University Press.

Gibson, C., Folley, B., & Park, S. (2009). Enhanced divergent thinking and creativity in musicians: a behavioural and near-infrared spectroscopy study. *Brain and Cognition, 69*, 162–169.

Gough, H. (1979). A creative personality scale for the adjective check list. *Journal of Personality and Social Psychology, 37*, 1398–1405.

Gray, N., Fernandez, M., Williams, J., Ruddle, R., & Snowden R. (2002). Which schizotypal dimensions abolish latent inhibition. *British Journal of Clinical Psychology, 41*, 271–284.

Gray, N. S., Pickering, A. D., Hemsley, D. R., Dawling, S., & Gray, J. A. (1992). Abolition of latent inhibition by a single 5 mg dose of d-amphetamine in man. *Psychopharmacology, 107*, 425–30.

Green, M., & Williams, L. (1999). Schizotypy and creativity as effects of reduced cognitive inhibition. *Personality and Individual Differences, 27*, 263–276.

Guilford, J. (1967). *The nature of human intelligence.* New York: McGraw-Hill.

Holt, N. (2012). The muse in the machine: creativity, anomalous experiences and mental health. In C. Simmonds-Moore (Ed.), *Exceptional experience and health* (pp. 131–170). Jefferson, NC: McFarland.

Holt, N., Simmonds-Moore, C., & Moore, S. (2008). Benign schizotypy: investigating differences between clusters of schizotype on paranormal belief, creativity, intelligence and mental health. In S. Sherwood (Ed.), *Proceedings of presented papers* (pp. 82–96). New York: Parapsychological Association.

Howanitz, E., Cicalese, C., & Harvey, P. (2000). Verbal fluency and psychiatric symptoms in geriatric schizophrenia. *Schizophrenia Research, 42*, 167–169.

Howard-Jones, A., Blakemore, S., Samuel, E., Summers, I., & Claxton, G. (2005). Semantic divergence and creative story generation: an fMRI investigation. *Cognitive Brain Research, 25*, 240–250.

Jamison, K. (1993). *Touched with fire.* New York: Free Press.

Jaracz, J., Patrzala, A., & Rybakowski, J. (2012). Creative thinking deficits in patients with schizophrenia: neurocognitive correlates. *Journal of Nervous and Mental Disease, 200*, 588–593.

Kaufman, A., Kornilov, S., Bristol, A., Tan, M., & Grigorenko, E. (2010). The neurobiological foundation of creative cognition. In *The Cambridge Handbook of Creativity* (pp. 216–229). Cambridge: Cambridge University Press.

Kéri, S. (2011). Solitary minds and social capital: latent inhibition, general intellectual functions and social network size predict creative achievements. *Psychology of Aesthetics, Creativity and the Arts, 5*, 215–221.

Kerns, J. (2005). Positive schizotypy and emotion processing. *Journal of Abnormal Psychology, 114*, 392–401.

Kinney, D., Richards, R., Lowing, P., LeBlanc, D., Zimbalist, M., & Harlan, P. (2001). Creativity in offspring of schizophrenic and control parents: an adoption study. *Creativity Research Journal, 13*, 17–25.

Kottler, J. (2006). *Divine madness: Ten stories of creative struggle*. San Francisco, CA: Jossey-Bass.

Kyaga, S., Landén, M., Boman, M., Hultman, C., Långström, N., & Lichtenstein, P. (2013). Mental illness, suicide and creativity: 40-year prospective total population study. *Journal of Psychiatric Research, 47*, 83–90.

Kwapil, T., Barrantes-Vidal, N., & Silvia, P. (2008). The dimensional structure of the Wisconsin Schizotypy Scales. *Schizophrenia Bulletin, 34*, 444–457.

Kwapil, T., Brown, L., Silvia, P., Myin-Germeys, I., & Barrantes-Vidal, N. (2012). The expression of positive and negative schizotypy in daily life: an experience sampling study. *Psychological Medicine, 42*, 2555–2566.

Ludwig, A. (1998). Method and madness in the arts and sciences. *Creativity Research Journal, 11*, 93–101.

O'Reilly, T., Dunbar, R., & Bentall, R. (2001). Schizotypy and creativity: an evolutionary connection? *Personality and Individual Differences, 31*, 1067–1078.

Martindale, C. (1999). Biological bases of creativity. In R. Sternberg (Ed.), *Handbook of Creativity* (pp. 137–152). Cambridge: Cambridge University Press.

Martindale, C., & Hasenfus, N. (1978). EEG differences as a function of creativity, creative process and effort to be original. *Biological Psychology, 6*, 157–167.

Mason, O., Claridge, G., & Jackson, M. (1995). New scales for measurement of schizotypy. *Personality and Individual Differences, 18*, 7–13.

Mednick, S. (1962). The associative basis of the creative process. *Psychological Review, 69*, 220–232.

Mednick, S., & Mednick, M. (1967). *Examiners manual for the remote associates test*. Boston: Houghton Mifflin.

Merton, T., & Fischer, I. (1999). Creativity, personality and word association responses: associative behaviour in forty supposedly creative persons. *Personality and Individual Differences, 27*, 933–942.

Mihov, K., Denzler, & M. Förster, J. (2010). Hemispheric specialization and creative thinking: a meta-analytic review of lateralization of creativity. *Brain and Cognition, 72*, 442–448.

Miller, E., & Chapman, L. (1983). Continued word association in hypothetically psychosis-prone college students. *Journal of Abnormal Psychology, 92*, 468–478.

Miller, G., & Tal, I. (2007). Schizotypy versus openness and intelligence as predictors of creativity. *Schizophrenia Research, 93*, 317–324.

Mohr, C., & Leonards, U. (2005). Does contextual information influence positive and negative schizotypy scores in healthy individuals: the answer is maybe. *Psychiatry Research, 136*, 135–141.

Mohr, C., Graves, R., Gianotti, L., Pizzagalli, D., & Brugger, P. (2001). Loose but normal: a semantic association study. *Journal of Psycholinguistic Research, 30*, 475–483.

Nelson, B., & Rawlings, D. (2008). Relating schizotypy and personality to the phenomenology of creativity. *Schizophrenia Bulletin, 36*, 388–399.

Nettle, D. (2006). Schizotypy and mental health amongst poets, visual artists, and mathematicians. *Journal of Research in Personality, 40*, 876–890.

Panells, T., & Claxton, A. (2008). Happiness, creative ideation, and locus of control. *Creativity Research Journal, 20*, 67–71.

Prentky, R. (2000–2001). Mental illness and roots of genius. *Creativity Research Journal, 13*, 95–104.

Preti, A., & Vellante, M. (2007). Creativity and psychopathology: higher rates of psychosis proneness and nonright-handedness among creative artists compared to same age and gender peers. *Journal of Nervous and Mental Disease, 195*, 837–845.

Rawlings, D., & Locarnini, A. (2008). Dimensional schizotypy, autism, and unusual word associations in artists and scientists. *Journal of Research in Personality, 42*, 465–471.

Rawlings, D., & Toogood, A. (1997). Using a 'taboo response' measure to examine the relationship between divergent thinking and psychoticism. *Personality and Individual Differences, 22*, 61–68.

Rawlings, D., Twomey, F., Burns, E., & Morris, S. (1998). Personality, creativity, and aesthetic preference: comparing psychoticism, sensation seeking, schizotypy, and openness to experience. *Empirical Studies of the Arts, 16*, 153–178.

Richards, R., Kinney, D., Lunde, I., Benet, M., Merzel, A. (1988). Creativity in manic-depressives, cyclothymes, their normal relatives, and control subjects. *Journal of Abnormal Psychology, 97*, 281–288.

Ross, S. R., Lutz, C. J., & Bailey, S. E. (2002). Positive and negative symptom schizotypy and the Five Factor Model: a domain and facet level analysis. *Journal of Personality Assessment, 79*, 53–72.

Rubinstein, G. (2008). Are schizophrenic patients necessarily creative? A comparative study between three groups of psychiatric inpatients. *Personality and Individual Differences, 45*, 806–810.

Schlesinger, J. (2009). Creative mythconceptions: a closer look at the evidence for the 'mad genius' hypothesis. *Psychology of Aesthetics, Creativity, and the Arts, 3*, 62–72.

Schuldberg, D. (1990). Schizotypal and hypomanic traits, creativity, and psychological health. *Creativity Research Journal, 3*, 218–230.

Schuldberg, D. (2000–2001). Six subclinical spectrum traits in normal creativity. *Creativity Research Journal, 13*, 5–16.

Shrira, A., & Tsakanikos, E. (2009). Latent inhibition as a function of positive and negative schizotypal symptoms: evidence for a bi-directional model. *Personality and Individual Differences, 47*, 434–438.

Silvia, P., & Kaufman, J. (2010). Creativity and mental illness. In J. Kaufman, & R. Sternberg (Eds.), *Cambridge Handbook of Creativity* (pp. 381–394). Cambridge: Cambridge University Press.

Smith, D. (2007). *Muses, madmen and prophets: Hearing voices and the borders of sanity.* New York: Penguin.

Smith, G., & van der Meer, G. (1994). Generative sources of creative functioning. In M. Shaw, & M. Runco (Eds.), *Creativity and affect* (pp. 147–167). Norwood, NJ: Ablex Publishing Corporation.

Weisberg, R. (2006). *Creativity: Understanding innovation in problem solving, science, invention.* New York: Wiley.

Weinstein, S., & Graves, R. (2001). Are creativity and schizotypy products of a right hemisphere bias? *Brain and Cognition, 49*, 138–151.

Wuthrich, V., & Bates, T. (2001). Schizotypy and latent inhibition: non-linear linkage between psychometric and cognitive markers. *Personality and Individual Differences, 30*, 783–798.

Part IV
Future directions

13 Old thoughts: new ideas: future directions

Gordon Claridge

The previous chapters of this book have assembled considerable evidence for how, as a dimensional construct, schizotypy can inform our understanding of schizophrenia. The exact nature of that dimensionality was not addressed in detail by any of the contributors: that was not their brief. But when, as in several cases, authors did have cause to raise the issue, it was satisfying to see that they invariably phrased the prevailing opinions in the debate in a form similar to that stated in my 1997 book on schizotypy, and referred to in this book's Introduction. Two different perspectives on dimensionality were mentioned. One, named 'quasi-dimensional', refers to schizotypal features (clinical or subclinical) as literally forming part of the schizophrenia spectrum, manifest as mild disease. The other view, called 'fully dimensional', sees schizotypy as a set of adaptive healthy personality traits that can (but need not) transform into disease at their extreme. That idea seems to have survived the ravenous appetite of some wolfish critics: if only among the present editors' selection of (eminent) researchers in the field.

When I originally proposed the fully dimensional model, I also raised another question about schizotypy, asking whether the term was too narrowly focused on schizophrenia and whether a broader term, taking in all forms of psychosis, might be better. That issue has been less well publicised and, when it has been discussed, has generally been misinterpreted or received a lukewarm response. It therefore seemed appropriate in the final chapter of this book to revisit the question and offer the suggestion again as a thought for future theorising and research. Doing so will clear up some misunderstandings that have bedevilled the topic, and also help to elucidate some further aspects of dimensionality, as it relates to psychological disorder.

Given the focus of this book, and since Meehl was the first psychologist to use the term 'schizotypy', it is appropriate to start by examining where his (quasi-dimensional) theory lies in the historical landscape of attempts to dimensionalise serious mental illness (see Figure 13.1). As shown in the figure, two main themes can be recognised. On the right is what can broadly be designated a *medical* tradition of thought, represented here by Eugen Bleuler whose redefinition of Kraepelin's *dementia praecox* as schizophrenia

218 *Gordon Claridge*

marked the beginning of an era of systematic clinical description. At the time, under the influence of Kraepelin, a firmly stated categorical classification of mental illness was in place. Even so, some sense of 'dimensionality' was evident in the thinking of both men. Bleuler (1911/1950) – and even Kraepelin (1913/1919) himself – noted that some individuals could show schizophrenic-like characteristics that did not amount to the symptoms of the full-blown illness (see Chapter 1 for further discussion). This was often true of the relatives of clinically diagnosed schizophrenics. Bleuler used the term 'schizoid' to describe such people. The eventual emergence of the notion of a 'schizophrenia spectrum' was an obvious development and Meehl's adoption of schizotypy offered a scientific approach to measurement and definition, based on statistical analysis. His main innovation was the development of taxonometric methods that claim to identify individuals within a population who are schizotypes – as distinct from non-schizotypes. Logically, this opens up a methodology for comparing people who fall within and outwith the schizotypy taxon for evidence – biological, behavioural, cognitive – of the features responsible for schizophrenia.

Chronologically in parallel with this medical movement, there was another research tradition that also sought to dimensionalise psychopathology, but more radically (see left side of Figure 13.1). Here the starting point was not mental illness, but individual differences in personality. According to that view, psychological disorders could be seen as extreme expressions of personality and temperamental dimensions underlying

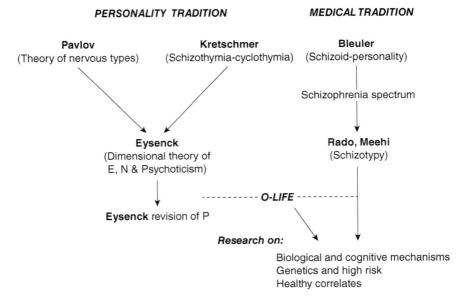

Figure 13.1 Two historical traditions in proposals to dimensionalise psychosis.

health. As an ideology it was also more broadly based – not narrowly focused on schizophrenia. Here the significant historical figure was Ernst Kretschmer (1925) who was a near contemporary of Bleuler. As a psychiatrist himself, he formed a bridge between the medical and personality traditions depicted in Figure 13.1. Indeed, his work can be seen as more a contribution to the field of personality psychology than to psychiatry. Especially relevant was his proposal for connecting types of psychosis to normal temperaments through a dimension of 'schizothymia–cyclothymia'. The endpoints of this dimension were defined by, respectively, schizophrenia and manic depression ('bipolar disorder' as it is now called), but its continuous nature allowed for corresponding differences in normal temperament, as well as, towards the two extremes, clinically 'borderline' variants of schizoid and cycloid.

Kretschmer's writings greatly influenced Hans Eysenck who, in the modern period, was the person who did most to pioneer the idea of psychological disorders as extensions of normal personality. Eysenck is best known for his attempt to explain milder, neurotic, disorders – considered to reflect different combinations of his two major personality dimensions of neuroticism (N) and introversion-extraversion (I-E) (Eysenck, 1957). However, from the very beginning of his career, Eysenck (1952b) had postulated a third dimension of 'psychoticism', or (P). At that stage P was considered to be comparable to N, as a descriptor of general traits that all forms of psychosis have in common. Types of psychosis – schizophrenia and manic depression – could be accounted for by reference to variations along the I-E dimension; in a manner *exactly* comparable to the explanation of neurosis as combinations of N and I-E. Eysenck arrived at this theory by rejigging, through factor analysis, Kretschmer's schizothymia–cyclothymia dimension (1952a). It is worth noting that in proposing this general psychoticism construct Eysenck was not stating anything new: he was merely adopting the unitary (or *Einheitpsychose*) construction of psychosis, which, until Kraepelin came along, was a commonly held view of madness during the nineteenth century (Berrios, 1995).

Despite the very different conclusions to be drawn from their work, as contemporaries, Eysenck and Meehl had curiously similar research aims and methodologies, at least up to a point. Both used statistical techniques to establish a subject matter of interest within psychopathology; and then they applied laboratory techniques to examine the biological and behavioural origins of the variations they had identified. Here the parallel ends, however. On the statistical front, Eysenck sought to establish fundamental, orthogonal and fully continuous dimensions of personality that could define all forms of serious mental illness; Meehl to develop measurement techniques that could identify qualitatively distinct types of people whose nature was uniquely 'schizophrenic'. Matching this distinction, their explanations of biological causation were also entirely different in form. Consistent with the medical model of schizophrenia, Meehl proposed an explanation of schizotypy that drew upon a similar *broken brain* view of its neurobiology and genetics (see Chapters 3 and 5 for further reference). In contrast, Eysenck – finding inspiration in Pavlov's theory of 'nervous types' (see Figure 13.1) – believed that the biology of both normal and abnormal personality lay in *naturally occurring variations* in brain function: personalities simply have different kinds of brain.

There is a final point to be noted in Figure 13.1. The diagram portrays the later convergence of the medical and personality traditions as an eventual confluence of research effort on the dimensionality of psychosis. This is misleading in one respect. The *unitary psychosis/psychoticism* theme on the left side of the diagram – and, in particular, concern with the dimensionality of bipolar disorder – has largely disappeared from view: attention has shifted almost entirely to the schizotypy–schizophrenia connection. Insofar as this gap in research effort was accounted for by Eysenck's influence, it can easily be explained. On returning after several decades to his third major dimension, Eysenck set out to specify psychoticism (P) more precisely (Eysenck & Eysenck, 1976). He did so in the most unexpected way, defining it in terms of antisocial traits, most commonly found in psychopaths –far removed from the cognitive and affective characteristics that most writers, irrespective of their stance on other issues, would consider central to psychosis, especially the schizophrenias. Psychoticism and the P-scale, Eysenck's questionnaire measure of his supposedly broader dimension, actually became narrower in scope and more idiosyncratic in content. Over several versions its items gradually moved away from those typically found in the schizotypy questionnaires of the time and became more slanted towards impulsivity, aggressiveness and non-conformist behaviour. This formulation of psychoticism was heavily criticised (Claridge, 1981, 1983) but it remained Eysenck's theoretical position to the end of his life. So, in his latest statement (Eysenck, 1992), he presented a model of psychosis consisting of a continuum ranging from criminality, through affective disorder, to schizophrenia. True, a unitary dimensional theory linking schizophrenia and bipolar disorder, but deeply flawed as a comprehensive account of psychotic traits and states. And far removed from 'Version 1' of Eysenck's theory in which psychoticism supposedly collected together elements that the two major psychoses had in common, while preserving the differences between them.

This ill-considered revision of his theory left Eysenck and his P-scale isolated from mainstream research in the area. As the preceding chapters in this book demonstrate, scientific enquiry was consolidated around clinical schizophrenia as the reference point, with schizotypy questionnaires as measures of its dimensional features. There were increasingly few studies using the P-scale that could seriously expect to reveal insight into schizophrenia, or even psychosis in a broader sense.[1] The side-lining of the P-scale by serious schizotypy researchers had its impact on questionnaire development and interpretation. Illustrative here is the research leading up to and including the development of the Oxford-Liverpool Inventory of Feelings and Experiences (*O-LIFE*); (Claridge et al., 1996; Mason, Claridge, & Williams, 1997), an inventory that was intended to bridge the gap between the personality and medical traditions. Work on the questionnaire was unique in including the most comprehensive set of scales hitherto subjected to statistical analysis, in order to try and establish, definitively, the factorial structure of psychotic traits. The items and scales that were included covered not just regular schizotypy measures but others to do with hypomania and borderline personality (and Eysenck's P-scale). As well-recorded in previous chapters and elsewhere, these analyses identified the three main factors now named in the O-LIFE as Unusual Experiences (UnEx), Cognitive Disorganisation (CogDis), and Introvertive Anhedonia (IntAn) – scales generally accepted as comprehensively defining schizotypy.

However, the O-LIFE data set also contained a fourth factor – eventually labelled Impulsive Non-conformity (ImpNon). This additional factor is mostly ignored by workers using the O-LIFE – presumably being regarded by them as a statistical aberration, a best ignored distraction from retaining the neat schizotypy structure traditionally supplied by the other three factors. Yet it has become increasingly obvious that the presence of ImpNon in the so-called 'schizotypy' domain seriously questions whether the schizotypy–schizophrenia spectrum can be studied in isolation from other psychotic features. In other words, should we not be considering a more inclusive formulation of psychosis and psychotic traits, closer to Kretschmer's? And, dare I say it, closer to Eysenck's (Version 1) theory?

One reason for stating this comes from the pattern of factor loadings found in the analysis of scales used in the construction of the O-LIFE (Claridge et al., 1996). The ImpNon factor was, not unexpectedly, partly defined by Eysenck's P-scale. But, more interestingly, other scales also had high loadings, notably a hypomania scale included in the study. Furthermore, this same fourth factor contributed strongly to the main positive symptoms factor (Perceptual Aberration Scale) that is used, as we know, to describe a major feature of schizotypy. In other words, ImpNon was *not* some isolated artefact of the analysis: instead, having connection to manic-depressive traits, it intermingled with and contributed in a real sense to the domain we have been accustomed to label 'schizotypy'. Of further interest here is the behaviour in the factor solution of another scale: the Borderline Personality Scale (STB) (Claridge & Broks, 1984). Like hypomania, the STB also cross-correlated with the other factors, particularly CogDis, again suggesting shared variance with 'schizotypy'. This result chimes with earlier reports that the STB correlates highly with the Schizotypal Personality Scale (STA), the better known schizotypy scale, developed at the same time by Claridge and Broks. In their paper they refer to STA/STB correlations as high as 0.59 (Rawlings, 1983) and +0.71 (Claridge, Robinson, & Birchall,

1983), putting beyond reasonable doubt the extendability of schizotypy beyond its usually accepted boundaries.

Why are these results for borderline personality of interest here? Two reasons. One is that some authors have argued that some types of borderline personality – although not necessarily all (it is a notoriously difficult concept to define) – might represent attenuated forms of bipolar disorder, forming part of its spectrum (Akiskal, 1996; Perugi, Fornaro, & Akiskal, 2011). Second (more a mystery than a reason), in its early history the attempt to characterise psychiatric states that fell on the edges of full-blown psychosis was an inchoate mixture of features found in schizophrenia, manic depression and everything in between – and generating many different labels that captured a mixture of schizophrenic, affective, neurotic and personality disorder characteristics (see Claridge [1995] for a discussion of this topic). Subsequent attempts to bring order to the field revealed the existence of two clusters: 'schizotypal borderline' and 'borderline borderline' (Spitzer, Endicott, J, & Gibbon, 1979). These were separate yet overlapping, exactly like the pattern of correlations for STA and STB described earlier. Oddly – and this is where the mystery lies – when using those data to set up new diagnostic guidelines for personality disorders in *DSM-III*, the committee of the American Psychiatric Association assigned one form (schizotypal) to the 'Mad' (A) cluster and the other (borderline) to the 'Bad' (B) cluster. What this effectively did was to take out of the arena for debate – or, put more crudely, deliberately cause to be ignored – the question of whether the two forms of borderline might share common descriptive and aetiological features across psychosis. In short, despite the evidence, 'borderline borderline' was no longer seen to be part of a psychosis spectrum.

Returning to ImpNon, this has recently been shown to correlate significantly with independently assessed bipolar symptoms (Alminhana et al., submitted; Nettle, 2006); its place as a measure of psychotic traits in the affective sphere is therefore well established. However, Nettle goes further than that in addressing the overall structure of psychotic traits. Writing in the context of creativity research, he proposes 'thymotypy' and schizotypy as forming two related subdimensions, of equivalent status, that relate to creativity (Nettle, 2001). It is an interesting suggestion, given that creativity is an expression of psychotic traits where the influence of both schizophrenic and bipolar features – often overlapping or intermingling – is particularly evident (see Chapter 12, this volume). Two recent examples illustrate the point. Both used the O-LIFE to assess psychotic traits, in one case in comedians (Ando, Claridge, & Clark, 2014) and in the other case in poets (Mason, Mort, & Woo, 2015). In the former study, the comedians were found to have very high scores on all the O-LIFE scales. But most notable was their performance across the scales: very high on both IntAn and ImpNon, a combination that was interpreted to signify in comedians a predominantly manic-depressive (bipolar) personality profile. The Mason et al.

study extended these results by showing with Hirschfeld's (2000) Mood Disorder Questionnaire that the poets had a very high incidence of bipolar symptoms. On the O-LIFE, although unlike the comedians not differing from controls on IntAn, the poets did have significantly high scores on the other three scales.

This evidence from questionnaire data exists against a background of increasing support for a unitary view of clinical psychosis, an old idea that was strongly resisted for much of the twentieth century but which has seen a revival in recent years (Marneros & Akiskal, 2007). That, together with a general loosening of categorical boundaries supposedly defining distinct psychiatric diseases without overlap, and a greater acceptance in psychiatry of dimensional models, further strengthens the case for subsuming the schizophrenia and bipolar spectra under the same heading. Whether 'psychoticism' is a suitable overarching label for that spectrum is a moot point. Eysenck's idiosyncratic use of the term still lingers and continues to cause confusion whenever the matter is discussed by psychologists. However, this will hopefully fade with time and 'psychoticism' does seem the most obvious term to use. It is also significant that 'psychoticism has found its way into *DSM-5* as one of five dimensions in the so-called PID-5 for assessing personality disorder traits (American Psychiatric Association, 2013). There it appears to describe a dimension of lucidity versus poor reality testing. This may not precisely coincide with the usage intended here, but it does at least draw away from Eysenck's later definition of P.

Another quandary is how best to designate and measure the subdimension that sits alongside schizotypy in the broader spectrum of psychoticism (or whatever we might decide to call it). As we have seen, there are several possibilities. One is ImpNon from our own O-LIFE, but that seems to be too psychometrically grounded to be suitable. The same is true, to a lesser extent, of borderline personality and anyway, conceptually, it is a very amorphous construct; features that overlap with psychosis would need specifying more precisely. Historically, 'cyclothymia' is the obvious choice but nowadays that seems to have morphed into a description of a clinical subsyndrome of bipolar illness, rather than a personality trait or dimension as it was traditionally used. Cyclothymia's only appearance in the broadly personality literature seems to be as a subscale in the TEMPS-A temperament scale described by Akiskal and his colleagues (Akiskal et al., 2005): opportunities otherwise for measuring affective traits it might tap are through hypomania or mood rating scales, such as the Mood Disorder Questionnaire (Hirschfeld, 2000) used by Mason in his study of poets described earlier. One research task for the future, therefore, is to consolidate measurement, terminology and theory around a concept that sits alongside schizotypy, symmetrically and of equal status as a second subdimension of the psychosis spectrum. My own best guess for a likely candidate is Nettle's use of 'thymotypy', referred to earlier.

A final word on the quasi- versus fully dimensional issue. This has continued to be a bone of contention, often eliciting strong statements, especially from critics in the US who through their loyalty to Meehl are fierce adherents to the 'quasi' model. An illustration was a recent exchange in the journal *Personality and Individual Differences*. The trigger was a paper published by Rawlings, Williams, Haslam, & Claridge (2008a) throwing doubt on the idea of schizotypy as a universally observed distinct taxon. A reply from members of the Meehl school was brutally dismissive (Beauchaine, Lenzenweger, & Waller, 2008). Yet – and here I naturally write from a partisan position as originator of the fully dimensional approach – much of the argumentation in that exchange was based on two misunderstandings by Beauchaine and his colleagues (see Rawlings, Williams, Haslam, & Claridge, 2008b). The first arose through their conflation of the pure dimensional issue with that pertaining to the influence of Eysenck's theorising about (P) – a confusion I hope I have cleared up here for good. The second was their failure to understand that the quasi- and fully dimensional models are not mutually exclusive. If the two models are judged as rivals, it is only true insofar as the fully dimensional model is the more comprehensive: it includes the features focused upon by quasi-dimensionalists, but adds to them. Thus, full dimensionality refers to *healthy traits* when describing variations in the personality domain and shifts to specifying *unhealthy symptoms* at the illness end of the spectrum. What this means statistically is whether a dimensional or a taxonomic picture is revealed in data will depend on the kind of individuals sampled: fully dimensional and trait-like in the mid-range of the population; dichotomous and quasi-dimensional in people further up the spectrum who are pre-psychotic, or in the zone of risk. Traits and symptoms certainly have different properties: the former are more continuous, follow normal distributions and are ego-syntonic; the latter are ego-dystonic and more often dichotomous and skewed in their distribution. But this does not mean that they cannot lie on a continuum with one another – or a pseudo-continuum if one wants to be pedantic about it. (See a recent position paper by Mason [2014] for a detailed analysis of the implications of these points for measurement and theory in schizotypy research.) There are many instances when this is true, where personality and illness connect (Claridge and Davis, 2003): trait anxiety and anxiety disorder are a case in point. There is good evidence that schizotypy and schizophrenia (or psychoticism and psychosis) merely form another example.[2]

The central question therefore is *not* whether trait-like features and symptom-like features can exist in adjacent related domains of variation, one describing healthy and the other a failure in function (and one defining risk for the other). The more interesting question is how trait becomes symptom: under what conditions healthy adaptation becomes illness. It is a universal question, not confined to psychopathology. In the Introduction to this book, briefly attempting to clarify the quasi- and fully dimensional distinction, we mentioned the analogous situation of blood pressure and essential hypertension: how the former can exist as a healthy trait, yet also constitute a risk for the pathologically high blood pressure that can issue in a serious failure of function, such as heart failure or stroke. Anticipating much of what in a different context I have tried to convey here – and in a passage that I have had occasion to quote on a number of occasions – W.B. Cannon, the famous psychophysiologist, once wrote about the phenomenon as follows:

> There are many systems in the body which, because of misuse or misfortune, may have their services to the organism as a whole so altered as to be actually harmful. Thus vicious circles of causation become established which may lead to death...The development of pathological functions in a system is quite consistent with its usual performance of normal functions. (Cannon, 1953).

Notes

1 An exception, I could (immodestly!) claim, is a linked group of early experiments by me and my colleagues showing a common theme in the psychophysiology of schizophrenics, high P subjects, and LSD drug-induced effects (Claridge, 1972; Claridge & Chappa, 1973; Claridge & Clark, 1982). A slightly unfortunate combination of strategies, given the eventual marginalisation of P and criminalisation of LSD, and the difficulty in finding first-episode drug-free psychotic patients.
2 Raine (2006) is one writer who disagrees, however. In an attempt, seemingly, to avoid incorporating healthy personality traits into his construction of schizotypy, he has proposed the notion of 'pseudoschizotypy'. He claims that this mimics true schizotypy but has no connection to the aetiology of schizophrenia. The idea seems a redundant addition to theory: one wonders whatever happened to Occam's razor (the principle of parsimony)!

References

Akiskal, H. S. (1996). The prevalent clinical spectrum of bipolar disorders: beyond DSM-IV. *Journal of Clinical Psychopharmacology*, 16, Supplement 1, 4–14.

Akiskal, H. S., Mendlowicz, M. V., Jean-Louis, G., Rapaport, M. H., Kelsoe, J. R., Gillin, J., & Smith, T. L. (2005). TEMPS-A: validation of a short version of a self-rated instrument designed to measure variations in temperament. *Journal of Affective Disorders*, 85, 45–52.

Alminhana, L. O., Farias, M., Moreira-Almeida, A., Menezes Jr. A., Zanini, A., Claridge, G., Cloninger, R.C. (submitted). Psychobiological model of temperament and character: criterion to mental health and schizotypy in individuals with anomalous experiences.

American Psychiatric Association. (1987). *Diagnostic and statistical manual of mental disorders (DSM-IIIR)* (3rd ed., rev.). Washington, DC: Author.

American Psychiatric Association. (2013). *Diagnostic and statistical manual of mental disorders (DSM-V)* (5th ed.). Arlington, VA: Author.

Ando, V., Claridge., G., & Clark, K. (2014). Psychotic traits in comedians. *British Journal of Psychiatry, 204*, 341–345.

Beauchaine, T. P., Lenzenweger, N. F., & Waller, N. G. (2008). Schizotypy, taxometrics, and disconfirming theories in soft science. Comment on Rawlings, Williams, Haslam, and Claridge. *Personality and Individual Differences, 44*, 1652–1662.

Berrios, G. E. (1995). Conceptual problems in diagnosing schizophrenic disorders. In J. A. Den Boer, H. G. M. Westenberg, & H. M. van Praag (Eds.), *Advances in the neurobiology of schizophrenia* (pp. 7–25). Chichester: John Wiley.

Bleuler, E. P. (1950). *Dementia praecox or the group of schizophrenias* (J. Zinkin, Trans.). New York: International Universities Press. (Original work published in 1911.)

Cannon, W. B. (1953). *Bodily changes in pain, hunger, fear, and rage*. Boston: Charles C. Branford.

Claridge, G. (1972). The schizophrenias as nervous types. *British Journal of Psychiatry, 121*, 1–17.

Claridge, G. (1981). Psychoticism. In R. Lynn (Ed.), *Dimensions of personality. Papers in honour of H. J. Eysenck* (pp. 364–387). Oxford: Pergamon Press.

Claridge, G. (1983). The Eysenck Psychoticism Scale. In J. N. Butcher, & C. D. Spielberger (Eds.), *Advances in personality assessment* (Vol. 2). Hillsdale, NJ: Lawrence Erlbaum Associates.

Claridge, G. (1995). *Origins of mental illness*. Cambridge, MA: Malor Books.

Claridge, G. (Ed.). (1997). *Schizotypy: Implications for illness and health*. Oxford University Press.

Claridge, G., & Broks, P. (1984). Schizotypy and hemisphere function – I. Theoretical considerations and the measurement of schizotypy. *Personality and Individual Differences, 5*, 633–648.

Claridge, G., & Chappa, H. J. (1973). Psychoticism: a study of its biological basis in normal subjects. *British Journal of Social and Clinical Psychology, 12*, 175–187.

Claridge, G., & Clark, K. (1982). Covariation between two-flash threshold and skin conductance level in first-breakdown schizophrenics: relationships in drug-free patients and effects of treatment. *Psychiatry Research, 6*, 371–380.

Claridge, G., & Davis, C. (2003). *Personality and psychological disorders*. London: Arnold.

Claridge, G., Robinson, D. L., & Birchall, P. M. A. (1983). Characteristics of schizophrenics' and neurotics' relatives. *Personality and Individual Differences, 4*, 651–664.

Claridge, G., McCreery, C., Mason, O., Bentall, R., Boyle, G., Slade, P., & Popplewell, D. (1996). The factor structure of 'schizotypal' traits: a large replication study. *British Journal of Clinical Psychology, 35*, 103–115.

Eysenck, H. J. (1952a). Schizothymia-cyclothymia as a dimension of personality. II. Experimental. *Journal of Personality, 20*, 345–384.

Eysenck, H .J. (1952b). *The scientific study of personality*. London: Routledge and Kegan Paul.

Eysenck, H. J. (1957). *Dynamics of anxiety and hysteria*. London: Routledge and Kegan Paul.

Eysenck, H. J. (1992). The definition and measurement of psychoticism. *Personality and Individual Differences, 13*, 757–785.

Eysenck, H. J., & Eysenck, S. B. G. (1976). *Psychoticism as a dimension of personality*. London: Hodder & Stoughton.

Hirschfeld, R. M. A. (2000). Development and validation of a screening instrument for bipolar spectrum disorder: The Mood Disorder Questionnaire. *American Journal of Psychiatry, 157*, 1873–1875.

Kraepelin, E. (1919). *Dementia praecox and paraphrenia.* Edinburgh: Livingstone. (Original work published in 1913.)

Kretschmer, E. (1925). *Physique and character* (W. J. H. Sprott, Trans.). London: Kegan, Trench, & Trubner.

Marneros, A., & Akiskal, H. S. (Eds.). (2007). *The overlap of affective and schizophrenic spectra.* Cambridge University Press.

Mason, O., Claridge, G., & Williams, L. (1997). Questionnaire measurement. In G. Claridge (Ed.), *Schizotypy: Implications for illness and health.* Oxford University Press.

Mason, O. J. (2014). The duality of schizotypy: is it both dimensional and categorical? *Frontiers in Psychiatry, 5,* 1–4.

Mason, O. J., Mort, H., & Woo, J. (2015). Research letter: investigating psychotic traits in poets. *Psychological Medicine, 45,* 667–669.

Nettle, D. (2001). *Strong imagination.* New York: Oxford University Press.

Nettle, D. (2006). Schizotypy and mental health amongst poets, visual artists, and mathematicians. *Journal of Research in Personality, 40,* 876–890.

Perugi, G., Fornaro, I., & Akiskal, H. S. (2011) Are atypical depression, borderline personality disorder and bipolar II overlapping manifestations of a common cyclothymic diathesis? *World Psychiatry, 10,* 45–51.

Raine, A. (2006). Schizotypal personality: neurodevelopmental and psychosocial trajectories. *Annual Review of Clinical Psychology, 2,* 291–326.

Rawlings, D. (1983). An enquiry into the nature of psychoticism as a dimension of personality. DPhil thesis. University of Oxford.

Rawlings, D., Williams, B., Haslam N., & Claridge, G. (2008a). Taxometric analysis supports a dimensional latent structure for schizotypy. *Personality and Individual Differences, 44,* 1640–1651.

Rawlings, D., Williams, B., Haslam N., & Claridge, G. (2008b). Is schizotypy taxonic? Response to Beauchaine, Lenzenweger, and Waller. *Personality and Individual Differences, 44,* 1663–1672.

Spitzer, R. L., Endicott, J., & Gibbon, M. (1979). Crossing the border into borderline personality and borderline schizophrenia: the development of criteria. *Archives of General Psychiatry, 36,* 17–34.

Index

ABC-analysis model of delusions 171
aberrant salience 14, 26; childhood trauma 108; delusional beliefs 171; dopamine 35; genetics 56, 58; *see also* salience
Aberrant Salience Inventory (ASI) 14, 26
Abramson, L. Y. 103
abuse 2, 99, 100, 101–103, 104, 106–107, 108, 118, 122
Acar, S. 200
action potentials 34
addiction 34; *see also* substance use
Addington, J. 183
ADHD *see* attention deficit hyperactivity disorder
adolescents: borderline personality disorder 91; developmental perspective 85, 86, 88, 92–93, 94; genetics 52; schizotypal personality disorder 187; substance use 134, 137, 140–141
affect 142–143, 185, 207; *see also* emotions
affective dysregulation 12, 20, 121
affective pathway model 108
Afifi, T. O. 101
aggressiveness 15, 122, 220
Aghevli, M. 185
Ajdacic-Gross, V. 101, 102
Akiskal, H. S. 223
alcohol 132, 133, 136–137, 141, 142–143
Aleman, A. 149
alexithymia 150, 156
alleles 50–51, 53–54, 55, 126

Alloy, L. B. 103
Alvarez-Jimenez, M. 87
Alzheimer's disease 183
ambiguous auditory environments 148–153
ambivalence 17, 18, 26, 85
ambulatory schizophrenia 7
American Psychiatric Association (APA) 165–166, 222
amphetamine 33, 38, 42, 137
Anglin, D. M. 102
Angst, J. 101
anhedonia 11, 12, 13, 84, 188; depression 183; developmental perspective 89; family environment 118; genetic effects 52; inducing psychotic-like experiences 154; introvertive 11, 19, 221; Physical Anhedonia Scale 10, 16, 20, 72; Revised Social Anhedonia Scale 10, 17, 20, 74, 75, 89; schizotaxia 85; trait negative affectivity 185
animals 57, 116, 121
anomalous perceptions 93, 94, 151, 156–157, 170–171, 172, 188–189; *see also* unusual experiences
antisocial behaviour 11, 15, 220
antisocial personality disorder 38
anxiety 183, 184, 224; childhood trauma 99, 108, 124; delusional beliefs 173; help seeking 140; insecure attachment 123; lack of 38; negative beliefs 108; Referential Thinking Scale 18; substance use 109, 134, 136, 142; *see also* social anxiety

APA *see* American Psychiatric Association
Appiah-Kusi, E. 122
appraisals 171–172, 175, 191
Aristotle 197
ARMS *see* at-risk mental state
Arntz, A. 101
arts 202, 203, 204, 207, 208
ASD *see* autistic-spectrum disorders
Ashcroft, K. 122
Ashford, C. D. 122
ASI *see* Aberrant Salience Inventory
assessment: childhood trauma 106–107; creativity 198–199; delusions 174; experience sampling methodology 120, 126–127; *see also* psychometric assessment
Atchley, R. A. 75
at-risk mental state (ARMS) 9, 180–181, 187, 190, 191
at-risk people 9, 83, 84, 183, 190
attachment 10, 108, 119; delusional beliefs 173; insecure 122, 123; mentalisation 124
attention 11, 17, 73–76; asymmetries 63; emotional processes 173; selective attention 39; THC effect on 139
attention deficit hyperactivity disorder (ADHD) 34
attributional style 172
auditory hallucinations 148–153
autistic-spectrum disorders (ASD) 3, 186–187
autosomes 50
Avramopoulos, D. A. 15

Baker, L. A. 52
Barkus, Emma 2, 124, 132–146
Barneveld, P. S. 187
Barrantes-Vidal, Neus 2, 10, 20, 92, 116–131
Barron, F. 209
Battaglia, M. 51–52
Battle, C. L. 102
Bayer, U. 70–73
Beauchaine, T. P. 224
beliefs: confirmation bias 173; delusional 93, 165–179; flexibility 169, 174; metacognitive 189–190; negative 108, 185; negative cognitive schemas 122–123; obsessive-compulsive disorder 184; paranormal 24, 71, 74–75, 104, 150, 155–156, 157
Bell, V. 187–188
Benishay, D. 13, 20–21
Bennett, M. E. 18
Bentall, R. P. 119, 124, 152, 171
Berenbaum, H. 101, 102, 103
Berenz, E. C. 102
Bernstein, D. P. 101
bipolar disorder 183, 185–186, 199, 219, 222; childhood trauma 99; Eysenck 220; genome-wide association studies 55; poets 223; substance use 142
Birchwood, M. 171, 175
bizarreness 166, 167
Blakey, S. 203
Blanchard, J. J. 185
Bleuler, E. P. 7, 186, 217–218
Boden, M. T. 101, 102
borderline personality disorder (BPD) 38, 90–91, 221–222, 223
Borderline Personality Scale (STB) 19, 221–222
borderline schizophrenia 7
Borge, A. 72
Borroni, S. 86
BPD *see* borderline personality disorder
Bracha, H. S. 75
Bradley, C. 101
Brady, F. 150, 153, 154
brain: broken brain view 220; cannabis impact on the 139; cognitive functions 40, 43; creativity 206–207; dopamine 35; emotional processes 173; environmental adversity 119–121; genetics 52–53; hemispheric asymmetries 62–80, 206; naturally occurring variations 220; neurochemical transmission 33; out-of-body experiences 155; prepulse inhibition 39; turning behaviour 37
Brasfield, J. L. 187
Braun, J. G. 74
Bredemeier, K. 101, 102
Briskman, J. 198
Broks, P. 11, 19, 71, 221–222

Brown, J. 150, 155–156
Brown, L. A. 14
Brugger, P. 71, 74, 75
Bryson, F. M. 75
bullying 99, 100, 104–105, 106, 108, 118, 122, 124
Bunton-Stasyshyn, R. 151, 156–157
Byron, George Gordon 199

CAARMS *see* Comprehensive Assessment of At-Risk Mental States
Cain, Charlotte 2
cannabis 33, 108, 109, 134–135, 138, 139–140, 142, 143
Cannon, W. B. 225
CAPE *see* Community Assessment of Psychic Experiences
Caputo, G. B. 151, 157
Carlson, E. A. 91
Carpenter, L. L. 103
Carson, S. 205, 206
Castro, A. 70, 72
Cattell, J. P. 20
causality 118–119, 132, 133–134
CBTp *see* cognitive behavioural therapy for psychosis
Chadwick, P. 171
Chapman, J. P. 10, 16, 17, 20
Chapman, L. J. 10, 16, 17, 20, 201, 203
Checklist of Schizotypic Signs 19–20
Chen, H. 102
Chermahini, A. S. 208
childhood maltreatment 17, 99–100, 101–103, 105–106, 116, 124; *see also* abuse
childhood trauma 2, 99–115, 118, 119; dissociation 124–125; gene-environment interaction 126; insecure attachment 123; neurobiology 119–120; social cognition 124; social defeat hypothesis 121; substance use 141
children: auditory hallucinations 148; borderline personality disorder 91; developmental perspective 84, 85, 89, 93; family environment 117–118; insecure attachment 123; multiple complex development disorder 187; psychotic-like experiences 181

Chumakov, I. 53
Chun, Charlotte 2, 7–32, 120
Cicero, D. C. 14, 17
Claridge, Gordon 1–3, 8, 10–12, 19, 48, 62, 71, 74, 150, 153–155, 203, 217–227
clinical method 9
cocaine 138
co-dominant alleles 51
cognitive behavioural therapy (CBT) 190
cognitive behavioural therapy for psychosis (CBTp) 175
cognitive biases 169, 172–173
cognitive control 25
cognitive disorganisation 11, 19, 221; *see also* disorganisation
cognitive flexibility 68
cognitive functions 43, 62
cognitive schemas 122–123
cognitive slippage 17, 25, 58, 85
Cognitive Slippage Scale (CSS) 17, 25
Cohen, A. S. 14, 185
Cohen, P. R. 102
Colangelo, M. 103
Colbert, S. M. 169
Coleridge, Samuel Taylor 201
Collins, L. M. 185
Combined Schizotypal Traits Questionnaire (CSTQ) 19
comedians 222–223
common pathways model 52, 120
communication impairments 17
Community Assessment of Psychic Experiences (CAPE) 15, 25
comorbidity 182
Comprehensive Assessment of At-Risk Mental States (CAARMS) 180
Compton, M. T. 187
COMT 50, 56, 57, 126, 139–140
confirmation bias 169, 173
constricted affect 13, 14
conviction 166, 169, 173, 174
coping strategies 189, 190
corpus callosum 67, 68
CPS *see* Creative Personality Scale
Cre recombinase 57
Creative Personality Scale (CPS) 198
creativity 3, 8, 10, 15, 197–214; affect

and motivation 207–208; definition of 198; experience seeking 208; implications for health and wellbeing 209; mixed-handedness 68; neurocognitive models 205–207; overview of literature 200–205; psychometric assessment 19; psychopathology 199–200; 'right-hemisphere hypothesis' 66
Crow, T. J. 65, 69
Csikszentmihalyi, M. 208
CSS *see* Cognitive Slippage Scale
CSTQ *see* Combined Schizotypal Traits Questionnaire
Cunningham, S. M. 103
curiosity 12, 208
cyclothymia 203, 207, 218, 219, 223

Daneluzzo, E. 186
Daniel, Christina 3, 147–161
Das-Munshi, J. 121
Davis, K. L. 35, 37
Davis, O. S. 48
Day, S. 24
Debbané, Martin 2, 83–98
Delespaul, P. 174
delusions 3, 93, 165–179; anomalous experiences 170–171; appraisals 171–172; childhood trauma 105, 107; cognitive biases 172–173; on a continuum with normal beliefs 166–168, 175; dissociation 124; emotional processes 173; multidimensionality 168–170, 173, 175; persecutory 21; Peters Delusional Inventory 23, 24, 25, 167, 169; prevalence 147; psychiatric definitions of 165–166; psychological interventions 174–175; understanding 174
dementia praecox 7, 217–218
depersonalisation 24, 103, 104, 124, 125
depression 185; aggression 122; childhood trauma 99, 108, 124; delusional beliefs 173; psychometric assessment 15; Referential Thinking Scale 18; substance use 109, 134, 136, 142; symptoms 183
development disorder 187
developmental perspective 83–98

diagnosis 55, 86
Diagnostic and Statistical Manual of Mental Disorders (DSM-III) 13, 20, 52, 222
Diagnostic and Statistical Manual of Mental Disorders (DSM-IV) 117, 165–166
Diagnostic and Statistical Manual of Mental Disorders (DSM-V) 26, 165–166, 169, 173, 175, 223
dimensionality 217–218, 220, 223, 224; *see also* fully dimensional perspective; quasi-dimensional approach
disorganisation 84, 221; bipolar disorder 185, 186; childhood trauma 103, 104; creativity 204; developmental perspective 89–90, 94; dopamine 42; genetics 56; psychometric assessment 25
dissociation 17, 124–125; anxiety 173; childhood trauma 104, 109; 'flow' 208
distress 169, 170, 174, 184, 188
distrust 17, 108
divergent thinking (DT) 198, 200, 201–202, 203, 204, 207–208
DNA 49–50, 126
domestic violence 99, 107, 124
dominant alleles 51
Dominguez, M. D. 94
dopamine 14, 33–47, 57, 58; basic behavioural functions 36, 37–39; cannabis use 109, 139; childhood trauma 108, 120; cocaine 138; cognitive functions 36, 40–41, 43; delusional beliefs 171; divergent thinking 207–208; dopamine-salience hypothesis 168; dysregulation 119; genetics 52–53; methods to assess the role of 36; molecular imaging 41–42; salience 120–121; social defeat hypothesis 121; substance use 141–142; treatment effects in schizophrenic patients 34–36
DSM see Diagnostic and Statistical Manual of Mental Disorders
DT *see* divergent thinking
Dudley, R. E. J. 172
dysthymia 183

early identification 83
early intervention 88, 95, 190
eating disorders 100
eccentric behaviour 11, 13, 14, 26, 93; childhood trauma 101, 104; developmental perspective 93
Eckblad, M. 16, 17
Edelman, A. 71
Edinburgh High-Risk Study 181
Edmundson, M. 8
educational attainment 141
egocentricity 15
electromagnetic fields (EMFs) 151, 156–157, 158
Elliott, G. C. 103
Ellis, H. D. 187–188
EMFs *see* electromagnetic fields
emotional abuse 99, 101–103, 104, 122
emotionality 12, 14
emotions: asymmetries 63; creativity 207; delusional beliefs 168, 173; emotional processing 17; emotional regulation 142–143; negative beliefs 108
empathy 15
endophenotype approach 88, 91–93
environment 99, 116–131; gene-environment interaction 49, 51, 58, 118–119, 126, 127; macro-environmental risk factors 116–117; mediating mechanisms 118–119, 125; micro-environmental risk factors 117–118; neurobiology 119–121; psychological mechanisms 122–125; psychosis-proneness-persistence-impairment model 189; smoking 136; social defeat hypothesis 121–122
epigenetics 126
epilepsy 3, 187–188
EPQ *see* Eysenck Personality Questionnaire
equifinality 90
Ericson, M. 52
ESM *see* experience sampling methodology
Esterberg, M. L. 187
ethnic minorities 117, 121
Ettinger, Ulrich 2, 33–47
executive control 17, 25, 197, 204
exons 49, 50

experience sampling methodology (ESM) 120, 126–127, 185
experience seeking 208
extraversion 12, 219
eye tracking 10
Eysenck, H. J. 15, 85, 205, 218, 219–220, 221, 223, 224
Eysenck Personality Questionnaire (EPQ) 71, 72
Eysenck, S. B. G. 15

familial method 9
family environment 117–118
fantasy proneness 152, 158
Fathi, M. 71
Faust, M. 71
Feelgood, S. R. 148, 149
Fenigstein, A. 22
FEP *see* first-episode psychosis
Fernandez-Rivas, A. 149
Fernyhough, C. 124
Fink, A. 205–206
first-episode psychosis (FEP) 87
Fisher, Helen L. 2, 99–115, 122
flexibility of beliefs 169, 174
'flow' 208
fMRI *see* functional magnetic resonance imaging
Fonseca-Pedrero, E. 10
Fossati, A. 86
Fowler, D. 122
Freeman, D. 22, 93, 122, 171, 172, 175
Freeman, J. L. 23
French, C. C. 151, 156–157
fully dimensional perspective 8, 19, 48, 86, 87, 217, 218–220, 224–225
functional impairments 189
functional magnetic resonance imaging (fMRI) 39, 42, 92, 139; *see also* neuroimaging

Galdos, M. 149
Garety, P. A. 24, 169, 171
gender 73, 140
gene of interest (GOI) studies 53, 55, 58
genes 48, 50, 53–54, 55–56, 58; gene-environment interaction 49, 51, 58, 118–119, 126, 127; handedness 67; XY Gene Hypothesis 65, 69, 73

Index   233

genetic knockout (KO) method 57
genetics 43, 48–61, 99, 118–119, 126; cannabis use 139; handedness 67, 76; hemispheric asymmetries 65; heritability of schizophrenia 51–53; identifying genetic loci of the schizotypy continuum 53–57; relatives 181; substance use 141–142; terminology 49–51
genome-wide association studies (GWAS) 49, 53–56, 58, 67
Gibb, B. E. 103
GOI see gene of interest studies
Gooding, D. C. 74, 75
Gottesman, I. I. 51
Gould, T. D. 51
Goyal, M. 149, 153
Grant, C. 122
Grant, Philip 2, 48–61
Graves, R. E. 71, 72, 74
Gray, J. A. 41
Gray, N. S. 41
Green, C. E. 167
Grimshaw, Gina M. 2, 62–80
Gross, G. M. 20
Gross, M. 103
Gruzelier, J. H. 65
guilt 108
Guo, S. 65
Guralnik, O. 103
GWAS see genome-wide association studies

Haker, H. 101
Halligan, P. W. 187–188
hallucinations 11, 171; adolescents 92; animals 57; childhood trauma 105, 109, 119; creativity linked to 200–201; dissociation 124–125; inducing 148–153, 154, 157, 158; prevalence 147; sensory deprivation 153–154
handedness 62, 63, 66–68, 69, 76
Hans, S. L. 92
Hanssen, M. 15
Haque, U. 151, 156–157
Hasin, D. 136–137, 141
Haslam N. 224
'Haunt' project 151, 156–157
Hausmann, M. 70–73

Haworth, C. M. 48
Hay, D. A. 52
Hayashi, M. 153
hemispheric asymmetries 62–80, 206
Hengartner, M. P. 101, 102
Heriot-Maitland, Charlie 3, 165–179
heritability 51–53, 57, 67, 99, 142; see also genetics
Heron, J. 185
Herzig, D. A. 71, 74
heterozygotes 50–51
high-risk research 84, 181
Hirschfeld, R. M. A. 223
Hoch, P. H. 20
Hodgekins, Jo 3, 180–196
Holmes, E. A. 186
Holt, Nicola 3, 197–214
Hommel, B. 208
homozygotes 50–51, 67
Hori, T. 153
Howes, O. D. 35, 52
HPA see hypothalamic-pituitary-adrenal (HPA) axis
Humphrey, M. K. 75
hybrid vigour 51
hyperdopaminergia/hypodopaminergia 35, 37, 38, 40, 120–121
hypocrisia 85
hypomania 12, 202, 221
hypothalamic-pituitary-adrenal (HPA) axis 90, 107–108, 120

immigrants 117
impulsive non-conformity 11, 19, 202–203, 221, 222, 223
impulsivity 11, 15, 17, 38, 220
inattentiveness 17
incorrigibility 166, 169, 173
infrasound 151, 156, 158
inhibition 66, 184, 188; latent 39, 205–206, 207–208, 209; prepulse 39
insecure attachment 122, 123
intentionality, appraisal of 127
interactionalist position 2
interference with functioning 170
interhemispheric interaction 64, 65, 76
interpersonal relations 84, 85
interventions 190–191

introns 49, 50
introversion 219
introvertive anhedonia 11, 19, 221
intrusions 107, 184, 186
Irwin, H. J. 103

Jackson, M. 11, 19, 20
Jaspers, K. 165
Johns, L. C. 167
Johnson, J. G. 102
Joseph, S. 24
'jumping to conclusions' 172

Kanner, L. 186
Kapur, S. 35, 52, 168
Kaufman, J. C. 12
Kelleher, I. 105–106
Kelly, M. M. 103
Kéri, S. 205, 206
Kerns, J. G. 14, 17
ketamine 137–138, 139, 140
Knutelska, M. 103
Kraepelin, E. 7, 21, 217–218, 219
Kranz, Laura 2, 62–80
Kravetz, S. 71
Kretschmer, Ernst 218, 219, 221
Krummenacher, P. 71
Kwapil, Thomas 2, 7–32, 120

Laguerre, A. 185
Landis, T. 71
Langdon, R. 150, 155–156
language 17, 40, 63, 64, 65, 68, 69–73
latent inhibition (LI) 39, 205–206, 207–208, 209
lateralisation 62–63, 64, 65, 68, 70, 76
Launay-Slade Hallucination Scale (LSHS) 148, 149, 150, 152, 154
Leboyer, M. 185
left-handedness 66, 67
Lehmann, D. 71
Lentz, V. 101
Lenzenweger, M. F. 9, 18
Leonhard, D. 71
Leung, W. W. 185
Lewandowski, K. E. 183, 184
Lewis, E. 150, 153–154
lexical decision task 69–70

LI *see* latent inhibition
Li, M. 54
Liberman, R. 190
Lilenfeld, L. R. 18
Lin, A. 183
Lin, C. C. H. 52
Linder, M. 103
linkage studies 53
Linney, Y. M. 12, 52, 56
Liouta, E. 75
listening tasks 68, 70
Lloyd, D. M. 150, 153–154
Lobbestael, J. 101
LoC *see* locus of control
Locarnini, A. 202
locus of control (LoC) 124
Lovatt, A. 189
LSD 225n1
LSHS *see* Launay-Slade Hallucination Scale
Luh, K. E. 74, 75
Lynn, S. J. 152

Ma, X. 57
Maffei, C. 86
Magical Ideation Scale (MIS) 10, 16, 20, 71, 72, 74, 75
magical thinking 84; artists 208; childhood trauma 103; creativity 201; obsessive-compulsive disorder 184; psychometric assessment 11–18
Maguire, N. 122
Maher, B. A. 171
Martindale, C. 206, 207
Maryland Longitudinal Study of Schizotypy 188
Mason, Oliver J. 1–3, 10–12, 19, 62, 74, 99–115, 147–161, 222–223, 224
Matthews, R. A. 14
McCaffrey, P. 56
McCarthy, D. M. 14
McCoy, L. 137, 140
McCreery, C. 150, 153, 154–155
Meary, A. 185
mediating mechanisms 118–119, 125
medical-biological approach 86, 217–218, 219–220
medication 34, 36, 41, 87
Mednick, S. 201

Meehl, Paul E. 7–8, 19–20, 48, 50, 51, 85, 217–218, 219–220, 224
memory 17, 25; antipsychotic compounds 41; asymmetries 63; childhood trauma 107; creativity linked to 209; emotional processes 173; THC effect on 139
men 73, 140
mentalisation 92, 123, 124
mephedrone 138
Merckelbach, H. 149, 152
metacognitive beliefs 189–190
methodological issues: childhood trauma 105–107; inducing psychotic-like experiences 158
Miers, T. C. 17
Milanek, M. E. 101, 102
Miller, E. 201, 203
Miller, G. 208
Minnesota Multiphasic Personality Inventory (MMPI) 10, 21
minority status 117, 121
mirror gazing 151, 157, 158
MIS see Magical Ideation Scale
Mishlove, M. 17
mixed-handedness 66, 67–68, 76
MMPI see Minnesota Multiphasic Personality Inventory
Mohr, Christine 2, 33–47, 71, 74, 75
molecular heterosis 51
molecular imaging 36, 41–42
monoamines 34
mood 109, 185, 186, 189, 203, 204, 207–208
Mood Disorder Questionnaire 223
mood disorders 183, 185, 188
mood-congruent processing 173
moodiness 11
Morikawa, T. 153
Morrison, A. P. 171, 180
motivation 63, 207
Muller, M. 102
multifinality 90
Munafò, M. 71, 74
Myin-Germeys, I. 102, 120

NA see trait negative affectivity
Najolia, G. M. 14
Najt, P. 70–73

NAPLS see North American Prodrome Longitudinal Study
naturalistic experiments 155–156
negative affect 143, 185, 188, 189, 207
negative beliefs 108, 185
negative cognitive schemas 122–123
negative schizotypy 84, 188; childhood trauma 104, 118, 123; creativity 200, 203–204; developmental perspective 89, 94; latent inhibition 205; psychometric assessment 10, 12, 20; spontaneous eye blink rate 37–38; stress 42; trait negative affectivity 185
neglect 99, 100, 101–103, 104, 107, 118, 121
Nettle, D. 202, 203, 222, 223
neurobiology 119–121; see also brain
neurochemical transmission 33
neurocognitive models 205–207
neuroimaging 10, 76, 88, 207; see also functional magnetic resonance imaging
neuroleptics 34
neuronal resilience 49, 53, 54, 58
neuroscience 88; see also brain
neuroticism 17, 21, 184, 219
neurotransmitters 33–34, 189
Newman, T. K. 126
Newport, F. 167
nicotine 132, 133, 134, 135–136, 141
non-conformity 11, 19, 202–203, 221, 222, 223
norepinephrine 34
North American Prodrome Longitudinal Study (NAPLS) 9

OBEs see out-of-body experiences
obsessive-compulsive disorder (OCD) 183–184, 187, 190
odd behaviours 84
O'Donovan, M. C. 54
O-LIFE see Oxford-Liverpool Inventory of Feelings and Experiences
Oltmanns, T. F. 168
openness: experience seeking 208; mixed-handedness 68
O'Reilly, T. 207
out-of-body experiences (OBEs) 150, 153, 154–155

Over, D. E. 172
Overby, L. A. 72
Oxford-Liverpool Inventory of Feelings and Experiences (O-LIFE) 11, 19, 218, 220–221, 223; anxiety 184; ARMS criteria 180; disorganisation measures 25; genetics 57; hemispheric asymmetries 71–72, 73, 74–75; latent inhibition 39; Short Forms 12

panic attacks 134
Papousek, I. 74, 75
paranoia 119, 184, 188–189; childhood trauma 103, 104, 108, 109, 119, 120; delusional beliefs 167, 170, 173; inducing psychotic-like experiences 154; insecure attachment 123; negative cognitive schemas 122–123; psychometric assessment 18, 21–24; social cognition 124; virtual reality experiment 172
Paranoia Checklist 21, 22
Paranoia Scale 21, 22
Paranoia/Suspiciousness Questionnaire (PSQ) 21, 23
Paranoid Thoughts Scale 167
paranormal beliefs 24, 71, 74–75, 104, 150, 155–156, 157
paranormal experiences 147
parental loss 99, 100
parental separation 100, 102, 118
Parkinson's disease 34, 37
PAS *see* Perceptual Aberration Scale
Pavlov, Ivan 218, 220
Payne, J. 150, 153–154
PCCS *see* Poor Cognitive Control Scale
PDI *see* Peters et al. Delusional Inventory
PDI-21 *see* Peters Delusional Inventory
Pearson, D. 148
Pearson, H. 49
Pearson, R. 70, 72
Perceptual Aberration Scale (PAS) 10, 16, 20, 52, 71–72, 74–75, 221
perceptual aberrations 11, 12, 15, 17, 18, 84; childhood trauma 103; developmental perspective 93; inducing psychotic-like experiences 154; obsessive-compulsive disorder 184; virtual reality experiment 172
perceptual asymmetries 62, 63, 68–69, 76
perceptual dysregulation 26
Perona-Garcelán, S. 124–125
persistence 189
personality 7, 10, 33, 62, 83–84; environmental risk factors 125; experience seeking 208; fully dimensional perspective 8, 217, 218–220; genetics 49; mixed-handedness 68; premorbid 182; substance use 139, 142, 143
personality disorders 8, 100, 133, 199, 219, 222, 223
Peselow, E. 132, 134
PET *see* positron emission tomography
Peters, Emmanuelle 3, 23, 24, 165–179
Peters Delusional Inventory (PDI-21) 24, 25
Peters et al. Delusional Inventory (PDI) 23, 25, 167, 169
Pha *see* Physical Anhedonia Scale
physical abuse 99, 101–103, 104, 107, 122
Physical Anhedonia Scale (Pha) 10, 16, 20, 72
Pickering, A. D. 41
Pizzagalli, D. 71
Plath, Sylvia 199
PLEs *see* psychotic-like experiences
Plomin, R. 48
poets 199, 201, 202, 203, 223
Poincaré, Henri 201
Polito, V. 150, 155–156
polymorphism 50, 53–54, 55–56, 58, 139
Poor Cognitive Control Scale (PCCS) 17, 25
Poreh, A. M. 72
positive schizotypy 84; anxiety 184; childhood trauma 102, 104, 118, 123; cognitive functions 40–41; compensatory mechanisms 43; creativity 200–203, 204, 209–210; developmental perspective 89, 94;

gene-environment interaction 126; genetics 53, 57, 58; handedness 67; latent inhibition 39, 205; negative cognitive schemas 122; paranoia 21; psychometric assessment 10, 12, 17, 20; 'right-hemisphere hypothesis' 66; spontaneous eye blink rate 37–38; stress 42; substance use 134, 137–138; women 73
positron emission tomography (PET) 36, 41, 42
postdrome 182
post-synaptic processes 34, 35
post-traumatic stress disorder (PTSD) 99, 109, 186
Poulton, R. 181
poverty 117
Powers, A. D. 101
PPI *see* prepulse inhibition
precognition 104
Prentky, R. 206
preoccupation 169, 170
prepulse inhibition (PPI) 39
Preti, A. 208
Price, L. H. 103
priming tasks 70
prodrome 8, 9, 10, 35, 182, 184
promoters 49–50
pseudoneurotic schizophrenia 7
pseudoschizotypy 225n2
PSQ *see* Paranoia/Suspiciousness Questionnaire
psychiatry 142, 223
psychoanalysis 85
psychological mechanisms 122–125
psychometric assessment 9–26; inducing psychotic-like experiences 149–151; paranoia 21–24
psychopathology 3, 9, 86, 180–196; clinical implications 190–191; cognitive factors and individual differences 189–190; creativity 197, 199–200, 207; descriptive 7; developmental 90–91, 93, 95; dopamine 34; environmental risk factors 125; fully dimensional perspective 8; hemispheric dysregulation 206; persistence 189; schizotypal subtypes 188–189; secondary 133
psychosis: at-risk mental states 180–181; brain correlates 33; childhood trauma 100, 104–105, 108–109, 118, 120; cognitive behavioural therapy for 175; cognitive models 188–189; conceptualisation of schizotypy 8; creativity 209; delusional beliefs 165, 166–167; developmental perspective 83–84, 85–87, 88, 94, 95; dimensionality 220; dissociation 124–125; dopamine 34–35, 168; environmental adversity 116–118, 119, 121–127; Eysenck 220; final common pathway model 52; genetics 49, 53, 54, 55, 58; hallucinations 152–153; handedness 67; hemispheric asymmetries 62; HPA axis 108; inducing psychotic-like experiences 147; insecure attachment 123; interventions 190–191; negative cognitive schemas 122–123; psychometric assessment 10, 14, 15, 19, 25; psychosis-proneness-persistence-impairment model 189; schizotypy after 181–183; schizotypy before onset 181; social anxiety 184; social defeat hypothesis 121–122; substance use 2, 132, 133–134, 136, 142; traumagenic neurodevelopmental model 120; unitary view of 220, 223; XY Gene Hypothesis 65; *see also* psychoticism; psychotic-like experiences; schizophrenia
psychosocial factors 116–118, 119, 121, 126
psychoticism 85, 223; dopamine 34–35, 36, 37, 38, 41; Eysenck 219, 220; prepulse inhibition 39; psychometric assessment 13, 15, 26; *see also* psychosis
Psychoticism Scale 15
psychotic-like experiences (PLEs) 180–181, 190; cannabis use 139; causality 118–119; childhood trauma 100, 105–106, 118; developmental perspective 89, 93, 94; family

environment 117; high-risk research 84; inducing 147–161; insecure attachment 123; locus of control 124; persistence 189; social defeat hypothesis 121; stress 120; temporal lobe epilepsy 188; urbanicity 116–117

quasi-dimensional perspective 8, 86, 87, 217–218, 224–225

Rado, S. 7, 48, 218
Raine, A. 13, 20–21, 52, 86, 121, 182, 225n2
Ramesar, R. 126
Randell, J. 149, 153
Rantzen, A. J. 148, 149
Raulin, M. L. 16, 17, 18
Rawlings, D. 23, 71, 72, 202, 203, 208, 224
reality distortion 116
receptors 34, 35, 41–42
recovery 182–183, 190–191
Referential Thinking Scale (REF) 18, 25–26, 168
Reiter-Palmon, R. 12
relapse 87
relatives 7, 181, 218; bipolar disorder 185; cocaine use 138; creativity 199–200; dopamine 35; family environment 117–118; family studies 9; heritability of schizophrenia 51, 99; smoking 135
religious beliefs 168, 169, 170
remote associations 201, 202, 203, 204
response inhibition 41
Ressler, K. J. 101
Revised Social Anhedonia Scale (R-SAS) 10, 17, 20, 74, 75, 89
Rhue, J. W. 152
Ribolsi, M. 75
Richardson, A. J. 62, 66
'right-hemisphere hypothesis' 65–66
Ripke, S. 54
risk factors 134, 181; borderline personality disorder 91; delusional beliefs 166; developmental perspective 83, 90, 91, 95; environmental 116–118, 119, 121, 125, 189; genetic 48–49, 53, 54

risk markers 88, 89–90
RNA 49–50, 57
Robertson, M. 190
Rodgers, S. 102
Roethke, Theodore 201
'rollback phenomenon' 182
Ross, S. 132, 134
Ross, T. P. 72
Rossi, A. 186
Rössler, W. 101, 102, 137
R-SAS *see* Revised Social Anhedonia Scale

salience 14, 26, 191; childhood trauma 108; delusional beliefs 171; dopamine 35, 52–53, 120–121, 168; genetics 56–57, 58
Sandor, P. S. 71
SAS *see* Schizotypal Ambivalence Scale; Social Anhedonia Scale
Saunders, J. 149, 153
Savitz, J. 126
SBR *see* spontaneous eye blink rate
schemas 122–123
schizo seed 85–86, 87
schizogene 7, 85
schizophrenia 2, 7, 217–218, 222; alcohol use 136, 137; bipolar disorder comparison 186; clinical evaluation 83; conceptualisation of schizotypy 8–9; creativity 199–200, 209; dopamine 34–36, 40, 42, 207–208; endophenotypes 91–92; Eysenck 220; first episode psychosis 87; genetics 48–49, 50, 51–53, 54, 99; hemispheric asymmetries 62, 64–66, 67, 76; heterogeneity 8, 9; negative affect 143; neurodevelopmental hypothesis 88; neuronal changes 43; obsessive-compulsive disorder 183; personality tradition 219; prepulse inhibition 39; psychometric assessment 10, 16, 20; smoking 135; spontaneous eye blink rate 37; stereotyped behaviour 38; substance use 133, 142; traits and symptoms 224; *see also* psychosis
schizotaxia 7, 48, 51, 85
schizothymia-cyclothymia 218, 219

Schizotypal Ambivalence Scale (SAS) 18, 26
schizotypal personality disorder (SPD) 38, 39, 52, 187; childhood trauma 100, 101–103, 104, 118; HPA axis 108; poverty linked to 117; psychometric assessment 20
Schizotypal Personality Questionnaire (SPQ) 13, 20–21, 54, 56, 86, 182; adolescents 94; bipolar disorder 185, 186; disorganisation measures 25, 42; epilepsy 187; genetics 52; hemispheric asymmetries 71, 72, 75; social anxiety 184
Schizotypal Personality Questionnaire Brief (SPQ-B) 13, 21, 103
Schizotypal Personality Questionnaire Brief Revised (SPQ-BR) 14, 21
Schizotypal Personality Scale (STA) 19, 71, 72, 75, 221–222
Schizotypal Symptoms Inventory (SSI) 182–183
Schizotypal Traits Questionnaire (STQ) 10, 19
schizotypy 1–3; childhood trauma 99–115; conceptualisation of 8–9; creative advantage 197–214; definition of 199; developmental perspective 83–98; environmental factors 116–131; future directions 217–227; genetic basis for 48–61; hemispheric asymmetries 62–80; heterogeneity 8, 9; history of 7–8; inducing psychotic-like experiences 147; measurement of 9–26; multidimensional nature of 8, 9, 26, 84, 106; psychopathology 180–196; role of dopamine 33–47; substance use 132–146; versus at-risk mental state 180–181; *see also* negative schizotypy; positive schizotypy
Schizotypy Personality Scale (STA) 11
Schmeidler, J. 103
Schofield, K. 71, 74
Schuldberg, D. 203, 209
Schulter, G. 74, 75
Schurhoff, F. 185
screening 9–10, 19
scrying 151, 157

SD *see* social defeat hypothesis
secondary psychopathology 133
secondary substance use 133
selective attention 39
self-consciousness 18
self-control 11
self-esteem 108, 124, 168, 173, 190
self-medication 133, 135, 136, 137
self-monitoring 18
Selten, J. P. 121
semantic activation 25
semantic networks 40
semantic processing 63, 66, 70, 76
Sen, S. 200
sensation seeking 12
sensory deprivation 147, 150, 153–155, 158
serotonin 34, 56–57
sexual abuse 99, 101–102, 104, 107, 119
Sheinbaum, Tamara 2, 116–131
Shevlin, M. 119
Shrira, A. 205
signal detection theory 40
Silvia, P. J. 12, 20
Simeon, D. 103
Simons, C. 149
single photon emission computed tomography (SPECT) 36, 41
Sirof, B. 103
Slamar-Haldbedl, M. 205–206
Smirnis, N. K. 15
Smith, A. D. 75
Smith, G. 209
Smith, M. 151, 157
smoking 69, 132, 133, 135–136, 141
social anhedonia 185, 188; family environment 118; genetic effects 52; psychometric assessment 11, 12, 14, 17, 20; *see also* anhedonia
Social Anhedonia Scale (SA) 71
social anxiety 182, 184; childhood trauma 101, 104; disorganisation 204; psychometric assessment 11, 13, 14, 20; substance use 140
social capital 121
social cognition 10, 122, 123–124
social defeat (SD) hypothesis 121–122
social desirability 18, 152
social isolation 84, 93, 103, 170

240 *Index*

social phobia 17, 183
social skills training 190
social withdrawal 183, 188, 203, 204
sociodevelopmental-cognitive model 108–109
somatic symptoms 17
Somers, M. 66, 67
Sommer, I. E. C. 103
SPD *see* schizotypal personality disorder
SPECT *see* single photon emission computed tomography
speech: odd 13, 14, 93, 94; speech processing 63
spiritualism 104
spontaneous eye blink rate (SBR) 37–38
SPQ *see* Schizotypal Personality Questionnaire
SPQ-B *see* Schizotypal Personality Questionnaire Brief
SPQ-BR *see* Schizotypal Personality Questionnaire Brief Revised
Sprong, M. 187
SSI *see* Schizotypal Symptoms Inventory
STB *see* Borderline Personality Scale
Steel, C. 186
Stefanis, C. N. 15
Stefanis, N. C. 15, 56
Stefansson, H. 53
Stein, D. J. 126
stereotyped behaviour 38–39
Stirling, J. 137, 140
Straub, E. 53
Straub, Richard 55, 56
Strausberg, M. 167
stress 42, 107–108; childhood trauma 120; individual differences 189; neurobiology 120; psychotic-like experiences 120; social defeat hypothesis 121; substance use 142
Su, B. 54
substance use 2–3, 69, 87, 109, 132–146; artists 208; association with schizotypy 134–138; childhood trauma 99–100, 108; subjective effects of 138–140
suggestibility 157, 158
superstition 104, 184
suspiciousness 13, 14, 21, 23, 24, 108, 140
Suzuki, A. 71

sweat lodge ceremony 155–156
symptoms 182–183, 224
synapses 33
Szoke, A. 185

Tabak, N. T. 188
Tal, I. 208
taxonic models 8, 48, 86–87
Taylor, K. I. 75
temporal lobe epilepsy 187–188
Terhune, D. B. 151, 157
THC 139
Theory of Mind (ToM) 92, 123–124, 172
therapy 174–175
Thomas, K. M. 101
Thompson, R. J. 101, 102
thought problems 84
thymotypy 222, 223
ToM *see* Theory of Mind
Toogood, A. 203
Tower, P. 171
Tracy, J. 71, 74
trait negative affectivity (NA) 185, 188, 189
traits 52, 224; *see also* personality
trauma 2, 90, 99–115, 118, 119; appraisal of intentionality 127; causality 118–119; dissociation 124–125; gene-environment interaction 126; insecure attachment 123; neurobiology 119–120; psychosocial factors 126; social cognition 124; social defeat hypothesis 121–122; substance use 141; *see also* post-traumatic stress disorder
traumagenic neurodevelopmental model 120
Trotman, H. D. 187
Trower, P. 175
Tsakanikos, E. 205
turning behaviour 37
Tuvblad, C. 52
twins 50, 51, 52, 99
Tyrka, A. R. 103

Unterrainer, H. 205–206
unusual experiences 57, 184, 221; childhood trauma 104; delusional

beliefs 170–171; psychometric assessment 11, 19, 26; *see also* anomalous perceptions
urbanicity 116–117
Usher, M. 71

Van de Ven, V. 149, 152
Van der Meer, G. 209
Van der Merwe, L. 126
Van Os, J. 15, 117, 166–167, 174
Vanable, P. A. 22
Varese, F. 119, 124
Velikonja, Tjasa 2, 99–115, 118
Vellante, M. 208
verbal fluency 41
verbal hallucinations 148–153
Vercammen, A. 149
victimisation 99, 100, 104, 119, 124, 167
violence 11, 99
virtual reality 172
visual backward masking 92
Voglmaier, M. M. 72
voices, hearing 105, 148, 171, 173

Walker, E. F. 187
war trauma 99
Waxman, R. 101
Weinberger, D. R. 54, 55
Weinstein, S. 71, 72

Weisman de Mamani, A. G. 188
Weiss, E. 205–206
Wheeler, R. 103
white noise 149–151, 152, 153, 157, 158
Whitman, D. R. 72
Wickham, S. 119
Widiger, T. A. 8
Wigert, B. 12
Williams, B. 224
Williams, H. J. 54
Williams, L. 10
Wilson, L. 150, 153–154
Winterstein, B. P. 12
Wisconsin Card Sorting Test 38
Wisconsin Schizotypy Scales (WSS) 10, 12, 20
witchcraft 104
women 64, 73
word associations 201, 202, 203, 204, 209
WSS *see* Wisconsin Schizotypy Scales
Wyche, M. C. 103

XY Gene Hypothesis 65, 69, 73

Yasuda, Y. 56
Young-Wolff, K. 52

Zäch, P. 75

eBooks
from Taylor & Francis

Helping you to choose the right eBooks for your Library

Add to your library's digital collection today with Taylor & Francis eBooks. We have over 50,000 eBooks in the Humanities, Social Sciences, Behavioural Sciences, Built Environment and Law, from leading imprints, including Routledge, Focal Press and Psychology Press.

Choose from a range of subject packages or create your own!

Benefits for you
- Free MARC records
- COUNTER-compliant usage statistics
- Flexible purchase and pricing options
- All titles DRM-free.

Benefits for your user
- Off-site, anytime access via Athens or referring URL
- Print or copy pages or chapters
- Full content search
- Bookmark, highlight and annotate text
- Access to thousands of pages of quality research at the click of a button.

Free Trials Available
We offer free trials to qualifying academic, corporate and government customers.

eCollections

Choose from over 30 subject eCollections, including:

Archaeology	Language Learning
Architecture	Law
Asian Studies	Literature
Business & Management	Media & Communication
Classical Studies	Middle East Studies
Construction	Music
Creative & Media Arts	Philosophy
Criminology & Criminal Justice	Planning
Economics	Politics
Education	Psychology & Mental Health
Energy	Religion
Engineering	Security
English Language & Linguistics	Social Work
Environment & Sustainability	Sociology
Geography	Sport
Health Studies	Theatre & Performance
History	Tourism, Hospitality & Events

For more information, pricing enquiries or to order a free trial, please contact your local sales team:
www.tandfebooks.com/page/sales

www.tandfebooks.com